YESTERDAY'S COUNTRYSIDE

Country Life as it Really was

VALERIE PORTER

David & Charles

WEIGHTS AND MEASUREMENTS

As this book is largely about yesterday's countryside, imperial measurements have been retained and there has been no attempt to give metric equivalents. For the sake of a younger generation, the following definitions and conversions might help.

Definitions

perch = 5½ yards, or 16½ feet
rod = perch or pole
square pole = 30¼ square yards, or 272¼ square feet
dwt = pennyweight (weight of a silver penny) = 24 grains of troy weight. 20dwt = 1 ounce (troy)
gr = grain (average weight of a grain of corn). There are 7,000 grains to one pound avoirdupois
stone = 14 pounds (but varied widely in different regions and for different commodities; for example, 1 stone of meat = 8 pounds)
cwt = hundredweight = 112 pounds
pint (of corn) = approximately 568cc (UK)
bushel = dry measure of 8 gallons (but varied in some places)
shillings and pence: 12 pence (12d) = 1 shilling (1s); 20s = £1
guinea = 21s (£1 1s)
half-a-crown = 2s 6d
bob = 1s
tanner = 6d
farthing = ¼d

Conversions

1 inch (1in) = 25.4mm
1 foot (1ft) = 12in = 0.3048m
1 yard (1yd) = 3ft = 0.9144m
1 perch, rod or pole = 5½ yd = 5.029m
1 rood = ¼ acre = 101,171m^2
1 acre = 4840 sq. yd = 0.4047ha

1 pint (1pt) = 0.568l
1 quart (1qt) = 2pt = 1.136l
1 gallon = 8pt = 4.546l
1 ounce (1oz) = 28.35g
1 pound (1lb) = 16oz = 0.454kg
1 stone = 14lb = 6.351kg
1 hundredweight (1cwt) = 50.802kg
1 ton (1T) = 20cwt = 1.016 tonnes
1 grain (1gr) = 64.799mg
24 gr = 1 pennyweight (1dwt) = 10oz (troy)
1 bushel = 0.036m^3

A DAVID & CHARLES BOOK

Hardback first published in the UK in 2000
Reprinted 2001, 2003
First paperback edition 2002
Reprinted 2003 (twice)

A catalogue record for this book is available from the British Library.

ISBN 0 7153 0968 4 (hardback)
ISBN 0 7153 1420 3 (paperback)

Printed in Italy by Stige
for David & Charles
Brunel House Newton Abbot Devon

Contents

Introduction

For many decades, there has been an enormous nostalgia for the 'traditional' British countryside – a dreamy place full of birdsong and meadow flowers, purple heather and misty hills, honest old gaffers exuding wit and wisdom, eccentric squires and lairds playing at and with life, cottages nestling in the landscape, cosy self-sufficient villages, children thriving in the fresh air ... and all that. Of course, it is largely in the imagination, but versions of it have served as an inspiration to many since Roman poets, condemned to city life, wrote lyrically of the countryside. Poets and other artists have continued the theme ever since.

Then there is the reality. For some born and bred in the country, the dream was to escape from it – but to where? All too often they were lured to the towns and cities, in search of work and better conditions, but never found their pots of gold there. Within two or three generations their descendants had reversed the dream and sought to return. The continuity had been broken, however; they found that they were strangers in the landscape and the dream, being a dream, remained elusive.

Some of us have been lucky enough to spend our childhoods in the country and discover our own reality, untainted by expectations. We have followed the natural urge to leave the nest and explore the wider world and, if we are truly lucky, we have come back, rejecting the undoubted attractions of urban life for the simpler but more deeply felt joys of a rural one. With our eyes wide open to reality, we have perceived the changes in the countryside – some of them deplorable, some of them to the greater good. This book seeks to highlight the ways in which living in the country, in all its aspects, has changed, as seen through the eyes of an older generation still living and through the written words of generations long gone. It also seeks to be optimistic about the future, where that is possible.

The biggest change, perhaps, is that country dwellers are very much in a minority now. The Domesday Book showed that the total population of England in the eleventh century was 2 million people, of whom about 90,000 were cottars and bordars – peasants living in country cottages in return for labour. Most people in Britain at the time lived in rural areas and this would be the case until the industrial revolution began to swell during the eighteenth century. By 1850, for the first time in Britain's history, as many people were living in towns as in the country but their roots remained rural; most town-dwellers still had close relatives in the countryside and liked to make day-trips there for fresh air and the scenery.

By the outbreak of the Second World War, only one in five of the UK's population of more than 45 million people lived in rural areas. By the 1990s the population had increased to about 57 million and the 'rural' proportion was less than 20 per cent.

The definition of rurality can be a problem when statistics come into play. With the rapid growth in the sizes of villages in many parts of Britain, their tendency to stretch out towards each other and the tendency of suburbs to spread far beyond their natural bounds, it can be difficult to decide where the countryside truly begins. Perhaps it is a matter of the heart. If you feel that you live in the countryside, then you do.

1

Country Living

THE COUNTRY COTTAGE: what an evocation of the lost idyll of a past that we never really knew; and what a deception, what a romantic hoodwink!

During the Second World War, some people returned to the countryside as evacuees from the cities and rediscovered the reality of it, which proved to be very different from the picturesque scenes that slid past their railway-carriage windows.

Before the war, there had already been an exodus of country weekenders, caravaners, hikers, touring motorists and charabanc outings, and so country cottages became highly desirable. Actors, authors and politicians had to have their 'country cottages', even though some of these became country mansions with twenty bedrooms, formal gardens and swimming-pools, and barns converted into playrooms. Here the famous person would pose for illustrated articles about their 'country' lifestyle and talk about earth closets and inglenook fireplaces. Younger, poorer escapists found a semi-detached rented labourer's home for ten bob a week, or rented a summer caravan in the field.

In a down-to-earth book, *Living in the Country*, written before the war and published in 1940 to open wistful townee eyes to the realities of their dream, Frederick Smith and Barbara Wilcox discussed the real old country cottages 'which our grandfathers are reputed to have bought for £50 and sold to townsfolk for £500 ... The countryman is so alive to the situation that he often tries to overcharge what he calls "the town mug". He knows that the old cottage which he often rather despises has a strange attraction for the townsman and he puts the price up accordingly.' In particular, the authors warned against sellers who described their 'insanitary hovels, derelict small-holdings or dreary villas' as 'ripe for conversion'.

THE COUNTRY IDYLL

EVERY ESCAPING TOWNEE WANTED A PERIOD COTTAGE WITH CHARACTER, FACING SOUTH, WITH A VIEW AND A GARDEN IN THE FRONT, AND WITH MAINS WATER AND ELECTRICITY, FOR NOT MORE THAN £500 IN THOSE INTERWAR YEARS AND PREFERABLY 'ISOLATED' BUT NEAR ENOUGH TO LONDON AND OTHER CITIES TO SOFTEN THE ISOLATION.

PREVIOUS PAGE
Arlington Row, Bibury, Gloucestershire

RIGHT
Preparing for the reaper

THE MORE HONEST estate agents of the 1930s would tell them that very few cottages faced south (cottages were built wherever there happened to be a spare bit of land, and actually often faced east so that the rising sun hit the sleeping labourer in the eye and got him out of bed early) and that cottages had been built for landworkers earning about ten bob a week, not city dwellers with good incomes and high living standards. The workers' cottages were usually utilitarian boxes, two up, two down. 'Period cottages at £500 belong to your grandfather's time, not yours,' the honest 1930s agent would say. The garden was more likely to be an awkwardly triangular twenty perches than a pleasant half acre; the view was likely to be a limited one, as cottages were generally built in valleys, not on hills, because that was where the water source would be and shelter from the weather. Whatever the increasingly frustrated town buyer might finally lay hands on would need a lot more spent on it to make it weatherproof, sanitary and free from rising damp, and probably radical reconstruction to bring it up to modern standards even in those interwar years.

The hamlet of Rickford, near Blagdon Hill, Somerset, in the mid 1930s

The Second World War brought many more suburbanites to the country, and these tended to be civil servants, teachers and the like who were somewhat shocked to find themselves without electricity and with a bus only twice a week. The war also brought airmen, soldiers and others to a wartime rash of aerodromes, camps and hospitals, and some of them stayed on in the countryside after a war that became a major turning point in the British way of life.

Today, when even more of us live in urban and suburban areas, the dream of a cottage in the country maintains the powerful grip it has held over us for at least 150 years. Seduced by a host of Victorian artists and writers, the town-dweller imagines a small(ish), cosy, pretty and intimate little home. It is probably made of mellow local stone or tile-hung brick, or half-timbered or of comfy Devon cob, tucked under a thatched or mossy-tiled or lichen-splashed stone slab roof or one of rain-slicked slate, with diamond-pane windows glinting irregularly in the sun and potted geraniums scarlet on the windowsills. Warmth is suggested by woodsmoke curling gently from the chimney and the whole vision snuggles quietly and discreetly into its rural surroundings. It is frocked with flowers in a blowsy, abundant garden with a patch of healthily organic and weedfree vegetables and country idyll

ripe fruit for the picking; perhaps a few gentle cows in a buttercup meadow beyond the honeysuckle and wild-rose garden hedge, a few homely brown hens pottering in the dust of the lavender-hemmed garden path.

This pastel place is close to a friendly village where you are greeted by name in a shop whose owner has time to chat; there is a friendly little school where children learn in small classes and play safely in the fresh air; there is a maternal church, a snug pub with a roaring fire of scented logs, all just a stroll or gentle cycle ride away down a lane whose hay-scented verges are sprinkled with wild flowers in yellow, white, blue, pink and purple. Ah yes.

ROMANCE AND REALISM

Was it ever like this? Helen Allingham (1848–1926), perhaps the most familiar of the romantic cottage painters, escaped from Chelsea to Surrey and painted hundreds of local exteriors, invariably depicted in high summer, invariably with flower-filled gardens, clean and happy children, dignified and cheerful women with time to chat, kittens playing, hens and ducks wandering in the wheel-free dusty lanes. But her own large and far from vernacular Surrey home at Sandhills, near Witley, was nothing like these wavy-roofed thatched or tiled, lattice-windowed old cottages; and the real cottages were often nothing like as pretty as she painted them, her artistic eye glossing over the leaking tiles, draughty doorways and ill-fitting window casements. She did not paint poverty and dirt. The people in her paintings were rarely the real (and often sickly) inhabitants; she chose prettier women and sweeter children and dressed them in cleaner, unfrayed clothes that would have been far too good even for Sunday best.

In 1909, in a joint book with Allingham, Stewart Dick noted that old England was changing fast in those early years of the twentieth century. 'The life that the old cottage typifies is now a thing of the past, and is daily fading more and more into the distance. Twentieth-century England, the England of the railway, the telegraph, and the motor-car, is not the England of these old cottages. Our point of view has changed. We no longer see the old homely life from within, but from the outside.'

'Today, when even more of us live in urban and suburban areas, the dream of a cottage in the country maintains the powerful grip it has held over us for at least 150 years.'

OLD COTTAGES Allingham's neighbour in Surrey was Myles Birket Foster, whose finely engraved Pictures of English Landscape were published in 1862. The engravings were accompanied by text by Tom Taylor, who was clear-eyed in his poem 'Old Cottages'. First he described the romantic vision of picturesque cottages in flowery gardens. Then:

All these I know, – know, too, the plagues that prey
On those who dwell in these bepainted bowers:
The foul miasma of their crowded rooms,
The fever that each autumn seals its dooms
From the rank ditch that stagnates by the door;
And then I wish the picturesqueness less,
And welcome the utilitarian hand
That from such foulness plucks its masquing dress,
And bids the well-aired, well-drained cottage stand,
All bare of weather-stain, right angle true, –
By sketchers shunned, but shunned by fevers too.

country idyll

'There must also be lots of light and sun and wide views, and no ants or other crawling things.'

KATE GREENAWAY (1846–1901) was another painter of pretty cottages. Esther Meynell, writing in the 1930s about her own search for the ideal Sussex cottage, explained how the Greenaway paintings had set her standard:

> *... embowered in cherry trees, set on the edge of a village green haunted by geese, yet as convenient and habitable as if it were designed by the most accomplished modern architect. It must have tiny casement windows in which gay curtains the size of a pocket-handkerchief flutter in the breeze, and these windows should be set preferably in age-deep thatch. But there must also be lots of light and sun and wide views, and no ants or other crawling things. Cosiness is essential to the perfect cottage, yet there must be space to house many books and a cherished Blüthner grand piano. There must also be much hot water and lots of cupboards.*

Under the spreading chestnut tree in Stanford-in-the-Vale, Oxfordshire

Not surprisingly, she failed in her quest for the ideal old cottage and built a new one instead, in an old cabbage field.

Nor were the painters alone in the deception. In the 1920s the photographer Graystone Bird of Bath posed his own prettily plump and healthy models, costumed in 'country' clothes, bearing assorted water pitchers, wooden hay rakes, rustic baskets and three-legged milking stools as rather obvious props while they pretended to be cottage and village women decorating his scenes of picture-postcard Castle Combe in Wiltshire. In Sussex, photographer George Garland posed some of his own friends chatting casually with his favourite 'country characters', the latter often genuine shepherds and farmworkers looking slightly uncomfortable at the falseness of the scene.

In the 1930s and 1940s there was a plethora of books about village homes and village people, chronicling the yearning to live in 'the country'. But it goes much further back. Flora Thompson, a stonemason's daughter born in 1876 at Brackley, Northamptonshire, and who died in 1947 at the age of 70, moved to the Surrey village of Grayshott (Heatherly in her writings) in 1897 at a time when the region had become 'civilised'. This heathy countryside around Hindhead had been an area of squatters' hovels, sheep-stealing gangs, smugglers and highway robbers who made the most of the old coaching road between London and Portsmouth, but then it became fashionable: Tennyson and his set escaped to the bracing fresh air around Hindhead (though hardly to live in cottages); other poets had fled further, to Somerset and the Lake District. All over Surrey, the 'gentry' had been moving into the countryside during the nineteenth century; some of them had simply enlarged and modernised existing farmhouses; a few took over old agricultural and squatters' cottages and knocked them down to build finer homes for themselves to enjoy on summer weekends.

Flora Thompson discovered that few of those who lived in Grayshott had been born there or had lived there as children. Several of the shopkeepers had Brummy, London or

country idyll

Shropshire accents; and most of the working people had come there simply to earn a livelihood. None of them had 'had time to get rooted in the soil, even if they had had the inclination'. She was surprised; she had spent her own childhood in a more essentially agricultural area where people did not change; where 'those born on the land, with very few exceptions, lived and died on the land. ... The old family names survived generation after generation in the villages.' She found that her adopted Surrey village was very different: the so-called villagers, 'having broken with their own personal past and come to a place without traditions, appeared to live chiefly for the passing moment'. Remember, this was towards the end of the nineteenth century, not the end of the twentieth: the suspicion that incomers superficially browse on local life is nothing new.

The smaller village homes in Grayshott were occupied by those who worked at the larger houses, or by tradesmen and their families; and the larger by doctors and other professionals. To meet the true Surrey natives, Flora had to head out of the village and on to the heath, where the poorer families could still eke out a living from their tiny smallholdings with the help of commoners' rights and besom-making, dwelling in old and definitely humble homesteads. All over the country, people had built themselves rough huts on the commons, legitimately or otherwise. There was an old theory that if you built your shelter overnight and had a fence around your 'garden' and smoke rising from your chimney before dawn, you secured squatter's rights to live there.

In Elizabethan times, one John Symons or Symonde secured land at Betchett Green on Holmwood Common, in Surrey. Frances Mountford's delightful book about the home he built there as it developed during the next four centuries (*A Commoner's Cottage*) reveals that he applied successfully to the Court Baron in nearby Dorking and was granted a rood (quarter of an acre) of land in 1592 as a copyholder. He built his home from local oak trees, infilling the wooden framework with wattle and daub since bricks from the abundant local clay were far too expensive for him then. His cottage was probably no more than a central hearth-room from which the main fireplace's smoke drifted out through a roof hole; there was a back service room and an outshot, and a ladder to a family sleeping loft over the central room.

The farmer's wife

Mary Russell Mitford was born in Alresford, Hampshire, in 1787, a century earlier than Flora Thompson. She was the daughter of a doctor and had a far more comfortable upbringing than Flora until her father gambled away the family's money and they moved to Three Mile Cross, near Reading. During the 1820s she wrote evocatively and honestly about village life, describing every building and every inhabitant with warmth and wit – especially the cottages, with the villagers 'whose faces are as familiar to us as the flowers in our garden; a little world of our own, close-packed and insulated ... ; where we know every one, are known to every one, interested in every one, and authorised to hope that every one feels an interest in us'. Her village societies in Hampshire and Berkshire were far more traditional than Flora's in Surrey.

Back-along in a Wiltshire village

COTTAGES AND LANDLORDS

SIR CHARLES TAYLOR (1770–1857), A CLOSE FRIEND OF THE PRINCE OF WALES AND A MEMBER OF THE CARLTON HOUSE SET, WAS RIDING IN HIS CARRIAGE THROUGH SUSSEX WHEN HE BECAME SNOWBOUND ON THE SLOPES OF A HANGER LOOKING OVER A BROAD VALLEY TOWARDS THE SOUTH DOWNS, WITH A GLIMPSE OF GOODWOOD IN THE FAR DISTANCE.

'They were building semi-detached stud-and-mud cottages for £30 each . . .'

CAPTIVATED BY THE VIEW, he built himself a thatched cottage here – but not remotely of the type that the locals inhabited. Oh no. He commissioned John Nash and Humphrey Repton to create a *cottage ornée* on that very spot, with eight bedrooms (excluding those for the servants), a billiard room 21ft long, a library 23ft long, a large oval drawing room, an octagonal boudoir, a huge dining room, a 'noble' inner hall, a conservatory, aviary, orangery, water closet and more – country living with all mod cons of the period.

Over several years as the eighteenth century turned into the nineteenth, the national Board of Agriculture commissioned a series of county-by-county surveys to report on agriculture in England. These comprehensive and readable reports also looked at roads, landlords, housing, welfare and other rural matters, and they were often damning. In Worcestershire, W. Pitt wrote that the labourers' cottages had 'nothing particular to recommend them; in the ancient villages and common field parishes, they often consist of timber and plaster walls covered with thatch, and are merely a shelter from the weather, without any particular attention having been paid to comfort and convenience, but with the addition of a garden for potatoes and other vegetables.' Here and there a good landowner's conscience had been pricked and much better homes had been built, some with 'well cultivated gardens, potatoe grounds, and pigs, but no cows' and some with fruit trees.

Kate Jones's isolated old stone cottage

The Devon surveyor, Charles Vancouver, did not like what he found. While mansions were built of the stone that was available in most parts of the county, cottages and farmhouses were built of cob, 'this dull, heavy, and deforming material ... without rough-cast, or white-wash to conceal the native colour of the loam'. He said that for about £60 a good rough and white-washed cob cottage could easily be built, including a fireplace and oven in a main room 14ft square, with two small rooms to store fuel and provisions, and with two apartments upstairs for parents and children. Some landlords, he noted with approval, did indeed build good cottages: Lord Clifford was singled out for praise because he included windows for light in the upper storey, as well as a garden and fruit trees for self-sufficiency. Others, in areas where there was an acute shortage of cottages, allowed existing ones either to be grossly overcrowded or to tumble down from neglect. In Chilworthy, for example, 'three mud walls and a hedge-bank form the habitation of many of the peasantry', yet in Bridestow the local rector had built splendid new stone cottages, their walls 20in thick up to 8ft high and above that of thick cob under a slate roof. Each had a large downstairs room with fireplace and oven, an understairs pantry, and lean-to storage areas for fuel, tools

landlords

and the cottage pig, all for a rent of a shilling a week but with the threat of instant eviction if the tenant should be 'disorderly' or should fail to 'frequent the church, and behave themselves soberly, and carefully, and as good neighbours to each other'.

In Lincolnshire, Arthur Young noted that the cottages in the low country were commonly built of what was called stud and mud, 'the stud-pieces as large as a man's arm', but at Brotherton a Mr Cartwright had built a row of twenty-nine brick-and-slate cottages, each with a useful pantry and 'a necessary and pig-sty, with a small back yard for coals and wood, and a small garden in front'. To build this row cost £2,538 15s 2d. At Folkingham, as a result of the enclosures, every cottage was assigned 'at least three acres of land, including a garden, upon which, for the most part, they keep a cow, and are much better labourers for it'. At Frieston they were building semi-detached stud-and-mud cottages for £30 each, one room on each floor: 'the entrance is into a small room for washing, a sort of common open store-room; by this means, the keeping room is much warmer than if the house door opened directly into it; the other room is a little dairy, in which also the beer is kept'. At Reevesby a brick cottage for two families could be built for 80 guineas, or a smaller one for one family for £50, or one-third less if of stud-and-mud.

In Sussex, the Reverend Arthur Young (no relation to the Lincolnshire surveyor) wrote:

> *The miserable construction of cottages in many parts of the kingdom, and the too great exclusion of comfort, are circumstances which ought to be remedied. No signs of prosperity like new-built cottages: the dwellings of the poor are, in most counties, but mud-cabbins, with holes that expose the inhabitants to the rigour of the climate. In the Weald of Sussex they are in general warm and comfortable, and many of them built of stone; and on the Downs with flints. Certainly the lower class of people are here in much more eligible circumstances than in many other parts of England which might be named.*

MISERIES OF THE COTTAGE

In Sussex, the Hon John Byng wrote in 1788 about 'How wretched do the Miseries of a Cottage Appear'. He had taken refuge in a cottage near Lewes, where he found:

Want of Food, want of Fuel, want of Clothing! Children perishing of an ague! and an unhappy Mother unable to attend to, or relieve their wants, or assuage their pains, nor to allow time sufficient even for the Reparation of their Rags. Whilst the worn-down melancholy Father (perhaps A Shepherd) pinched by Cold and pining with despair, Returns at Evening Close to a Hut devoid of Comfort, or the smallest renovation of Hope.

For cottagers, it was something of a lottery: the availability of good cottages depended on the conscience and wealth of the local landlords. The successor to Sir Charles Taylor in 1866, buying what was by then an estate of more than 4,000 acres, was the Victorian engineer Sir John Hawkshaw, who extended Taylor's *cottage ornée* hugely, giving it castle-like turrets and massive baronial doors.

Kentish cottage set among hop gardens near Chilham

Hawkshaw was a philanthropical squire: he built numerous traditional Bargate-stone cottages to very high standards on his large estate for the many who worked on his land or in his house, and created an attractive settlement of individual cottages around a little green, with a school for his employees' children.

In the late 1890s Edward Lamb, MP for Leominster but a near neighbour of Hawkshaw's, was so appalled at the state of the cottages in his area even at that late date that he too set about building new ones fit for the locals. Like Hawkshaw, he built with an eye for good looks and vernacular style, and he built solidly and well in the local stone and brick. Today those workers' cottages are highly desirable residences that sell for huge sums on the rare occasions when they come on the market. (That is the current dilemma in rural areas. Homes are no longer affordable for the rising generation whose parents have lived locally all their lives.)

landlords

IN 1872 YOUNG Richard Jefferies (1848–1887) wrote to *The Times* about the Wiltshire agricultural labourers whom he knew so well and would write about frequently until his early death at the age of 38. Having described a typical labourer in build, gait, clothing and eating habits, he turned to the cottages:

> *The cottages now are infinitely better than they were. There is scarcely room for further improvement in the cottages now erected upon estates. They have three bedrooms, and every appliance and comfort compatible with their necessarily small size. It is only the cottages erected by the labourers themselves on waste plots of ground which are open to objection. Those he builds himself are, indeed, as a rule, miserable huts, disgraceful to a Christian country. I have an instance before me at this moment where a man built a cottage with two rooms and no staircase or upper apartments, and in those two rooms eight persons lived and slept – himself and wife, grown-up daughters, and children. There was not a scrap of garden attached, not enough to grow half a dozen onions. The refuse and sewage was flung into the road, or filtered down a ditch into the brook which supplied that part of the village with water.*

'There are those who can remember sleeping head to toe like sardines in a tin, several to the bed ...'

It is shocking to realise that those crowded children, had they reached a reasonable old age, would have been alive well within living memory and their own children are probably still alive today. And it is shocking to realise that among the latter generation there are those who can remember sleeping head to toe like sardines in a tin, several to the bed, in their country cottages, though they often claim to have had a far happier childhood than many. 'What you never had, you never missed,' is a common remark.

Another observant young writer of the Victorian period was Arthur Gibbs, educated at Eton and Oxford before living a quiet country life devoted to literary pursuits, and who died at the age of 31 in 1899. He wrote about his own Cotswold village of Ablington, which he did not claim to be 'one whit prettier or pleasanter or better in any way than hundreds of other villages in England'. He sought only to 'record the simple annals of a quiet, old-fashioned Gloucestershire hamlet and the country within walking distance of it ... It is often said that in books like these we paint arcadies that never did and never could exist on earth. To this I would answer that there are many such abodes in country places, if only our minds are such to realise them.'

RIGHT
Going, going: a house sale forced by eviction

landlords

Unlike Richard Jefferies, an author he much admired, Gibbs was virtually a commuter. His book opens:

> *London is becoming miserably hot and dusty; everybody who can get away is rushing off, north, south, east, and west, some to the seaside, others to pleasant country houses. Who will fly with me westwards to the land of golden sunshine and silvery trout streams, the land of breezy uplands and valleys nestling under limestone hills, where the scream of the railway whistle is seldom heard and the smoke of the factory darkens not the long summer days?*

And so he climbed on to one of the trains whose whistle he had just deplored and steamed away on the Great Western Railway express racing at sixty miles an hour through the countryside, until at last he arrived at Cirencester, so 'clean and fresh and picturesque' after the dirt and smoke of London. The city man had come home to the country.

SOCIAL HOUSING

THE TUMBLING INSANITARY COTTAGES THAT VARIOUS BENEFICENT LANDOWNERS REPLACED THROUGHOUT THE NINETEENTH CENTURY WERE THE REAL COTTAGES – PLACES FROM WHICH THOSE WHO WERE BORN IN THEM WISHED ONLY TO ESCAPE. THE BUILDINGS WERE USUALLY SET ON LOW-LYING LAND THAT HELD THE WET AND THE SEWAGE AND IN GENERAL THE HOMES WERE COLD, DRAUGHTY, SMOKE-FILLED, CROWDED, DAMP, DARK, EXTREMELY UNCOMFORTABLE AND UNHEALTHY, AND VERY DEMANDING ON THE HOUSEWIFE IN PARTICULAR.

WHEN COUNCIL HOUSES were first built during the 1890s, the cottagers led the stampede into what for them was pure luxury and found it hard to understand the counter-stampede of town dwellers into their discarded homes. The country cottagers knew the reality of life in the cramped buildings they had shrugged off like unwanted carapaces, and they pitied the incomers.

In the late 1930s, when there were continuing attempts to improve conditions under the Rural Workers' Housing Act of 1926, a programme was broadcast on BBC radio (in those days 'wireless', of course) about housing design – a subject that concerned many a good-hearted social worker. A village group of men and boys listened to the broadcaster praising the beauty of older houses and disparaging the rash of bungalows that were appearing on village outskirts. The villagers discussed the broadcast in a typically roundabout rural way, but the most telling comments came from one old man. 'What 'ee say about Tudor 'ouses and the like be all right, but I'll give all these 'ere cottages, thatch an' all, for one of them there bungalows.' 'With water laid on,' said another. 'And a ceilin' you don't bust you 'ead on every time you stand upright,' commented a third. In the early 1950s, a grateful local wrote a short poem (published in *The Countryman* in 1952) to the rural district council that had built bungalows for old people:

Thatcher at work at Godshill, Isle of Wight

Before our bungalows were built
We lived in one large room
No gas, no water, no proper stove
For two years was our doom.

But now all this has changed and we
Have light and heat and space,
With baths and stoves and other helps –
The world's a pleasant place.

In 1947, writing about housing the country worker, Michael Tilley (a young architect who was the son of a farmer) lambasted the way that council houses had been built almost in isolation on the edges of villages between the wars and made a very good case instead for modernising existing old village housing. He pointed out that the Second World War had brought vast numbers of townsfolk into the countryside, on a scale never known before, and that many people who had practically forgotten that a countryside existed had been finding out the reality of the country way of life.

> *Many of the things that they have found have caused them great displeasure. Things to which the countryman had become painfully inured, such as dry wells in summer, rat-infested larders, leaky roofs, and damp walls in winter, all these drawbacks and many more, are being met for the first time.*

Every townsman seemed to think he knew how to cure the problems, whether in an official capacity or as a whimsical letter-writer to the newspapers, and all were agreed that housing for the country labourer in the past had been utterly miserable. With his own agricultural and architectural background, Tilley pointed out that the countryman's needs differed from those of the towndweller and he approved of the fact that RIBA's evidence to the government had stressed that

social housing

rural housing should not be treated the same as urban housing. Tilley was particularly alarmed at the 'sporadic and fortuitous layout of housing estates, related neither to each other, nor to the village, nor to the industries which they have to serve. There has been no overall conception of the village as a social and economic unit in the life of the countryside.' One wonders how much the planners, local councils and government have learnt about village housing in the intervening half a century.

THE REALITY

So what was it really like to live in the country? And how is it different now? Was Dr Johnson right when he said, 'No wise man will go to live in the country unless he has something to do which can be better done in the country'? Or, as F.G. Thomas put it in 1938 at the University College of the South-west in Exeter: 'Has the tradition and experience of urban life destroyed the capacity to live happily except in towns and cities?'

Begin with the distant view. Before the railways made feasible the transporting of bricks countrywide, there was a time when it was easy to recognise just where in the country you were by the style and substance of the local buildings. The substance relied heavily on what was locally available, and that was largely a matter of geology. In stone regions, for example, the houses seem to grow out of the landscape, as they were indeed built from its local stone, though the material was rarely used in earlier times for mere cottages. Even better-class houses were sometimes of wattle and clay right into the seventeenth century, by which time so much timber had been felled that it became as cheap to use local stone. William Harrison, in his *Chronicle* of the small Essex village of Holinshed, wrote in 1577:

> *In times past men were contented to dwell in houses builded of sallow, willow, plum-tree, hardbeane, and elme, so that the use of oke was in maner dedicated wholie unto churches, religious houses, princes' palaces noblemen's lodgings, and navigation, but now all these are rejected, and nothing but oke anie whit regarded.*

He foresaw the great oak shortage that became a reality within a generation: in 1604, for example, the use of timber had to be forbidden for the frontage of all buildings in London as there was not enough wood left.

In heathland regions people sometimes embellished the mortar of their stone houses with small chips of black ironstone, known locally as witches' eyes. In wooded regions the homes might be half-timbered, perhaps infilled with plastered brick, or with wattle, which consisted of vertical hazel rods 'sprung' into grooves and interwoven with smaller horizontal rods like basketwork, then daubed with a mixture of muddy clay, straw and cow dung or chalk or lime.

In clay regions, homes in due course were built in tile-hung brick. On the chalklands they might be studded with the flints that littered the chalk; sometimes chalk was laid out over winter to be broken down by the frost and then combined with straw and water and trodden in, producing something like the two-foot-thick cob walls of the West Country. In some eastern counties they used sun-dried lumps of clay; in Wiltshire and Dorset there was an old custom of building walls with sun-baked mud covered with plaster and a yellow wash.

Each region had its own local materials for walls and roofing and each had its own local (vernacular) building styles. Today, as you journey across the country, you are likely to see endless boxes in similar styles and materials whether you are in Caithness or Cornwall, Carmarthen or Cambridge. The sense of place is dying.

Iron railings like these largely disappeared during the Second World War, when they were donated for the war effort

'As you journey across the country, you are likely to see endless boxes in similar styles and materials ... The sense of place is dying.'

COUNTRY BUILDERS

THE ALMOST SUBURBAN UNIFORMITY BETWEEN NEIGHBOURING VILLAGE HOUSES IS A STRIKING MODERN FEATURE, IN CONTRAST TO THE OLD VILLAGES WHERE, APART FROM THOSE BUILT IN ONE GO BY A LOCAL ESTATE OWNER OR INDUSTRY, EACH HOME IS DIFFERENT, AT LEAST IN AGE AND DETAIL, BUT SOMEHOW GROUPS NATURALLY WITH ITS NEIGHBOURS EVEN WHEN THEIR ROOFLINES ARE APPARENTLY QUITE RANDOM. THEIR HARMONY ARISES THROUGH THE USE OF THE LOCAL MATERIALS AND OVERALL STYLE OF BUILDING.

Farmhouse at Lower Treneague, Cornwall, in 1910

OPPOSITE Trimming excess clay from a hand-moulded brick

AS WELL AS THE economics of building on a large scale, this new uniformity has probably been encouraged by the planning laws that have evolved since the first Town and Country Planning Act in 1948. Old cottages did not need planners and architects: they grew organically; they were built as simply as possible to meet basic needs for shelter and storage – one main room (low of ceiling for the sake of warmth), with somewhere to store things and a wash-house, and perhaps sleeping lofts in the roof space; bits were added on when needed, or fell off when not, and yet they had a cohesiveness about them and an individual identity. The building style was passed from one generation to the next almost by osmosis; the buildings themselves suited the landscape and became part of it, rather than marching blatantly across it.

There was a time, of course, when people built their own homes. In the seventeenth century, for example, Daniel Defoe described how post-plague Londoners took only a few days to build themselves a shed as shelter on commons and in the woods, later turning it into a cottage with upstairs sleeping loft and thick earthen walls, and a chimney with a bread oven beside the hearth. In the nineteenth century Richard Jefferies described how a man could build his own home, with the help of a few friends – living room, fireplace, chimney, lean-to bakehouse, bedroom, whitewashed walls, thatched roof and earth floor, far superior to some of the typical wattle-and-daub hovels that still existed, and improved with the addition of a well-hedged garden. But cottage building gradually became a matter for builders, not DIY dabblers, and builders needed to be paid for their expertise and labour, and they began to dictate what would be built.

FARMHOUSES

Many of the older cottages that remain were never the humble homes of genuine cottagers; they are often much too big to be called cottages, even those with only three bedrooms. They were more often the homes of farmers than farmworkers, or of tradesmen who considered their status to be well above that of the agricultural labourers that formed the very broad base of the pyramid of rural society. Conversely, farmhouses are often no more than cottages in style but developed to a much greater degree of comfort and spaciousness. Typically the farmhouse would be the focal point for a scattering of workers' cottages, forming a little community of their own. Some of the older farmhouses are still magnificent, with a huge main room big enough to seat a dozen or so at meals, since it was the custom for unmarried labouring men to 'live in' in the farmhouse. There would be an enormous fireplace, a big fat chimney built on later, a roomy bacon loft over the fire, a large cellar for home-brewed beer and cider (virtually every farm made its own beer until about the 1820s, and many country people made their own cider, country wines and ginger beer well into the twentieth century), a cool dairy for making and storing cheeses and butter, a big yard with outhouses, stabling and cavernous barns, and no doubt a duckpond as well.

In contrast to most cottages, farmhouses had the benefit of a roomy back kitchen with a sink and draining-board. In the coolest part of this room, in the absence of a cellar, would be stored the barrels of home-brewed beer and cider. Sides of bacon hung in a draught from a beam along with cured hams stitched into flyproof canvas, and drying bunches of herbs; bags of flour would be stored on low shelves there too. Every beam and post had nails for hanging useful things on.

BRICKS

There are older builders who can still tell you exactly where your house's bricks were made, just from the look of them – not merely which region of the country but the very brickyard. In the broadest terms, certain regions specialised in types of brick that depended on the local geology: for example, yellow bricks based on London clay, or blue bricks from the iron-oxide coal clays of the West Midlands and Staffordshire. In addition to the base clay, colour could be added during the clay-mixing process by including minerals such as barium carbonate or manganese dioxide; colour was also affected by controlling the amount of oxygen during the firing process, producing greys, purples and ochres as well as a wide range of reds.

The oldest bricks give away their age because they contain ash: they hark back to the days when bricks were baked in clamps, such as when Eton College was first built in the 1440s. Brick sizes were variable until 1769, when legislation set the standard as 8¼ x 4 x 2½ inches, but because the government levied a duty on bricks per thousand in 1784, bricks became bigger until the government doubled the tax on larger bricks. Then in 1850 the brick tax was finally abolished; brick sizes became properly standardised at 9 x 4½ x 3 inches and they became mass-produced rather than hand-made.

As every child knows, the Romans knew all about brick-making, but it seems to have become a lost art; no Saxon brick kilns have yet been discovered, though there were medieval ones here and there producing bricks for grander buildings. During the sixteenth and seventeenth centuries the use of brick began to drip down to vernacular buildings, spreading very slowly across the country in the same manner as most other 'fashions': downwards through the social levels, and fanning geographically from the continent-influenced south-east of England, on a time scale that might be as long as half a century from south-east to north-west. In clay areas bricks were made on a very local scale, with many a village and estate having its own brickworks, so that the houses were made literally from local mud.

Even in clay areas local cottages were rarely made solely from brick until the eighteenth or nineteenth century – it was simply too expensive a material for a whole cottage, though brick might be used as quoins on a stone building, straightening and strengthening the corners, door jambs and window frames. In London, the Great Fire of 1666 had led to the creation of byelaws stipulating that all rebuilding must be in brick, to reduce the likelihood of a similar inferno, and by then there were already various regional decrees that chimneys, even in small homes, should be made of brick or stone, not the traditional and far-from-fireproof wattle and clay. By the eighteenth century, most cottages had a good, solid brick or stone chimney, very often built on to the outside – partly because there was no space for a chimney breast indoors and partly so that the neighbours could see that you could afford the bricks.

Transport was the biggest problem; hence the need to make bricks locally. A horse and cart could carry only a few hundred bricks, and it was not until there was a good network of canals and railways that brick transport became more practical. Here again, 1850 or thereabouts was the turning point. The Victorians fell in love with brick; the railways enabled them to transport them all over the country, and it rapidly became cheaper to use mass-produced bricks from elsewhere than to produce them by hand locally. So all over the country harsh red bricks began to dominate, ousting even the local bricks that had reflected the nature of the land from which the clay was dug; and the origins of the Victorian mass-produced bricks became meaningless.

country builders

'Until the fifteenth century, cottagers' homes were usually one-roomed hovels ...'

BUILDERS (whether professional or DIY) often hid something during their work, building a talisman into the wall or chimney to protect the inhabitants. Typically this might be a shoe (usually a child's), a coin or something against witches such as knives or pins. Although there seem to be plenty of old cottages still standing and lived in, they are as nothing compared with the number that have disappeared – the ones made of flimsier and combustible materials or the ones that crumbled to pieces in times of economic depression, or were swept away by frequent floods or by landowners whose view was spoilt by their presence. Until the fifteenth century, cottagers' homes were usually one-roomed mud hovels, roughly thatched, with an open fire in the middle of the room whose smoke drifted out through the many gaps in the roof and whose sparks frequently set the thatch alight. (You can often tell a really old cottage by the pitch of its roof: the steeper the roof, the older the cottage. Thatch, made from various local materials, used to be the universal roof covering until perhaps the late sixteenth century, and it needed a much steeper pitch than do tiles.)

The major era of new cottage building was in Elizabethan and Jacobean times, especially in the period 1575–1625. The boom in building new cottages (usually for yeomen rather than simple cottagers) faded after about 1650, and it became more a matter of adding to or altering what was already there. In general it was not until the nineteenth century that there was another major rash of building new cottages, but these tended to be utilitarian and rather characterless – a vast improvement in terms of quality of life for their occupants but not in the least picturesque.

THE HUMOROUS BUILDER

Sometimes builders had a sense of humour. Once, when a farmhouse was being extended, the owners discovered a pouch built into the wall. On a scrap of paper within it were the following words, in faded pencil:

> This house was built by J. Holder
> Sheet
> Started 14 Nov 1904
> Finished 14 Feb 05
> Worked on the job
> Horace Andrews/Albert Halls/Mac Mace/Tom Jackson/
> Harry Wincome/Jack Shephard/H. Stanley/J. Liccome
> Whosoever may find this is to be the owner of this house from that time evermore the money buried under ...

The rest of the paper had been deliberately torn off by the builder and the hiding-place of the 'treasure' remains unknown.

country builders

THE COTTAGE WITHIN

THE OLD COTTAGES WERE ALWAYS CROWDED – FAMILIES WERE MUCH LARGER THAN THE PRESENT AVERAGE OF TWO OR SO CHILDREN, EVEN WELL WITHIN LIVING MEMORY, IN CONTRAST TO THE TOWNS IN WHICH THE AVERAGE IN 1900 WAS MUCH AS IT IS TODAY. IN MANY A VILLAGE, THOSE WHO ARE NOW IN THEIR SEVENTIES OFTEN COME FROM FAMILIES OF EIGHT, TEN OR MORE, EACH FAMILY CRAMMED INTO A COTTAGE, OR HALF A COTTAGE.

RIGHT
Repairing the rendering at Bovey Tracey, Devon

IN EARLIER TIMES rural homes tended to be empty by day, when both parents might be working and the children would often be doing the same, if they were not at school. With limited artificial light, bed was the place to be once it was dark; there would be no sitting around in a living-room at leisure, though the occupants might be bent over some cottage industry work to bring in a few extra pennies. The furnishings and decor of the cottage were minimal; they could not be afforded, there was little need for them anyway and they were rarely aspired to. Whatever was within the cottage was functional, essential to everyday life, and had little to do with comfort or aesthetics. Home was simply somewhere to escape from the cold and wet of outdoor work, somewhere to eat a hot meal and to sleep.

> *'Plaster on the walls was something of a luxury …'*

The key to rural domestic life was improvisation, creating for yourself what was needed from resources close to hand and preferably costing nothing. This was easier in the country than in the town. Perhaps the biggest contrast with the interior of the modern home is in uniformity: today goods are mass-produced, readily available all over the country and much the same whether you are in the Orkneys or the Isle of Wight, the Welsh hills or the Northumbrian coast. Wherever you live, you can recognise a cooker or a refrigerator immediately for what it is. There is no longer much need (or so much scope) to be ingenious in creating something out of nothing, recycling anything and everything to make for yourself whatever you require; or exploiting (say) the fact that natural running water or a hole dug deep in the soil can keep perishable goods cool – an option not usually open to town-dwellers.

Teatime at a farmhouse in Radnorshire, 1923; note the wallpaper and the dresser

WALLS

Plaster on the inside walls was something of a luxury in cottages for a long while, but a householder who wrote to *The Field* in the 1980s was intrigued to find that the reeds which bedded the plaster of a cottage built in 1787 were still in perfect condition 200 years later, preserved by a combination of the natural silica in the reeds and the lime in the plaster.

Sometimes there are surprises when the paint of later decades is rubbed back a century or two or three. It was not all whitewash, or dirty cream; indeed, some cottagers had a passion for bright colours on their walls and *cottage within*

woodwork, inside and out. Regional rural fashions included deep blue or yellow ochre in the north of England, light green in Derbyshire and red ochre in northern Ireland. The basic limewash that was usually applied to external cob or wattle-and-daub walls to protect them was (and is) often coloured in locally favoured hues of pink, red, yellow ochre, blue, greenish-blue or lime-green by adding certain minerals to the slaked quicklime, already boosted with melted animal fat or linseed oil or milk and curds to make the wash more rainproof. A typical 'country way' of making limewash was as follows: put a bushel of quicklime and twenty pounds of tallow in a rainwater barrel and slake it with hot water; cover it with sackcloth to retain the steam, let it cool and then sieve it before applying.

Indoors, despite the problem of smoky fires that encouraged the use of dark colours, cottagers might use a plain, cheap whitewash (crushed chalk powder in water with a binding agent such as starch): it was a quick and easy way to brighten a dull room, and also acted as a disinfectant. In 1854, *The Field* suggested that the whole of London could do with an external coat of whitewash to lighten the gloomy pall of smoke, narrow streets and tall buildings.

Colour could be added with a stain that mixed red ochre with bull's blood or something equally imaginative. The poet Samuel Taylor Coleridge's cottage at Nether Stowey, Somerset, which he rented for £7 a year for three years as a young man in the late 1790s, was recently restored to the original decor discovered by scraping away wallpaper and paint: his limewash was found to be a bright orange-yellow on the walls, with pale olive green on doors and woodwork. The cottage was described by his wife Sara as a 'miserable hovel', draughty and damp; it was also infested with rodents, but Coleridge said it would be 'an abuse of hospitality' to get rid of them.

In the early nineteenth century, walls were sometimes decorated with stencilled patterns; in the later years of that century mass-produced wallpaper gradually became a more affordable option for some, or cheap prints, or pictures cut from calendars and journals, or home-made samplers and embroidery. Sometimes cottagers used cheap deal to panel their rooms as a practical way of covering the ubiquitous rising damp and as added insulation – which is exactly why the grander houses used panelling in the first place.

FLOORS

The oldest cottages, some of them into the nineteenth century, were so much a part of the land that their floors were simply the bare earth – dusty when dry, slippy when the rain blew in, and frequently flooded with rainwater or even sewage when, as was often the case, the floor was below the outside ground level. The earth could be raked, watered and then beaten with flat pieces of wood to make it smooth and hard. It could then be strengthened, and at the same time decorated, by pressing bone fragments into it; a favourite was to set a pattern of pig's knuckle-bones. Sometimes the floor was given a gleaming finish with the help of oxblood or soot, or simply by regular sweeping.

'... their floors were simply the bare earth.'

Cottagers proudly displaying their new linoleum floor

cottage within

'It was customary to scatter soft rushes over the floor ...'

The dust, even from a well-beaten earth floor, settled everywhere and the trick was to sprinkle it with water before the dust rose. It was customary to scatter soft rushes over the floor, which produced their own dust, and these too would be dampened to lay the dust and also to reduce the risk of a spark from the fire setting them alight.

Some floors were a rammed mixture of lime and ash, almost like plaster. Those who were lucky enough might find local stone, slate or baked clay (bricks or tiles) to lay direct on their earthen floors, but with no underlying insulation these were often cold, damp and uneven. Initially only heavy-duty areas would be protected in this way, and women liked to enhance stone thresholds and hearths with the help of whiting (ground chalk), or to darken the cleaned stone with milk and then pattern it with light-coloured sandstone or wet white clay, or daub it with damp pipeclay in spots, squares and flowers, or sprinkle the dampened stone with swirls of coloured sand. Special floor sand could be sprinkled on brick floors each week to keep them dryer.

The next stage in flooring was boards, which were of unaffordable hardwood until cheap deal was imported in the eighteenth century. The more artistic painted their planks in solid colours, or with patterns. Floorboards were initially used only upstairs, laid loosely over the joists to form sleeping lofts.

It was not until the nineteenth century that floors began to be carpeted, with canvas floor cloths which, in better homes, were painted with pigmented linseed oil, and later factory-printed. In cottages the 'carpet' was more likely to be old potato sacks, or home-woven mats of rushes and straw, or cheap and cheerful rag rugs made from strips of old clothing.

Linoleum was invented in 1860 and became widespread in country cottages – so much easier to keep clean! Proper carpets, although being mass-produced in the nineteenth century, were out of reach for most cottagers until well into the twentieth century.

DOORS

A major problem in old cottages was draughts, against which there was a running battle using rolled-up mats, paper, straw and anything else that might remedy ill-fitting woodwork that alternately swelled with damp and shrank when it dried out, while slowly crumbling with decay from woodworm and rot.

At first, doors were not even fixed: they were merely boards propped across the gap when required, and many a cottage has retained the idea of doors that can easily be lifted off their L-hinges to be placed in a different doorway when the wind changes.

In fact, cottage 'doors' would often have been no more than a piece of that ubiquitous sacking, or woven straw or rush matting, hanging from hooks above the doorway, or of sturdier woven hazel hurdles or bundles of brushwood bound together and hung by means of plaited straw 'hinges'. In some regions these makeshift doors remained the norm for cottages even in Victorian times.

Typically, the outside door opened straight into the main room, so that the weather came in full blast every time the door was opened and seeped in through the gaps when it was closed. Smoke from the fire, however, never seemed to find those same gaps as a means of escape, and many a fireplace was so poorly designed that it was necessary to fling open the door to let the smoke escape whenever the wind was in a certain quarter – usually the coldest.

LOCKS & BOLTS

It was not until the nineteenth century that country cottagers generally used locks or bolts for their doors, because it was often not until then that they had anything worth stealing. More pretentious households locked their doors at a much earlier period and in his Holinshed Chronicle of 1577, William Harrison scoffed at the need for such measures. Harking back to times past, he wrote: 'In those days the courage of the owner was a sufficient defence to keepe the house in safetie but now the assurance of the timber double doores, lockes, and bolts, must defend the man from robbing.'

cottage within

WINDOWS

The word 'window' comes from 'wind eye' or 'wind hole'; originally the window was the escape hole for the fire's smoke (in an age when the fire was simply laid on stones in the middle of the room, with no fireplace or chimney) and would have had no glass. Nor were windows for opening: the fresh air had free access, along with insects, bats, rodents, pollen, field dust, rain and anything else that cared to enter. Windows to admit daylight were simply barred, mullioned, latticed or shuttered to repel larger intruders; sometimes they might be made a little weatherproof by the use of parchment or waxed linen, or the very small lantern panes that could be made from cattle horn. Cottagers usually resorted to open-weave sacking.

By the late seventeenth century smaller houses began to have glazed windows – small offcuts from that deliciously distorting 'bottle' glass for the less than wealthy, held in place with the pliable metal of leaded lights kept rigid in metal frames. And it was not until the middle of the eighteenth century that cottage windows even became openable. Most cottagers could not really afford glass in them anyway until the nineteenth century, when glass was plate rather than spun and could be cut into larger panes. By that magic date of 1850, glass was being mass-produced, almost unwavy and more affordable – especially in the following year when the window taxes that had existed since 1696 were finally abolished. Cottagers often continued to stuff their window gaps with paper; they certainly did not embrace the suburban fashion for stained-glass windows that began to spread from the 1860s and lasted up to the First World War. If you find old stained glass in your cottage, it was probably introduced by a refugee from the suburbs.

Even in Victorian times curtains were usually too extravagant of material for most cottagers, though they might make their own cloth blinds if they could no longer stand the sight and dust of that sacking.

'Cottagers often continued to stuff their window gaps with paper ...'

HEAT AND POWER

In Elizabethan times, Bishop Hall described a cottar's home:
Of one bay's breadth God wot a silly cote
Whose thatched spars are furred with sluttish soote,
A whole inch thick, shining like Blackmore's brows
Through smoke that downe the headlesse barrell blows.
At his bed's head feaden his stalled teame,
His swine beneath his pullen o'er the beame.

'The hearth … usually the only source of rural domestic warmth until the twentieth century.'

The idea of keeping your horses and cattle close to your bed is comfortably warming, though perhaps one could do without the pigs rootling on the floor and the chickens sitting above your head on the beam. You can still find evidence of old wattle-and-daub cottages that are closely skirted by catslide outshots which originally housed livestock on the other side of the family wall.

But, oh, those smoking fireplaces! A major attraction for would-be cottage dwellers from the towns is an inglenook fire, burning sweetly scented logs from an old apple tree, the flames leaping cheerfully, throwing up little showers of sparks now and then with a comforting crackle, offering glowing red embers below for toasting bread and marshmallows or roasting chestnuts and potatoes. The reality tends to be more smoke than flame, and smoke that is determined to belch into the room rather than up the chimney. Modern cottagers prefer the efficiency of a woodburning stove, if wood is the fuel of choice: the stoves don't smoke, they don't sulk and they throw the heat into the room instead of up that chimney.

Taking a break from sheep-shearing: the kettle on the range was always ready for brewing tea

The hearth may have been the heart of the home, and usually the only source of rural domestic warmth until the twentieth century, but it was too often the cause of early death, either from lung disease exacerbated by the smoke or from the very real threat of the place catching fire. (Those with thatch on the roof would whitewash the thatch to make it less flammable.)

Many people actually believed that inhalation of smoke kept you healthy. Rector Harrison bemoaned the wimpishness that he perceived in many sixteenth-century households thus:

> *Now we have manie chimnies, and yet our tenderlings complaine of rheumes, catarhs, and poses. Then had we none but reredoes, and our heads did never ake. For as the smoke in these daies was supposed to be a sufficient harding for the timber of the house, so it was reputed a far better medicine to keepe the goodman and his familie from the quacke or pose, wherewith as then verie few were oft acquainted.*

Originally the fire was set in the centre of the room, with no fireplace and no chimney. By Harrison's time the fire was more usually against a wall, with a hood over it of wattle daubed with clay and plaster to channel the heat and power

smoke up to the roof. Two centuries later most homes, even country cottages, had proper chimneys, though chimney builders rarely understood the basic proportions of the chimney throat that are necessary to avoid smoke problems. Count Rumford, at the end of the eighteenth century, was one of the first to understand these principles but his ideas took a long time to filter out to rural areas. His secret was to reduce the throat to only four inches deep; he also made the fireplaces themselves less deep, so that more heat was thrown into the room instead of going straight up the chimney. The huge inglenook fireplaces, with their cosy built-in wooden seats, had big wide chimneys to match, virtually ensuring that they would billow smoke into the room. Cottagers did their best by draping little curtains from the inglenook beam, and by letting the fire ash build up as high as possible so that the fire itself was raised and its smoke more likely to find the chimney.

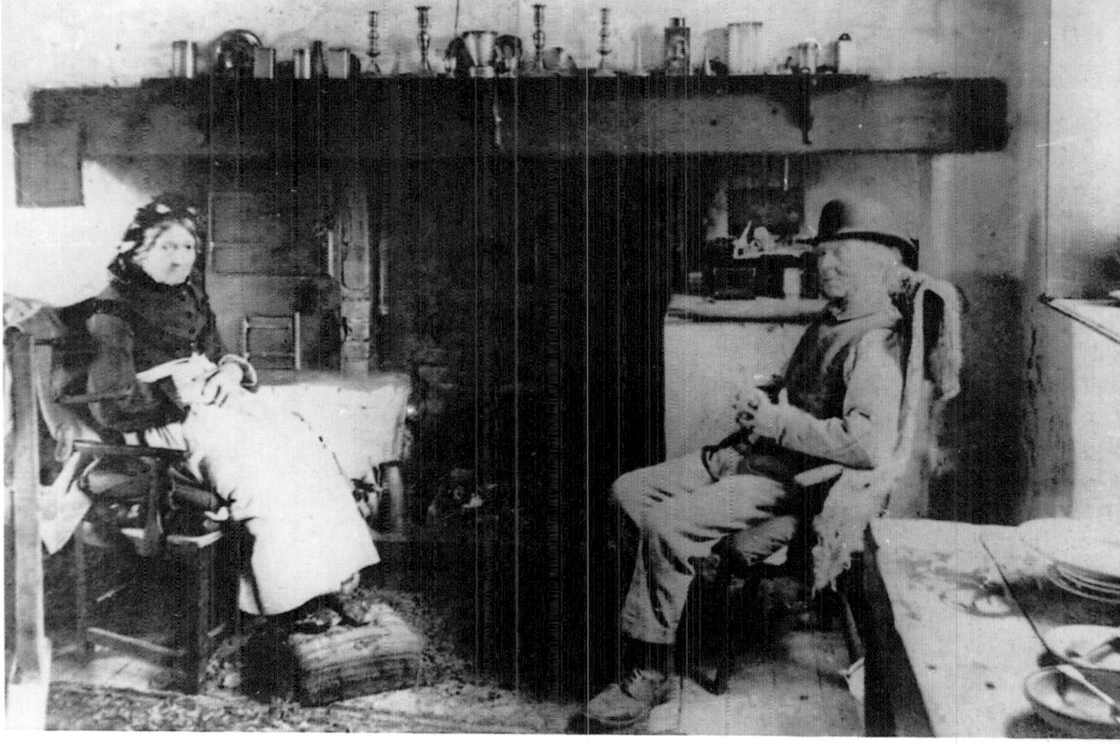

Sitting by the range in a Dorset cottage, 1890

The fire was not simply for the pleasure of reading dream pictures into the flames, or keeping warm if you were close up to it (the old problem of fire-mottled face and shins but frozen back and kidneys). It was where kettles were boiled and family meals were cooked; it was often the main source of light in the evening; and it had a psychological, almost religious significance: many people insisted on keeping the fire burning continuously, summer and winter, night and day, because it was unlucky to let it die, as well as being a considerable labour to relight it and bring it up to a high enough temperature quickly. Even today, some of the older generation keep their faithful Rayburn burning year round, and feel empty and lonely without its comforting background presence.

COOKING AIDS

Open fires, set in big wide fireplaces, were furnished with all manner of ironwork, in the days when blacksmiths were thriving in every village and roving tinkers could mend your broken pots and pans. There was the essential heavy, cast-iron, fat-bellied cooking pot hung over the fire on its chain or ratcheted hanger, dangling from a wooden bar that was fixed some six or seven feet up the chimney, or the pot simply stood in the ashes on three stubby legs; whole cottage meals could be stewed in these hard-working cauldrons. A kettle might dangle from an 'idleback', a device that allowed you to tip the kettle for pouring from it without burning your fingers by taking it off its hanger. Quite elaborate wrought-iron chimney cranes were ingeniously created so that you could easily place cooking implements higher or lower over the fire or swing them from one side to the other or away from the fire altogether. There might be a gridiron, or a flat iron griddle or bakestone hanging over the fire for baking oatcakes.

'Many people insisted on keeping the fire burning continuously, summer and winter, day and night ...'

heat and power

IN MORE AFFLUENT homes there would be skillets made of brass or of bell-metal (copper and tin), set on trivets. Skillets developed into flat-based brass or copper saucepans, if you were rich enough to afford them and remembered to have them 'tinned' on the inside to avoid copper-poisoning. Poorer households used cast-iron saucepans long into the nineteenth century and gradually adopted enamelled vessels in the latter half of that century. They also used cheap wrought-iron frying pans with long handles or with hanging handles; and handled stoneware or earthenware pipkins.

Home baking in a sixteenth-century Essex farmhouse in 1949

'... in some regions they burned dried animal dung as fuel.'

There might be a meat-roasting spit resting on tall iron fire-dogs, turned by a wide range of devices – pulley-wheels, geared weighted winches driven by gravity, smoke-jacks driven by the fire's hot air, clockwork-spring mechanical bottle-jacks and the like; in poorer cottages they would simply rig up a system of twisted string. Very occasionally a farmhouse might even have a dogwheel for turning the spit – quite literally a small dog scampering like a hamster in a treadmill. (Dogs also helped to churn farm butter; and where a bigger house had a particularly deep well a donkey or horse would trudge around and around to raise the water.)

It is always interesting to look at inventories of household items, to see what implements people used to use. For example, after the death of Arthur Bettesworth, gentleman, in 1670, the inventory for his long-since-vanished seven-bedroom farmhouse included a pair of andirons in each room, along with assorted fire shovels and tongs; in the kitchen there were five spits, a jack, two iron dripping pans, two pairs of pot-hangers, four iron pots, an iron kettle, two pairs of gridirons, a rack, three brass kettles, two brass pots and more; in the brewhouse he had a brass furnace and brass cauldron, a brewing vat, a cooler, four kivers, a tunn, three tubs, four buckets and a cheese press, not to mention all sorts of baking troughs, salting troughs, salting tubs and barrels in the cellar.

Before the cooking could begin, the fire had to be lit and kept alight. Friction matches were not invented until 1826, and to strike a spark from a tinderbox was something of an art. But first, there was all the labour of finding something to burn; the luckier cottagers had commoners' rights to gather firewood, peat or turf for the hearth and in some regions they burned dried animal dung as fuel. Coal was already being used in some smaller country homes by the mid seventeenth century if it was mined locally; in the rest of the country coal did not become a common fuel until the railways made its transport cheap two centuries later.

In cottages, much of the food was boiled, or stewed. The iron pot might be kept simmering for days, more bits being chucked in to enrich the broth at intervals. Boil-in-the-bag was common well into the twentieth century: you set your joint of bacon (the cottager's staple meat) to simmer in the pot; after a while you would add potatoes tied in cotton bags (reclaimed from the village shop, which sold dry goods in them) and other garden vegetables in a separate cotton bag, and no doubt a suet pudding wrapped in a piece of old white sheet. The

heat and power

bacon would be eked out for several meals in different guises, and was inevitably a piece of your own pig, which had been living the good life at the end of the garden.

As many country people relied heavily on the pig for their protein and winter-warming fat, large chimneys often housed a bacon loft, or the sides of bacon were just hung in the chimney to smoke after being salt-cured. Homemade sausages often dangled in the smoke and were cut down for cooking as and when they were needed.

BAKING

Small loaves and cakes could be baked straight on the hot ashes, covered by an upside-down redware pot to act as a miniature oven, with more hot ashes heaped over the pot. In older and better cottages and farmhouses you might still find evidence of a bread oven, probably long since bricked off or converted into a cupboard. The oven, generally next to the main fireplace and sometimes built as a little extension bulging on the outside of the home, was usually a tunnel-like cavity, with a gently arching ceiling and an iron door. The method of baking was this: first, bavins or faggots must be gathered from the woods and commons – these were bushy twiggery, bound together in small bundles. The faggots were loaded into the oven and allowed to burn fiercely, with the door closed. When they had burned out, the oven was hot enough to start baking: the ashes were raked out before the dough was slipped into the oven on a long-handled paddle-like 'peel'. You often found pieces of charcoal stuck to the bottom of your loaf.

Built-in bread ovens were something of a luxury as bricks were expensive. West Country cottagers might use portable earthenware ('cloam') ovens, the last of which were made in Truro in 1937. Elsewhere people created an instant baking oven by turning the iron cooking pot upside-down on the fire and surrounding it with hot ashes, and these developed into lidded cast-iron baking pots or 'camp ovens', known in Yorkshire as yetlings.

Farmers' wives continued baking longer than most cottagers, who by the nineteenth century usually bought their bread or took their own dough and cake batches down to the ever-warm ovens of the village baker; he would also roast their Sunday joints. According to a national food inquiry in 1863, only 20 per cent of rural labouring families still baked their own bread, but home-baking persisted longer in areas where coal was readily available as a cheap source of fuel.

'You often found pieces of charcoal stuck to the bottom of your loaf.'

Baking oatcakes on the bakestone

heat and power

GRATES AND RANGES

'Cooking over an open fire gave way to the challenges of the range ...'

With the growing affordability of coal, more efficient methods of cooking began to be developed. Although wood can be burnt on the hearth itself, or slung across firedogs, coal fires require grates, allowing the ashes to drop away from the coals. Grates became quite common in coal country in the seventeenth and eighteenth centuries, and in places like London, where wood was hard to come by but coal could be brought in by sea.

The fireplace began to change: the old all-purpose inglenook, spacious enough to accommodate wooden benches so that you could huddle right over the fire for warmth, became a much smaller area. Slow-burning grates on firebrick bases were being used all over the country in the final decades of the nineteenth century and the hearth became more suited to merely keeping you warm than being a place for cooking and bacon-curing as well. Cooking over an open fire gave way to the challenges of the range, but rather later in country cottages, with their one main living room, than in town homes with their fancy parlours. Where wood was still plentiful, for example in southern Britain, cooking on the big old open fireplace persisted. Country people, well within living memory, often continued to cook on open fires but out of doors: typically a bonfire would be made up for cooking the vegetables, especially in summer when it was too hot to cook inside. The garden barbecue is nothing new.

In coal country, although you might have a hob grate for boiling a kettle (ironworks in Coalbrookdale, Shropshire, and in Falkirk were both famous for their hob grates), grates were more often found in kitchens. They were used for cooking, and by the eighteenth century they were usually described as ranges, in comparison with 'stove grates' for heating living rooms. The open range, which was initially developed late in the seventeenth century, became an open coal fire with an iron baking oven on one side and a boiler on the other (if you were lucky) to replace the old portable copper, both with cooking hobs but also with the old beam for dangling your kettle over the open fire, where you could also roast the meat. It was not the most efficient method for either heating or cooking, and the next development was to contain the central fire under a cast-iron hotplate that kept the smoke and ashes away from the food and kept the heat where you wanted it. Traditionalists at heart, many country families claimed that the meat tasted wrong from such a range and they preferred to roast on the old open fire. Then during the nineteenth century manufacturers put iron doors across the front to make the closed range, which was particularly popular in the Midlands (where they were often called 'kitcheners'), but many cottagers disliked not being able to see those warming flames, nor could they quite get the hang of dampers.

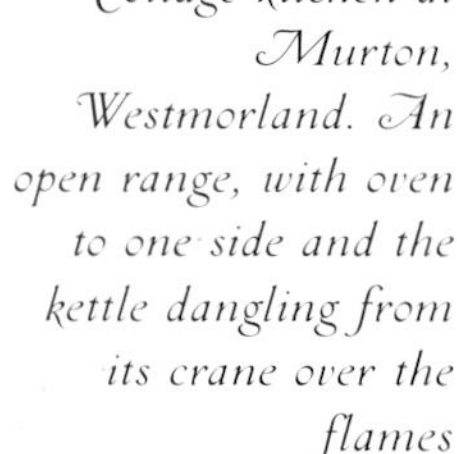

Cottage ktichen at Murton, Westmorland. An open range, with oven to one side and the kettle dangling from its crane over the flames

heat and power

Manufacturers persisted, and created small, cheap ranges ideally suited to cottages. They also began to make portable ones; in the first half of the nineteenth century ranges were built in, at one with the fireplace brickwork, but later portable ones stood on their own legs and were completely encased in iron, which meant they could even stand in the middle of the room, if you built an appropriate flue pipe to the old chimney. This type became far more popular in Scandinavian countries than in Britain.

Just after the First World War, farm kitchens in Cornwall, for example, had nearly all retained their open fireplaces, with a cloam oven alongside for baking, but some had by then installed an iron range as well for quick cooking on the weekly baking day. Most country households had a range of some kind by then, even if they still cursed and swore at the sweat and sootiness of them.

In 1929 the first Aga cookers, burning coke, came into Britain and proved ideal for farmhouse kitchens, though far too expensive for cottages. The latter eventually opted for the smaller, cheaper Rayburns that many still run today; they fitted perfectly into the smaller cottage fireplace and they were much easier to clean and more efficient at burning fuel than the old ranges. Anthracite was the ideal fuel, cleaner than coal and burning slowly enough to keep the fire in all night, but it was usually too expensive for cottagers. Nor did they benefit from the new fuels that town-dwellers took for granted: piped gas still has not reached many country areas even now, and mains electricity did not come to the villages until at the earliest the 1920s and more usually not until the 1950s or later, though many big country houses generated their own electricity supplies right from the beginning of the twentieth century. For example, the Hawkshaw house described earlier had a private electricity supply in 1901 and central heating from 1910; it also boasted a private indoor telephone connecting the big house, stables and lodge in 1917, and a public telephone system in 1924.

Even when electricity was attainable, many rural households distrusted it. Some chose oil stoves, which were often highly temperamental and filthy, with a tendency to set light to things and blow soot all over the kitchen. There were frequent problems with electricity power cuts in rural areas, as branches and trees fell on overhead power lines, usually just as the Sunday roast was beginning to sizzle. In the south of England, for example, the great storm of October 1987 proved to be a blessing in disguise. The 'hurricane' winds brought down huge numbers of trees, and blacked out large swathes of the countryside for days on end (people with solid-fuel cookers were much in demand). The aftermath meant a great deal of new cabling throughout the grid system and it has been noticeable since then that power cuts are now rare, whereas they used to be regular features of country life.

'In 1929 the first Aga cookers, burning coke, came into Britain ...'

Most cottagers swept their own chimneys; in the old days they used a bundle of goose feathers

heat and power

'The countryside, as ever, was several decades behind the town.'

LIGHTING

In 1925, Gertrude Jekyll (1843–1932) wrote: 'We who are accustomed to strike a match when we want a light can hardly realise what a difficult job it was a century and a half ago. We now have brilliant and clean light from electricity ...'

This renowned gardener was living near Godalming, in Surrey, at the time. Less than 20 miles away, my own Sussex village had no electricity until the 1950s, despite the fact that Hugh Gaitskell, Minister for Power and Light, owned a farm here. So people were still 'striking a light' instead of flicking a switch. The countryside, as ever, was several decades behind the town. As recently as 1999, an elderly couple living in rural Leicestershire still had no electricity, gas or mains water. They used oil-lamps for lighting, an open stove for cooking and heating, and garden spring-water for drinking. Their situation became known when they asked the local council for help in digging a well. They grew most of their own food, and used a 50-year-old army motorcycle and sidecar if they needed to shop for extra items. And they are by no means the only ones without all the modern conveniences that are taken for granted by most but either rejected by or unattainable for the few even now. Mind you, the rejection may not be bilateral: I know of one couple in which the husband frequently complains to visitors about his wife's poor performance as a dish-washer. Yet all he has allowed her is a very old-fashioned cold-water sink in the corner ....

Rushes from the Windrush being dried. These are probably for rushwork baskets and mats; different types of rush were used for rushlights

In the big country houses, candles were the means of providing artificial light in the first part of the eighteenth century. Many cottagers could not afford even tallow candles, let alone wax ones, until perhaps the 1830s, and some not even until the end of that century. Instead they relied on the flicker of firelight or, as ever, they improvised: they made their own candles from rushes gathered from the meadows in summer. Rushlight has been used for many centuries – it was known to the Greeks and Romans, and it continued to be used in many English cottages throughout the nineteenth century and in some Welsh ones well into the twentieth.

The long, tubular rush leaf is not much thicker than a grass stem, and the art was to peel away its green 'rind' to expose the fine network of white pith within, leaving just a sliver of rind so that the whole core did not simply fall apart. The rushes were dried in the sun and then steeped in scalding-hot animal tallow – preferably mutton fat skimmed from the cooking pot (mixed with a little beeswax if the cottager kept hives). With the fat set hard, the rush was placed in a special holder (it was too frail to support itself) and lit, to burn like a weak candle. According to Gilbert White of Selborne in the 1770s, if you had to buy your dried rushes and your grease, you could have 800 hours of light for only three shillings. He said that, foolishly, 'the very poor, who are always the worst economists, and, therefore, must continue very poor, buy a halfpenny candle every evening which, in their blowing, open rooms, does not burn much more than two hours. Thus they have only two hours' light for their money instead of eleven.' William Cobbett, writing in 1822, said that his own grandmother 'never burned a candle in her house in her life' – she only used rushes.

To light your rush, or your candle, you either pushed a spillikin into the flames of the eternally burning fire or you tried to use a tinder box. The fire was easier.

The smell of melting tallow was not pleasant, but candles used the same type of fat. Most cottagers could not spare any tallow from their infrequent meat meals; they put their dripping on bread and ate it, rather than

heat and power

wasting it as light, and anyway relied on bacon, rather than the fat from sheep and cattle that made the best candle tallow. Farmers, of course, had the advantage of keeping their own livestock, and could easily make their own tallow candles, though they usually preferred to buy them ready-made, or became part-time candle-makers themselves to supply local villages and towns.

Beeswax was vastly superior to tallow for candles, both in the light it produced and its lack of smell and smoke, but wax candles were far too expensive for everyday household use. In the late eighteenth century candle-makers began to use spermaceti (sperm-whale oil) but this too was expensive. Then in the second half of the nineteenth century mass-produced paraffin-wax candles became widely available; these produced a steady, long-lasting and almost smokeless flame, and they were affordable. All sorts of candle holders and candle lanterns were invented, to suit the purposes of reading and working by candlelight or carrying your light around with you as you moved about the home, pottered up to bed, went along the garden path to the privy, took a journey by coach or ventured out into the weather to check your livestock or milk your cows.

By then, however, there was more competition in lighting. Oil lamps had become increasingly sophisticated, and again it was paraffin that led the way – it was cleaner and easier to use than the various fish, vegetable and other oils that were customary. Then came gas lighting (though rarely in rural areas except in the big houses) and at last, clean and instant electricity, which relegated the use of candles to festive occasions and power cuts.

Women collecting coal from a mine's waste heaps before a threatened coal strike, 1912

'Wax candles were far too expensive for everyday household use.'

FURNISHING

Except in the grandest houses, furnishing was minimal until the Victorian period, when all classes began to fill their homes with bits and bobs. Even the poorest cottagers then began to accumulate knick-knacks, perhaps picked up at country fairs, such as china mantelpiece ornaments, and then dressers to exhibit their collections.

Yet in the Holinshed Chronicle of 1577, Harrison the rector had noted that not only were the gentry decorating their homes with tapestries, 'Turkie work', pewter, brass, plate and fine linen but even the farmers (forever aspiring to become gentlemen) were putting tapestry and silk hangings in the bedroom, showing off cupboards full of plate, and adorning their tables with carpets (carpets were originally designed for tables, not for floors) and fine 'naperie'. 'There are old men yet dwelling in the village where I remaine, which have noted three things to be marvellouslie altered in England, within their sound remembrance.' The first of these was the 'multitude of chimnies latelie erected'; the second was 'the great though not general amendment of lodging, for, said they, our fathers and we ourselves also have lien full oft upon straw pallets, on rough mats, covered onelie with a sheet, under coverlets made of dogswain, or hapharlots (I use their own termes), and a good round log under their heads in steed of a bolster or pillow. ... Pillows, said they, were thought meet onelie for women in child-bed.' The third change the old men noticed was 'the exchange of vessell as of treene platters into pewter, and wooden spoones into silver or tin'. In their time, they had depended on wooden tableware, but now it was all fancy pewter, silver and 'a dozzen of spoones to furnish up the sute'.

The Bettesworth inventory of 1670, mentioned earlier, listed tables, couches, stools and 'joyned stools', chairs, 'cubbards', carpets, curtains and 'quishorns' (cushions) in most of the rooms. The several bed chambers each had 'bedstedle matt and cord', often with 'valence and curtens'; each 'bedstedle' had a feather bed and feather bolster, usually a pair of blankets, perhaps some feather pillows, and there was generally a chest or trunk of some kind in the chamber for storage. He also had flock beds in two rooms and a couple of trundle beds in another (no doubt for servants). In the linen cupboard were eight pairs of sheets ('at 13/4d a pair') and eight pairs of coarse sheets (at 6/8d). This was a wealthy household; most cottagers would have had no more than truckle beds with straw mattresses and certainly no sheets, with perhaps a coarse blanket or sacking thrown on top to keep you a little warmer. No wonder they kept the fire in all night!

WATER SUPPLIES

Household water – pure, fresh, essential – is taken for granted now: a turn of the tap, and there it is, straight into the glass or kettle with no thought as to where it came from. Most households, even country ones, are now 'on the mains' for water supplies, though many rural ones still have private sewage disposal systems, just as they always did.

In many villages, mains water was unknown even fifty years ago. In the early 1940s, 25 per cent of rural parishes had no piped water and 50 per cent had no sewage disposal systems. According to the 1951 census, 20 per cent of all private households in Britain still had no piped water supply, and it needs to be borne in mind that the majority of those would have been in rural areas, where about 20 per cent of the population of Britain still lived.

For most unpiped households, every drop of water for drinking, cooking, house cleaning, bathing, brewing and laundering had to be drawn manually and often laboriously – caught from springs, dipped from streams and ponds, drawn from rainwater tanks and butts, hand-pumped or wound up from garden wells.

The village pump

PUMPS AND TANKS

Some homes had pumps outside the back door, or within the scullery – who needs a gym workout when they could be pumping water for their cold morning shower? But pumps had their own funny little ways and it was important to understand them. In particular, their pipes tended to freeze solid in winter. Bigger pumps (hydraulic rams) were employed on big estates to push water uphill to the house from streams and ponds in the marshy valley below.

Where groundwater levels were uncertain, people built underground water storage tanks which, in theory, retained enough water to last through the summer, though it was hardly fresh. Such tanks were rare for rural cottages until perhaps the 1920s or 1930s. Instead, smaller homes might rely on the waterbutt by the back door, collecting roof rainwater and all that went with it – moss, lichens, twigs, leaves, insects and algae, for example. In a good season you could store enough rainwater for all the household's everyday needs, perhaps even a bath once a week if the bathwater was shared by all the family. But not in summer.

Town dwellers had piped water long before those in the country, and it seems a little unfair that, according to old Eddie Taylor (eighty-four when he was remembering in 1950), 'they pumped Wolmer Pond dry when Brighton built their new pumping station on Race Hill'. Wolmer Pond, some 40 miles from Brighton, was on West Sussex's northern borders with Hampshire in an area of heaths and hangers renowned as Sussex's watersheds. The local population in this remote rural area did not have its own mains water until after Mr Taylor's time.

LEFT
Welsh farmhouse interior at Builth Wells, with a splendid table lamp

water supplies

WATER PURITY

'Wells became fouled by dead rodents ...'

Water purity was a major problem. Wells became fouled by dead rodents or by being too close to the privy; rainwater tanks, unless soundly sealed and lightproof, bred bacteria and insects; streams and ponds were also where livestock drank and paddled, cartwheels were dipped to swell them to fit their iron rims again, steam engines sucked up their water supply, sheep were washed before shearing, children swam, ducks and geese defecated, rats loitered – and those ponds were often the source of the water in the bowsers that were drawn by horse for delivery to your door. There is a theory that country people, living in constant association with polluted water, developed an immunity to it; and indeed this was highlighted during the Second World War when evacuees, instantly succumbed to local water impurity in their temporary 'country-fresh' homes.

Only the lucky homes had access to pure spring water. In 1808 Charles Vancouver, waxed lyrical about Devon's local water supplies.

> *All the springs rising below the foot of Dartmoor are collected with great care ... There can be no purer or more wholesome water anywhere, than that which is generally to be met with in this district; the springs which supply the town of Dartmouth are peculiarly inviting to the eye, and agreeable to the taste, and although the stream which is conveyed over Rodborough-down is at all times slightly tinged with a copper-colour, it seems in no respect complained of, but affords an ample and inestimable supply to the shipping and inhabitants at Dock.*

Elsewhere in the county,

> *Of all the streams with which this part of the county seems so highly favoured, the river Bray and its superior branches, hold the first rank for clearness and salubrity, as well for domestic use, as for the purposes of irrigation. The streams ... are little if at all inferior for any purposes to 'which the most crystal fountains or the purest streams can be applied.*

Lower Slaughter, a Cotswold village

WELLS

Good welldiggers were men of skill and indeed courage. Many a country well is as much as 60–100 feet deep and today those who repair them usually wear wetsuits and carry gas masks and full climbing gear. The old welldiggers knew the risks but had to take them, with only a candle to warn them of unbreathable air. Cyril's uncle was one of those who ran out of luck and was overcome by gases down the well; others slipped on the wet walls and drowned.

There is an art to using a well. Novices who simply drop the wooden pail on its rope find to their surprise that it bobs about on top of the water. The knack is in persuading it to tilt so that the water can begin to spill over the brim. Well pails were traditionally of wood, built in the manner of a cask, with wooden staves bound by iron bands; it was not until late in the Victorian period that galvanised metal buckets began to be used.

Those same well novices have probably already knocked themselves out on the flying windlass handle when they let it go. Then there is the sheer hard work of winching the full pail up again and of carrying it indoors time and time again without getting yourself soaked by the slopping water. Yes, there is even an art to carrying a pailful of water. The usual vessel was heavy and wooden, narrower at the top to reduce spillage; sometimes two such 'stoups' might be carried with the aid of a wooden yoke across the shoulders; or a tub of water would be slung on a pole carried by two women; or perhaps a pitcherful of water might be carried on the head, biblical style. (Ponder on these matters next time you are complaining about a hosepipe ban in your area, and think about the fact that a pail would probably contain 2 gallons of water – about what a modern toilet flushes in one go!)

'My first chore in the morning, before going to work on the farm, was to draw water for the house – enough to last the day,' says Bill. 'We had this well, 90 feet deep. Carry all the water to the house, and then carry it all out again when it was done with, tip the dirty water in the garden.' Bill's routine was typical for many country dwellers.

For some cottagers the well was conveniently just outside the door (in some farmhouses it was actually inside the kitchen, under a big flagstone) but for many the well would be across the yard or garden, or even further away in a neighbour's garden or across the fields. In outlying rural areas each cottage usually had its own well, but in villages or where cottages were grouped together on the big country estates the drawing of well water became a communal activity and a chance for a good old chat.

George Sturt, writing before the First World War, remarked that in times of drought water often had to be carried long distances in pails, usually by women, and that many cottages had no water unless the weather was wet anyway. He learnt that in his own Surrey village people were 'saving up the cooking water of one day to be used over again on the day following' in a dry summer.

Wells were far from infallible. Beverley Nichols, writing in the early 1930s, described the dreaded day when his cottage well in Huntingdonshire ran dry during the 'Great Drought'. He did have a bathroom but all the water for it had to be pumped up from the well into a cistern in the roof before the tap could be turned on. It was 'lovely brown water, as soft as silk' and, the cistern being small, it had to be used with frugality, a fact that his frequent town visitors failed to appreciate. One day he turned the tap and 'nothing happened except a noise that is best spelt "Hich"'. He looked down the well – it was as dry as a desert. In despair, he went to see the formidable Mrs M., who had the best well in the neighbourhood, 80 feet deep and producing as much as 500 gallons an hour of clear sparkling water, pumped up by a small donkey engine. She knew all about underground streams; she quickly discovered that his dry well was not on a spring, but relied on water randomly filtering through the soil. They summoned an ancient water-diviner, 'a man with curious eyes ... very liquid, and faintly shot with green', who produced a twig from his pocket, looked straight ahead and began to walk, very slowly, with his arms rigid to his side. His forked hazel twig did indeed twitch violently to indicate the place to dig a new well, only 14 feet below ground, which instantly produced copious clear water.

water supplies

In his Worcestershire survey of the same period, W. Pitt said that the best of the cottages were 'very properly built near a perennial stream of clear water, an object of considerable consequence, and which should be always had in view in the erection of cottages'. In some parts of the country, it is still possible to trace evidence of a few steps on the bank of a stream, down which the cottagers would have carried their water pails.

'... no wonder so many rural families in the nineteenth century only drank tea or beer, never water.'

In the late 1870s George Dew, a local Relieving Officer in Oxfordshire, had to visit Scotland Cottage, Ardley, where eight people were ill with typhoid fever, the father of the family, a shepherd, having just died of the disease at the age of forty-six. Dew took a sample of their drinking water from the pump: 'The water appeared as if very slightly tinged with soap-suds, & on holding it up in the bottle before the sun there could be seen an immense quantity of filaments resembling what is sometimes called flue; but the chief feature belonging to the water was a greasy film which immediately settled upon its surface.' No wonder the cottagers were dying like flies, and no wonder so many rural families in the nineteenth century only drank tea or beer, never water.

Even when mains water did come to the countryside (in many places not until the 1950s), old habits died hard. Yes, it was a joy to turn the tap and watch the water splashing merrily into the sink, but could you trust the stuff enough to drink it? Oh no, not unless you boiled it first, especially if you knew that it had been stored in the local concrete water tower that was a landmark for miles around. Even after boiling, the taste depended on the local water source, and most of us still habitually run the cold-water tap for a while in the morning to get rid of funny overnight tastes and sediments. How many of us today have any idea of the source of our mains water? We are merely thankful for its quality and its convenience.

water supplies

DRAINS

A derelict cottage in Sussex woodland had a typical arrangement. There was an old sink outside, next to the back door and beside the well. In this case the sink was simply a stone container in which a wooden tub or baked-clay redpan would sit. There was no plug-hole because there were no drains: you filled the tub by hand and you emptied it by hand, into the garden. Many cottages had wooden sinks (sometimes lead-lined) or earthenware ones; later they might be of galvanised iron or, rather more grandly, of enamelled porcelain as the Victorian period progressed. By the interwar years of the twentieth century, sinks were more likely to be enamelled or glazed, with a wooden or slate draining-board alongside, and with a plugged drainhole emptying into a bucket underneath or, at last, directly into a drain, albeit one that ran into a soakaway.

Most of us now pull out the bath plug or flush the toilet with never a thought as to where it all goes, but some of us in rural areas still rely on our own sewage-disposal systems in the garden – more advanced than of old, but stern reminders about being profligate with water.

Today those systems are likely to be septic tanks – a series of covered chambers acting like a miniature sewage works and from which, in theory, potable water eventually trickles into the local streams. Nobody ever inspects them to see that this is so, and often they pong with a sickly sweet smell, especially in summer. Septic tanks rely on beneficial bacteria, and modern habits tend to be antagonistic to those bacteria; detergents, bleach, chemicals used for cleaning toilets and baths, hormones from women taking contraceptive pills, and various other substances that a household on mains drainage flushes away with gay abandon, leaving the problem to the water companies, must be used much more cautiously when you have a septic tank.

At least we now have pipework to remove soiled water from the house. In the nineteenth century most country homes had no such thing. The waste water, whatever its source, might be chucked into an open ditch just outside the back door, creating a considerable health hazard to the residents and their neighbours. If you look in country churchyards you will see evidence of the epidemics of typhoid fever and cholera that resulted.

In the Oxfordshire village of Lower Heyford, George Dew noted in his diary in the late 1870s the state of the cottages up Bicester Hill owned by Corpus Christi College, Oxford (seemingly the most lackadaisical of landlords). Complaints about the 'sanitary state' of the cottages had been running on for years and many of the inhabitants suffered from assorted fevers and illnesses, largely due to an open communal sewage ditch beside their homes. Dew wanted each cottage to be given a strip of land at the back as a garden 'for sanitary purposes'. The college's refusal to do so was seen by him as 'a bar to health, pleasure, & morality to nearly half the cottages of the village'. Without a garden, the cottagers had nowhere to dispose of their own waste except in the open ditch.

Plumbing comes to the countryside: sink with hot and cold taps

Most Victorians realised that something must be done, in both the country and the town. During the 1870s there was an attempt to bring mains drainage to some rural areas but unfortunately it was so badly designed that it polluted local water supplies and put country people off the idea of public sewage systems for a very long time. In 1956, the National Federation of Women's Institutes published a survey of its member organisations: nearly every village at that time still put the improvement of sewage facilities at the top of its list of concerns, closely followed by water quality and availability (indoor WCs and running water from taps were eagerly requested) and electricity supplies. In a similar survey in 1999, when more than 80 per cent of the institutes still classified themselves as rural, there was no mention of sewage, water or electricity in the improvements demanded.

'The waste water … might be chucked into an open ditch just outside the back door …'

water supplies

As for those squares of old newspaper hanging from a string in the privy …

PRIVIES

In towns, in the latter part of the nineteenth century, the local councils would remove 'night soil' from people's privies on a fairly regular basis and cart it away into the countryside for dumping, or for selling to farmers as manure. In the country there was no such system. People dealt with their night soil themselves: dad would dig a pit and empty the contents of the privy into it when necessary. If you have a strongly growing patch of nettles at the end of your garden, that is probably where the night soil ended up.

The privy was usually a simple wooden or corrugated iron shed (or brick if you were lucky) within which would be a scrubbed plank to sit on, with a square hole or two cut into it. Instead of the customary country dock-leaf, pieces of cut-up newspaper (the *Daily Mail* for preference as its ink was less likely to come off in use) might dangle from a string or nail for your convenience. Beneath the plank there might be no more than a hole in the ground, with a simple soakaway dug out by dad, and a bucketful of dry earth or ashes which you could sprinkle over the effluent to soak it up. At intervals a new hole would have to be dug and a corrugated privy could readily be shifted to cover the new site.

The daily trudge carrying water from the well

Privies were usually down the garden (there was no space indoors for an earth closet), which meant creeping out in all weathers, at night as well as by day, though a chamber pot under the bed was useful at night except that you had to empty it into the garden in the morning. Imagine traipsing down the dark garden path in the early hours in the rain, with slugs and toads squelching underfoot, owls hooting, bats flying, bogeymen lurking … and being unable to see the spiders, beetles, snails and roosting hens that you knew lived in the privy. Many a child evacuated to the countryside during the Second World War would soil their bed rather than face such a challenge.

In the more refined privy, the effluent would go straight into a galvanised lavatory bucket; you still had to sprinkle the stuff with ashes or earth, and dad then had the labour of emptying the bucket when it was full, tipping it into his trenches and planting vegetables on top to make the most of the manure. The next refinement was the use of chemicals in the lavatory bucket, which liquidised solids but failed to disguise the stink.

As for those squares of old newspaper hanging from a string in the privy, many will remember the hard, shiny, non-absorbent toilet paper that replaced the comforting softness and absorbency of newsprint. The hard stuff, which you couldn't even read in idle moments, came in sheets or in due course in rolls, with brand names like Everest ('The "Peak" of Toilet Papers'), Bronco and Izal. By the 1950s this noisy, rustly paper had found its way into every cottage, and remained there for at least the next twenty years, when gradually it was replaced by the rolls of soft toilet tissue known today, first white and then in colours to match pastel bathrooms. Well, now – what would the Rector of Holinshed have said about such a thing?

Privies continued to be used by cottagers until they had access to mains water and plumbing, which, as already noted, might have been only fifty years ago in many rural areas, and as recently as the 1960s in some. Wash-down indoor water closets were widely available in the late nineteenth century if you did have the plumbing, but cottagers continued with their privies or used indoor Elsans. Many have fond memories of the privy as a place to which you could escape, sitting in peace, listening to birdsong and gazing at the flowers in your garden ….

BATHING

When mains water first came to the countryside, most people opted to plumb a lean-to or outhouse. Gradually they found space for a bathroom (just a tiny one), because of course plumbing meant not only cold water on tap but hot as well, if you had

water supplies

an appropriate boiler. This was bliss indeed. No more firing up the copper to boil the bath water and then ladling hot water into a successionally shared portable tin bath in front of the fire for the weekly dunking! No more emptying the bath by hand into the garden! No more showering under the cold water from the pump outside the back door!

The plumbing trend was led by the middle-class town-dwellers who migrated to their 'romantic' country cottages and were shocked at the lack of facilities they had taken for granted in their urban homes. For example, in an anonymous article written for *The Countryman*, a 'retired professional woman' described her hunt for a 'Victorian spinster's cottage with a veranda and a little sitting-room on either side of the front door, a kitchen at the back, four bedrooms above and a shut-in garden' in the West Country. In the 1940s she eventually found one, in a considerable state of decay, with a pump outside at the back, 'a sink clinging forlornly to it, unconnected to any drainage'. Her first essentials were 'an indoor lift-and-force pump, to supply water tanks in the roof, and a water-closet'. The pump, installed by a local builder, produced only a thin trickle of pea-soup water which, on analysis, proved to contain 'every kind of impurity', as did the water supply for the rest of the village.

Apart from that possible weekly bath, cold water was usually the order of the day for personal hygiene – under the pump, or using plain enamel or prettily decorated Victorian jugs and washbowls. At boarding school in the 1950s some of us still endured the morning and evening routine of filling your pitcher with hot water from a tap a long way down an unheated corridor and carrying it back to the dormitory to tip into the washbowl, then carting all the dirty water away afterwards in a pail to tip it down the communal sink. At least it was hot water then: not much earlier it would have been cold, and probably turned to ice in the pitcher overnight.

'Cold water was usually the order of the day for personal hygiene . . .'

Durham coalminer's ablutions in the 1930s

water supplies

WASHDAY

The modern habit of using a washing-machine almost daily would have amazed a generation born before the Second World War and would have been unthinkable for earlier generations. The same would be said for bathing more frequently than once a week.

'There were, of course, no detergents for washing clothes or dishes …'

Even in the nineteenth century, most country people had few clothes and not much bedding; and what there was tended to be cumbersome to wash and likely to disintegrate if washed too often. Consider the time, labour and sheer drudgery of hand-washing when there was no soap except what you could make yourself from basic raw materials; no instant means of collecting the water, let alone heating it; no drains to take away the waste water; no means of drying the washing except by passing it through a hand-turned mangle and draping it on a hedge out in the fresh air or in front of a smoky fire. It is hardly surprising that the washing was at the most a weekly event; in the eighteenth century it was often only a quarterly one.

The labour of drawing water was one thing, but then came the labour of heating it – for washing your body or your clothes. No wonder many country women simply took their laundry to the local stream or river and gave it a thorough pounding in cold water!

On a typical washday, first the water needed to be drawn from the well or other source, and carried by hand to be poured into the copper – a very large and very heavy container (sometimes of iron rather than actual copper) with a rounded base, set into a brick plinth in the scullery, if you were lucky enough to have such a place. The copper had its own tiny fireplace beneath, fuelled with bavins, and its own little chimney. Washday had to start early: it took a long time to get the fire going enough to heat such a large volume of water, and then the whole room (very often the living-room), even the whole cottage, would fill with steam the day long.

Next came the sorting. There would be a row of earthenware redpans: one for white bedding, with a blue-bag in the water to whiten the material; one to soak dirty working clothes in soapy water; one for coloured clothes and maybe another for underwear. Then it was a

The wash-tub

water supplies

matter of scrubbing the dirtiest clothes, rubbing them against a corrugated washboard with a brush or your red-raw knuckles – or you could dump the clothes in a wooden barrel and bash them with a wooden dolly to loosen the dirt first. To bleach whites, the country trick was to mix hen manure with urine, or simply let the sun bleach your sheets instead.

Pegging out the washing at Little Barrington, Gloucestershire

Each pan had to be filled with water from the copper, carefully transferred in a pitcher, and hand-emptied afterwards; usually the water was thrown into the garden. Then the clothes had to be wrung out (twisted by hand unless a hand-wound mangle could be afforded) and pegged with gipsy-made split wooden pegs on a clothesline made of wet-heavy hemp, or by about 1900 a line of galvanised wire that sometimes leaked rust. Bedlinen was often flung over a hedge to dry. All this was fine in summer, but in winter the drying would be indoors, so that already cramped and usually damp quarters were full of heavy clothes and bedding steaming gently in front of the fire for days on end.

Then came the labour of ironing. Before electricity, heavy flat-irons would be heated by the fire or range (you spat on them to test the heat) and the 'ironing-board' was usually the kitchen table covered with an old sheet. 'What a deal of work!', as William Cobbett would say.

In the 1920s, women's magazines were advertising washing-machines, but these could only be afforded by those who could already afford someone else in the village to do their laundering for them. Washing-machines also needed piped water and plumbed drainage. Mains drainage helps, too: septic tanks object to the use of too much detergent, letting you know their views by stinking. We who live with septic tanks are perforce 'green' in our use of water.

There were, of course, no detergents for washing clothes (or dishes) until recently. You might make your own washing lye by steeping wood-fire ashes in soft water, or laboriously make soap by first melting mutton fat, then separately mixing caustic soda and water, stirring the mixture in an earthenware vessel with a wooden stick while it spontaneously heated itself, before adding this lye slowly to the fat, still stirring, and finally pouring it all into moulds to set. Or you might buy hunks of concrete-hard carbolic soap from the carrier's cart in green, yellow or brown, from which you cut off pieces as required. Then you grated it before use, or boiled it to a jelly. Fairy, Sunlight Lifebuoy – names to bring a tear to a washerwoman's eyes – and Monkey Brand, which told you it wouldn't wash clothes anyway.

water & waste

PLUMBING

'... the joy of pulling the plug or yanking the chain!'

Plumbing: what a boon it was, once it came, to people who were used to carrying every drop of water they needed and carrying away every drop of wastewater! The joy of turning a tap for instant water, even if the quality was less than perfect; the joy of pulling the plug or yanking the chain! Yes, you might still have to arrange for the emptying of your cesspit every month, or your septic tank once or twice a year, when the 'lavender man' would come along with his cart and pump out the sludge for subsequent spreading on farmers' fields, but with luck you would be linked to a communal village sewage works and, eventually, to the mains sewage system so that your waste was no longer your own problem, nor even that of your local community. You need give it no more thought and you could start wasting your water as merrily as any townsman.

TRASH

'Cottagers seemed to have perpetual fires for burning rubbish ...'

In the decades after the Second World War, we all became less green in our recycling of rubbish, though there is a trend back to the old ways now. In the country, the disposal of rubbish used to be entirely your own concern; there were no council collections from your bin, no communal dumps, no recycling centres. Whatever waste you produced, you had to find a place for it yourself. There was far less of it than now, largely because most people could not afford to be profligate. They used things until they were worn out, and then they turned them into something else. Consider your own rubbish now: most of it is paper-based or plastic or glass, mainly from packaging; or it is reading matter; or it is food waste.

There was very little unwanted packaging of goods bought from shops until after the First World War: you took your own containers with you for loose groceries, or bought goods packed in biodegradable materials such as cotton, sacking and paper bags; and anyway in the country you produced most of your own food. Very few people read newspapers and magazines, and if they did it was probably the communal edition in the village reading room. Waste paper was recycled as toilet paper, or used to stuff draughty gaps or to decorate the walls, or as a last resort would be composted or burned – cottagers seemed to have perpetual bonfires for burning rubbish, and also for cooking up scraps for the chickens and the family pig. Waste food that was not recycled through the pigs and chickens was put on the compost heap.

There was no plastic and there were no polythene bags, of course. Empty tins and jars, such as there were, might be buried at the bottom of the garden or in the hedge

water & waste

bank, or in nearby woods or wasteland, and today you might find fishpaste pots rather than treasure under the soil. The more careful cottager saw empty jars and bottles as either reusable in their obvious storage role or as decoration, perhaps in the garden to edge or form a path, or to make a bottle wall. Broken crockery was simply thrown into the garden soil for good drainage, and today gardeners turn up endless pieces of decorated chinaware as they dig.

So the main methods of waste disposal were, first of all, recycling; then composting, burning or burial, depending on what the rubbish was. Whichever method was chosen, it was done essentially on your own premises, so that you were constantly aware of it. Today, like waste water, rubbish is dumped miles away and is somebody else's problem.

Town councils were collecting rubbish from urban dustbins in the 1930s. Such a service came much later in rural areas, where the old habits of frugal recycling and using items until they really could no longer be patched and tinkered lingered on, and sometimes still do. Most of a country bin would be filled with ash from the coal fire or the range; it was not as useful as wood ash, which could be spread in the garden or used to make soap, though clinkers were handy for surfacing garden paths.

A horse-drawn dust cart at East Hendred, Berkshire

2 Country Gardens

countryside gardens

IN THE EARLY 1950s the London Gardens Society aimed 'to make a permanent contribution towards the beautification of London by the growing of flowers, more particularly in those parts which are dull and ugly; to provide a healthy and civilising interest for those who have little opportunity for self-expression; and to give the humblest citizen an opportunity of performing a civic function by taking part in a movement for the improvement of his surroundings'. Through its thirty-nine affiliated garden societies, the LGS asked country dwellers not to burn or compost their thinnings from overcrowded borders but to request addresses of old people's welfare societies, nursery schools and housing societies 'to whose members any roots or cuttings will give pleasure out of all relation to the trouble of dispatching them'. Town-dwellers carried the countryside with them by creating gardens, however small.

Despite the flowery image of the romantic country cottage, in reality a cottage garden was essentially practical. It was a place in which to grow food in the form of vegetables, fruit, poultry, pigs, goats and perhaps a cow or two; it was a self-sufficient medicine cupboard where you grew herbs and other home remedies; it was a dumping ground for rubbish, ashes and dirty water; it was the home of the pump or the well; it was where you built beehives, sheds, wood-piles and compost heaps and recycled the contents of the privy. It was also a refuge from the openness of the working countryside; hence the garden was often firmly enclosed by walls, hedges or fences, and sometimes there would be protective mountain-ash trees to ward off the witches. In 1677 John Worlidge wrote that 'there is scarce a cottage in most of the southernmost parts of England but hath its proportionate garden, so great a delight do most men take in it'.

country gardens

COTTAGE GARDENS

IT SHOULD BE REMEMBERED THAT COTTAGE GARDENS HAD ONCE BEEN LARGE — VERY LARGE. IN THE SIXTEENTH CENTURY IT WAS DECREED THAT ALL NEW COTTAGES MUST HAVE AT LEAST FOUR ACRES OF LAND, TO ACCOMMODATE GARDENS AND COTTAGE LIVESTOCK, BOTH OF WHICH WERE ESSENTIAL TO THE COTTAGER'S SELF-SUFFICIENCY AND WITHOUT WHICH HIS FAMILY WOULD PROBABLY STARVE.

'A typical cottager would cultivate about twenty perches for vegetables and put quarter of an acre down to fruit trees, and run a flock of perhaps fifty poultry and a pig ...'

RIGHT
A smallholder's family

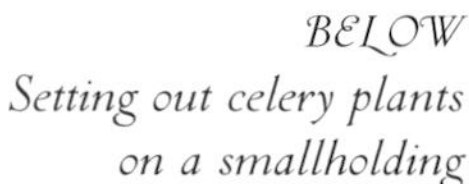

BELOW
Setting out celery plants on a smallholding

GRADUALLY THIS ALLOCATION shrank, especially with the enclosures that began later in that century and peaked between about 1760 and 1820, depriving cottagers of common-land grazing for their animals and reducing their gardens very often to small patches around the home that needed to be planted intensively if they were to feed the family at all.

In the late nineteenth century the Liberals, in their ideas for the formation of grass-roots parish councils, found an election winner among rural labourers when they said that parish councils should be allowed to hold and let to villagers a certain amount of land as allotments and that each allottee should be 'limited' to four acres (three pastoral and one arable). Four whole acres for your family's allotment! The Act by which parish councils were created became law in 1894 but very few councils could come by enough land to offer four-acre allotments.

Thus the severely reduced cottage garden gave preference to essentials such as vegetables, fruit trees and beehives. In practical terms, a typical cottager would cultivate about twenty perches for vegetables and put quarter of an acre down to fruit trees, and run a flock of perhaps fifty poultry and a pig, in order to be reasonably self-sufficient: the cottage pig along with meat and eggs from the poultry reduced the butcher's bill,

cottage gardens

and both types of livestock did well on household scraps with a little supplementary meal, while their manure fed the vegetable patch.

Maud Bridger, born in 1910, remembers her childhood home in Sussex. The cottage was divided into two: on the other side lived a spinster, whose garden was basically vegetables, with a few flowers round the edges. Maud's half was mostly vegetables (potatoes, swedes, cabbage, onions, carrots), strawberries and mint, with chicken coops, wooden beehives, 'flowers for Granny' (delphiniums, sweet peas, marigolds and the like) and plenty of apple trees (Granny Smith, Blenheim Orange, one called 'Nanny' 'which went soft – you had to eat them off the tree', and a tiny sweet apple whose name she can no longer recall). Granny would stake out her goats in the orchard but well out of reach of the trees that they loved to ring-bark.

The cottage that Maud moved into on her marriage in 1930 had the green dual-purpose apple called Hereford, the great big Peasegood Nonesuch and various russets. There were some beautiful Belcony plum trees from which she made a hundred pounds of jam one summer. But above all her husband was devoted to vegetable-growing: potatoes, cauliflower, cabbages and broccoli that grew huge on a diet of pig manure and the contents of privy buckets and kitchen slop buckets. Maud loved her childhood flowers and she soon planted a border along the length of the garden path, with delphiniums and pinks; she planted lots of lilies; she grew roses and honeysuckle, and rockery plants on the old stone garden walls; she planted raspberries, gooseberries and currants, grown from cuttings. Her husband extended the vegetable garden into the neighbouring field, where he grew large crops of carrots, parsnips, cabbages, Brussels sprouts (from his own seed), rhubarb and strawberries – the villagers used to walk up the lane simply to admire it all, as well as buy fresh vegetables, which he also sold on market days in the local town.

TOP
An imaginative duck house
ABOVE
Tackling the vegetable garden

TOP LEFT
Gloucester Old Spot: the typical cottager's pig

FARMHOUSE GARDENS

Farmhouse gardens were similar to cottage ones except in scale; farmers and their wives rarely had time to garden for pleasure. But some farmhouses were occupied by wealthier yeomen; for example, Evelyn Willis remembered living at Foscote Farm in Wiltshire, where she worked in the kitchens for Mr E.G. Harding, 'one of those rich farmers' who rode around the farm on a horse to inspect his prize herd of Shorthorn cows. He always wore a buttonhole, picked by his wife, when he drove to Chippenham Court each Friday (he was in fact a judge). Evelyn remembered the garden especially:

The Farmhouse was lovely, large, with a drive with ten walnut trees, from which we made walnut pickle – delicious, black when kept six months in vinegar. The front of the turretted House there were pink Roses and White jasmine. The perfume was wonderful. The Kitchen window looked out on the front, so we were able to enjoy the perfume. There were lawns, crazy paving, a Rosebed, a stone Table and Bird bath where Wood Pigeons bathed and cooed. A large vegetable garden, a Gardener, a tennis-court, a summer-house. The daughter grew violets in a large cold-frame, which she sold to friends and shops at Bath. There were plenty of vegetables – asparagus, celery, beetroot which we bottled, sliced, in vinegar (popular to give to friends, who lived in town, no vegetable garden). every kind of apple and pear trees, a large Filbert tree at the end of the garden. Many marvellous big dark brown nuts each autumn. A stile led into the fields.

WALLED GARDENS

walled gardens

It was only the bigger houses that could afford to employ gardeners and grow plants for the sake of their beauty, and only the very biggest that could run to hothouses for exotic flowers and fruits. The dream Victorian walled garden, with its pampered vegetables, fruit and flowers, needed an army of gardeners to maintain it.

'The dream Victorian walled garden, with its pampered vegetables, fruit and flowers, needed an army of gardeners to maintain it.'

The rule of thumb was two or three gardeners per acre, with one acre producing enough vegetables and fruit for a dozen people, which often included house staff and perhaps those on the estate as well as the employer's family. The walled kitchen garden was expected to supply produce all year round, and a third of the area would usually be devoted to glasshouses, frames and pits to extend the season and variety of fresh produce.

These kitchen gardeners became highly knowledgeable in the ways of manure and compost, potting mixtures, pest control, stoking the boiler, harvesting and presenting produce properly to the cook, the secrets of irrigation and the labour of carting water in horse-drawn bowsers from the nearest natural source or an estate reservoir.

Walled gardens were highly popular throughout the nineteenth century and right up to the Second World War, after which wages rocketed and employers were also able to buy readily available and cheap vegetables and fruit from all over the world. Those employers had rarely gardened themselves until the war brought about such significant social and economic changes that even the moderately wealthy had to get dirt under their fingernails – and discovered that gardening could also be a pleasure.

Walled gardens often had well-stocked herbaceous borders for a supply of cut flowers, with espalier fruit trees against the wall behind

VEGETABLES

IN THE 1940S AND 1950S MANY VILLAGES HAD PRODUCE ASSOCIATIONS WHICH CATERED FOR GROWERS OF FOOD CROPS IN GARDENS AND ALLOTMENTS, AND ALSO FOR SMALLHOLDERS WHO KEPT BEES, RABBITS AND POULTRY. WITH THE WAR STILL A FRESH MEMORY, HOME FOOD-GROWING REMAINED POPULAR AND WOULD EVENTUALLY ENCOURAGE THE 1960S/1970S INTEREST IN SELF-SUFFICIENCY.

THE ESSENTIAL CROP in any kitchen garden was the potato, which first came to Britain in the late sixteenth century but remained an 'exotic' species well into the eighteenth. In the 1820s William Cobbett lectured cottagers who allowed potatoes to supplant bread as their staple food, and he abhorred the idea of allotting labourers a potato patch in part payment of their wages. In contrast, the publisher J. Baxter of Lewes, writing in the 1830s, sang the praises of the potato, whether for man or beast and 'either as smoking in solitary importance on the labourer's humble board, or as taking its customary place among the viands of the great'.

Turnips, carrots, parsnips and beets were other standard cottage vegetables, all neatly buttoned in rows with nary a weed in between, along with all kinds of onions and of course greens, especially cabbages, spring greens, kale, spinach, broccoli and cauliflower. Brussels sprouts did not become widely grown until the nineteenth century. Broad beans were always popular, along with peas, runner beans and haricot beans.

The vegetable patch might also grow food for a smallholder's animals, such as cow cabbage, chicory, swedes, buckwheat (its blossom for bees and its seed for pigs and hens) and hemp (seeds for greater egg production, and the fibre for huckabuck cloth and homemade rope). The rhubarb patch, too, tended to find a home in the vegetable plot.

Runner beans were sometimes grown as much for their clambering scarlet flowers as for their pods. Borage was grown as a vegetable (for its boiled roots and young shoots) a herb and a bee-attracting flower; it had the added attraction of self-seeding profusely. Horseradish was another multi-purpose plant, for those who had a damp piece of ground for it: the hot roots were grated for horseradish sauce and also added to a grease to relieve rheumatism and sprains. Ordinary radish seed pods could be pickled, or the roots could be eaten raw for their hot flavour or to solve bladder problems, or applied as a cure for warts and corns. Onions could be rubbed on bald men's heads with honey to make the hair grow, or applied to chilblains to ease them. Lettuces were more than a salad plant: you could dry the juice and use it as a mild opiate.

'Turnips, carrots, parsnips and beets were other standard cottage vegetables, all neatly buttoned in rows with nary a weed in between ...'

HERBS

SWEET HERBS WERE GROWN AS MUCH FOR MEDICINAL AS CULINARY PURPOSES AND EVERY COUNTRY 'GOODWIFE' KNEW FROM HER MOTHER AND GRANDMOTHER WHAT PLANT TO USE FOR WHAT PROBLEM WELL INTO THE VICTORIAN PERIOD, THOUGH FOLK REMEDIES HAD BEEN FIGHTING A LOSING BATTLE WITH ORTHODOX MEDICINE SINCE THE EIGHTEENTH CENTURY.

'Countrywomen knew that chamomile could relieve all manner of digestive problems ...'

TOWN-DWELLERS HAD FORGOTTEN their herbalism but countrywomen knew that chamomile could relieve all manner of digestive problems, mint did its trick for indigestion and bad breath, rosemary was the ideal rinse for brunettes, lavender was a moth deterrent and room sweetener (as pot pourri or burned like joss sticks), sage cleaned your teeth and made a good gargle with vinegar and honey, marjoram battled with colds – the uses for cultivated herbs were endless, and that was before you took your pick of the wild plants that filled the woodland, hedgerows and field margins beyond the garden gate.

The First World War inspired the government to encourage the growing of medicinal herbs again, largely because it was no longer possible to import them. Quite a few enterprising people began herb farms, and came into their own again during the Second World War. The most important cultivated herbs included aconite, balm, belladonna, burdock, caraway, colchicum, comfrey, dandelion (roots were required in large quantities), elecampane, foxglove, henbane, horehound, hyssop, lily-of-the-valley (all parts were of medicinal value – it was even said that a distillation of the flowers could restore speech to those with 'the dumb palsie' – and you could also get a good return by picking the flowers and getting them into market early for the florists), marigold, marsh mallow and mullein.

During the First World War, when women were encouraged to attend gardening schools, a Women's Herb Growing Association was

Chicory flowers. The plant can be 'blanched' to provide heads for salads or for stewing in orange juice; the roots were ground as a coffee substitute

herbs

formed with the aim of cultivating and marketing medicinal herbs on co-operative lines. The supply of these herbs had hitherto come mainly from Germany and Austria, and there was a very strong demand for drugs from medicinal herbs during the war. The association sought to encourage women gardeners to organise themselves as herb-growers at a time when prices for the herbs were rocketing. They wanted to create a central drug farm where some of the herbs most urgently needed could be grown in large quantities, but also to encourage women to grow herbs in their own gardens, large or small, and to provide them with an established system of collecting and marketing the small amounts they would be able to harvest. The herbs particularly required were monkshood roots, chamomile flowers, deadly nightshade leaves and roots, thorn-apple leaves and seeds, henbane leaves, foxglove leaves (you could gather up to two tons from an acre), fennel seeds, opium-poppy heads and valerian roots. Also needed were balm, feverfew, dandelion, yarrow, barberry bark, common nightshade branches, broom branches, henbane, sweet-flag rhizomes and red poppy petals.

It was not just the women who took up herbery. Between the two World Wars, Walter Murray had been living in a poky third-floor London flat when he felt the urge to escape to the countryside to live alone there, close to Nature. He rented an isolated and virtually derelict cottage known as Copsford for three shillings a week – an amazing bargain at a time when country cottages were so desirable that they could command a higher rent than a country mansion. His advantage, on the rental market, was that the cottage was a long way from the 'ordinary services and comforts of civilised life' (too far for most romantics) and had been uninhabited for at least twenty years. There were few slate tiles left on the roof, no panes of glass in the frameless windows, no plants to soften the bare brick walls, no garden to protect the house from the encroaching pastures, no bridge across the brook below, no source of drinking water, no drainage, no other buildings within sight, and it was a crow's mile to the nearest lane (with not even a footpath across the fields and woods) and two miles from the village. Despite the large army of rats that inhabited Copsford, it was ideal for this freelance journalist and potential herbalist. For it was to harvest wild herbs that Murray had taken Copsford: he intended to earn his living by drying and selling them. First he sought out hedgerow clivers, which some call cleavers or goosegrass: he gathered fifty pounds in his first afternoon and then set about experimenting in the drying of them. Next came woodland foxgloves for heart problems, then centaury for indigestion ('like the scent of fresh tea with something else added, something essentially English – the sweetness and fragrance of the woodlands of this England'), then rough-pasture sweet agrimony with its honey-lemon scent, downland traveller's joy or old man's beard, streamside mints, meadowsweet for children's ailments, strong-smelling tansy, tiny blue-flowered eyebright on heathy banks, ferny yarrow from fallow cultivated ground, and, for variety, the fruit of sweet chestnuts for roasting and blackberries for eating from the bush.

Red campion, a wildflower often allowed to grow in cottage gardens; there are also cultured varieties

'The First World War inspired the government to encourage the growing of medicinal herbs ...'

SHRUBS & HEDGES

HEDGES WERE PLANTED AROUND COTTAGE GARDENS TO KEEP OUT MARAUDING LIVESTOCK AND WILDLIFE AND TO SATISFY THE AGE-OLD HUMAN NEED TO DEFINE PERSONAL SPACE: THIS IS *MY* PATCH! THE HEDGE SENT OUT THAT MESSAGE LOUD AND CLEAR TO NEIGHBOURS, STRANGERS AND ANIMALS, AND IT COULD BE A PRODUCTIVE FEATURE OF THE GARDEN AS WELL.

RIGHT
Wild dogrose, common in garden hedges

BELOW
Topiary on a grand scale in a country churchyard. The men clipping the trees were often paid in beer!

ELDER WAS ONE of the most useful country plants: both berries and flowers could be made into wine, and the flowers could be fried in batter, or made into lotions and ointments with a wide range of applications. The hollow stems were turned into whistles or pea-shooters, and the wood itself was used to make toys, pegs, meat skewers and angling rods. Elder grows easily and fast, and the quickest way of establishing squatters' rights was to plant an elder hedge around your 'property'.

Blackthorn was another invaluable plant, for hedging and also for its sloes. Hawthorn was planted as a hedge and its young leaves made a tasty snack or could be brewed as a tea, while may-blossom was another basis for a country wine. Holly was an excellent defensive hedge in areas where it seeded itself freely.

Other popular hedging plants included the flowering currant, which was easy to 'set' and was pretty in spring with its pink flowers. But it smells like tomcats and is no good for keeping livestock in or out, nor does it produce edible fruit. In some areas cottagers have dug up wild rhodendron in the woods and used that as a hedge; it has large mauve flowers in spring and is evergreen, but is poisonous to livestock. Laurel became popular in Victorian times and grew very fast each year, making the cutting of it something of a labour. Lilac, winter-flowering scentless yellow jasmine, snowberry, japonica and privet were other favourites in garden hedges, especially when cuttings and self-layering plants could be taken from friends and neighbours for free.

FRUIT

THE MORE FAR-SIGHTED LANDLORDS ENSURED THAT EVERY COTTAGE GARDEN HAD AT LEAST ONE FRUIT TREE – ALWAYS APPLES, BUT ALSO PEARS, PLUMS, DAMSONS, GREENGAGES AND CHERRIES WHERE SPACE PERMITTED. MANY AN OLD GARDEN WOULD HAVE MEDLARS AND MULBERRY BUSHES (BOTH COULD BE TURNED INTO A LAXATIVE SYRUP), NUT BUSHES AND AROMATIC QUINCES.

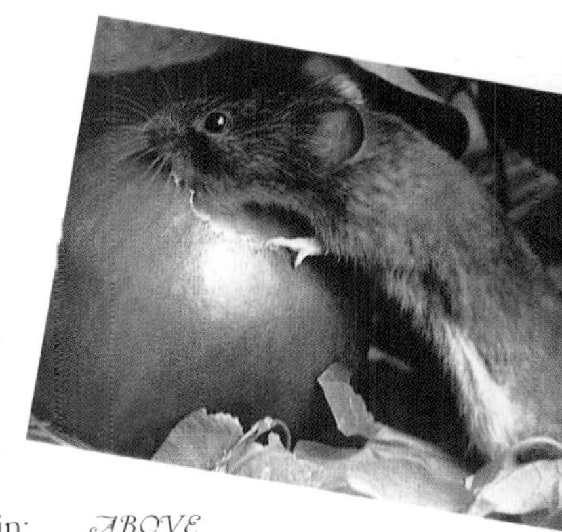

ABOVE
Field mice and yellowneck mice relish garden apples

LEFT
Growing raspberries: experimenting with new techniques

SOMETIMES, WANDERING THE HEDGEROWS or light patches of woodland, you might come across an ancient apple tree that was once part of the garden of a long-vanished cottage, and you probably will not recognise the variety. Recently the range of different apples available to buy as fruit in the shops or to buy as saplings from the nurseries has dwindled sharply.

Baxter's *Library of Agricultural and Horticultural Knowledge* (1834), under the heading 'The common or cultivated Apple', detailed more than 170 varieties of cooking, dessert and cider apples and said that 1,400 were described in the Horticultural Society catalogue. They varied considerably in shape and colour, and their seasons ranged from July (Spring Grove Codlin; White June-eating or Jenetin) to May (Hambledon Deux Ans; Fullwood Green; Cornish Gilliflower; Coe's Golden Drop; Golden Harvey; Newtown Pippin; Old Nonpareil and Pomme-poire; Rostocker; Powell's Russet; Winter Majetin; Young's Seedling) and even June (Beaufin Norfolk, 'excellent for drying'). In regions where appropriate apples could be grown, when most farmers and many cottagers made their own cider. Cider apples included glorious names such as Foxwhelp Knotted Kernel, Sweet Copin and Cap of Liberty. They also made their own perry, but the list of pears in Baxter was a little shorter, as only 600 varieties were catalogued by the Society. Wild crab apples were eagerly gathered for jelly-making, and their verjuice was used on sprained limbs.

More common in cottage and farm gardens were bush and cane fruits such as black currants (valuable for their vitamin C content), red currants, white currants, gooseberries and raspberries. Gooseberry growing became highly competitive in some villages. Baxter said that there were more than 700 varieties of gooseberry, and as his choice for small gardens he gave details of two dozen of them with evocative names such as Clewor h's White Lion, Saunders' Cheshire Lass, Moore's White Bear, Edwards's Jolly Tar, Hamlet's Kilton, Knight's Marquis of Stafford and Farmer's Roaring Lion. 'The cultivation of "Prize Gooseberries", as they are termed, is an object in which so many are interested that we subjoin a list of the principal varieties that obtained the prizes for 1833, arranged according to their colours, the weight of a single berry being alone given,' wrote Baxter adding that the heaviest single gooseberry in 1832 was 'the Bumper, weighing 30 dwts, 18grs, above an ounce and a half'. (The abbreviation 'dwts' is for 'pennyweights' and 'grs' is for 'grains', based on the average weight of a grain of corn. There are 24 grains in a penny-weight.) His hefty tome then went on to give detailed instructions on the cultivation of the gooseberry, uses for its fruit and how to preserve the berries through the winter.

'Wild crab apples were eagerly gathered for jelly-making, and their verjuice was used on sprained limbs.'

HORTICULTURAL SOCIETIES

Six Lewes men in 1832 were members of a small horticultural society in the nearby Sussex village of Ditchling, which boasts the oldest village fruit, vegetable and flower show in England. Its story is told in Richard Morley's *Red Roughs and Copper Kettles*. The informal Ditchling Horticultural Society was formalised in 1831, having probably developed gradually from a monthly club inaugurated in 1773 at The Bull in which the members exchanged corn and seeds, and a Ditchling Society for the Prosecution of Thieves formed at the same inn in 1784. The aim of the latter society was to raise funds for prosecuting murderers, robbers and defaulters and also to meet annually at The Bull for dinner at two shillings a head.

During the 1820s the Ditchling Horticultural Society held informal shows at which members would bring along 'some Specimen of Fruit, Vegitable or flowr' [sic]. In 1831 they held a separate show for apples, pears, potatoes, grapes 'grown in the open air', dahlias and china asters. The members were a mixture of skilled artisans, tradesmen, farmers and the gentry (whether of the old type or nouveau riche who had profited from the Napoleonic Wars). In 1829 the local paper reported that the 'Ditchling Fruit Society' had been formed five years earlier for the purpose of 'encouraging the culture of useful fruits and plants in the garden and neighbourhood, but more particularly as a stimulus to the working classes of society, who have hitherto sadly neglected this profitable and amusing employ'. Amongst the exhibits of the members' English fruits on that occasion, the newspaper said that 'the gooseberry was the most deserving of notice, since the size and weight of the berries have been more than doubled in the short space of four years that this institution has been formed'.

From then on it seemed that gooseberries and currants dominated the show, and by 1833 the paper was reporting on the 'Annual Ditchling Gooseberry Shew' which that year was attended by 'many cottagers, being the class of person for whose advantage this useful shew was instituted and is now kept up. Although under the humble title of Gooseberry Shew, its chief aim is the improvement in the growth of cottage fruits and vegetables.' Gooseberries and currants apart, there were some splendid cauliflowers (which gave rise to jealous questions about 'what artificial means had been used' to produce them) and 'some immense bouquets of wild flowers'. The spirit of competition between cottagers grew with the size of their gooseberries, and many became great experts in selecting seed, nurturing young plants, feeding and pruning their bushes and creating new varieties, encouraged by special prizes. In 1833, for example, the prizes included a copper kettle for the heaviest pint of Red Rough gooseberries, an iron kettle for the best vegetable, and prize money totalling £8 14s 6d for assorted gooseberries and currants, seedling gooseberries, fruit, vegetables, bouquets, dahlias, cucumbers, carnations, pinks, picotees, stocks, roses, geraniums, apples and grapes.

Finally there were 'A Friend's Prizes ... to the Cottagers of Ditchling exclusively': a copper kettle for the best fruit of any kind, a kettle and spoon and 1s 6d for the best vegetable of any kind, and other prizes for baskets of vegetables and bouquets of wild flowers. The following year there was a compensation prize for the most deserving unsuccessful exhibitor. The copper kettles were joined by copper boilers, steamers, metal coffee pots, steel forks, nailed boots and gardening tools; the classes expanded to include all sorts of vegetables and flowers, strawberries and raspberries, bunches of mixed herbs, the biggest cabbages and more.

The committee also began to inspect cottagers' gardens; they instituted prizes for the best cultivated garden, for length of servitude of male and female servants, for the best management of 'pigs, bees, poultry, etc.', for 'general habits of industry, economy and cleanliness apparent in cottages' and for 'the man or widow wheoman who has brought up the largest family with the least assistance from the parish', as well as a system of fixing fair prices for cottage produce. All this from a horticultural society interested in gooseberries! Typical cottage reports in 1843 read: 'Good garden, well cropped. 1 good pig. Cottage clean. 7 children'; 'Garden well cropped with Potatoes, Peas, Onions, House and French Beans, and Cabbage. A very fine flower garden. 2 good pigs. Cottage clean'; 'Garden well cropped with Peas, Beans, French Beans, Onions & Cabbages. 13 hives of Bees. 2 pigs. A faggot stack. Cottage clean.'

FLOWERS

ONLY SOMETIMES WAS THE GARDEN MADE MORE CHEERFUL WITH COTTAGE FLOWERS, USUALLY BY THE WOMAN OF THE HOUSE AND ORIGINALLY ONLY WITH THE FLOWERING PLANTS THAT HAD MEDICINAL PROPERTIES. AFTER ALL, IN THE CENTURIES BEFORE THE WIDESPREAD USE OF HERBICIDES, THE MEADOWS AND VERGES WERE FULL OF WILD FLOWERS AND THERE WAS NO NEED TO GROW YOUR OWN.

'Those who did develop a passion for flowers tended to cram them into every corner of the garden ...'

Primroses and primulas are cottage favourites

BUT THE LOVE OF FLOWERS for themselves increased and when this was so the effects were striking. William Cobbett (1763–1835), the politically minded farmer's son and radical pamphleteer who was always on the side of the agricultural labourer, published his *Cottage Economy* in 1823 and then a treatise on gardening (ostensibly for Americans). In his better-known *Rural Rides* of 1830 he gave high praise to some parts of West Sussex, where the labourers' dwellings had 'an appearance of comfort ... that is very pleasant to behold ... The houses are good and warm'; their gardens were 'neat and full of vegetables of the best kinds' and he 'saw a pig at almost every labourer's house'. More generally he referred to 'those neatly kept and productive little gardens round the labourers' houses, which are seldom unornamented with more or less of flowers' all over England. Those who did develop a passion for flowers tended to cram them into every corner of the garden, in amongst the vegetables, along the garden path, clambering over the porch and the low-dipping roof. Indeed, the smaller the garden, the more densely would it be packed with flowers, crammed in wherever there happened

GERTRUDE JEKYLL

Gertrude Jekyll (1843–1932) was always ready to admit her considerable debt to the cottage gardens she had known since childhood, which greatly influenced this famous gardener. She found the informality and bounteousness of cottage gardens far more inspiring than the carefully manicured beds of bigger Victorian gardens, and she loved the scented flowers that were so typical of rural gardens: wild honeysuckle, pinks, violets, lily-of-the-valley, apple blossom, night-scented stocks, tobacco flowers, primroses and old-fashioned cottage roses. She also found that cottage gardens were a secret repository for a huge variety of plants that had become rare.

flowers

to be a space, so that there was a gloriously random riot of mixed colour and form but an unplanned overall sense of harmony.

Gradually, then, the flowery cottage garden depicted by Helen Allingham and her contemporaries became a reality, with its hollyhocks, delphiniums, wallflowers, everlasting pea, dame's violet, pansies, violets, snowdrops, crocuses, primroses, roses and honeysuckle. In the end it was often the cottagers who became the most adventurous flower growers, developing single-minded passions for pinks or dahlias or auriculas and creating new varieties by the score. And it was often the cottagers who swept the board at the local horticultural show with their prize flowers and vegetables. They rarely bought their stock; rather, they drew on stock in the wild or swapped cuttings and seeds with their friends. Many a cottage gardener can still remember who gave their grandparents which plant.

J. Mantell, writing in Baxter's *Library of Agricultural and Horticultural Knowledge*, pondered:

> *Who can pass even the poor man's cot, where the hand of industry has tastefully entwined the rose, the honeysuckle, and the briar around the very threshold of his home, without associating in his mind the idea of comfort and happiness within; but, if the weeds of indolence are seen towering in luxuriant growth over the loveliest gems of Flora's Temple, choking up, as it were, the very approaches of the habitation, who will not, with emotions of regret, conclude that waste and prodigality are the inmates there. How important is it then to induce a taste for the cultivation of flowers!*

Mantell's theory was that a man who grew flowers would not waste his leisure hours in 'revelry abroad, whilst his family is suffering from want and penury'. Eager to persuade the cottager to become a flower-grower, he then proceeded to explain how to grow stove plants (tropical exotics that required hothouses warmed by circulating hot water through metal pipes – somewhat out of reach for a cottager!), greenhouse plants (in which 'no fire is required except in damp weather or to protect the plants from the effects of frost') and finally hardy plants, be they trees, shrubs, perennial herbaceous plants, or annuals and biennials.

His extensive catalogue of plants ran to many pages, but he devoted substantial sections to the cultivation of 'florists' flowers', among which he included dahlia (first introduced to England in 1789 and lost through lack of interest until it was re-introduced by Lady Holland in 1804), tulip (the finest of which ever raised in England he decreed to be the Fanny Kemble), auricula and polyanthus, anemone and ranunculus, carnation and pink, pansy, 'Cape bulbs' (gladiolus, amaryllis and others), geranium, heather and of course rose ('the child of nature, has, from the remotest antiquity, uniformly found a place in every garden, and is equally the delight and ornament of the palace and the cottage').

Bluebells, another woodland plant often found growing naturally in cottage gardens

Old-fashioned geranium or meadow crane's-bill – a much daintier plant than the pelargonium 'geraniums'

In 1618 a Yorkshireman, William Lawson, published his own sixteen-chapter gardening book, which had taken him nearly half a century to write. He clearly loved his flowers:

> *The rose red, damaske, velvet, and double double province rose, the sweet muske rose double and single, the double and single white rose, the faire and sweet-scenting woodbine double and single; Purple cowslips, and double cowslips, and double double cowslips; Primrose double and single, the violet nothing behind the best for smelling sweetly . . .*

GRASS

THERE WAS NO PLACE IN A COTTAGE GARDEN FOR GRASS, EXCEPT AS PASTURE FOR LIVE-STOCK AND GRAZING FOR GEESE. IN THE GROUNDS OF GRANDER HOUSES, HOWEVER, GRASS SET OFF FINE BUILDINGS AND PLANTINGS. THE PROBLEM WAS ONE OF MAINTENANCE.

'Country gentlemen may find in using my machine themselves an amusing, useful and healthy exercise.'

THE ORIGINAL MEANS of keeping grass cut was the scythe, and this could be done by an expert to a degree that turned a potential meadow into something approaching a lawn, though there tended to be scalped patches here and there and the job took a very long time indeed.

Edwin Budding, a carpenter near Stroud in Gloucestershire, who worked as a freelance engineer for various mill owners, conceived the first grass-cutting machine, possibly inspired by rotary cutters he had seen being used to cut the nap off wool cloth. He patented the idea of a cylindrical grass cutter in 1830 and his partner John Ferrabee manufactured the first machine to this patent at his Phoenix Foundry near Brinscomb. The machine was seen not merely as an efficient way of cutting grass: 'Country gentlemen may find in using my machine themselves an amusing, useful and healthy exercise.'

By 1841, ponies were pulling lawn mowers instead: they could cut a lawn at the rate of an acre an hour. In the early years of the twentieth century, leather-booted ponies, donkeys and horses were still mowing parks and the lawns of country houses and continued to do so in some places right up to the Second World War.

By the late nineteenth century, there was also a wide range of hand-pushed mowers to choose from. In the 1890s steam-powered mowers were patented for the first time but petrol-driven mowers were already being designed and would become increasingly popular after the First World War. In 1896 the first mains-powered mower was produced, though it was not until the early 1960s that battery-powered and electric mowers became widely accessible.

After the First World War, it seemed that every suburban householder aspired to a patch of lawn and the great ritual of weekend mowing began, with countless less-than-fit men manfully pushing and sweating with their hand-mowers. Gradually (as ever) the idea spread to country cottages as well.

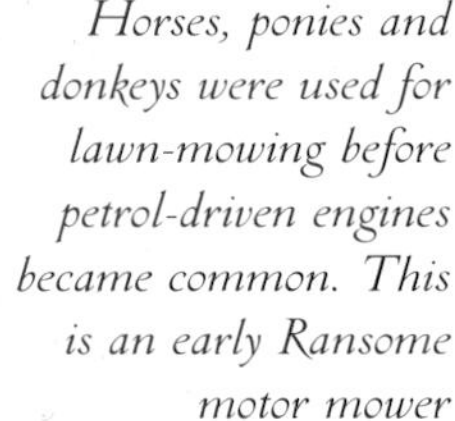

Horses, ponies and donkeys were used for lawn-mowing before petrol-driven engines became common. This is an early Ransome motor mower

TOOLS & MACHINERY

IN THE COUNTRY THERE WAS GREATER INTEREST IN HEFTY ORCHARD GRASS-CUTTERS LIKE THE ALLEN SCYTHE OR IN PETROL-POWERED CULTIVATORS THAN IN LAWN MOWERS; THEY WERE INVALUABLE ON SMALLHOLDINGS AND IN LARGE GARDENS AND ALLOTMENTS WHERE FOOD-GROWING WAS A SERIOUS MATTER.

IN 1940, THOSE INTENDING to live in the country were advised to make use of mechanical power if they had more than twenty perches; for example, you could plant a hundredweight of potatoes in half an hour by machine, whereas the hours that it would take by hand were unthinkable.

In pre-mechanised days, employed gardeners had a very wide range of equipment, often made by the village or estate blacksmith. Each item was carefully chosen for the job in hand, and for the hand that held the tool. Each gardener had his favourite designs, many of them to a traditional local pattern, to cope with trenching, digging, forking, weeding, raking, turfing, trimming, pruning, cutting, scything, harvesting, planting, transplanting, dibbing, propagating. There were all sorts of different barrows, portable cloches, forcers, water-carts, watering-cans, rollers, sprayers, fumigators, syringes, containers and endless terracotta pots in the potting shed.

Cottagers made do with a trusty spade and fork, their metal parts and wooden handles polished with constant use to a beautiful gleam. A rusting spade in the shed was a sure sign of a lazy gardener.

'A rusting spade in the shed was a sure sign of a lazy gardener.'

LEFT
Checking a scythe. This could be used for cutting garden grass (if you were skilled) as well as for mowing hay

BELOW
Using a swan-necked hoe in a sugarbeet crop

3

Country Journeys

IN 1922, ERNEST PULBROOK described country lanes as white roads winding through the great solitude of the countryside, with only occasional figures appearing at long intervals 'as spectres which come from nowhere and thither vanish; the labourer approaches a wayside cottage and is gone, the wagon is swallowed by the leafage of the lane, the fleeting motor-car dissolves in a cloud of dust'.

Most of the lane's users were on foot, picking up and distributing local and regional gossip as they passed, chatting with friends and strangers alike. Some of the more familiar traffic was already beginning to wane in those years immediately after the First World War: the big four-wheeled wagons pulled by teams of heavy horses no longer rolled on their long-distance journeys of several days, and horse-drawn coaches were being replaced by motorised vehicles. Even the famous Minehead-to-Lynton coach had been ousted by the 'remorseless motor-bus' from the road it had traversed for so long, and only middle-aged travellers had experienced the discomfort and drawbacks of coaching in winter.

Ironically, Pulbrook saw the motor car as awakening the road into life again in lieu of the vanishing figures that used to walk the lanes or plod on the backs of donkeys, or clip along on horseback. Today motorised vehicles – cars, lorries, buses and all – dominate the lanes to such an extent that those who persist in using their feet or their horses or bicycles feel they have no right to be there at all and are threatened by the killing power of motor traffic. But then, people have always complained about the traffic. In the 1660s, for example, Yorkshiremen were moaning about the large numbers of Scottish and Irish cattle on the roads; or more honestly, they were worried about the competition against their own animals in the marketplace. At the time, drovers were escorting huge herds to market, mainly along the broad upland greenways but often along roads that were no more than wide tracks across large unenclosed fields.

TOLLS & TURNPIKES

SOME OF THE LOCAL LANES WERE MAINTAINED BY FARMERS BUT MANY WERE NOT MAINTAINED AT ALL. PUBLIC HIGHWAYS, ACCORDING TO LAWS LAID DOWN IN 1555, WERE SUPPOSED TO BE KEPT IN REASONABLE ORDER BY STATUTE LABOUR.

'Parishes remained responsible for all the roads that ran through them for about 280 years after the 1555 Highways Act that had imposed this burden upon them.'

PREVIOUS PAGE
In the Dales near Burnsall, West Yorkshire

BELOW
Irish lane, leading to a farm overlooking Carlingford Lough in Co. Louth

EVERY FARMER HAD to fulfil the required number of man-hours each year, under the beady eye of the parish's highway supervisor; various individuals were bound to provide a cart, a team of oxen, donkeys or horses, and the requisite labourers and their tools. If you look through old vestry minutes, kept by the local church, you will find mention of appointments to this unpaid supervisory post – one which most did their best to avoid. You will also find deep resentment that the locals had to pay for the maintenance of roads used by outsiders passing through, and endless complaints about the state of local roads.

Parishes remained responsible for all the roads that ran through them for about 280 years after the 1555 Highways Act that had

tolls & turnpikes

imposed this burden upon them. When the main traffic was on foot or on four feet (donkeys and packhorses), the system just about coped, but wheeled vehicles – whether two-wheeled carts or carriages and coaches – needed better surfaces and standards and also caused a great deal more damage by carving indelible ruts.

There is a story of a carter taking coal to a gentleman's country house six miles from Poole in the 1820s: he started 'at earliest summer daylight' to load at Poole and did not get home until late at night as the roads were so terrible.

The first suggestion for levying a tax on heavily loaded vehicles was made by the village of Standon in Hertfordshire, which was fed up with its main street being damaged by through-traffic. Parliament passed an Act in 1663 that allowed Hertfordshire, Huntingdonshire and Cambridgeshire to impose tolls on road users passing through their counties, and the first toll-gate, or turnpike (the word originally described a spiked turnstile), was installed at Wadesmill in Hertfordshire. Thirty years later, other counties began to wake up to the advantages of such a scheme and a rash of turnpike trusts became established in southern England. The network grew gradually, spreading over the whole country, with the Great North Road becoming turnpiked over almost its entirety up to and beyond the Scottish borders by 1750. Stone huts and sometimes elegant little roadside tollhouses, often polygonal or semi-circular at the front for a good view of approaching traffic, were built to accommodate those who collected the tolls – and no doubt to protect them from dissatisfied customers, many of whom resented having to pay their way. New trusts continued to be formed into the early decades of the nineteenth century, until the creation of the railway network began to compete fiercely for the traffic. The last toll-gate closed in 1895.

From horse power to engine power: loading milk churns at Notgrove, Gloucestershire, in the 1930s

THE STATE OF THE ROADS

TRAVELLERS PAINTED A VIVID PICTURE OF LIFE ON THE ROADS. ONE OF THE FIRST TO RECORD HIS WANDERINGS WAS JOHN LELAND, A WILTSHIRE PARSON WHO AT THE BEGINNING OF THE SIXTEENTH CENTURY WAS INSTRUCTED BY HENRY VIII TO 'TRAVEL OVER ENGLAND IN SEARCH OF ANTIQUITIES, WITH POWER TO INSPECT THE LIBRARIES OF CATHEDRALS, ABBEYS AND OTHER ECCLESIASTICAL ESTABLISHMENTS'.

'There are old persons who are said to recollect when passengers used to breakfast at Knightsbridge, dine at Hounslow, and after a day's prodigious exertion, sup at Staines.'

Leland's Itinerary is sometimes regarded as one of the first 'road books'; he was followed by the likes of the naturalist John Aubrey in the late seventeenth century, the intrepid Celia Fiennes for several decades from the 1680s, the down-to-earth Daniel Defoe in the 1720s and the indefatigable country-loving William Cobbett a century later. All of them talked about the state of the roads.

Writing in 1822, J.B. Pyne remarked in his *Microcosm:* 'There are old persons who are said to recollect when passengers used to breakfast at Knightsbridge, dine at Hounslow, and after a day's prodigious exertion, sup at Staines.' What speed! In the mid seventeenth century, you could reach Dover from London by coach in four days, on the best roads in England; twice a week you could travel from London to Liverpool as a passenger in a stage waggon, ten days on the road, or you could reach York from London in a week.

Gertrude Jekyll described the long-distance coaches that used to pause at Godalming, halfway between London and Portsmouth, changing at Petersfield, Guildford, Ripley, Cobham and Esher on the way back. Sometimes a midnight coach from London would bring gangs of chained convicts on their way to Portsmouth to be embarked for transportation to the other side of the world. More frequent travellers were merry coachloads of sailors (four within and twelve hanging on outside) who had been at sea for three or four years and were now on

Delivering cottage loaves in the Somerset Levels, where floodwater is no barrier to a horse

the state of the roads

their way to London to spend all their money.

In 1754, the 'flying' coach ran between Manchester and London in four and a half days, at a maximum speed of five miles per hour. This tardiness was not the fault of the horses or their drivers, but of the road surfaces. The ruts were often so deep that the coach would sink to its axles in mud and water, making progress almost impossible. Country roads (and most town ones) were alternately mud or swirling dust, and for centuries it was the practice to 'lay' the summer dust by watering the road surface. As traffic increased, this simple routine was no longer adequate.

The series of county reports to the Board of Agriculture published at the beginning of the nineteenth century always had a section on the state of local roads. For Devon, Charles Vancouver in 1808 complained that the turnpike roads were not of the width prescribed by law, and being so narrow became 'so high in the middle, that without sides or bulwark to support them, they are, in a short time, by the traffic of the lime-carts, bilged, and forced out upon their sides, when the only passage remaining is confined to a narrow ridge on the top of the road, but which from the excessive coarseness of the materials of which it is made, is soon broken into so many holes and unevennesses, as very much to endanger the knees of the horse, and the neck of its rider.'

Devon's parish roads varied considerably, some being even worse than the turnpikes. Several parishes suffered heavy road rates for their inhabitants since the roads bore 'prodigious' traffic passing to and from Cornwall for the collection of sea-sand for manure. Vancouver was shocked that none of the 'resident gentlemen' in these parishes wanted to be highway supervisor or way-warden. He also remarked on the very Devonian feature of high hedge-banks along the narrow lanes, which created 'the idea of exploring a labyrinth rather than that of passing through a much-frequented country'. But the illusion was quickly dispelled, he warned, on meeting gangs of packhorses: 'The rapidity with which these animals descend the hills, when not loaded, and the utter impossibility of passing loaded ones, require that the utmost caution should be used in keeping out of the way of the one, and exertion in keeping ahead of the other.' Wheeled vehicles in these lanes were rare.

Devon lane near Buckland-in-the-Moor

TRAVELLER'S FARE

The food that some travellers stuffed down their throats at the coaching inns was prodigious. On his visit to England in the late seventeenth century the Russian Tsar Peter the Great and his entourage of twenty breakfasted on half a sheep, half a lamb, ten pullets twelve chickens, seven dozen eggs and the 'contents of two large salad beds', washed down with a gallon of brandy and two of mulled claret. For dinner a few hours later they chomped their way through three stone-weight of ribs of beef, a fat sheep, a lamb, two loins of veal, eight capons, ten rabbits, three dozen bottles of sack and a dozen of Bordeaux. A couple of English dukes, in about 1790, found the fare so good that they ate thirty-six mutton chops and drank ten bottles of claret.

the state of the roads

Dung cart and horses plodding up the hill

OPPOSITE Aston Tirrold, Oxfordshire

'It was claimed that the women and horses of the Weald had the longest legs in the country ...'

LINCOLNSHIRE WAS ONE OF the counties surveyed by Arthur Young (1741–1820), an East Anglian farmer who became the first Secretary to the Board of Agriculture and was one of the first to turn agriculture into a science. In the 1780s Young had undertaken a 20,000-mile tour of the country for his *Annals of Agriculture*, riding a blind white horse. In his Lincolnshire survey, published in 1813, he said that the roads in general were 'esteemed below par' and he said very little more about them, except that in 'the hundred of Skirbeck to Boston, and thence to Wisbeach' they were generally of silt or old sea-sand 'deposited under various parts of the country ages ago, and when moderately wet are very good; but dreadfully dusty and heavy in dry weather; and also on a thaw they are like mortar'.

In Sussex, the Reverend Arthur Young (a Sussex clergyman, and not the same Arthur Young as above) wrote in the same year that the turnpike roads were generally in good order and of excellent materials ('whinstone; the Kentish rag, broken into moderate sized pieces'). Other roads in the coastal areas were kept firm and dry with gravel or sea shingle but on the claylands of the Weald the roads were 'in all probability the very worst that are to be met with in any part of the island' – indeed it was claimed that the women and horses of the Weald had the longest legs in the country, as they were always having to drag their feet out of sticky mud. The Wealden roads also bore heavy loads of timber and corn, which quickly made them virtually impassable for wheeled traffic in winter, and conversely baked so hard in summer that animals' hooves suffered badly.

Quite apart from the nature of the clay itself, Young blamed the 'predilection which gentlemen have for their shaws and woods in a very stiff soil': he said that these prevented both the sun and the wind from drying the surface of the roads. He drew the contrast with what he considered to be the best roads in England, especially the 44 miles of turnpike from Bury St Edmunds to Huntingdon, and those around Newmarket; the splendour of these roads he attributed to the nature of the soil and the openness of the country. He also described the turnpike at Horsham, noting that 'the present road to London was made in 1756; before that time it was so execrably bad, that whoever went on wheels, were forced to go round by Canterbury, which is one of the most extraordinary circumstances that the history of non-communication in this kingdom can furnish'.

The Worcestershire report in 1813 claimed that the principal roads from town to town (all with toll-gates) were generally in good repair, though rather stony and uneven in hilly districts. Some of the 'cross' roads were very bad, especially in clay areas, 'where little attention is paid either to plashing hedges, opening ditches, or mending roads; many of these are scarcely passable from

the state of the roads

Christmas to Midsummer, either on horse-back, or with a loaded carriage'. While Worcestershire's public roads were improving, many of the parish ones lagged far behind. However, in the Vale of Evesham a Road Club was established in 1792, the members of which dined together on the first Thursday of every month 'at half past two o'clock', at various inns in rotation, for half-a-crown a head (plus another half-a-crown for liquor). Although the monthly meal was the subject of the first two Articles of the club, there was a lot more to it than having a good time. The members all agreed, 'feeling very sensibly the inconvenience arising from the bad state of the roads in our neighbourhood, and wishing to act cordially and unitedly, in the best manner, for the improvement of the said roads', that they would henceforth exert their 'utmost influence, by advice and example' to serve their turns as Surveyors of the Roads in their parishes and would be diligent in their service.

The Articles then went into considerable detail on how to make a 'good durable road'. First, the surface of the natural soil should be rounded so that the water could run into its drainage trenches; next small brushwood or furze, or both, should be laid cross-wise in a good thick layer; then large stones, covered by other stones graded to smaller and smaller sizes to gravel at the top. All the stones should have been exposed to the air for at least twelve months after quarrying. The hedges and ditches must be 'properly cut and opened, at the usual seasons directed by act of parliament for that purpose' on a regular basis; drains should be laid to divert any water that might injure the road. Sun and wind must be able to reach the surface of the road, thus hedges must be kept well trimmed and not planted on high banks. Narrow-wheeled carriages should not be allowed to be overloaded.

Repairs to the surface must be carried out immediately they became necessary; all obstructions and nuisances must be removed, and ruts filled and levelled. Labourers should be made available to take care of certain stretches of the road and keep them in perfect order at all times. What splendid ideals!

ROAD MAKING

It had taken a blind man, John Metcalfe, to draw attention to the need for good drainage and good foundations in road-making, an art known to the Romans but apparently lost in Britain thereafter. Metcalfe, of Knaresborough in Yorkshire, surveyed turnpike roads in three counties over forty years.

'Macadamised roads revolutionised transport, and steam rollers added to the improvements by consolidating newly made and repaired road surfaces.'

He began to use bundled heather for drainage under his road stones, finishing with gravel and cambering the surface so that rainwater was shed into roadside ditches, and built his first successful road on these principles in 1753. But he was ahead of his time.

Three or four years later, two men were born in Scotland who would take his ideas further in the early nineteenth century: John Loudon MacAdam and Thomas Telford. Gertrude Jekyll wrote in 1925 that 'no really sound roads such as we now know were made till in 1818 Loudon MacAdam's method of construction was adopted, and the first roads with good foundation of larger, and surface metalling of smaller stones, were built.' MacAdam (1756–1836) and Telford (1757–1834) both understood the importance of good drainage. Telford's rather more expensive roads were built on solid foundations: at the base were tightly packed stones up to about 10in long, covered by a 6in layer of broken stones, topped by small stones and gravel forming a slightly convex surface; there were drainage ditches along the side of the road, fed by culverts running at intervals beneath the foundations. MacAdam's principles were broadly similar but he used cheaper material, often recycling stone from earlier roads and grading it in size in successive layers. Dig under today's lanes and you will find the evidence still in place.

In both systems, the top layer of small stones and gravel was the renewable part, and many women and older men would be employed as stone-breakers, sitting at the side of the road by a large heap of stones and laboriously breaking them into smaller pieces with a stone-hammer. Sometimes they made themselves eye-protecting goggles out of walnut shells. Stone-breakers remained a familiar sight in rural areas well within living memory, always ready for a chat with passers-by and generally opening the conversation by asking the time. Some of them were no mere down-and-outs: for example, the stone-breaker at Saintbury in the Vale of Evesham was also the parish clerk and, by the way, a Greek scholar and musician. His mundane occupation gave him plenty of time for thought.

Macadamised roads revolutionised transport, and steam rollers added to the improvements by consolidating newly made and repaired road surfaces. Travelling roadmen would camp beside their steam rollers wherever they were working, spending the evening listening to one of their number playing a concertina or having a night out on the town or nearest village. Marian Robertson, born at the end of the First World War, remembers the steam engine housed in a huge shed in her village. 'It was quite a wonder when the steam engine started up ... they started the engine, polished it like mad, and it used to chug its way along the roads as a steam roller. Everybody ran to see the engine, all the smoke coming out of the tall chimney.'

Macadam remained the national road surface until tarring (tarmacadam, or tarmac) began to be used in some places in the early twentieth century. In country areas, as ever, such improvements came much later, except on the major roads. Lanes and village streets remained rutted and muddy in winter and dusty in summer. An elderly Sussex man well remembers the impassable sandy lane past his family's cottage in the 1920s: when the owner of the 'big house' wanted to drive along it in his automobile, he would slip the lad a few pence in advance to make sure that the surface was briefly good enough for the car not to get stuck.

It was motoring that eventually brought tarmac to all the lanes. Macadamisation had been a good start but it was not good enough for the rapidly increasing and speeding motorised traffic. At first tar was sprayed on roads simply to lay the dust – it was more

road making

effective than mere water, and tar-spraying was being widely used as early as 1910 in some places. Elsewhere, many villages did not have the benefit of tarmac until the time of the Second World War, and many country people can remember the coming of tarmac to country lanes: as children they would be encouraged by their mothers to stand by the great steaming barrels of pitch at the cross-roads, breathing in the harsh fumes, which were deemed to be good for the chest and for warding off colds. Even just after the Second World War, in many districts people still waded through mud, often ankle-deep, to reach the village shops or the school or pub (quite a few rural cottages did not even have a path to them across the fields) but farmers, who of old had happily rumbled their tumbrels along muddy, irregular surfaces, found that modern farm machinery was too sophisticated for such treatment and they began to concrete their farm tracks. Farm cottagers benefited: they could walk to the village by way of the new concrete roads.

Gang breaking stones for road repairs in the 1850s

MAINTAINING THE ROADS

road making

'*In those pre-mechanised days, hedges were trimmed by hand with the skilful use of sharp blades to keep the hedge dense and livestock-proof.*'

WHILE THE PARISHES were still responsible for the maintenance of local roads, you would have regularly seen gangs of local men repairing surfaces, clearing ditches and keeping the roadside hedges in good trim. Hedgecutting remained useful winter work for farm labourers at a time of year when there was little else they could be doing on the farm. In those pre-mechanised days, hedges were trimmed by hand with the skilful use of sharp blades to keep the hedge dense and livestock-proof. All the cuttings were cleared up and heaped on to a bonfire, which kept the men warm as well as disposing of the debris. Ditches were scoured out with ditching irons; and the 'grips' dug into the verges to channel water off the road and into the ditch were carefully kept clear. When county councils were first created in 1888, they took over responsibility for main roads in their county; six years later other rural highways became the responsibility of the new district councils, and the parishes breathed a heavy sigh of relief. Later, county councils took over minor roads as well.

Such is progress however that, in the interests of 'efficiency' and economy, most councils centralised their operations during the 1980s and 1990s and their gangs became roving ones with no particular interest in a village or parish. In recent years it has reached the rather ridiculous stage where pot-holes are not simply mended by the gang on the spot: instead, a surveyor must first come out to assess and paint a line around the pot-hole, then make a report; eventually a gang will come out to fill in the hole but this whole process can take several weeks. In some council areas the gangs no longer know where the grips should be or care to maintain them – a small detail, perhaps, but it leads to water lying where it should not and the early degradation of the road surface.

Budget cuts also mean that the grass grows freely down the centre of narrow and less used lanes, fed by the mud washing down from the hedgebanks that has been dislodged by vehicles too wide for the lane but persisting in using it. Increasingly, local lanes are hammered by ever-larger lorries that are sometimes delivering locally but equally often are simply cutting through on their way to elsewhere, choosing what might look on the map like a short-cut but which on the ground

road making

is unable to carry them, or is so narrow that invariably they must reverse on meeting other vehicles. Lane surfaces and especially old bridges are rapidly crumbling under their impact, and locals are frustrated that there seems to be no way of deterring the intruders. There is rebellion in the air.

As for the roadside hedges all country dwellers are well aware of the changes: hedges now are rarely seen as essential for the confinement of livestock and instead are a nuisance to farmers, most of whom now cut them by means of the dreaded tractor-driven flail that smashes its way through branches much thicker than it is designed to tackle, leaving them ragged and wide open to disease so that the hedges gradually die out. Usually the flails leave a carpet of thorny debris on the road surface – no one has time any more to clear up after the cut, and the thorns find their way into tyres and dogs' paws and the soles of unwary shoes.

BELOW LEFT
Repairing a laneside stone wall near Shap, in Cumbria

LEFT
Herb-rich verges in a leafy lane

THE LENGTHSMEN

For a golden while, county councils continued to employ lengthsmen or linesmen. Each man was responsible for a defined length of local lane (perhaps 15 miles) and it was his job and pride to keep it in good condition, and to make sure that local landowners did their bit by cutting the hedges. Everybody in the village knew him and would pass the time of day when they came across him by his little laneside bonfire or working close to the small handcart or wheelbarrow in which he carried his spades, forks, shovels, brooms and faghook. These familiar characters continued their responsibilities well within living memory, until councils began to replace them with mobile road gangs whose areas were rather wider. The last of the lengthsmen had retired by the 1970s. Even after mechanisation, council road gangs were local enough to know their patches well and be known, and they continued to take a personal pride in keeping the grips and ditches clear as well as dealing with pot-holes before they became a problem to traffic. Locals who noticed a problem would simply mention it to the foreman and it would be dealt with then and there.

ON FOOT

THE LANES WERE SOCIAL AREAS, PLACES WHERE YOU COULD HAPPEN UPON ACQUAINTANCES AND HAVE A CHAT STANDING IN THE SUMMER DUST OR WINTER MUD, OR CASUALLY AT THEIR GARDEN GATE; PLACES WHERE YOU CAUGHT UP ON LOCAL GOSSIP AND THE PHILOSOPHIES AND TALES OF PASSING STRANGERS. LANES WERE PLACES WHERE YOU COULD WANDER TO HARVEST HEDGEROW BERRIES FOR PIES, OR SLOES AND ELDERFLOWERS FOR HOMEMADE WINE, OR PICK FLOWERS TO PLONK IN A JAMJAR ON THE WINDOWSILL.

'Lanes were places where you could wander to harvest berries ...'

COUNTRY LANES TODAY are dominated by motorised traffic. Walkers, bikers and horse-riders are gradually giving up the struggle in the face of danger and pollution. Some of us resolutely continue to walk the lanes and refuse to leap into the ditch with every passing car, which is fine if the driver is local and has come to anticipate such idiots on the highway. But the lanes originally belonged to those on foot, be it two feet or four, and they seek to reclaim them.

Before combustion engines, before steam engines, before bicycles and before horses, if you wanted to get somewhere you walked. Before the Second World War people still often walked – to work, to school, to the village shop, to visit friends and relatives, to fairs and dances, even to the nearest town on market day, albeit ten miles each way. Between the wars, in particular, hiking was popular – townsfolk strode the lanes in unaccustomed boots, struggling with maps, and very clearly tourists.

In the nineteenth century and the early decades of the twentieth, you might also meet walking itinerants of various kinds:

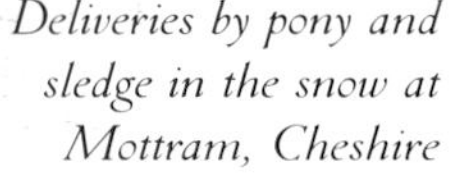

Deliveries by pony and sledge in the snow at Mottram, Cheshire

on foot

people who could mend chairs, umbrellas, pots and pans, or pedlars (literally, those who carry their goods themselves) with their knick-knacks in a waterproof backpack, doom-laden bell-ringing almanac sellers with a gaudy poster decorating their hats, sheet-music vendors, gypsies who made wooden clothes pegs and bunches of lucky heather, one-man bands knocking cymballed knees together and banging a drum behind their back while they blew on a penny whistle, tramps (women as well as men) with their bundle of worldly goods wrapped in a checked cloth on the end of a stick over their shoulder, roving fiddlers and ballad singers, beggars heading for holiday resorts in summer, sailors making their way to seaports, soldiers rejoining their regiments, and migratory agricultural labourers.

In the late afternoon and evening, women would be trudging home after a hard day's work in the fields, trying to be back in time to cook for their families, or bent double under bundles of deadwood and fircones for the fire, perhaps with small children clutching their skirts and toddling along with them as best they could. You might hear, as George Sturt described it, 'in the gathering dusk ... the buzz and rumour of manifold homecomings – tired children squalling, women talking and perhaps scolding, as the little chattering groups came near and passed out of earshot to their several cottages'.

Tramp, with all his possessions in a handcart made from an old pram

THE MOUCHER

With luck, you might even pass the time of day with a padding, bare-footed, bent-kneed moucher, out in all weathers to collect anything he could possibly sell – bundles of briar roots as grafts for garden roses, moss and peat for flowerpots, small snails as food for cage birds, small squares of turf for those who kept larks for their song, primrose 'mars' and rooted ferns to hawk from door to door in town along with violets and other spring flowers, frogs and lizards and snakes as pets, watercress from the brook, birds' eggs complete with nest to remind townsfolk of the countryside they no longer had time to wander in themselves, dandelion and other weed leaves for townees' tame rabbits, worms and grubs as anglers' bait, young rabbits or squirrels as pets, fledgling goldfinches and linnets as cage birds, bunches of 'blue-bottle' (cornflower) to sell in London at amazing prices, groundsel as cagebird seed, wild duck eggs for the farmhouse table, mushrooms of course and basketloads of blackberries. No tramp or thief was the moucher – just a man who knew his lanes and knew how to harvest them for a living. The lanes were so rich then.

on foot

'Lanes are sensual places – so much to see and touch, and smell.'

LANES WERE SAFE for children then. Richard Jefferies (1848–1887) remarked: 'As soon as ever the child is old enough to crawl about, it is sure to get out into the road and roll in the dust. It is a curious fact that the agricultural children, with every advantage of green fields and wide open downs, always choose the dusty hard road to play in ... the younger ones sprawling in the dust, their naked limbs kicking up clouds, and the bigger boys clambering about in the hedge-mound bounding the road, making gaps, splashing in the dirty water of the ditches.'

Lanes are sensual places – so much to see and touch, and to smell. The smells have changed over the years, of course. Once, it was the smell of dust or damp soil, dew on the grass, the subtle scents of wildflowers and tree bark, lichen and fern, the richness of ripe berries, the musk of passing wild animals (you can always tell when a deer, fox or badger has crossed the lane), the stable aroma of fresh horse-droppings, the warm friendly smell of a sweet-breathed milking herd on its way from the meadow to the parlour. For several

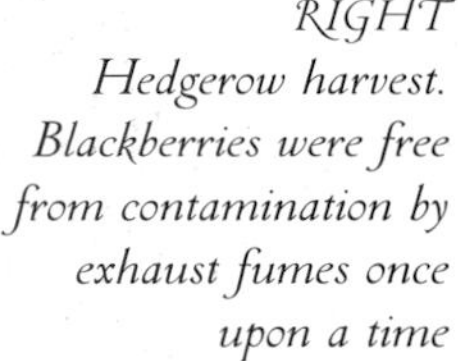

RIGHT
Hedgerow harvest. Blackberries were free from contamination by exhaust fumes once upon a time

FAR RIGHT
The post always gets through: three days before Christmas near Windermere in 1938

on foot

decades of the twentieth century the smells have been masked by the throat-catching harshness of exhaust fumes, yet even this is changing: if you walk the lanes now you will find that the smell of those fumes is sweeter, gentler, far less offensive and, they say, far less damaging to the health of the walkers and the environment as a whole. The noise of the engines, of course, still wipes out the high song of grasshoppers and warblers, but perhaps that too will change in years to come. Perhaps one day the cows (if any remain) will again wander down to the farmyard unmolested by road-rage drivers, and lane-walkers will once again find peace.

THE SCHOOL CROCODILE

In my own childhood we often walked along the lanes in pairs as 'crocodiles' from the village school, dawdling if the teacher let us and absorbing an outdoor lesson in nature without realising it was being taught. Today you'll be lucky to see a child on the road even on a bike, though they will flash by in a car, always in a hurry to be somewhere else, cocooned from the idle joys of discovery that lanewalkers can know even now – familiar lanes where you can see the progress of the seasons, greet the regular flock of sparrows that bounces over the hedge as you pass, and recognise diverse hedgerow plants – even the individual coltsfoot plant or lady's-smock in damp places; or unknown lanes that you can explore with a sense of adventure.

ON FOUR FEET

LONG GONE ARE THE DAYS WHEN HERDS OF LIVESTOCK FILLED THE LANES ON THEIR WAY TO MARKET, OFTEN TRAVELLING HUGE DISTANCES. DROVES OF CATTLE FROM ALL PARTS OF THE KINGDOM GRADUALLY FUNNELLED THEIR WAY TO THE BIG CITIES AND SHEEP STREAMING OFF THE HILLS AND DOWNS JOSTLED BETWEEN THE HEDGEROWS.

'The march of progress demands that the traffic must be kept moving, but the cows, bless them, are steadfastly maintaining the last vestige of life in a rural community.'

SMALL GROUPS OF wilful pigs were driven by agitated swineherds to woodland pannage in the autumn; large flocks of geese and other poultry walked for miles to market, sometimes with their feet shod in little leather boots for protection from the stones. Gone are the days when West Country farmers would bring their 'mobs' of cattle off the hills and drive them closer to the home farm along the lanes for the winter. Almost gone are the days when dairy cows wandered home along the lane at milking time, at their slow pace, sampling the herbage along

on four feet

the verges, pausing to consider life in general and gaze about them, often in company with no more than a small child.

In the 1960s, a Welsh villager noted that twice a day, morning and evening, there was a decrease in the rate at which the local traffic moved, especially in the evening when people were driving home after work. 'There is no policeman on duty, no traffic signals, and no roadman signalling his orders because roadworks are ahead. What is it that brings about this subtle change? Ah, the cows!' A herd of Friesians would be making its way from the pasture at one end of the village to the farm in the middle of the village, accompanied by the farmer and his dog and showing not a jot of concern for motorists impatient to get home. The cows would meander from one side of the road to the other without a care in the world, and all the vehicles in both directions were forced to a standstill until the cows had reached the familiar farm gate. 'The march of progress demands that the traffic must be kept moving, but the cows, bless them, are steadfastly maintaining the last vestige of life in a rural community,' wrote this Glamorganshire villager.

Most herds have now been chased right off the road by those impatient motorists, or by the complaints of incomers who dislike cowpats on the tarmac. It still seems almost surreal to see a herd of cows silhouetted overhead, crossing motorways along their very own footbridges – almost as unlikely as the herds of toads or families of badgers that pass beneath the traffic in their private tunnels. The ancestors of all these creatures had been using their routes for many centuries before the idea of motor vehicles was even an idle futuristic fancy, yet now they are banished.

Otherwise, unlike the major coaching roads, country lanes were relatively quiet places where the clop or splat of hooves was heard only occasionally. Two feet were far more common than four but you might have met the doctor riding to a patient, or a team

'Country lanes were relatively quiet places where the clop or splat of hooves was heard only occasionally ...'

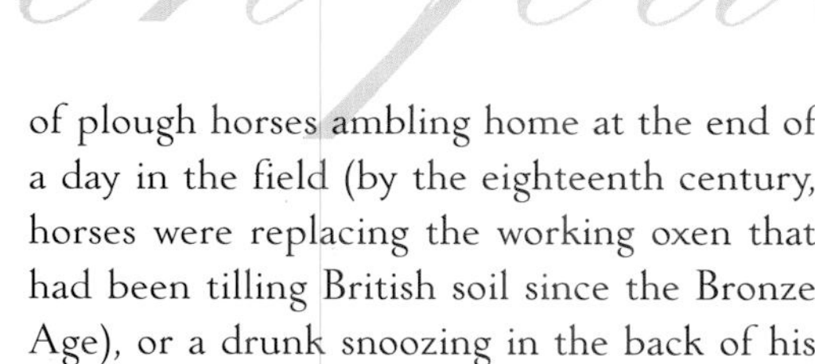

of plough horses ambling home at the end of a day in the field (by the eighteenth century, horses were replacing the working oxen that had been tilling British soil since the Bronze Age), or a drunk snoozing in the back of his cart while his horse found its own familiar way home, or a laden farm wagon on its way to market, or the nag-drawn carrier's van transporting household necessaries along its round and giving a lift to a housewife or two who wanted to get into town. The wise driver was wary of certain loads: carriers might have bundles of rod and strap-iron (brought out from the town for the local blacksmith) sticking out from the back of their hooded vans and difficult to see in the twilight; timber waggons might have long, slender larch poles whipping about at the back; and builders' vehicles would have long ladders and floor boards protruding, which tended to sway dangerously from side to side as the horses moved smartly downhill on uneven roads.

BELOW
Once a common sight: sheep being driven along the highway

BOTTOM
Devonian cowboy

In many areas, especially hilly ones, goods were carried on the backs of packhorses: they could pick their way where wheeled vehicles would come to grief, and in the nineteenth century trains of them were still heralded by the jangling bells of the lead horse. Many a bridge was designed for packhorses, with indented passing places. Bells were also worn by teams of wagon horses as a warning to other teams on stretches of road too narrow for passing: you often find, on old greenways, an unexpectedly wide verge that virtually doubles the width of the lane for a few yards, allowing a team to pull to one side as another passed in the opposite direction.

on four feet

An Irish milkman. Working donkeys were common all along Britain's lanes in the nineteenth century

DONKEYS AND STALLIONS

One of the biggest changes in lane life has been the disappearance of the donkey, the poorer man's horse. There were countless working donkeys in nineteenth-century Britain – the English neddy or dickey, the Scottish cuddy, the Welsh moke. They were a common sight in the lanes as pack animals, their panniers laden with goods for fairs and markets or for door-to-door delivery by gipsies and itinerant hawkers selling a wide range of wares and services. Donkeys also accompanied travelling entertainers of various kinds. Cottagers might afford to keep a donkey; they are easier and cheaper than horses, dependable, steady and long-lived and in many countries they act as the family's main means of transport, carrier of goods and worker on the land as well. Pannier-carrying donkeys continued in Ireland and were still quite common in the lanes of the West Country's coastal areas in the 1920s, but you no longer see them in Britain's lanes though there has been a revival of interest in donkey-driving for pleasure in recent years. Harry Rapley, who started school in 1905, described how he was going home one Saturday night: 'I wasn't drunk, and as I come to one bend I sees a light, just, you know, coming slow. When I turned the corner there was an old man, leading a donkey; he had a candle lit in a jam jar and he had a beard that went right down a long way.'

Sometimes you would meet a splendid 'travelling stallion'. Before the First World War, Old Bill Tull used to set off with his employer's very handsome and well-known Shire, Rock II, at the beginning of the week to visit mares that were ready for service. Bill would return home several days later; his wife would pack up another stock of food and ale for him, and off he would go again with Rock after a day's rest.

'... in many countries they act as the family's main means of transport, carrier of goods and worker on the land as well.'

GYPSIES

The donkeys and shaggy-maned piebald and skewbald horses of gypsies were once so familiar in rural areas. Many people were quite fond of 'their' gypsies; they understood and wryly admired their way of life, and came to know them quite well. Others saw gypsies as furtive and dishonest, apt to poach and a general nuisance to be watched closely by the village bobby and the game keeper. Gertrude Jekyll, writing in the 1920s, said that a distinction should be made between 'the true Romany and the rougher van-dweller, who is by no means always a real gypsy. The right people have a pleasant address and manner much like that of the Italian peasant; they are generally honest, and have a good deal of self-respect. It is to be regretted that they have to so large an extent given up their distinctive dress; the bright handkerchiefs for head and shoulders, and the long gold ear-rings. Now they dress in any old clothes that may be given to them, and wear on their heads any battered old hat with draggled feathers.'

Gypsies often made themselves 'benders' – shelters formed from hazel poles covered with heather, branches or canvas

Gypsies were very much a part of country life; they brought colour to the wastelands and commons with their romantic camps of brightly painted horse-drawn vans or quickly made 'benders' fashioned from supple hazel branches. The smoke of a gypsy's fire, to some, meant a welcome pause for a chat and a hot drink, once you had made friends with the dogs. The gypsies were courteous, kindly and hospitable to those who respected them but sometimes took advantage of those who did not. Gypsies knew where to find whortleberries, blackberries, sloes, nuts, watercress, mushrooms and wild plovers' eggs to harvest and sell; their nimble fingers could make pegs and besoms, or repair pots and pans; and they were forever offering lucky bunches of heather. (Why heather? Who knows?)

Gypsy caravan in Galloway

Gypsies came from a long tradition and the way of life was an ancient one. Today's New Age travellers, on the other hand, have come new to an itinerant life, of their own volition, and perhaps do not understand the unwritten rules of it. Like gypsies, they vary enormously in character and attitude, but the links with the past have been broken and the new country dwellers tend to distrust and resent these strangers on their land – especially when they arrive in numbers, in broken-down old vehicles that, however gaily decorated, cannot match the picturesqueness of the old gypsy vans. Those who take the trouble to get to know the 'hippies' usually find them gentle and peaceable, but not many take that trouble.

BICYCLES

Roads essentially liberate people: they enable you to travel from one place to another, by various means and at various speeds. In the country, your travels were generally limited by the endurance of your own legs; you went as far as you could walk. Then in 1817 Baron von Drais of Karlsruhe invented the hobby-horse, which was the forerunner of the bicycle.

And it was the bicycle that truly liberated country people, opening new horizons of independence and choice. On your bike you could travel to work far more quickly than on foot, you could travel to town, you could travel to meet new people, you could find marriage partners who were not simply recycled from the village gene pool.

The hobby-horse was not for country lanes; nor, realistically, were the four-wheeled and three-wheeled cycles of the 1820s or the 'boneshaker' velocipede of the late 1860s, nor indeed the 'Ordinary' bicycle of the early 1870s, with its outsize front wheel. Tricycles of the period became quite popular with more sedate cyclists, and as delivery vehicles, but it was not until the safety bicycle was produced in the mid 1880s that cycling for the ordinary country dweller began to become truly practical. In 1896 there was a great boom in cycle production, and once the fashionable folk had got over all the excitement, the ordinary working folk, be they in industrial or rural areas, had claimed the bicycle as their own essential steed.

Thinking back to before the First World War, a Welshman born in 1890 remembered cycling to an Eisteddfod in Liverpool. He was a harpist and singer. He started from Coventry at six in the morning, had dinner in Newcastle-under-Lyme at twelve and reached Liverpool at six that night after a ride of 110 miles. He won first prize the next day and cycled home again. Between the wars Ken Ainsworth, a farmworker from the Leicester area, thought nothing of cycling to Wales for lunch and then home again on his day off; when he became engaged he would put his fiancée on the back of a tandem and they would set off to Southampton to see her relations. With empty roads, long-distance cycling was a pleasure.

During the First World War, bicycles were pressed into service for more serious matters. Several coastal regiments had their own Cyclist Battalions, who patrolled their areas 'to prevent an enemy from landing unobserved and unreported'. Bicycles were ideal for the purpose: they were silent, swift and versatile and you could sling your rifle along the crossbar. Then came the motorbike – especially ones with sidecars in which you could carry your wife or your tools or your pig.

'With empty roads, long-distance cycling was a pleasure.'

WHEELED VEHICLES

In the relatively brief heyday of the horse, you might have met all manner of them in the lanes, especially agricultural and dray horses like the Old English Black cart-horse, the Suffolk, the improved Lincolnshire, the Clydesdale and assorted common cart-horses in every shape, size and colour.

Wheeled traffic at Stool End Farm, Langdale in the Lake District

Sometimes you would meet riding horses – the Charger, or the Covert, Road and Park Hack (each with a different role) and the Ladies' Horse. Or perhaps the fancy Carriage, Brougham or Cabriolet Horse, the Heavy Machiner (which pulled omnibuses and vans at a spanking six to eight miles per hour) and the Phaeton Horse, Gigster or Fast Trotter would hasten past between the shafts, though most were more likely to be seen in town. You might have seen a couple of children in a small governess's cart pulled by a trotting pony; you might have leapt into the ditch to avoid a careering rector driving hurriedly between his multiple churches.

Quite often, the barking of every local dog in the neighbourhood would herald the approach of another kind of draught animal altogether. Teams of large dogs, especially of the Newfoundland type, would pull yellow carts of fresh fish and salt bound for the London market. A team of four dogs could carry three to four hundredweight of fish, plus the driver, who would ride with his legs cocked up along the shafts. The dogs were generally left to roam freely about the village to scavenge for food while their master downed a pint or two at the inn; then he would blow a horn and his team would reassemble for harnessing. A dog team could travel as fast as a coach but there were so many complaints about the noise and nuisance they caused that a law banning the use of draught dogs came into effect in 1854.

THE CARRIER'S CART

LONG BEFORE THE RAILWAYS, A NATIONWIDE NETWORK OF CARRIERS SERVED COUNTRY AREAS. THE HORSE-DRAWN CARRIER'S CART TOOK GOODS TO ISOLATED COMMUNITIES, AND SOME WOULD DELIVER RIGHT TO THE DOORS OF REMOTE FARMHOUSES.

The carrier's cart and its market-day passengers

THE CARRIER ALSO took a few passengers, if you wanted to get into town or, more importantly, needed help in carrying goods home again from the market. (Anybody could walk to the market – five or ten miles was nothing – but with a load you needed help.)

The earliest form of the carrier's cart was in fact the enormous road wagon drawn by six horses: this would take cattle and sheep over long distances to London markets, and come back with loads of groceries or whatever else people needed on the way home. Many carrier services had started as a sideline to a main trade that already involved the carrier in transporting his own goods to market; he had a vehicle that would otherwise be empty on the return journey. Perhaps his goods were flour if he was a miller, or livestock and grain if he was a farmer, or he might have set up a coal delivery service, collecting coal from the railway depot and taking it round the houses. Trade directories also reveal carriers' dual roles as shopkeepers, publicans, blacksmiths and the like.

Carriers' carts were not exactly a comfortable way of travelling. They tended not to have shock-absorbing springs and bounced about heartily on the rough country lanes. You clambered up the steps at the back and sat on wooden benches along the sides of the cart, with no upholstery to take the bumps. Some were open two-wheeled tilt-carts; some were more solid wagons covered with canvas in the style of the Wild West. Other carriers fashioned a cabin on top of the vehicle, perhaps with dusty curtains between driver and passengers and usually with old paint peeling from the sides.

The horse knew where to go and where to stop as well as its driver, who was one of those invaluable characters, a mine of local information and gossip. Typically he would extend his job well beyond carrying market goods and people; he knew his customers well and often did small favours for them in town such as collecting debts. The older carriers could not read or write but always remembered their many commissions; a later generation needed notebooks. By the 1880s there were at least 200,000 carriers in the country, and they were still offering their services in the 1920s. But as the First World War broke out the system began to change: carrier's carts became motorised vans, or even buses packed with passengers and with hardly any room for the goods that were once the carrier's main trade.

'Anybody could walk to the market – five or ten miles was nothing – but with a load you needed help.'

MOTORING

In 1930 *The Field* gave details of 'Mr Norrison's new Code of the Highway'; this was the year before drivers were first required to take driving tests. The Code was aimed at motorists but applied equally to all road-users, be they cyclists, horse-driven vehicles or people in charge of animals on the road.

'So by 1930 two and four legs had already given way to motorised vehicles.'

'It is of the most vital importance, for instance, that everyone should know that, in future, all animals, ridden, led, or driven, must keep to the left, or near side, of the road, except when overtaking. Hitherto, of course, they have kept to the right, facing oncoming traffic. Use should be made of grass or other verges where these exist, and, when approaching a corner, drivers of flocks or herds should send someone on in advance to warn approaching traffic.' So by 1930 two and four legs had already given way to motorised vehicles. The article continued: 'But why should not the carrying of a lamp or lantern by the drover or shepherd be made compulsory? Nothing is quite so invisible as a black horse or bullock on a wet night.'

In the early years of the twentieth century, the battle for supremacy between horse power and motor power was in full swing. Steam traction had had its brief moment of glory, with steam engines chuntering at walking pace along the lanes (preceded by the proverbial man with a red flag or lantern) as the nineteenth century became the twentieth, and they continued to be valued by farmers for threshing for several decades to come.

The early history of mechanised transport is encapsulated by Reynolds, a furniture removals' company based at Bognor in Sussex. The firm was established when Samuel Reynolds opened a high-street furniture shop in the town in 1870. At the time, everything was transported by horse-drawn wagons, but by the turn of the century Reynolds had become the proud owner of a splendid Foden steam traction engine, jolting its driver along the road on its solid wheels as it pulled a miniature train of containerised furniture to and from its warehouses. By 1910 the company had progressed to a petrol-driven lorry, its fresh-air driver sitting with no protection from the elements at all; on the lorry's flat-bed behind him would be a container full of the contents of a customer's house. The container, winched on to the lorry at the warehouse, would be taken to the station and lifted complete on to a rail wagon for delivery to another part of the country. Soon the firm had Bedford vans; in 1929, for example, such a van was carrying luggage belonging to King George V along the cobbled streets of Windsor.

Horses and steam had had their day: for the transport of goods and of people, the petrol engine had won, even though there were still a few horse-drawn deliveries as late as the 1950s. While the general public seemed to welcome motorised goods' vehicles and public transport, such as cabs (the name comes from the horse-drawn cabriolet of the nineteenth century) and omnibuses ('omnibus' means, literally, 'for all'), the private motor car was not popular, especially in country areas. It was too noisy, it frightened the horses, and it went too fast. The old 4mph limit had been increased to

Garage catering for anything on wheels at Overton, 1910

motoring

12mph for vehicles of less than 3 tons in 1896, the year in which motor cars were first legalised as road vehicles (and the year of the first London-to-Brighton run).

In 1900 the Prince of Wales bought a Daimler and set the fashion for private motoring. In 1903 the speed limit for motor cars was increased to 20mph. In 1909 *The Times* warned car drivers that many horse drivers travelled with no lights at night, on the crown of the road, with the driver confidently sleeping in the knowledge that the horse could find its own way home. In 1910 the Sussex village of Aldingbourne was one among several that pleaded unsuccessfully for a 10mph limit. A few miles away the village of Poyning had decided in 1905 that 20mph was much too fast for public safety; in the late 1930s they begged for a 30mph limit through the village and did so annually until, in despair, in 1946 the parish clerk put up his own speed limit sign – at 10mph. Another village wanted a 6mph limit in 1907, to no avail. In fact all over the country villages deplored the danger of 'fast' cars but their pleas went unheeded, as they often still do today though at last county councils are listening and providing speed limits and assorted 'traffic calming' measures. The trouble is, some of the older residents complain at the proliferation of signs and some of the newer ones complain that the traffic-calming humps are a nuisance when they are late in getting the children to school. (By car? Why can't they walk?)

In 1905 there were 15,800 cars on Britain's roads. By 1914 this had increased to 132,000; by 1920 it was 200,000, by 1924 it was more than half a million and in 1939 there were more than 2 million private cars on British roads (and more than 400,000 motorbikes and 488,000 goods vehicles). Virtually all of them, of course, were black. Today there are more than 20 million cars on our roads, and very few are black.

Harking back to his youth in what is now the traffic-clogged Surrey village of Chobham, Frank Burningham recalled: 'There was no vehicles in the village, there was no traffic of any sort. If you saw three carts go through the village, trundling through with gravel on them from up on the Common, it was about all you saw all day long.' And there are many photographs from all over the country to prove it – empty village streets, perhaps a pony and trap or old Tarry Jack walking beside his donkey, or children playing with hoops in the road, or a dog lazily scratching itself at the crossroads. In 1925, Gertrude Jekyll remarked:

> *The road was a kind of world in itself, full of personal incident and human story. Now nearly all of this is swept away; much that went by road is now carried by rail and the roads are rendered offensive and unsightly by the petrol traffic and its needs. Our roadsides, formerly beautiful with wild flowers and grasses, are now defiled with heaps of rank-smelling tarred stones and collections of empty tar barrels, the roads themselves are offensive with a half-stifling reek of tar, and their edges are harshly defined by a pitiless line of cement blocks. So much for our modern improvement; everything for haste and hurry – nothing for peace and quiet enjoyment and use of life. Surely there was truth in the mouth of the wise man who said we were 'progressing backward'!*

Ah well, at least she did not have her view blotted by fields full of ranked caravans.

Motoring for pleasure was in full swing in the 1930s, especially on Sundays and Bank Holidays. Beauty spots within motoring distance of the cities were eagerly visited by people in double-decker omnibuses, people on motorbikes and in side cars, and richer people in their cars. In 1931 petrol was 1s 4d a gallon and the 20mph speed limit had just been abolished (the 30mph limit in built-up areas would be introduced in 1934). And proper signposts were being introduced so that you knew where you were going.

TOP
Having a picnic in the days when people still went for a Sunday drive in the country for pleasure

ABOVE
The village street as it used to be, traffic-free

ROAD SIGNS

BEFORE THE 1930S, THE ONLY SIGNPOSTS WERE THOSE PUT UP BY THE AUTOMOBILE ASSOCIATION FOR THE SAKE OF ITS MEMBERS. THE AA DEVELOPED WHEN A GROUP OF MOTORING ENTHUSIASTS GOT TOGETHER IN 1905 TO PROTECT THEMSELVES FROM THE GENERAL PREJUDICE AGAINST MOTOR CARS.

'To help its members, the AA also began to put up village name signs from 1906.'

RIGHT
Automobile Association's roadside hut, 1919

BELOW
Snow-blocked Peak District lane near Chapel-en-le-Frith

THE GROUP ALSO felt singled out by the police, who seemed to delight in setting speed traps for them; the AA salute was originally a way of warning fellow motorists that there was a policeman with a stopwatch lurking behind the next hedge – if a patrolman, on his bike, failed to salute, you knew that there was trouble ahead. To help its members, the AA also began to put up village name signs from 1906. Of course the locals knew where they lived, but touring motorists had no idea unless they asked. In 1906 the AA also put up its first 'Danger' and 'Warning' signs to help its members as they approached various hazards. Then there were signposts to direct you to where you wanted to go – fingerposts were peppering the landscape in the 1920s. AA men also leapt out of their roadside boxes to direct traffic at road junctions (traffic lights were not installed outside London until 1931).

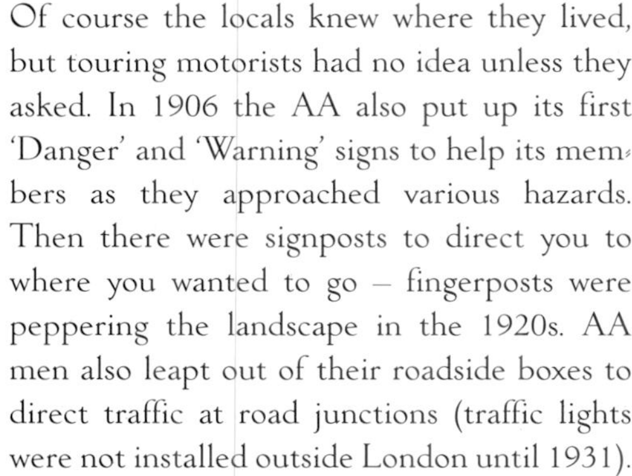

In 1930 a new Road Traffic Act allowed highway authorities to put up their own traffic signs, which had to be to Ministry of Transport specifications for size, type and colour. In 1964 these specifications became uniform all over Britain. Many villages, over the years, have objected to 'oversigning', which detracts from their rural character, but usually those objections are overruled. Sometimes the bureaucracy seems a touch arrogant; for example, in 1952 a county council sent a circular to its parishes about village name signs:

> *It is proposed to erect village place names throughout the County and for this purpose I enclose herewith a small map upon which I have marked the approximate position of the signs affecting your village. At each of the points marked in red on the map will be placed a peg. These pegs will have silver tops and the grass verge around the pegs will be cleared so you should have no difficulty in locating them. All pegs will be in position by the 26th inst. If any of your committee have any observations, please let me know before 2 Feb, when the erections will be starting.*

So the village was given only a week to decide where the signs should be; it had no option, apparently, about whether there should be a sign in the first place.

In the Second World War, of course, fingerposts and village signs were all removed, to fool the enemy. In 1925, here and there, white lines began to appear down the middle of some roads; in the first year of the Second World War they were extended to all trunk roads as 'aids to movement' dring wartime blackouts. 'Cats' eyes' were invented in 1934. How cluttered the lanes and verges were becoming!

ROAD ACCIDENTS

BEFORE THE SECOND WORLD WAR, VERY FEW COUNTRY PEOPLE COULD AFFORD A CAR ANYWAY, WHICH BRED A CERTAIN AMOUNT OF RESENTMENT AGAINST THE MOTOR TOURISTS WHO BEGAN TO FILL UP THE LANES, CHOKING THE LOCALS WITH ROAD DUST AND TERRIFYING HORSES AND CYCLISTS BY THEIR VERY PRESENCE.

YET IN THE 1930s the major roads were still quite empty; you could cycle with your sweetheart, side by side, arms entwined, along the trunk roads, still able to breathe pure country air and with little fear of being forced into the ditch by the traffic – if you were lucky. With motoring came road accidents. There had always been accidents, of course, usually involving bolting horses that toppled their carriages, but with motoring the accidents became more frequent.

In 1877 George Dew recorded in his diary that two runaway horses with a dung cart 'running at furious speed' had followed him on his daily journey along the Oddington road from Islip; he nearly put himself in a ditch trying to get out of their way:

> *The fore horse was fastened to the shafts of the cart by one trace only, & as soon as he saw my cart he left the beaten road & stopped behind me, the other horse attempting to rush by & we were brought into collision instantly, the trace throwing over my cart into the hedge & myself with it. My horse I found, on creeping out, to be rolled up in the ditch under the cart horse's belly & near the wheel of the dung cart; & had either of them commenced kicking my horse had been trampled to death. Fortunately myself & horse escaped with a few scratches & bruises but much shaken.*

This stretch of road brought Dew another accident the following year, when the harness bridle and blinkers slipped off his horse's head:

> *The horse bolted & in getting out trying to stop him, or rather in clinging to the cart to keep pace, I was thrown down, seriously bruising my arm & otherwise shaking me.... The horse galloped away at a furious pace, &, strange to say, turned three sharp corners without overturning the vehicle, & was stopped in Oddington village by a boy without any injury.*

It was about this time that our George decided to learn how to ride a bicycle: 'No person who had not tried to ride can imagine how difficult it is at first to preserve the balance ... I never saw one till about 12 or 18 months ago, & now there are several in Heyford.'

Within the month he was cycling 20 miles a day on his rounds, despite complaining that the public roads were 'abominably muddy & bad'.

In 1853 James Tracey, a veterinary surgeon, was brought before the courts on the charge of 'furious driving': he had run over a child with his horse and cart, driving at the wicked rate of 9mph and apparently completely out of control of his horse. He was fined 40 shillings. At the time, and until 1896, the maximum permitted speed for vehicles other than those drawn by horses was walking pace, 4mph.

The first person to be killed by a motor car in Britain was Bridget Driscoll in 1896. In 1906 the worst motoring accident in Britain to date occurred at Slaugham, Sussex. A top-decker motor bus had driven through Handcross's high street at 12mph carrying passengers on the fire brigade's annual outing from Kent, heading for Brighton. Seven minutes later, its brakes failed as it began to descend the hill at Slaugham and thirty-six people were killed.

More typically, in 1924 two girls were cycling along a twisty lane when a car coming in the opposite direction, driven by a 'London visitor', struck one of the bikes, flinging its rider into the hedge; the car ended up in the ditch. Fortunately, in this case, the only injuries were bad bruises and shock. The nightmare of drivers speeding down country lanes as if they were motorways was still a long way off.

'At the time, and until 1896, the maximum permitted speed for vehicles other than those drawn by horses was walking pace, 4mph.'

Blinding snow caused this accident in 1939

GARAGES

In 1950, the tables were turned in the village of West Dean. In cinemas across the land, Pathe News reported on a little local story. A black London taxi cab drew up outside a blacksmith's shop. The back door of the cab was opened, and out stepped Joey, a small pony.

'Garages began to spring up in every village with the growing popularity of motoring. Some had started out as the village smithy'

He stood patiently while the smith gave him four bright new shoes, then he climbed back into the taxi and rode home. Joey's owner and cabbie, Les Brockhurst, ran his own garage and so he knew all about horsepower.

Garages began to spring up in every village with the growing popularity of motoring. Some had started out as the village smithy – it was almost a natural progression from hammering iron on the forge to welding bits of car together. In the very early days of motoring, fuel would be purchased from oil shops or ironmongers, and so journeys needed rather careful planning. When cars broke down, it was generally a matter of do-it-yourself (or get the chauffeur to do it, as most early motorists were rich enough to employ staff) or asking a passing horse to drag your crestfallen vehicle to the nearest bicycle shop for help. Many such shops developed into garages for motor vehicles, and one or two of them combined with local coachbuilders whose experience with horse-drawn vehicle bodies was readily transferred to those of motor vehicles.

RIGHT
Fatal accident in dense fog near Haseley, Warwickshire, 1934

At first these businesses were in cities and larger towns, accessible to the richer folk who were able to afford motor cars and as close as possible to railway stations, as fuel and spares would be delivered by rail. The word 'garage' was eventually adopted for these new ventures. Apparently the word originally applied to the wide passing-places in French canals and was then used on French railways to refer to train sheds, thence to places for motor cars. The term was in use in Britain by 1900.

After the First World War, mass production of motor cars and commercial vehicles boomed and village garages began to open at crossroads or on a field that had become dirt cheap during the agricultural depression. They provided cars for hire, with or without chauffeurs; they ran taxis and they often provided bus services; they towed fire-engines, they carried the mail, and they could fix anything that needed soldering. Some of them even generated electricity, using oil-powered generators, for the locals to recharge their batteries.

Filling stations began to pop up – scattered roadside pumps in the middle of nowhere along busier roads, often to the horror of locals at these blots on the landscape. The AA started to provide its own filling stations, the first at Aldermaston in 1919. In 1927 there was legislation for the licensing of roadside petrol pumps, and a year later county councils were given powers over the appearance of garages in general, many of which had strongly featured corrugated iron. Some entrepreneurs, especially on tourist routes, developed their filling stations with tea-rooms and other attractions for the weary traveller. Others began plastering the area with signs – not just on site but along the road to catch your eye as you approached them.

As agriculture became increasingly mechanised between the wars, country garages built up a steady business with local farmers, repairing implements as well as tractors, to tide them through to the time when cars became essential in rural life. Otherwise they had lean times in the 1920s and 1930s, when poverty in the countryside put cars well beyond reach of most. And the Second World War had a severe effect on country garages – for a start their mechanics were called up and petrol was rationed. But many family businesses did survive, and continued to play an important part in the life of the village.

BYPASSES

With the phenomenal increase in traffic, countless villages have found that their streets no longer belong to them. Vibrations from heavy lorries shake old cottages to their very foundations; crossing the street becomes a problem; gossiping on the pavement floats away unheard over the roar of the traffic; exhaust fumes hang like a perpetual mist, hemmed in by the buildings; ducks that used to waddle across to the village pond lie squashed in the road; town-based burglars and vandals have much readier access to (and quick escape from) village and rural properties.

In the pretty Dorset village of Corfe Castle, the traffic that thundered through during the 1960s became almost intolerable. Summer tourist traffic ground to a halt in the crowded streets; bothered motorists fumed like their own exhaust pipes, gears clashed, horns sounded in frustration, radiators boiled. In addition, heavy lorries carrying Purbeck stone and coal rumbled through the village, taking loads that were no longer sent by rail. Incomers who had moved into the old cottages and spent considerable sums in modernising them were the first to object vociferously about the lost peace that they had come to find here.

The story was repeated in many villages throughout the country. This invasion of through-traffic has had a highly destructive effect on community life in rural areas, countering the advantages that transport has brought in the way of broadening horizons, importing goods and ideas and freeing the individual. The car that passes down your lane driven by somebody else, especially somebody you don't even know (in the country, you know everybody), is an intruder and a nuisance, even more so if the vehicle is a clean high-seated four-wheel drive clearly bought to impress rather than as a practical farmer's wagon. Ironically the car driven by you is an essential part of your life, and you do not see yourself as part of the 'traffic problem'.

It is little wonder that so many villages have pleaded for bypasses in recent years. In some cases those pleas go right back to the 1920s. For example, at Twineham in Sussex they drew the county council's attention to 'the large increases in the amount expended on the Main Roads and as most of the wear is caused by through Traffic which does not contribute towards the upkeep, the Parish Council suggest that the County Council should press for the nationalisation of the chief through roads, especially the main London to Brighton Road.' In the 1920s and 1930s Twineham's parish council persistently complained about a dangerous crossroads, or about the inconvenience of large charabancs using narrow lanes, or about the slippery road surfaces being a danger to agricultural horses. In 1928 there was a proposal for a 'motor road' or 'motorway' from London to Brighton, which was designed to run along a former turnpike road in the parish of Albourne. The parish council objected strongly, saying that a motorway would cut several fields in half and render them useless; it would also involve the demolition of a beloved old cottage or two. The 'motorway' was duly built anyway in the 1930s as the A23, but it was so dangerous that the locals dubbed it Blood Alley. It was not until 1991 that the locals won their battle for a bypass.

There was a similar situation in another Sussex village, Washington, where the powers that be wanted to demolish cottages in order to realign the A24. The saga began in the early 1950s and also involved the loss of the parish tennis courts and the compulsory purchase of National Trust land. Several other Sussex villages campaigned for thirty years before achieving their bypasses but at last in the early 1990s they were able to feel like proper villages again. The story is repeated all over the country, and the feeling always is that we who live here in rural areas must give way to the greater 'good' of getting traffic from one area to another through the heart of our communities, however much that destroys the community. The age-old resentment of through-traffic that, one way or another, takes from us without giving back lingers on and the doormats resent their role. After all, we live here.

THE COUNTRY BUS

THE COUNTRY BUS WAS ANOTHER GREAT LIBERATOR FOR RURAL POPULATIONS. BY THE EARLY 1920S IT HAD MORE OR LESS REPLACED THE FRIENDLY OLD CARRIER'S CART BUT GENUINE BUSES WERE LIMITED IN THEIR ROUTES.

'... or you might go to market in a small van fitted with benches, where you would be joined by assorted livestock and packages.'

MORE COMMON WAS the motorised van, and typical in rural areas was the cheaper-to-run open lorry, with padded seats, a roof for storing packages, and canvas sides that could be dropped down to keep out the rain (they had celluloid portholes as windows). Others were converted furniture-removal vans, with a drop-down tailboard for easy loading of goods and folding seats for a passenger or two; or you might go to market in a small van fitted with benches, where you would be joined by assorted livestock and packages. As Pulbrook explained, 'Fifteen miles in a tiny crowded van with pigs as companions can be enjoyed only by rural folk and those seeking adventure.'

Such a journey could provide considerable entertainment as the passengers exchanged conversation, shouting loudly above the rattle of the van. As on any country bus, this was where you heard the local gossip, exchanged witty remarks (usually rather personal), aired unusual or prejudiced views on topics of the day, discussed prices and the state of your crops and everybody else's, and let your imagination run wild about the new tenants of the local farm.

During the First World War many men were trained as mechanics and drivers, and those who returned from the killing fields often put their new skills to good use in civilian life by setting up village taxi or bus services. Their vehicles would be highly individual, converted from all manner of motors, and many of the men worked indefatigably, on the road all day, going wherever their customers needed to go and providing a service in the true sense of the word – meeting people's needs. They knew that half of the young would want to go the town cinema or dance hall by a certain time, and that they also wanted to be brought home afterwards, so the bus would be there for them. ('Nobody ever left behind!' was the slogan.) They knew that the women wanted to go to town on market day, and needed the bus to be parked conveniently nearby so that they could leave some of their packages (including baskets of live poultry and the like) safely on the bus while they completed their shopping. They knew where people lived and would drop you right at your gate so that you did not need to plough through the mud from a village bus-stop. And they knew that children enjoyed the thrill when the driver accelerated over the hump-back bridges that still existed, before the humps were deemed too uncomfortable for speeding motor cars.

With the increasing popularity of the private car, rural bus services were already deteriorating in the late 1940s; companies found that they were running at a loss and began to reduce their timetables, exacerbating the situation. Bus services became too few, and the times did not suit the needs of the passengers.

In the 1960s, the village of Drigg in

Heading for the Welsh border at Bishops Castle. Headlights were masked during the war

the country bus

Cumberland reported that because bus and train services were inadequate, most families owned a vehicle of some kind. 'In some cases each member of a family has a means of transport, eg, one house has two cars and two motorcycles, each vehicle belonging to a son. Their mother uses a bicycle.' In the Devon village of Colyton, only 12 per cent of the 2,000 population owned cars; but in Northamptonshire 59 per cent of the villagers of Little Houghton had cars, and included one four-car family. It was something of a chicken-and-egg situation: which came first – the deterioration in bus services leading to the need to have your own car in rural areas, or the desire to be a car owner leading to the demise of public transport? A rash of bus strikes in the 1960s didn't help: suddenly the service was unreliable and you might not be able to get to work that day.

One problem for the bus companies was that, unlike the railway companies, they were not underpinned by income from the transport of goods, only from that of passengers, and their profit margins were very low. Hence they reduced uneconomic services, cutting out Sunday buses, reducing evening services so you could not go out on the town at night, and eventually leaving most villages (unless they were lucky enough to be on a main road) with perhaps one or two bus runs a week, whereas before they had had several buses a day.

Yet it is in rural areas that a good bus service is the most essential; in towns you are generally within reasonable walking distance, if not of your destination then at least to the railway station. The small minority in rural areas who do not have access to a private car now experience considerable difficulty in meeting their most basic needs: so many village post-offices have closed that they cannot fetch their pension without a bus to the town; many villages do not have services such as a doctor's surgery or chemist, and increasingly villages no longer have a shop of any sort.

Some villages try to beat the bus problem by running their own minibuses, driven by volunteers, to ensure that older people in particular have a degree of mobility, but all too often voluntary schemes wane after the initial enthusiasm. It is a problem that many have tried to solve but few have succeeded in doing so, and it has resulted in many rural families becoming multiple car owners, to ensure that people can get to work and to the shops, children can get to school, and everybody can escape to find leisure activities that, like so many other needs, are not met within the village. The lack of good public transport is one of the many factors that have been slowly undermining village life.

The Newbury bus

AN ESSENTIAL SERVICE

Sometimes a bus would take the whole village on a day's outing. Such buses were often 'sharrybangs' (charabancs – open vehicles fitted with rows of benches), which also brought tourists from the towns and cities into the countryside. The tourists brought money with them, and wily locals soon learned to take advantage of their desire to spend it on teas and meals and bed-and-breakfast. By the 1930s buses were comfortable saloons with pneumatic tyres – a decade earlier many buses had iron wheels, which made the ride far from easy. The new buses still carried everything their passengers wished to carry and became greatly loved as well as essential to village life. One villager's memories of the 'wonderful' bus are typical of many: 'Jack Eggleton's, tuppence each way, thruppence return.' When grandmother needed to visit grandpa in hospital, the busman drove up on to the common to pick her up at her garden gate, dropped her at the hospital door, and then picked her up again at the hospital afterwards and drove her all the way home, still for threepence return.

CANALS

THERE WAS A PERIOD WHEN TRANSPORT BY WATER WAS SEEN AS THE SOLUTION TO THE ETERNAL PROBLEM OF AVOIDING IMPASSABLE LANES WHEN GETTING HEAVIER GOODS FROM ONE PART OF THE COUNTRY TO ANOTHER. QUITE APART FROM EXISTING RIVERS AND THE SEA, IT MADE SENSE TO CREATE A SYSTEM OF ARTIFICIAL WATERWAYS SO THAT THERE WAS A PROPER NETWORK FOR WATERBORNE GOODS.

'It was much cheaper and easier by water than by land.'

CANALS WERE BUILT extensively in the 1770s and 1780s. Sussex, for example, was a rural rather than an industrial county, with the main products being corn, timber, charcoal, chalk, lime, marl, iron, marble, limestone, cattle and sheep – all of them bulky goods for which transport could be very expensive. It was much cheaper and easier by water than by land. In the old days, huge loads of timber had been sent laboriously by land, over the terrible Sussex roads, to the coast for export; lime, likewise, was carried from the Downs by land; corn was sent in large quantities to Portsmouth, and so on. The rivers Rother and Arun were partly navigable, but the network had been greatly improved by cutting new canals in the early nineteenth century. To enhance the benefits of the new canals, the Earl of Egremont at his own expense undertook to make the Rother navigable as far as Midhurst; his eventual aim was to link Sussex directly with London for the exchange of goods. The net result of these waterway improvements was that far more timber was accessible, thus land values increased considerably in that woodland previously left untouched because of transport problems could now be felled and exported. Not only could Sussex export its products; it was also now easier to bring in coal from other parts of the country – initially to replace locally grown furze used by farmers to fire their lime kilns, and thereby releasing furze land to the plough for growing more grain. Another bonus was in employment: two hundred native Sussex men, said Reverend Young, were employed in cutting the canals. In many parts of the country, however, canal-cutting gangs were dreaded: they tended to be

canals

mobile teams, not of local men but of outsiders and foreigners whom nobody trusted and who caused riots and general mayhem wherever they went.

In Devon, the Reverend Coham of Black Torrington described how, instead of a 'most forbidding wild, and in a manner uncultivated desert, calculated only for the grazing of lean bullocks, and horses of the smallest and hardiest kinds' in the country that was surrounded by the circuitous course of the river Torridge, there were by 1808 extensive cornfields, luxuriant pastures, sheep-covered uplands and the continual creation of new enclosures and improved drainage and grazing on the moors. All this was apparently due to the improvement of the roads (largely thanks to one man, George Bickford Esquire of Darsland), which allowed wheeled vehicles to bring in large amounts of sea-sand as manure. However, Coham felt that far greater improvements could yet be made with the help of canals, because 'oxen do not possess strength and agility sufficient for heavy draughts and long journies' to bring in the necessary manure; while horses, which some were at that stage advocating to supplant oxen, would have to be kept as expensively large teams. But if everything went by canal instead, the horse teams could be reduced, road repairs would be required less often (and travel on them by others would be more pleasurable) and everybody would be happier!

In Lincolnshire, of course, they knew all about waterways and there were canals aplenty. The complaint was directed at the canal engineers themselves, 'for after giving their plans, they leave you to yourselves; and then difficulties arise in which the people are ignorant, and upon application to them, and ready to pay, cannot have their attention'. Nevertheless, a very fine canal from Grantham to Nottingham, thirty-three miles long, had been completed in 1795 at a cost of £100,000 and it was expected to bring in 'very great returns'.

'Another bonus was in employment: two hundred native Sussex men ... were employed in cutting the canals.'

RAILWAYS

THE IMPACT OF THE RAIL NETWORK ON RURAL AREAS WAS FAR GREATER THAN THAT OF CANALS AND FAR MORE SUDDEN THAN THAT OF ROAD IMPROVEMENTS. THE BUILDING OF THE RAILWAYS BROUGHT LOCAL EMPLOYMENT APLENTY, AND MONEY IN THE POCKET OF MANY A LAND OWNER WHOSE LAND WAS REQUIRED BY THE RAILWAY COMPANIES.

Moving an entire farm by rail from Wales to Surrey (livestock, machinery, furniture and all) in 1947

RIGHT The end of the line for horses and carts? This is at Calvert, Buckinghamshire, in about 1899

'The railways were not just escape routes for pleasure: they were also a means of finding work in new areas...'

IT ALSO BROUGHT fast, cheap public transport – initially of goods but very soon mainly of passengers – so that the countryman who had never travelled much further than his legs would take him found he could take the whole family, indeed the whole village if you booked an excursion train, for outings to the seaside or anywhere else they fancied. The railways were not just escape routes for pleasure; they were also a means of finding work in new areas; and they would eventually introduce the concept of the commuter. Village life would never be the same again.

The railway companies also introduced the concept of national time. Time had been a relatively unimportant and slow-moving local matter. The church bells let you know when it was time for certain important things like coming in from the fields or turning up for a church service (they also let you know when there had been a death in the village, and whether it was man, woman or child; and gave news of battle victories and suchlike) but there was no need to know what time it was elsewhere in the country unless you were one of the few to travel by the mail coaches that had begun to race from London to Bath and elsewhere in the late eighteenth century. Otherwise, all you needed to know was what the church bells told you, and rural time revolved around natural phenomena. Each town had its own time, based on the sun's local noon, and each village often decided its own time too.

The railways were more demanding: trains ran more or less to a timetable and in 1840 the Great Western Railway instructed all its stations to synchronise their clocks with London time. The other railway companies soon did the same and in 1849 an electric clock was installed at Greenwich Observatory which by 1852 was transmitting a time signal to Lewisham station and thence via the railways and telegraph stations to post offices and public clocks all over the country. Even the

railways

LEFT
Railway halt on the Thaxted branch, Essex

remotest rural villages came to accept that their time should be the same as that in the rest of the country, ie London time, which made catching the right train much simpler.

The first main railway routes were created in the 1830s. By 1850 far more freight and long-distance passengers travelled by rail than by canal or by road. The spread of the rail network continued throughout the rest of the nineteenth century, and by the 1870s there were cheap fares for workers, enabling them to find work wherever they pleased. The chains of village life had been broken. And then the town and city dwellers discovered the countryside through the windows of their railway carriages. Theirs were usually through-trains, but there soon developed a system of country trains that stopped at every station and wayside halt, sometimes by request – for example, a large land owner might flag down the train at his private halt, perhaps to load on horses, riders and hounds for the local hunt. These same land owners had often financed the building of rural branch lines in the first place.

Initially the railway was designed for the carriage of bulk freight, and instantly brought new markets for rural goods wherever there was a country station. Relatively few villages had their

LEFT
Station master and his staff

LOCAL & GLOBAL

Time was not the only rural horizon broadened by the coming of the railways. In the 1861 census for the Shropshire parish of Highley, a quarter of those registered were railway navvies and their families lodging temporarily in the parish, and their own places of birth included 23 different counties. Highley had become almost cosmopolitan overnight. Some of the navvies' children had even been born in France, while their fathers were building French railway lines. Imagine the effects of such an influx into villages whose inhabitants had often travelled no further than ten miles from home in their entire lives, and who had not even read about foreign lands. Villages on main coaching routes were more wise in the ways of the world; they had seen all sorts passing through and had heard many a traveller's tale over a pint at the local inn. But for villages in more remote parts of the country, the coming of the railway was a major and life-changing event.

railways

own railway depot and these ones often began to grow quickly with this new asset. The station was sometimes a mile or so outside the village, and the village began to stretch towards it. Farmers soon began to accompany their livestock on the trains and found it a convenient way of getting into town for other business. All sorts of farm workers and tradesmen joined in the fun, and to find work elsewhere. Increasingly the country train became a passenger train, though with far less profit to the railway companies than freight. Rail travel became cheaper and faster, wages increased with the scope for choice of work, working hours decreased and more and more people had time and money to take a train journey for leisure as well as for work. Huge numbers of people would flock to major events all over the country by train – race meetings, exhibitions, visits to the seaside.

It was boomtime for the countryside, and it lasted quite a while. It brought new buyers for country homes within commuting distance of the cities; it brought new businesses to cater for those buyers; it brought goods and ideas and so much more. And so the boom continued, until that black day when Dr Richard Beeching, Chairman of the British Railways Board (1963–65) wielded his axe and peremptorily severed a large number of what had been essential arteries feeding the countryside, all in the interests of 'economy', with no comprehension of the far more important social role of public transport. It was to prove a devastating blow for many villages, though the effects were slow to be recognised.

The deserted stations were converted into dwellings and the now-silent tracks reverted to nature and became artificial greenways for walkers, riders and cyclists. At Lavant, in Sussex, the parish council was informed in 1986 that 'a "gentleman" together with a "lady" are residing in a tree house built in an evergreen oak on the Railway Track near Oldwick Meadows.' The gentleman's presence was causing some concern to locals, as he was sometimes the worse for drink and he frightened people. But surely he was just another rich character, so many of which have disappeared from rural areas in an increasingly uniform world?

'Huge numbers of people would flock to major events all over the country by train – race meetings, exhibitions, sports events, visits to the seaside.'

RIGHT Loading punnets of strawberries into rail wagons

railways

AIRCRAFT

The two world wars brought a new presence to the countryside, this time something that flew. At first it was fun, watching planes made of brown paper and string cavorting in the skies, manned by ex-cavalry officers who, for the First World War, were told that because they could ride a horse they could fly a plane without being taught how.

'The wars brought a new presence to the countryside, this time something that flew.'

Rich young men began to buy private planes that they landed with dangerous imprecision in grassy fields when attending country-house weekends, but that, too, was an enjoyable spectacle for the locals.

With the Second World War, aircraft became threatening instead. Many rural areas were used by home-bound German aircraft as dumping grounds for their undelivered bombs – almost more frightening in their unexpectedness than the regular drubbing suffered by some of the big cities for which those bombs had been destined. In many places people had ringside views of the dogfights in the skies. New airfields were built, not only for British craft but also for large numbers of Americans and others, which had a considerable effect on many small communities. But still people were basically on the side of aircraft, and after the war one of the more pleasant sounds of high summer was the background drone of friendly propellers across a blue sky above the meadows.

Then came the rapid growth of the commercial airlines and the new mass habit in the past thirty years or so of spending holidays abroad and getting there by air. Jet engines replaced props and the sound became intrusive rather than soporific. Military jets began to scream very low over the fields, terrifying animals and people alike (hot-air balloons, so innocent, also stampede the animals); the heavy vibration of military helicopters throbbed menacingly as the big bugs loomed suddenly over the horizon and skimmed farmhouse rooftops. Flying became a hobby for more people; light planes flitted about the skies in increasing numbers – again a pleasure to watch but sometimes too much and too often. Then came the age of the spy in the sky – at first merely opportunists taking aerial photographs and trying to sell them to house owners, increasingly annoyed at being caught out in what until then had been a private garden. The aerial photographs, often published in local papers as a bird's eye view of a village, revealed areas that had previously been hidden from view except by invitation. And now there are satellites up there, watching your every move and able to zoom in so finely that they know the colour of your eyes.

Loading strawberries into the 'Cardiff Dragon' biplane at Weston-super-Mare

COMMUNICATIONS

THE WHOLE OF THIS CHAPTER ON COUNTRY LANES AND TRANSPORT HAS BEEN ABOUT COMMUNICATION, AND ITS DRAMATIC EFFECT ON LIFE IN THE COUNTRYSIDE. IT IS APPROPRIATE, THEREFORE, TO INCLUDE A SECTION ABOUT THE FORMS OF INTERPERSONAL COMMUNICATION THAT HAVE HAD AN EVEN GREATER AND MORE DIRECT EFFECT.

FOR CENTURIES, THOSE who lived in rural areas were isolated and introverted. They knew little about the world beyond the village, or beyond the nearest market town. It is really only within the nineteenth and particularly twentieth centuries that their eyes have been opened – first by education, especially learning to read, so that books, journals, political pamphlets and advertisements became accessible to all.

LIBRARIES

In Worcestershire in the very early years of the nineteenth century, it was realised that 'ignorance is one of the greatest obstacles to improvement' and that 'the way to remove it must be the dissemination of useful knowledge'. The interest originally was in the improvement of agriculture and to this end, long before the education of children became compulsory, Worcester put forward a plan for village and parish libraries. It was proposed to establish small libraries in every village, 'consisting chiefly of books on agriculture, history, modern voyages and travels, and other subjects of rational instruction and general utility'. The library would be managed by the resident clergyman; the schoolmaster would have use of the books for his own reading, and the books would be kept at the vestry room, or in the clergyman's home, or at any other room accessible to the library's subscribers. Each person could keep a book for one month, with a penalty of a penny a day thereafter, but magazines and reviews could only be kept for five days. A list of suitable books to form the basis of each library was suggested.

It was a fine idea but it was not until after the First World War that county councils began to provide rural library services, placing books in accessible rooms in the villages identified by a sign of the flaming torch of knowledge.

The mobile library

Long before then, worthy Victorians had created village reading rooms from about the middle of the nineteenth century, usually funded by a local benefactor, with the aim of 'improving' the locals: the rooms were places where 'the artisan, labouring and other poorer classes' could benefit from lectures and classes of further education. The rooms were also used for various entertainments (no alcohol allowed) such as lantern lectures and penny readings by the parson. Lucky villagers!

'... ignorance is one of the greatest obstacles to improvement.'

communications

Braving the floods at Elmstone Hardwick, Gloucestershire, in 1936

MAIL BY RAIL

The mail usually came by rail, along with newspapers, and with the railways also came another new and exciting form of communication in the 1840s: the electric telegraph. It was based at the local railway station because originally the system was used to pass messages concerning only railway matters down the line. Soon the station master found himself also acting as an agent for postal telegrams on behalf of the post office. The railway system also brought national newspapers and weekly journals hot off the city presses into the countryside, opening more eyes to the rest of the world.

POSTAL SERVICES

The ability to read and write opened an immediate line of communication through letters. A country-wide penny post was introduced in 1840 and contracts for running village post offices were first offered in the 1840s and 1850s, but by the 1870s most villagers still so rarely received post that when something was delivered, be it a letter or a mail-order circular, it would be read time and time again, carefully folded and kept in an apron pocket or on the mantelpiece in the meantime. In 1872 John Dew, 'Builder &c', successfully applied to be the village post master at Lower Heyford in Oxfordshire and proudly had a letter box fixed to the front wall of his home, setting aside the back parlour as the post office itself. About half of all village post offices in the 1850s had been connected with a shop of some kind, and these shops were the ones that would survive when the heyday of the general village shop began to wane in the early 1920s.

Postmen have always been popular in rural areas; for some isolated dwellings, the 'postie' is the only person they see for days on end. Postmen and postwomen have quite an important social role in rural areas: they tend to know a lot about what is going on in most of the households they visit, and are often the first to notice that someone is ill, or depressed, or in need of help. They can scan faces as they deliver the mail and are generally aware of whether an envelope contains a bill or a love letter! In times

'Postmen have always been popular in rural areas: for some isolated dwellings, the "postie" is the only person they see for days on end.'

RIGHT Exmoor postman Gerald Winzer fording the Exe on his Exford round in 1962

communications

gone by the postman would blow on his whistle as he passed a house, to give the occupants a chance to send a parcel or buy some stamps from him; today you cannot help but hear the familiar sound of the red van bouncing up the track and are relieved to be able to hand over outgoing post without having to walk two miles down the road to the postbox.

TELEPHONES

Next came the magic of the telephone. At first only the select few installed them in the home – people like doctors, who needed them, and city weekenders, who were used to them. In the 1930s farmers began to find them useful, and various tradesmen. Between the wars those familiar red telephone kiosks began to dot the countryside; private phones were still limited mainly to the middle classes and it was not until after the Second World War that they generally found their way into cottages. By then, every part of the countryside was delineated by stout telegraph poles, their multiple wires singing in the wind as if with the hum of the countless voices that chattered across the land, and dark green GPO lorries wandered the lanes with new poles protruding over their cabs. There were many complaints about the presence of these festooned dead trees in the landscape, but in general they followed the line of the roads and were accepted more readily than the dominating rows of huge electricity pylons that eventually marched menacingly across swathes of open countryside, destroying the view forever. Today there is another threat: masts for mobile telephone systems are springing up all over the countryside, and sometimes the insult is even greater when the companies try to disguise them as plastic trees.

Mail horse at the Blue Ball Inn, Countisbury, in North Devon. Postmen also used donkeys for their delivery carts

'Between the wars those familiar red telephone kiosks began to dot the countryside …'

communications

RADIO

By the 1940s the wireless was well and truly ensconced in every home. Radio particularly proved its worth during the Second World War, when ears would be glued to the sound of the news that reached the homeland almost instantaneously with the actual event. The BBC had begun its radio broadcasts in 1927. In due course programmes such as 'Mrs Dale's Diary' seemed to reflect a life people recognised; and 'The Archers' really did help farmers, always an isolated group, to learn about current farming practices. But there were those who were wary even of radio. In 1951, for example, a study of English life and leisure, begun in 1947, warned severely about the effects of 'continuous radio'. The report's authors stated that one woman had suffered a nervous breakdown from her husband's prolonged and loud playing of the radio, so that the family doctor instructed him to sell the infernal machine. In other cases, students had abandoned their studies, unable to concentrate when their parents had the radio on; wives almost divorced husbands for 'sitting by that blessed radio' and listening to whatever programme was broadcast, however dull (something the report described as 'domestic tyranny'); family arguments over which programme should be heard were frequent dear, dear, dear! Background radio – whatever next?

Farm workers in Cleeve, Gloucestershire, take a break from sowing seed to listen to a broadcast of the royal wedding of the Duke of Kent and Princess Marina of Greece on a portable radio, 1934

communications

TELEVISION

Next came television, with the BBC's first broadcast as early as 1936. Television brought new blots on the rural landscape – not just masts but forests of aerials on venerable country rooftops. It offered an even wider scope for new knowledge, though many distrusted it for 'doing away with family life', fearing that children would sit silently in front of the set rather than joining in with the rest of the family to play instruments, play games, read books and chat. (The thought of daytime television was too shocking to contemplate in rural areas, where daylight was far too precious to be wasted indoors.) Television sets were still rare even in middle-class homes in the 1950s, when several families would cluster round the only set in the village and peer at its tiny black-and-white screen.

An elderly man in Westmoreland in the 1960s had been a fiddler, and his brother a piccolo player. He was right against television; he said it had killed off all the fun they used to have, getting out their fiddles and dancing around the kitchen. Henceforth, music would be recorded, or broadcast; it was not *made* at home. The television generation became watchers rather than participants – in music, in sport, and in so many other aspects of their lives.

Would children become slaves to the television screen or would they enter a whole new world of knowledge?

THE NEW REVOLUTION

With the advent of computers, and particularly with the internet, not only is the village linked easily with the rest of the world but also many individuals can work from home in whatever part of the country they prefer. They are no longer tied to the workplace, no longer obliged to travel daily to their jobs, no longer forced to live in an area simply because that is where the jobs are. They can choose to work from home, and that means they can also choose to take part much more actively in the everyday life of their community.

It is perhaps this above all that will revitalise rural areas, though in 1965 Paul Jennings had expressed doubts about its coming: 'Is there now a tide before which even those protecting Welsh mountains will crumble, will the electronic village, in an irresistible process, worldwide, a mechanical and electronic culture, endlessly universal and homogeneous, obliterate the diversified life of villages as we have remembered them, all rural and all different?' Will the man who stood outside in the moonlight to watch and listen to a nightingale singing on a television aerial still see the real bird and hear its real song, or will he only see the virtual reality of it on the screen?

'It offered an even wider scope for new knowledge, though many distrusted it for "doing away with family life" …'

4

Country Markets

WHEN COUNTRY ROADS were difficult to negotiate and most people had no means of transport other than Shanks's pony, much of such shopping as they did came direct to their homes – on the backs of pedlars, or in panniers on hawkers' donkeys, or in carts. The carrier's cart would bring ordered goods from town shops and every now and then country people would go themselves to the local market town or to a fair to stock up. Village shops were fairly thin on the ground until the nineteenth century, and country people were perforce self-sufficient to a large degree, either by 'growing their own' or by ensuring that somebody else nearby did so and would exchange goods by barter.

Itinerants who brought their assorted goods to the country dweller were known by the general term of 'chapmen' (and chapwomen – trading was by no means limited to men) or packmen. They tended to buy in bulk in the towns and cities and then sell for whatever they could get in the country.

Those on foot, carrying their wares on their own backs, werepedlars, who 'peddled' their pedlary (isn't English spelling perverse?); those who could afford a donkey or pony to carry their panniers or pull a cart were hawkers. It was estimated that there were about 45,000 pedlars and hawkers in the country at the time of the 1871 census.

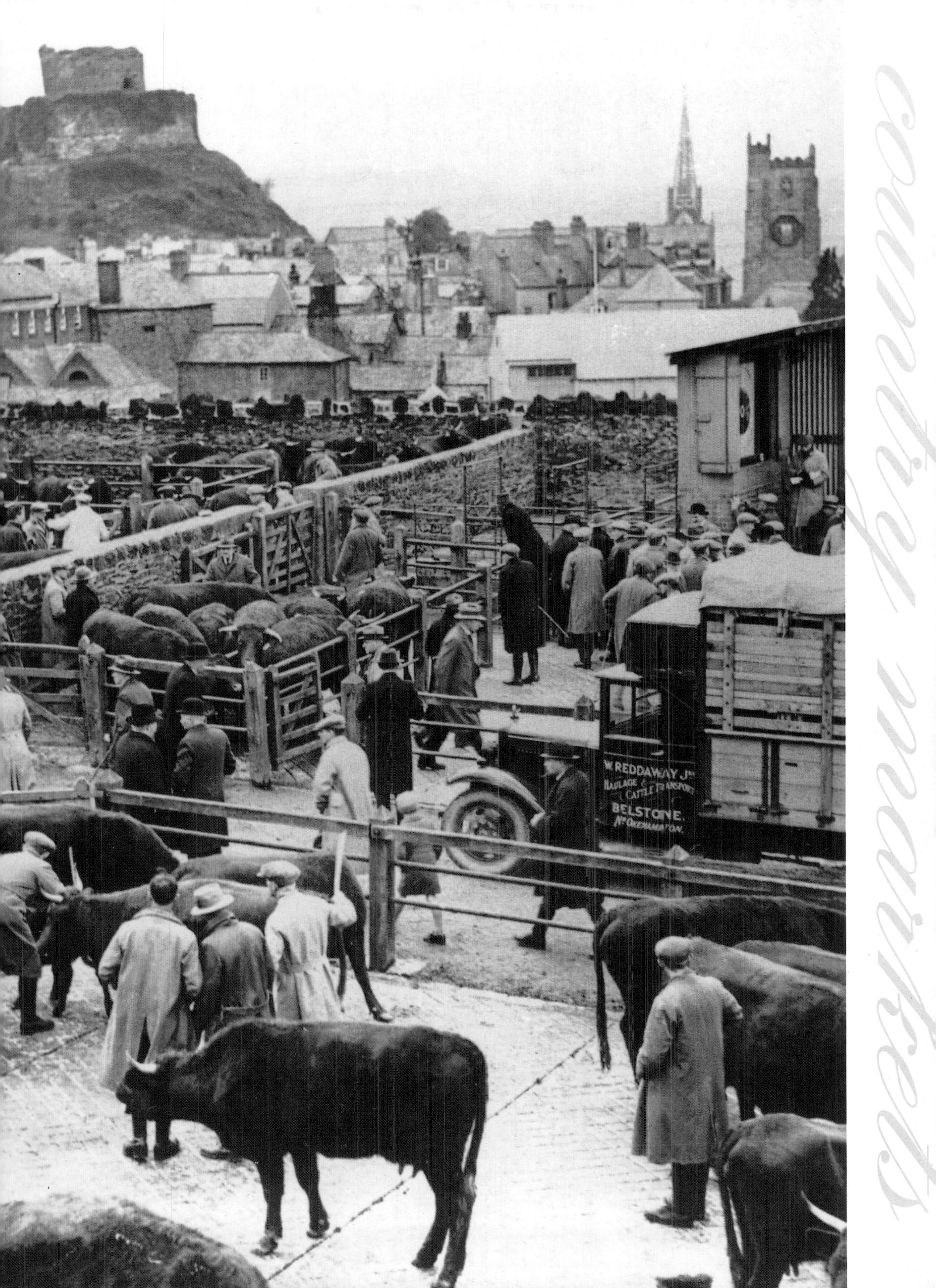
W. REDDAWAY Jnr
BELSTONE.

ITINERANTS

PEDLARS WALKED THE LANES CARRYING THEIR GOODS IN A SACK OR BASKET, OR IN A LEATHER BOX THAT DOUBLED UP AS A DISPLAY CABINET WHEN SWUNG ROUND TO THE FRONT AND OPENED. INSIDE WOULD BE USEFUL BITS AND PIECES SUCH AS NEEDLES, THREAD, RIBBON AND OTHER HABERDASHERY, MATCHES, CHEAP TOYS, ALMANACS, SONGSHEETS AND PERHAPS BITS OF CHEAP JEWELLERY.

PREVIOUS PAGE
Launceston cattle market

RIGHT
Gypsy woman whittling 'chrysanths' from pithwood

'Cheapjack' at Carmarthem market, demonstrating how to make an omelette!

HAWKERS COULD CARRY bulkier items, such as ornaments, crockery, baskets, ironmongery, brushes, pots and pans. 'Cheapjacks' were not what the name implies: they tended to be hawkers with a better class of goods who bought tools, cutlery, cooking utensils, leather items and so on from industrial areas and sold them widely across the country. The name arose because cheap Jacks and cheap Johns always claimed to be giving you a good bargain.

Typical of the cheapjacks was a Sheffield cutler's agent who would turn up in villages in Oxfordshire in the spring and autumn during the 1880s and 1890s, driving a covered wagon drawn by two large black horses. He would remain locally for a month, setting up his van on the village green in the evening to display pocket knives, billhooks, hoes, garden spades and other essential tools. A local lad would be paid a penny or two to ring a bell and shout the news of the cheapjack's arrival all over the village.

The various itinerants also set up their stalls at fairs and at towns' weekly markets. Travelling widely, they were an excellent source of information about the larger world, and usually good raconteurs who were quite happy to entertain locals with an evening of songs and stories. They often stayed a night or two at a farm and lent a hand with the farmwork while they were there.

Gypsies might come to the door selling their besoms, clothes-pegs and split-willow baskets or offering to tell your fortune (dukkerin').

Near the coast you might be lucky enough to come across fishwives walking the lanes with baskets of crabs, winkles or fresh fish for sale. In the big fishing ports, such as Brixham in Devon (where in the early nineteenth century the fishing fleet was a hundred vessels strong), which sold mainly to London, Bath and Bristol, there was the custom of processing any summer glut of fish such as whiting, flounder, gurnet and 'thornback' by gently salting and then drying the fish in the sun. Known as 'buckhorn', this was much in demand by the Navy. If you didn't have a fishing boat, you gathered cockles and mussels at low tide; in doing so, many women earned a great deal of money.

itinerants

SERVICES

Other itinerants included those who gave a service, such as the travelling tailor who moved from house to house within a more limited area. Typically a farmer might buy himself a length of cloth when he happened to be in town and would then wait for the tailor to stay at the farm for a few days to stitch the material into something useful, hunched over the kitchen table and being paid by the day to make new clothes and repair old ones. Some tailors did well enough to work from their own cottages, visiting the big houses at their request to measure up for a suit for the squire or 'uniforms' for keepers and hunt servants.

Chairmenders came with bolts of rushes on their backs and fixed the rush-bottomed chairs that were common in many farmhouses and cottages. Knife-grinders came with their heavy barrows: there would be a treadle-worked wheel to turn the grindstone for sharpening knives, razors and scissors. Wandering umbrella-menders had simpler equipment.

Tinkers usually had a donkey cart, raised high enough for there to be a hand-pumped set of bellows under the cart to make a draught for a pan of glowing charcoal. The tinker would sit by his cart, pumping his bellows now and then and working with a grindstone, an anvil and a small vice. Despite often being skilled craftsmen, tinkers did not charge very much for mending pots and pans and took some of their returns in food instead of cash. They might set up camp locally, making a simple bender for shelter.

THE HIGGLER

Trading was not just one way. The higgler came to the door of farmhouses and cottages to collect your butter, eggs, poultry and other home produce; he'd pop the birds into wicker crates and pile the rest in the back of his cart to sell the goods in town on your behalf. The village butcher, delivering his meat to your door, might perform the same favour.

Another itinerant, though more often seen at fairs than in the villages, was the travelling quack selling unlikely potions claimed to cure every illness or discomfort that could possibly occur. He was less likely to persuade country folk, as most of them had their own traditional remedies based on herbs and probably knew a lot more about it than he did; they also preferred to consult the 'wise woman' they already knew rather than the visiting stranger But some of these travelling 'doctors' were qualified pharmacists; they might have a shop in town, spending the winter behind the counter but the summer on the road, and some built up such a good reputation that they could live on their itinerant summer earnings, supplemented by a private mail-order business. Such men were still quite common in the lanes even in the 1920s, advertising their itinerary in the local press year after year and setting up their temporary consulting rooms in a spare room at the pub. The best of them had the integrity to advise their patients to see a qualified doctor where necessary; the real charlatans, however, took care not to return to an area for a very long time, whether they claimed to be doctors or mere tooth-pullers.

Travelling knife-sharpener, Joe Smith, driving his equipment by pedal power

Three-card trickster at the annual three-day Puck Fair, Co. Kerry

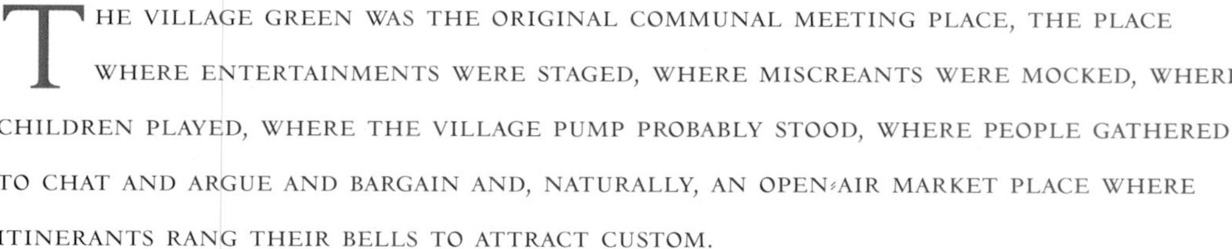

FAIRS AND MARKETS

THE VILLAGE GREEN WAS THE ORIGINAL COMMUNAL MEETING PLACE, THE PLACE WHERE ENTERTAINMENTS WERE STAGED, WHERE MISCREANTS WERE MOCKED, WHERE CHILDREN PLAYED, WHERE THE VILLAGE PUMP PROBABLY STOOD, WHERE PEOPLE GATHERED TO CHAT AND ARGUE AND BARGAIN AND, NATURALLY, AN OPEN-AIR MARKET PLACE WHERE ITINERANTS RANG THEIR BELLS TO ATTRACT CUSTOM.

New Forest pony sale, 1951

MANY A VILLAGE would have an informal weekly market on the green, and many will no doubt do so in the future if they can negotiate the tangle of red tape that seeks to deter them.

FAIRS

Sometimes the green was also the site of a fair – a time of great local excitement which attracted the crowds from miles around. Fair days were almost the only weekday holidays into Victorian times; fairs slotted into the calendar as regular as clockwork and punctuated the mundanity of everyday rural life. For a day, or two, or three, the site of the fair was buzzing with life and excitement and crowds, and the next day it was all over until the next time, gone, quiet again and back to the old routine.

There is a painting by Sir David Wilkie, dated 1804, which shows a fair in full swing in the small Fifeshire village of Pitlessie. The village itself remains recognisable from the painting even today, except that the population has dropped from 700 to 330; the butcher, baker and cobbler have gone; and the two annual fairs have long since ceased to bring the village to life. In 1985, to celebrate Wilkie's bicentenary, the villagers dressed themselves up in period costume and did their best to recreate Pitlessie Fair for one last time.

Some fairs had a specific purpose: say, a sheep fair, a horse fair, a toy fair, a simple pedlary fair, a hiring fair where people looked for new jobs, a cheese fair. Some fairs combined many purposes, and threw in a wide range of entertainment for good measure. But above all a fair was a market of some kind, and you went to the fair prepared to spend your money or to make it. You also went to have fun and to meet lots of people.

The animal fairs would mean herds and flocks filling the lanes and spilling over the hills for days beforehand, all heading for the fair, and all splitting off in different directions afterwards in the hands of new masters. Lewes Sheep Fair would attract up to 30,000 sheep in the nineteenth century, and not far away the ancient Findon Fair on the South Downs filled its pens with more than 10,000 sheep (nearly all of the Southdown breed) in the 1920s, with the added attractions of roundabouts, coconut shies and refreshment tents. In 1925, for the first time, sheep due to travel a long distance after Findon Fair were sent by rail, drifting over the Downs to the station at Steyning: Southern Railway laid on a special shunting engine with fifty-six trucks to transport them all over the country. In 1928 the first lorries were seen at Findon, loading sheep to and from the fair; until then the animals had used their own legs to get there. At its peak in 1950 some 18,000 sheep were sold at Findon Fair, most of them travelling in lorries (rail transport would cease entirely when the Steyning line was closed in the 1960s), but today only a fraction of that

Farmers taking their cattle through Modbury, Devon, on their way to the market in the 1930s

LEFT
The famous Appleby Horse Fair

BELOW
Taking Irish horses to Brough Hill Fair

number of sheep, of various breeds, comes to the fair, though buyers still come from all over the country.

Any fair would mean the convergence of a wide range of itinerants, eager to set up their pitches and bringing the lanes alive, mingling with the crowds who tramped fairwards with cheerful anticipation of selling a wife, buying a bonnet, seeing a bearded lady, chancing their arm against a wrestler, hearing their fortunes, shying coconuts, bowling for pigs, taking a turn in the dancing booth, watching a dancing bear or an organ grinder with his monkey, drinking themselves silly, finding a new lover, making faces at caged wild animals, and from the middle of the nineteenth century also enjoying the thrills of steam-driven fairground rides. Oh, those were the days!

'... mingling in the crowds ... with cheerful anticipation of selling a wife, buying a bonnet, seeing a bearded lady ...'

ABOVE RIGHT
Farmers at Clitheroe Cattle Market, Lancashire

RIGHT
Farmer's market at Uckfield, Sussex

BELOW
Gossiping at Hereford Butter Market

DIRECT SALE Cottagers, in their self-sufficient way, sell their produce at the cottage gate even now, however illicitly. There has been a gentle attempt to return to the true country market by creating 'farmers' markets', in which farmers sell their produce direct to the general public – a public which otherwise hardly connects farmers with the food they buy. The whole scheme is hedged with endless regulations

laid down by Europe but it is a step in the right direction. Some villages would like to follow suit, if only they could come to grips with all the legalities. Some would like to return to the simple but once highly popular Women's Institute weekly produce markets, but again most of these have been defeated by bureaucracy. How sad.

MARKET DAY

A more serious business was the weekly market day in town, when country people would bring in their goods and livestock for sale – a very important source of income. They would spend as well, of course. Almost every village was within walking distance of a market town, in the days when ten miles there and ten miles back in the same day was considered very reasonable.

Market days were all abustle, with sheep and cattle being herded into their pens, auctioneers shouting, men prodding flesh, chickens squawking indignantly, women bartering at top pitch, others ensconced in the market hall with their panniers of vegetables and fruit and their bowls of cream and butter, the occasional loud argument between buyer and seller, and plenty of good gossiping in between. Later in the day there would be the bustle of homegoing – bewildered livestock being herded by their new owners for the long walk to the farm, dogs barking, carriers trying to find their passengers, horses and carts getting in each other's way, and many loth to leave the liveliness of the market.

Market was where you met friends you only saw on market day, and in some market towns today those of an older generation have not broken the habit of coming in from the countryside every Wednesday to meet those friends, have a pint at the pub and wander round markets that have now almost lost their point. Today's mar-

kets rarely have livestock in them; they have fruit and vegetables bought wholesale in city markets and recycled, rather than local produce; they have racks and racks of cheap mass-produced clothes and shoes and bits and pieces.

While you were in town you would buy goods that were not available in the village or from the itinerants. Very few Victorian villages had apothecaries, for example, and so you might visit the chemists and druggists to marvel at the coloured bottles in the window or to buy the shop's own remedies or patent medicines. You could also buy perfume there, and hair lotion, rouge, tooth powder, foods for infants and invalids, cold cream, and a surprisingly wide range of other goods such as pickles, spices, tea, cocoa, ink, tobacco, matches, candles, dyes and varnishes. You might need medicine measuring spoons, invalid feeding cups, eyebaths, bronchitis kettles (for steaming away your lung congestion – remember Friar's Balsam?), sputum mugs, self-applied enema syringes, bedpans and urinals for invalids, pap warmers and pap boats for bread-and-milk sops, tea warmers for herbal tisanes, babies' feeding bottles, breast relievers and fly traps.

Chemists often doubled up as wine merchants, in that they sold 'tonic wines' anyway and it seemed only natural to sell alcoholic ones as well, which they did well into the twentieth century. More often you bought your alcohol in the village, or made your own. 'Small beer' was the medieval answer to the problem of contaminated drinking water: you boiled the water, flavouring it with common plants such as nettle or dandelion, and left it to ferment. Such brewing continued into the eighteenth century and here and there into the nineteenth; and the brewing of stronger ales and country wines certainly persisted in the villages. A home favourite was ginger beer, which began to be a popular refreshment sold on town streets in the 1820s and remained a cottage brew for at least a century thereafter.

Such hopeful ventures, like existing town market stallholders, face fierce competition from supermarkets and hypermarkets, but so far the greengrocery stalls are holding their own. The big chains have driven greengrocers out of their shops but not yet out of the market square. And it is the weekly market that has so often been the lure to bring people in from the countryside to spend their money in town shops. Without the market, town centres can die

Market day at Holsworthy, Devon, in 1909

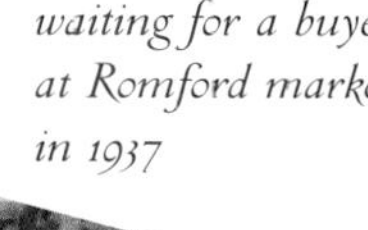
Christmas calves waiting for a buyer at Romford market, in 1937

VILLAGE SHOPS

MOBILITY HAS ALWAYS BEEN A MAJOR FACTOR IN THE ECONOMIC HEALTH OF THE VILLAGE SHOP, WORKING SOMETIMES IN ITS FAVOUR AND SOMETIMES DECIDEDLY NOT. IN THE EIGHTEETH CENTURY, WHEN MOBILITY WAS LIMITED AND ROADS WERE IMPASSABLE EVEN IN THE TOWNS, THE CUSTOMERS OF THE VILLAGE SHOP TENDED TO BE WEALTHY: GOODS MIGHT INCLUDE SILKS AND SPICES AND THE THEN LUXURIES OF TEA AND COFFEE.

Selling flowers at the cottage door

THE REST OF THE VILLAGE relied on itinerant pedlars and hawkers, and occasional visits to fairs and markets, to supplement what they could not grow or make themselves or glean from commonland.

In the mid nineteenth century, with the railway network beginning to stretch across the countryside, the village shop gained access to goods that were mass-produced and therefore cheaper. In almost every village the number of shops increased dramatically between the 1830s and the 1870s, particularly the general stores that sold everything a villager might need. At the village store even the poorest could buy goods, albeit in small amounts and on tick.

What the nineteenth-century shops did not sell continued to come into the village on the carrier's cart or on the backs of pedlars, or was grown locally in gardens and allotments. Greengrocers, fishmongers (except in seaside villages) and dairies were rare in country areas – most people grew their own vegetables and fruit and had backyard poultry; many had a housecow or goat for their butter and cheese or went up the lane with a can dangling from their hands to the local dairy herd of ten or so handmilked Shorthorns.

'...the greater individual mobility of villagers by bicycle, bus and train, or later by car became one of the biggest threats to village shopping.'

Mobility brought the heyday of the village shop in the nineteenth century, but the greater individual mobility of villagers by bicycle, bus and train or, later, by car became one of the biggest threats to village shopping. People enjoyed the excuse of going to town now and then, pennies carefully counted, making a family outing to do a week's shopping on market day or on a Saturday evening (even when this meant a journey on foot) and meeting their friends in town streets for a chat and a drink at the Crown. With luck there would be a railway station within two or three miles of home and they could take a cheap return ticket to town, piling their goods into the carriage for the homeward journey and only having to carry the booty over the common.

village shops

DIVERSIFICATION

Village shopkeepers were well versed in diversification; indeed, they had to be, in order to survive. Butchers might also sell vegetables, grocers might offer material and seeds, or in those blissfully unregulated times a cottager might simply open her front room to sell sweets, honey, backyard chickens, rabbits, stitchery, home-made ginger beer, flowers, herbs and anything else she could muster to increase the household income. Many shopkeepers ran their shops as a sideline (ideal for keeping up with the local gossip) and had other jobs to keep them going, especially in a Victorian age when most people spread their luck to harvest a series of incomes.

In a Women's Institute scrapbook produced for the NFWI's Golden Jubilee in 1965, the Yorkshire women of Aldborough remembered the village shop into which Mrs Nicholson's father had moved in 1913. The family kept cows, horses, pigs and hens. The shop was open from 7am until 9pm every day except Sunday, yet the shopkeeper still found time to do a yeast round to all the villages in a seven-mile radius. He also took people to Boroughbridge station in the pony and trap, and drove the waggonette that carried villagers to whist drives and dances.

Butcher's shop in all its glory at Godalming, Surrey. Even village butchers would put on a huge display at Christmas

SMELLS, SIGHTS & SOUNDS

Each shop had its own special smell. In the days when many groceries were sold loose (well within living memory) the shop was fragrant with a strange mixture of shop-blended tea, freshly ground coffee, hand-sliced bacon, flour, soap, candles, tobacco, dried fruit, vinegar, linseed oil, grain, paraffin, hessian, leather and cloth, sometimes combined with the unmistakable smell of the cats employed to keep down scavenging rodents.

Sweet shops were a childish heaven; the cheerful jangle of the shop's bell triggered by opening the door (to let the owner know it was time to emerge from nursing a cup of tea in the back room) still evokes for many the kaleidoscope of tall jars of loose toffees, gumdrops, striped bull's-eyes, gobstoppers, fudge, pear drops; lollipops, pastilles and multicoloured boiled sweets. On the counter would be sticks of black liquorice to dip into triangular yellow paper packets of sherbet; there would be slabs of mintcake and butterscotch to be broken with a small hammer; there were red-tipped sugar cigarettes and, later, tubes of Refreshers and Polo mints and assorted chocolate bars. Those who remember sweet rationing after the Second World War (it finally ended in February 1953) valued every mouthful: Mars bars were carefully cut into seven chunks so that you savoured one piece a day for a week; lollipops were sucked for a while then put away for another licking later; loose sweets were bought by the quarter with saved-up pocket money and were stored in a paper bag in your pocket along with rubber bands, pebbles, marbles and other useful bits and pieces.

While the ubiquity of packaged, tinned and frozen food has put an end to most of those lovely old grocery aromas, the butcher's shop still has its own smell of raw flesh, sawn bone and sawdust. The old butchers delighted in dressing their shop windows with fully feathered and furred game from the local shoot as well as plucked festive turkeys and geese, half sides of beef, lamb and pork (it was always abundantly clear where meat came from) and strings of home-made sausages. You would always expect to wait at least a quarter of an hour to be served, because the butcher was a chatty man and his customers loved him for it; he would also be taking time to select the right piece of meat, trimming and tying it to suit the customer as necessary. He reared his own animals in fields behind the shop, slaughtering, hanging and butchering them himself when he decided they were ready – not for them the stress of being herded into a lorry to travel to the bewildering noise and confusion of a distant abattoir. Today the butcher's fields are under a housing estate, and the old shop has been converted into a home. Perhaps the ghosts of the animals still wander in the gardens, and if you listen hard enough you might catch up on the gossip of fifty years ago.

village shops

THE VANISHING VILLAGE SHOP

The demise of the village shop is not a new problem. Even in 1891, a sixth of the rural parishes in Oxfordshire (for example) had no village store. The real heyday was over more than a hundred years ago. There was a gentle revival in the 1940s, when petrol rationing reduced mobility and food rationing encouraged people to shop locally. If they were lucky, the village shop could supply them with under-the-counter country-fresh local luxuries such as cream, eggs, ham and cheese.

In some places village shops continued to thrive after the war. For example, in the 1960s the estuarine Welsh village of Laugharne, south-west of Carmarthen, was a community of about a thousand people. All of its shops were family businesses and there were seven grocers, two drapers, two butchers, a post office, a newsagent, a chemist, a baker, a sweetshop and a betting shop. Their customers could also buy tomatoes at the bakery, fresh lettuce at the chemist, pork chops at the grocer's, bananas at the butcher's and antiques at the newsagents. The fact that these were family businesses gave them an individuality; it meant that future generations would hear tales of old Jones the Grocer, and how Mother Williams would don a leather helmet and jump on a motorbike to deliver the meat. In many places today, village shops have lost that individual touch and become anonymous; the continuity of stories has been broken.

An English village, again with a population of about a thousand, serves as an indicator of the more typical changes in village shops. Well within living memory it had a cobbler's boot-and-shoe shop, at least two sweet shops, a clock repairer, a butcher, a baker, a post office, a blacksmith who sold hardware, and a glorious general stores which for a century sold everything from furniture to haberdashery, groceries and pigmeal. Like most villages, it was virtually self-sufficient and there was no need to go elsewhere for most of your everyday needs. But the smaller shops dwindled away and in the 1980s it lost its general stores. The village now has no shops at all, apart from the local garage selling a few sweets, biscuits and ice-creams.

In Rudgwick, Sussex, there was an old-fashioned grocer's that stocked a splendid range of cheeses and home-cured hams and bacon as well as all the usual commodities; they delivered weekly, even up the longest of dirt tracks, as did the local butcher (always willing to slip in a marrow bone for your dog) and the baker (no wrapped sliced loaves for him). During the 1970s the elderly white-coated owners of the Rudgwick grocery decided they really must retire, being by then the same age as the century, and it caused them intense grief when the only buyer they could find was a self-service chain. The elderly couple had been proud to serve their customers and regarded them as friends.

Diversification: the post office doubling as a taxi office

LEFT & FAR LEFT One of two village shops at Laxton, Nottinghamshire, in 1952. The village had been bought by the Civil Service when Earl Manvers was forced by death duties to sell

village shops

'*Without a shop the centre of the village is hollow.*'

SELF-SERVICE IS CONVENIENT for many but it loses the whole essence of the village shop, which is based on friendliness and knowing each other and all about each other. You were always greeted by name; the shopkeeper knew what goods you were likely to buy, and probably every detail of your life to boot. Those behind and in front of the counter chatted about babies, village events, newcomers, illnesses, scandals and all the rest of the cement that keeps the community together. In the self-service shop all that has gone; there are no chairs to perch on while you listen to another customer gossiping with the shopkeeper, and the self-willed wire trolley has superseded the comforting wicker basket that used to hang on your arm.

Yacht stores at Abersoch, North Wales

More recently taxes, increasingly stringent public health regulations and other government decrees and, of course, the overwhelming competition from supermarket chains in and outside towns have almost sealed the fate of the village shop. The demise has been swift. In 1961, throughout Britain, there were about 147,000 grocery outlets; only fifteen years later there were 39,000 and of these only about 9,000 were in rural areas. In Suffolk alone, 337 village shops were lost between 1961 and 1978; in Gwynedd, 47 per cent of the villages had no shop by 1982 after a drop in shop numbers by 19 per cent in just ten years; in Nottinghamshire and Dorset more than 40 per cent of villages had no shop at all in 1979.

In 1999 the National Federation of Women's Institutes produced a report in which it listed the closure of 474 village post offices, 178 pubs, 196 butchers, 71 greengrocers, 70 bakers, 58 grocers, 36 hardware shops, 29 mobile shops and 24 newsagents. The villagers' 'wish list' of improvements to village life numbered 'new shop' as high as fourth place, after improved public transport, slower traffic speeds and a higher police presence. In a similar NFWI survey in 1956, there was no mention of village shops in the top ten wishes – they were considered to be constants in village life then.

Once a shop has closed, the actual building is usually converted to a dwelling, so that a new venture requires new premises – which is simply not economical in terms of village shops, even if building space were to be available in a prime village site.

FIGHTING BACK

Many of the shops that remain are owned by people who are perhaps retired and content to earn very little, or have gone into shopkeeping romantically with their eyes less than wide open. Some are more realistic and are fighting back by specialising in a commodity for which they become well known over a much wider area, or by using their imagination in some other way to retain their viability. Again, diversification remains the key in many instances, but now they are up against a new and more far-reaching form of 'mobility' – shopping by internet, which will be an even fiercer competitor than the mail-order catalogues that came into village life several decades ago.

The villagers themselves are fighting for their own shops. In the early 1980s there was a major campaign of support for village shops,

village shops

A fleet of mobile shops arriving at Burford, Oxfordshire

with assorted agencies seeking to give advice and to publicise their importance. There had already been a movement towards community shops: in several places, the whole village formed its own co-operative to buy the village shop when it was about to close for lack of profit, which meant that everybody had a vested interest in keeping the shop going by buying their groceries from it on a regular basis. (This was very different to the 'Co-operative Society' of the interwar years, which was organised from outside the village rather than within it and thus distrusted for a long time.)

In other villages there have been informal arrangements to use the village hall as a twice-weekly shop and post office. In at least one instance the man behind the counter is the vicar, who has extended the concept by serving tea, coffee and homemade scones so that shoppers can sit down, keep warm and have a good old-fashioned gossip – which is what village shops are all about.

More ambitious villages have persuaded the enemy to help them out. Some of the supermarkets now open satellite shops in the village, thus keeping a few more cars off the roads and keeping the heart of the village pumping. Socially and environmentally, this is better than the home deliveries that some supermarkets are prepared to make (which in itself is a welcome return to an old tradition): the village shop is almost more important as a social centre for public information and informal encounters, discriminating against no one, than as a source of goods. Without a shop, the centre of the village is hollow.

Doing the accounts

DELIVERIES

ACCUSTOMED TO VISITS BY ITINERANTS AND BY THE CARRIER'S CART, RURAL HOUSEHOLDS CONTINUED TO RELY QUITE HEAVILY ON DELIVERIES EVEN AFTER MANY OF THEM HAD PRIVATE CARS. THE BUTCHER FROM THE VILLAGE WOULD VISIT OUTLYING COTTAGES AND FARMS IN HIS CART, USING THE TAILGATE AS A CHOPPING BLOCK AND COUNTER.

Changing from horse-power to motors: loading milk for delilvery at Tostock in Suffolk

FISH HAWKERS WOULD BRING their fresh herring and mackerel to homes near the coast, having spent the night close to the beach, sheltering under a boat or by a hedge, so that they could have the pick of the fresh catch as it was landed. Ice-cream vendors brought their loudly painted barrows and donkey carts to remote cross-roads long before the days of piped-music ice-cream vans, or in winter they might sell hot baked potatoes and chips .

Most deliveries came by bicycle, with a large basket on the front, or by van, and the custom persisted, just, into the 1970s. Up until the late 1950s the lanes were almost teeming with deliveries and quite a few of them were still by horse-drawn cart (gardeners rushed out to scoop steaming dung into their buckets). Boys on delivery bikes could earn five bob a week after school and Bernard Parke remembers carrying 'at least 28 pounds of sugar and a side of bacon from the grocery wholesalers down the High Street, only to find the back end of the bike rising into the air from the weight'. He recalls that customers were bound to use just one shop during the Second World War and up until the mid 1950s: they had to be registered with the shop because of the system of food and sweet rationing. Clothes were also rationed but only until just after the war.

'Up until the late 1950s the lanes were almost teeming with deliveries ...'

But then shopkeepers began to find that deliveries were no longer economical and the service waned, forcing people to take their own cars out more often. Those who relied on the declining bus service were seriously disadvantaged by the loss of delivery services.

Of course, the village shops themselves were disappearing. In the 1930s Sydney Jones mentioned that he had 'once made purchases under a thatched roof framed to cover a perfect study of timber beams and overhanging joists, panelled with plaster, flint, stone and herringbone brickwork' in the village of Bignor, Sussex. This marvellous building was a great favourite of photographers (George Garland featured it frequently, usually with his trade-mark motorbike and sidecar parked outside) and in 1999 it was on the market as a private house for £600,000. It was originally a single-bay Wealden hall house, dating from the mid fifteenth century and built for a yeoman farmer, and remains as probably the best preserved specimen of its kind in England. It still looks almost exactly as it did when Garland photographed it in the 1920s, except that it has long since ceased to be a shop.

In the 1960s the Leicestershire villages of Kimcote and Walton looked back at village life in 1846 and, with the aid of a local directory of the period, discovered how much more self-

deliveries

sufficient they had been then. By 1965 they had just one general store and post office; the baker, butcher and tailor had disappeared within living memory, though there were several mobile shops.

For a while there was a trend for mobile shops, visiting villages in rotation with a range of goods. In Essex, the village of Radwinter reported in 1965: 'The nearby towns bristle with cut-price shops where the cost of travelling out of Radwinter is amply compensated. The mobile grocery shops sent out by the town co-operative societies are a boon to people living out of the village centre, but they are an additional competition for the village shops to which the same people once walked.'

In the 1930s, F.G. Thomas discussed the Co-operative Society, whose vans were increasingly seen then in rural areas. 'The slow success of this society,' he wrote, 'is of some social significance because the countryman, on the whole, has resisted all forms of co-operative enterprise in the past. The idea of a Co-operative Society cut across the personal basis of village trading. In a village one goes, not to the grocer, but to Mrs. X's shop: or even just to Mrs. X.' The village shopkeeper 'not only sold goods, but retailed the village news ... This personal goodwill could not be broken by a Co-operative organized from outside the village, which threatened the livelihood of Mrs. X. Even though a shopkeeper was unpopular, group feeling was strong enough to overcome the temptation of "dividends".'

During the 1990s there were the beginnings of a return to home deliveries, when various entrepreneurs began to sell fresh and frozen fish, readymade frozen meals for gourmets and so on. But very few of the old regulars such as bakers, butchers, grocers and greengrocers continued to deliver. Only the milkman persisted (do you remember bottles with cardboard tops that you could make into toys or use for winding wool into pompoms?), extending daily doorstep deliveries to include soft drinks, bread and potatoes as well as a wide range of dairy produce. He certainly no longer comes with fresh milk from the farm carried in pails on a yoke, and you no longer see children carrying jangly milk-cans on their rounds, with eggs and butter in their baskets, as would have been common in the 1920s. Nor does the milkman come with a horse that knows which door to stop at while the milk is ladled into the householder's own receptacle, and he certainly no longer brings the milking animal itself (be it cow, goat or donkey) to be milked on the spot, fresh from the udder!

The news still gets through, of course. In the 1920s the Sunday newsagent brought the weekly journals to cottagers; most of the Sunday papers had their own agents who would collect the journals from the carrier and distribute them. Cottagers in particular looked forward to their weekly read of the often lurid papers, full of murders, battles and society gossip as well as politics and endless advice on every aspect of practical life. With improving distribution networks people began to take in daily papers as well and in many rural areas they would have been delivered by a boy on his bike, ringing his bell to announce his approach. In many places he has been replaced by the man in the van, driving at great speed to make the job pay at all, hurtling along the lanes, bumping alarmingly up rough tracks and squealing to a halt outside the houses.

A newcomer on the delivery scene is the courier, delivering parcels of goods or, more often now, items not entrusted to the post and needed by those who work from home – documents, computer disks and the like. Couriers in rural areas are more likely to be in vans than on motorbikes; the latter are reserved for fast-food deliveries enabling the country dweller to eat just what everybody else eats: Indian or Chinese, pizzas or fish-'n'-chips.

Doorstep delivery!

Market wagons piled high along the Bath road

VILLAGE TRADES

VILLAGES NEEDED TO BE SELF-SUFFICIENT AND, WHERE THERE WAS A LARGE ENOUGH POPULATION AND THRIVING LOCAL AGRICULTURE OR A LARGE LANDED ESTATE TO SUPPORT THEM, THE VILLAGE RELIED HEAVILY ON ITS OWN CRAFTSMEN.

'Almost all of these old village trades were gone by the 1920s …'

A diver, F.M. Nalder, at Burford Mill in 1928. The equipment is an air pump

IN THE LONG PAST, craftsmen often travelled together in bands over wide areas to supplement their income, as the village itself could not supply their living. Typically these included stonemasons and other building artisans.

All over the country there are villages that developed their own local industry and whose names became synonymous with their products; some continued to thrive and became more organised than mere cottage industries, but others gradually lost their skills and their trade to industrialised towns when mechanisation took over the manufacturing.

Most villages, within living memory though no longer, would have at least their own blacksmith and wheelwright, and no doubt a paper-hatted carpenter or two (often doubling as the village undertaker), several general builders and a well-sinker; many would have had millers, tanners, brick-makers, thatchers, masons; some would have a cobbler (or even a shoemaker), a clockmaker and winder, perhaps a potter, a saddler and a tailor, as well as a wide range of skilled individuals making baskets or lace, spinning and weaving, knitting garments, making gloves and buttons, plaiting straw bonnets, braiding fish nets, producing turnery and a range of other artefacts from wood (chair legs, rakes and pitchforks, hoops, tubs and barrels, hurdles, besoms and so much more), all of it of a practical nature, producing things that people *used*. Today villagers tend to offer services rather than goods, though in the 1960s there was a splendidly rural tannery in the Devon village of Colyton where much of the work was done by hand and where they still

village trades

used tapioca on bridles and stirrup leather after the leather had been stained.

Almost all of these old village trades were already declining or gone by the 1920s. For the blacksmith, be he farrier or forger, the demise of the horse was one blow (though for a while he could fix bicycles instead of shoes), and the mass production of agricultural implements another – of old the smith and the farmer would have designed implements together to suit a particular purpose. Going further back, the smith was no longer required to beat spears into ploughshares, or vice versa; one of his important roles in the past had been to make weapons. But smiths were usually quick to find new niches: several took the trouble to understand the workings of motor vehicles when they first came into the countryside, and developed a new trade for themselves.

Wheelwrights often followed suit; many of them were coach-builders and could adapt to panel-beating a car or repainting the sides of a motorised van or bus. In the 1920s, however, they still had work to do on horse-powered vehicles – the vicar's trap, the farmer's wagon and the carrier's cart might still need attention, and gardeners still needed wheelbarrows.

Villages are much quieter and less colourful places since the passing of the old trades, and more introverted – people tend to hide their work indoors now, instead of spilling out into the lanes and street. Often the garage is the only sign of activity in the village, and somehow the villagers do not find it as intriguing, skillful and romantic as the old forge and the wheelwright's yard.

TOP LEFT
Shoemaker at his last

ABOVE
Millwright sharpening a grinding stone at Coltsford Mill, Hurst Green, Surrey

TRANSACTIONS

IN VICTORIAN TIMES, LIFE SEEMED SIMPLER. BEFORE THE AGE OF ADVERTISING, YOU BOUGHT WHAT YOU KNEW FROM LONG EXPERIENCE TO BE GOOD AND TO BE WHAT YOU ACTUALLY NEEDED. PRODUCTS WERE SLOW TO CHANGE; A MANUFACTURER'S CATALOGUE COULD REMAIN CURRENT FOR YEARS, AND PRICES TENDED TO BE STEADY.

LARGER LOCAL SHOPS acted as wholesalers to smaller rural shops and traders, often employing travellers as go-betweens. Credit over several months was commonplace.

There was always the little problem of weights and measures, which varied from district to district, and sometimes on a very local scale. In one place you might buy by the pound, in another by the gallon. If you were buying a 'load' of wheat, it might be forty bushels, but if it was of oats it might be eighty. A 'stone' of meat in Sussex would be eight pounds, not fourteen as elsewhere. If you were interested in land, the acre was a minefield: a forest acre was nine score rods, a statute acre was eight score, a short acre was six score in some places and five score in others. And so it went on. John Cartwright, in Lincolnshire, said despairingly in the 1790s:

In village shops, customers frequently relied on credit, its term depending on their relationship with the shopkeeper. Some shopkeepers were too gullible, and not much good at book-keeping anyway, and might have to resort to putting up the little notice: 'People came and I did trust them; / I lost my money and their custom; / To lose them both did grieve me sore / So I resolved to trust no more; / And now I sell the best of goods / For money paid me when it should.'

Typically there would be a weekly get-together, on the evening that wages had been paid, when customers or clients would come and settle their bills, lured by the sound of the local band and the chance of a few drinks together. The combination eased the payment.

transactions

In that rude state of society, while all exchange of commodities is by barter, weights and measures are useless; but as soon as they become necessary, they ought to be sacred. Every departure should be watched with a vigilant eye, and opposed with a vigorous hand. Even in the infancy of commercial intercourse, divers weights and measures have always been found an evil; but in the present maturity of British commerce, when the same person may have occasion to transact business at a vast variety of distant markets at the same time, an almost equal variety of weights and measures must prove extremely vexatious, and frequently the cause of imposition and loss.

Cartwright suggested that the inhabitants of every parish should take an oath to use only standard measures laid down by Justices of the Peace, and that the parish itself should be bound to make good any deficiencies arising from the failure of its inhabitants to honour these principles; defaulting individuals should be punished by a doubling of their house and window taxes. But nobody heard him.

In the village shop, weights tended to be rounded, and if your joint of meat was a little short of the pound, a few sausages would be thrown in to make up the difference rather than entering into complicated calculations of fractions of a pound. In the 1920s, in more remote areas, village tradesmen could still survive almost entirely on a system of barter based on exchange, or 'contra accounts', settled every six or twelve months when the two parties would spend an evening comparing what each had given the other and then settle the difference – coals for meat, or milk and cheese for tea and flour, or a funeral for horsefeed or bread, or building repairs in exchange for household commodities, and so on. Here and there, seven decades later, a few villages revived the system of paying in kind.

A visitor still common in rural areas in the 1930s was the tallyman, employed by the 'credit draper' who would sell clothes on tick, a few pence a week. Clothes were expensive, valued and long-lasting, and wardrobes were far from extensive. A man's Sunday suit would probably last him his lifetime; a woman's best dress would be passed down to her daughters in her will; schoolboys often had no more than one pair of trousers – short ones until they were old enough at thirteen for longs.

The Victorians, ever worthy in social matters, created all manner of societies and clubs to help people in paying for this and that. Village benefit clubs were among them, and they often chose fair day for their own club day, when the members would unfurl the club's precious silk banner, with its logo and motto, to process around the village to the houses of prominent residents, who would contribute to the club's funds. Then the members could enjoy a good dinner among the fairground booths or at the local inn – though many a club's rules instructed its members to 'live and behave themselves on all occasions religiously, honestly, and soberly'. The benefit clubs were the forerunners of the 'friendly societies' and Orders of this and that, which also liked a good parade in those days.

The country junk shop

FAR LEFT
The Corn Exchange at King's Lynn Market

LEFT
Bidding for barley at Exeter market

ADVERTISING

THE SPREAD OF ADVERTISING (WHICH, AS EVER, AFFECTED RURAL AREAS RATHER LATER THAN URBAN ONES) RADICALLY CHANGED A LOT OF OLD BUYING HABITS. COMBINED WITH IMPROVED TRANSPORT, IT CREATED NOT ONLY A FAR WIDER CHOICE OF GOODS BUT ALSO MUCH MORE INTEREST IN TRYING THEM.

'Remember Eno's Fruit Salts. Robin Starch. Bisto. Ovaltine ...'

'People began to demand goods with brand names: instead of the loose-sold goods of old they wanted things already packaged ...'

LIKE EVERYTHING ELSE, the pace of change was quickening – alarmingly so, for some, used to decades or even centuries when everything had been much as it had been before.

In the national press and the journals, villagers could read about the latest fashions, the latest urban tastes in food, the latest gadgets for this and that, and all the modern conveniences they had not been aware they were missing. In the village street, enamelled advertising signs began to vie for attention – great big outdoor ones that could not be overlooked, window ones in the shops, more of them on the counters, folding boards outside the shop; so much colour, so much boldness, so much reading to be done, so many goods to be coveted. People began to demand goods with brand names: instead of the loose-sold goods of old they wanted things already packaged, and perhaps partly processed, emblazoned with names they had seen in the advertisements.

When you examine those advertisements today, health seemed to be at the top of the agenda: stomach powders, remedies for constipation and miraculous health drinks, hot and cold, jostled for their place among extolments of the excellence of cleaning materials and aids. Remember Eno's Fruit Salts, Benger's Food for Infants, Vick Vapour Rub, Milk of Magnesia, Robin Starch, Bronco toilet paper, Lux, Palmolive, Town Talk Silver Polish, Cherry Blossom boot polish? And food, of course – jars of paste, Grape-Nuts, Bisto, Ideal Milk, Ovaltine, Bovril, Bisto and Oxo, Spry, Spam, Camp Coffee, Horniman or Typhoo Tea, Huntley & Palmer, Macfarlane Lang, Peek Frean, Carr's, Fry's Cocoa, Rowntrees. Then there were all the fashions, corsets, cosmetics, shampoos and soap, Viyella and Chilprufe. The unhealthy side of life was just as appealing, with numerous advertisements for cigarettes and tobacco such as Capstan, Woodbine,

advertising

Senior Service, Player's, Will's Gold Flake and 'cool and fragrant' St Julien. Nestlé's even produced 'Smokers semi-sweet milk chocolate'.

How could the countryside resist? If the village shop didn't stock it, the town did, or you could find your heart's desire in mail-order catalogues. The catalogues have been coming through the letter-boxes of rural homes for decades, but increasingly are a way of life for those who either cannot or will not traipse to the towns in search of what they need. It keeps their cars off the roads, replaced by delivery services that can bring an order to the remotest farmhouse within 24 hours of a telephone call. And now there is shopping by internet too. Out here in the country, the wheel is turning its full circle back to doorstep delivery, if you wish, and there is the opportunity for country dwellers to become isolated again at their own volition, communicating with the rest of the world indirectly by disembodied voice or silently through the screen.

'The catalogues have been coming through the letter-boxes of rural homes for decades ...'

5
Country Women

MURIEL FULFORD was born in Hampshire in 1901. When she was four years old her mother died and her father, a farm labourer, brought her with him to the small Wiltshire village of Shrewton. And there she stayed, until she died at the age of 98, having never travelled further than she could on foot except when, aged 96, she was taken on a shopping trip to Salisbury ten miles from her home. Everything she needed was in her own village, and she was thoroughly contented there. Muriel had never married. She had worked with her father on the farm from the day she left school at fourteen until he died in 1957; she then worked as a domestic help for the local doctor until she retired ten years later. It might not seem like much of a life to some, but for this gentle, proud little woman it could not have been bettered.

Gertrude Jekyll, writing in 1904, had met several old folk who had never been more than ten miles from their birthplace and she loved to listen to them; 'indeed, their simple wisdom and shrewdness are in many ways quite equal to those of their brethren in the wider world. Their lives have been perhaps all the happier in that they have been concerned with few wants and few responsibilities.'

country women

WOMEN'S VOICES

MARIAN ATKINSON, BORN IN CUMBRIA FOUR YEARS LATER THAN MURIEL, MARRIED A FARMER IN 1924 AND RAISED FIFTEEN CHILDREN WITH HIM, WHILE AT THE SAME TIME HELPING WITH THE FARM WORK. SHE WOULD RISE AT FIVE IN THE MORNING TO BRING IN THE SEVENTEEN COWS AND MILK THEM BEFORE GETTING THE CHILDREN READY FOR SCHOOL; THEN SHE WOULD CLEAN OUT THE COWSHED AND FEED THE PIGS.

'Perpetually pregnant, she thought nothing of heaving hefty bags of cattle feed or digging sheep out of snowdrifts ...'

PREVIOUS PAGE *Landgirls grading seed potatoes at Bankhead Farm near Perth*

RIGHT *A Romany couple*

Farmer's daughters in the West Country

PERPETUALLY PREGNANT, she thought nothing of heaving hefty bags of cattle feed or digging sheep out of snowdrifts, or bringing in 600 sheep at lambing time and helping them with difficult births. She naturally cooked for her huge family, kept the house in order, did the laundry and all the other countless unpaid jobs that women did; she never had time to go anywhere else, never had time to be ill, never had time to rest before or after giving birth, but she always made time to picnic in a field with her children, eating bread and jam, singing songs, telling stories and making daisy-chains, and she always had time to notice the seasons, especially the beauty of autumn. She now has fifty grandchildren, eighty-two great-grandchildren and five great-greats, and her life was typical of many country women in the earlier part of the twentieth century.

Mrs Budd lived in a two-room cottage in a Surrey village. She had so many children that as each one reached eleven or twelve years of age they had to leave home and go into service to make way for the younger ones. In the same village, the Devonshire family consisted of twelve children, living in a slightly larger cottage but with only a front room, kitchen and wash house downstairs; the fourth eldest was Cath, who went into service when she was fourteen, as so many did. Later, she found herself living for eight years in the vacated Nissen huts of an old Army camp on the common. Many families lived there, initially in the hope of council houses. The huts had mains water and electricity (which local cottages did not) and the rent was eight shillings a week. She and her husband managed to put up their own dividing walls in their hut to form two bedrooms, a sitting-room and a kitchen, and planted a flower garden as well.

In 1965 a Welsh woman living in the Anglesey village of Llanedwen wrote in her diary on 4 March:

> *Snowstorm. Today is a day not to be forgotten. Snow-drifts everywhere. I, Pheena Thomas the local postwoman, got to work by 7.15am. Mailvan did not arrive till 8.15am with only a few local letters, he could not get any further*

womens voices

than the Finger cross-roads because of road blockage. Anyway the council workers cleared the road so traffic started to pass through round about 10.30am. I walked the round, cycling was out of the question. Anyway, everybody was very kind, some took letters that they could deliver on their way to work, and others offered me cups of tea and biscuits, everybody seemed more helpful and cheerful in the snow except for one old growser.

Miss Thomas had been asked to write the diary as her local WI's contribution to the collection of village scrapbooks created to celebrate the national federation's Golden Jubilee in 1965. She wrote at one point about something 'that was news to me and I am supposed to know everything that is going on around me to put in this diary. ... I wonder who will be writing one in another fifty years? My hobbies are gardening and gathering firewood when I have time.'

Another diary in the same year, kept by a woman living in a semi-detached bungalow on a new estate:

7.30am, rise and dress, feed cat, cook breakfast; 8am, husband leaves for work, wash up, put washing to soak, make beds; 8.30am, child's breakfast, finish washing, housework. Prepare lunch, shopping. 11am, child sleeps, time for interests – dress-making, knitting, embroidery etc. 1pm, lunch, wash up, amuse child. 2.30pm, take child for walk or visit friends. 5pm, child's tea and bath. 6pm, husband arrives home and puts child to bed. 6.30pm, high tea with husband. Most of vegetables are home-grown. Almost all mother's and child's clothes are made at home.

One wonders whether such a quiet, ordered and rather isolated life was preferable to that of the postwoman struggling through the snow but knowing everybody in her village. There was the story of a child living in Grampound, Cornwall, who went shopping in the village with a city child. Wherever they went people smiled, waved and gave them a cheery greeting – the expedition was more a sequence of friendly visits than a shopping afternoon. The city child was amazed; at home those among whom she lived were generally impersonal and indifferent to her. 'Do you really know all the people in Grampound?' she asked her country cousin. 'Why, of course I know all of them; they're my friends!'

The editor of the WI diaries, Paul Jennings, travelled some 10,000 miles to see the villages whose scrapbooks he had read and to talk to the villagers. He came away with a strong sense of the importance of the 'female' voice – not necessarily the voice of the women, but the rural voice that was passive, peaceful and life-producing, in contrast to the 'male side of a nation that has confronted other nations – the external, the formal, the territory-defending, the aggressive'. Yes, Britain was predominantly a place of cities and industry and, yes, there were major national problems in economics, defence and so on. But in the villages he found the 'domestic sense' of the land and also a powerful sense of 'living in two times, in an old and a new Britain, with an awareness, an agility in effortlessly leaping from one to the other'. The ordinary people living in the villages were a mix of old and new, but they were getting on with the business of living together, understanding the importance of everyday concerns and 'bringing up their children under a real sky, under real trees'.

If you want to know about the reality of everyday life in the countryside, then or now, listen to the women. On the whole, it was the women who held together the fabric of rural life (they still do) but too often their stories have been overlooked. Go and listen to the elderly women in your village; go and learn. In the words of a poem reprinted in Paul Thompson's book, *The Voice of the Past*, but of unclear source:

What do you see nurses, what do you see,
What are you thinking when you look at me?
A crabbit old woman, not very wise,
Uncertain of habits with far-away eyes ...
I'm an old woman now and nature is cruel,
Tis her jest to make old age look like a fool ...
But inside this old carcase a young girl still dwells
And now and again my battered heart swells,
I remember the jobs, I remember the pain,
And I'm loving and living life over again
So open your eyes nurses, open and see,
Not a crabbit old woman, look closer – see me.

TOP
A Dublin fortune teller in Lancashire

ABOVE
Elizabeth O'Sullivan of Killorglin, Co. Kerry

IN THE HOME

THE CHAPTER ON COUNTRY LIVING SETS THE SCENE FOR THE ENDLESS TOIL OF RUNNING A HOUSEHOLD IN THE DAYS BEFORE ELECTRICITY, GAS, MAINS WATER AND PLUMBING CAME TO THE COUNTRYSIDE. OF COURSE, SOME WOMEN KEPT THEIR HOMES SPOTLESS; OTHERS DIDN'T GIVE A DAMN OR WERE TOO WORN OUT WITH CHILDBEARING AND WORK TO COPE.

'Monday was washing, Tuesday was ironing, Wednesday was shopping ...'

CONDESCENDINGLY, PULBROOK WROTE in 1922: 'Good housewives usually go in colonies, for the slattern is an affront to the tidy, and a clean and particular woman cannot long endure bad company; yet it is surprising how the sloven can improve when set an example by new neighbours.'

KEEPING HOUSE

Eileen Halliday's family had lived in the same cottage in the Cotswolds village of Dudbridge for more than a century until the once-rural home found itself urbanised and both Sainsbury's and roadbuilders tried to demolish it (she fought them and won – the road and the supermarket were built around her instead). She remembers the regularity of her mother's life after marriage in 1915: Monday was washing, Tuesday was ironing, Wednesday was shopping at the Co-op in the village, Thursday was bedrooms and Friday was polishing and windows. 'Saturday was getting the vegetables all ready for Sunday baking, because Sunday was the big day when the big lunch would be cooked.' Mother was a great cake-baker and also a great faggot-maker – the smell of her faggots wafting down the lane would draw admiring comments from all those who passed. Mother kept ducks, chickens, goats, pigeons and rabbits in the backyard; she made all the children's clothes, made sure all the household bills were paid and looked after Granny, 'who always had to have her glass of brandy before she went to bed'.

FAR RIGHT Mary Graham of Wythop Hall Farm near Cockermouth in the Lake District, removing butter from the churn and then preparing the butter for weighing

RIGHT Drawing water from the well

FEEDING THE FAMILY

Quite apart from the labour of laundry and cleaning the house, getting meals on the table was a job in itself for most country women. Perhaps the nub of it all was that the country housewife needed much more space than the town dweller, because she needed to be more self-sufficient: she needed to grow and rear food, harvest or kill it, preserve or pluck and skin it as well as store and cook it. Ideally she needed all the working areas of a farmhouse, but in cottages such space was not to be had. If the cottager was lucky enough to have a scullery in which to prepare vegetables, dish up, wash up and fire the copper, there tended to be friction because men would come into the house through the back door into the scullery, kick off their muddy boots, peel off their wet clothes and wash away the day's dirt just where and when the wife was preparing a meal. Oh, for a utility room, or just a downstairs wash-room! (And that is one reason why so many cottages have downstairs bathrooms, preferably near the back door.)

The broadcaster C.H. Middleton, in his 1941 book *Village Memories*, devoted a whole chapter to 'Grub', starting with boyhood memories of the village shop. He looked back half a century to grandmothers who would scorn anything out of a tin or out of a foreign country, who made their own jam and cured their own

in the home

bacon and distrusted any foodstuffs that had not been produced at home. He pointed out that the food was generally 'far more wholesome and palatable than some of the stuff eaten by the present toothless generation'. Meat was all home-killed, with one weekly joint for a family at most; in between you ate your own bacon and ham, perhaps a rabbit from the fields and occasionally poultry from your own backyard, but rarely fish unless you lived near the coast.

Pig meat was the basis of the rural diet in the days when every cottager kept a pig or two at the end of the garden. The pigs were killed at home, cured at home and eaten at home. The local pig-killer would kill your pig and cut it into joints for half-a-crown. Pig-killing meant a time of plenty for the family: you would roast the fresh spare-rib as pork; you would make black puddings and sausages, basins of brawn from the head, faggots from unmentionable parts liberally flavoured with onion and herbs, and curly 'scraps' (little bits of skin) for breakfast. The chine of a large baconer would be rolled, cured and stuffed with herbs. The great slab of solid white fat (the 'leaf' or 'flare') would be cut into small pieces and melted down for lard to be used for cooking or to be spread on bread as dripping with pepper and salt. The bacons and hams that were the bulk of the carcase would be salted and cured at home (sugar, salt and black treacle usually came into the recipe) and then hung in the back kitchen for a year. If you had a good big inglenook fireplace, you could hang the meat in the chimney and preserve it by smoking.

In the many homes that did not have a back kitchen or space for an airy walk-in larder, fresh and hung meat might be kept in a meat-safe – a cupboard with perforated zinc sides or something similar that let plenty of air in and kept the flies and rodents out, preferably on an outside north-facing wall to keep it cool. Summer milk in some rural areas had to be delivered twice a day; it was unpasteurised and very likely to 'go off' rather quickly, which was only a benefit if you wanted it ripe enough to make butter or to turn it into cheese yourself.

When Middleton was a child in the late nineteenth century bread was still largely baked at home in his village. Many cottagers even grew their own grain on their big allotments, harvesting and threshing it by hand and then taking it to the local mill for grinding into flour in exchange for the bran. Middleton worked at the village bakehouse for a while when he left school and well remembered how people would bring along their Sunday joints on the way to church; the joints, on trays complete with the housewife's own batter puddings and potatoes for roasting, would be popped into the baker's ovens and churchgoers would collect their sizzling hunks of meat after church to carry them home again under a cloth.

THE MIDDAY MEAL

n Middleton's Northamptonshire village the butcher would kill a bullock one week so that everybody had beef; the next it would be a couple of three-year-old sheep so that every family had hunks of mutton. His mother had a leg-of-mutton ritual: the meat would be hung in the back kitchen for a week and each day she would push a knife between bone and flesh to pour in some home-made wine and vinegar. When the meat was adequately hung and pickled in this way she would roast it, fatty and full of flavour, on a jack in front of the fire. Bacon was equally fat and farmworkers ate bread and boiled fat bacon for their midday meal – fat is the perfect energy source to recharge a labourer's muscles and keep him warm in cold weather. In country areas, incidentally, the midday rather than evening meal was the main one of the day and this was still the case nationwide after the Second World War.

in the home

OPPOSITE TOP
Straw-plaiting for making bonnets. This woman had practised the craft for 75 years, in the footsteps of her parents and grandparents

OPPOSITE BELOW
Stitching, at a Lake District cottage known as 'Bend or Bump' at Hawkshead

VEGETABLES WERE STORED and preserved in various ways. Root vegetables could remain in the ground until needed, or be stored in clamps – heaps of earth and straw to protect them from the frost. Marian Robertson, born during the First World War, remembers how everybody used to grow their own vegetables and help each other out – if Mrs So-and-So down the lane hadn't got a cabbage or swedes or parsnips, her neighbours would give some of theirs. In her village they would take turves from the common to clamp their root vegetables under the hedges. Haricot beans were dried; an excess of runner beans would be salted down in big earthenware pots; cabbage could be pickled, but most preferred to eat it fresh from the garden. Fruit was eaten in season or preserved in jams and jellies; bottling in Kilner jars became all the rage for those who could be bothered with the sterilisation procedures, and for a while there was also home canning, until it became much cheaper and easier to buy ready-tinned food.

Tinned meat was available as early as the 1820s, if you could afford it; but it was not until the beef farmers of Argentina started shipping tinned corned beef that the idea really became popular. Then in the early 1880s they came up with refrigerated ships so that cheaply produced South American and Australasian beef and lamb carcases could safely cross the oceans, denting the homegrown British fresh meat market in the process.

Refrigerators came late to the cottages, and freezers much later, though it was possible to buy ice from a travelling ice-man in the nineteenth century or carve your own block from a frozen pond. If you put a block of ice in the cellar it would last for a while, and if you were really lucky you had an insulated ice chest. The best of the ice chests were still being sold in the 1920s, which was when home refrigerators first came to Britain, though they did not become commonplace until after the Second World War, or even later in many country homes as there was no electricity supply to power them.

Electricity brought convenience in the home, but the early electric kettles could take eighteen minutes to boil a mere pint of water and the first electric toasters had dangerously exposed live elements. Electric vacuum cleaners would become a boon, replacing the whole dusty business of carpet-beating out in the garden or the much-loved push-and-pull Ewbank carpet sweeper – not that many country homes pampered their floors with carpets.

Plucking poultry at Llanthony in the Welsh Black Mountains

STITCHING

One of the most treasured inventions was the sewing machine. Singer sewing machines were invented in the United States in 1850 and were first used in cottages by glove-makers, who would hire or hire-purchase treadle-operated machines to speed up production in their cottage industry. Home glove-makers, still stitching by hand earlier in the nineteenth century and ruining their eyes by candlelight, had supported whole families during times of agricultural depression. With home machines, the industry managed to continue in spite of foreign

in the home

competition, and new cottages were being built for glove-makers in Oxfordshire as late as 1926.

By the end of the nineteenth century sewing machines were also being used by another cottage industry, that of stitching plaited straw into bonnets and hats. Plaiting was an industry in itself and required no equipment other than your fingers; you could plait straw anywhere, any time, man, woman or child, and in 1930 people around Luton were still plaiting straw. Cottage hat-makers continued to use their treadle machines into the 1920s and naturally country women who were accustomed to making the family's clothes adapted to sewing machines with glee. By the 1920s, far fewer country women made their own clothes: they usually went to the village dressmaker.

Smock-making was a local industry in some places. Smocks were at their peak in the mid nineteenth century in both popularity and complexity. In the eighteenth century they had been rather plain working overshirts, sometimes described as frocks, but during the nineteenth century women began to embroider them and some became highly rated specialists in the art of smocking; for example, Mary Bufton in Hereford until her marriage in 1835. At the Great Exhibition at Crystal Palace in 1851, nearly 800 agricultural labourers and other countrymen from Godstone, Surrey, turned up in force in their smartest smocks, with their women in best Sunday dresses.

By the end of that century smocks were largely going out of fashion, though men persisted in wearing these thoroughly practical garments into the twentieth century in some counties, and wearing them with pride. Working smocks, usually produced in factories, were in shades of beige, or locally blue in the Midlands, or dark grey for shepherds, or black in some places, brown or green in others. White smocks, heavily stitched, were usually worn on special occasions and for Sunday best and were made by family members (typically a girl for her sweetheart) or by a woman in the village who was an expert. In some places families took the industry a step further: they grew and spun their own flax as well as making it into smocks, and then sold them through a local tailor.

COTTAGE INDUSTRIES

CLOTHES INCLUDED KNITTED GARMENTS, OF COURSE, AND ALMOST ANY WOMAN, COUNTRY OR TOWN, COULD KNIT BY HAND. MANY COTTAGE WOMEN USED KNITTING AS ANOTHER MEANS OF EARNING MONEY AT HOME; YOU WOULD SEE THEM KNITTING AS THEY GOSSIPED IN THE VILLAGE STREET, KNITTING ON THEIR WAY TO MARKET, KNITTING IN THE EVENING GLOOM WITHOUT NEEDING TO SEE THE STITCHES.

'Cottage industries were an essential part of life ...'

ABOVE LEFT
Lace-making

ABOVE RIGHT
The never-ending job of mending

IT WAS NOT CONFINED to women; many a shepherd became an expert knitter, for example. Hand-knitting continued as a well organised industry into at least the 1870s in the north of England, with children attending knitting schools and cottagers knitting underwear, stockings and jackets for fishermen and also caps, gloves, stockings and clothes for a more general market, but village hand-knitting industries had generally died out by the late nineteenth century except in the more remote coastal and fishing villages. In Dorset thousands of pairs of hand-knitted gloves were produced every week for the armed services during the Second World War. In Leicestershire there were still many village stockingers working in the 1920s, though by then they were using steam-powered rather than hand frames.

Cottage industries were an essential part of life throughout most of the nineteenth century and were often in addition to not only housework and child-rearing but also working in the fields or other jobs. Initially they were based on raw materials produced by the cottagers themselves; later the materials were bought in and many cottage industries were dominated by agents, who brought out the materials to the cottages and sold off their output in the appropriate market place at a substantial profit – for the agents. Sometimes that little bit of spare-time home work became the main earner for the household and developed into quite a thriving small business, especially where several women combined forces and were capable of marketing the goods themselves.

Conversely, increasing industrialisation began

cottage industries

to swallow up cottage industries, which simply could not compete with mass-produced goods unless they could make a virtue of being 'different'. The old Dorset button-making industry collapsed almost overnight in the early 1860s when button-making machines were invented, though it was revived artificially by the Arts and Crafts Guild for a while in the early years of the twentieth century. Home spinning and weaving had been decimated by the steam-power looms and factory spinning jennies earlier in the nineteenth century. The ancient lace-making cottage industry had virtually died before Victoria was buried, though here and there it continued: for example, there was a family of hereditary lace makers in East Sussex in the 1920s, but they no longer peered at their work by the light of a candle enhanced with a globe of water to concentrate the brightness. In West Dorset villages women were still braiding nets in the garden well into the twentieth century.

Women tend to keep their hands busy while doing something else, and of necessity they were constantly making things for the home as well as for sale. They were experts at recycling: many a cottage was carpeted with homemade rag rugs; many a bed or doorway was draped with a patchwork quilt. Some embroidered samplers and table-cloths; some had enough leisure for tapestry work, though inevitably this was more often a hobby for middle- and upper-class women.

BELOW LEFT
Stitching gloves with the aid of a treadle in Worcestershire

BELOW RIGHT
Knitting by the range

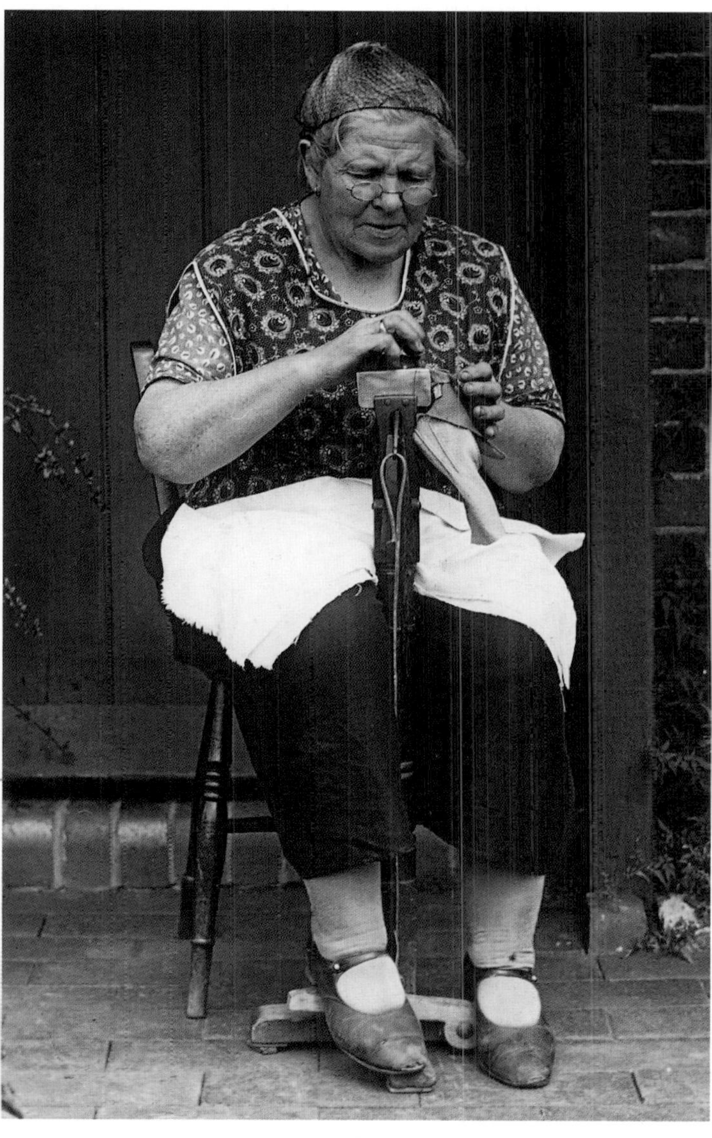

OUT AT WORK

Among cottagers, even those working at home to make extra money and caring for a large family were likely to be working outside the home as well. For generations, cottage women would clean other people's homes and launder their clothes and bedlinen; they would use their skills as needlewomen or at cooking special dishes to bring in the money.

Granny Cousins, a 'knocker-up' in Poole, Dorset. She was one of the last of her kind and more reliable than an alarm clock

Betsy Robert of Burrow Hill, in the years just after the First World War, would help not just with washing but also with childbirth – she was an early midwife, and was a good friend to many women in the village.

IN THE FIELDS

Women labourers were common in nineteenth-century fields, though earning much less than the men. Looking at annual earnings in Suffolk in 1795, a man might earn sixteen to eighteen pence a day and could make an average of £27 9s in a year; a boy of 12 would make £9 12s, a girl of 10 'spinning, pease and wheat-dropping, gleaning, &c' £4, and a wife £1 10s (type of work unspecified), so that the family's income for the year was £42 11s. In Worcestershire in 1794 a shepherd could earn 11 or 12 shillings a week, a carter 8 or 9 shillings, an old man 6 shillings a week, but a woman only sixpence or sevenpence a day. Wages in this county had shot up by 20 per cent in 1805; in 1807 a labourer at harvest time could earn sixpence a day plus meat, drink and a load of coal; at other times two shillings a day with beer; a man servant earned £10 10s a year but a dairy maid only £5 or £6 and an under-maid £3 to £5 a year. A Mr Fraser reported in the very early nineteenth century that he was concerned at the manner in which young females were sometimes treated and the 'severity of their servitude':

> *Scraping the roads, lanes, and yards, turning over mixings and filling dung-pots, is at best but a waste of time, and a feeble effort of infantile strength. What can a female child at the age of ten or twelve years be expected to perform with a mattock or shovel? or how will she be able to poise, at the end of a dung-fork, any reasonable weight, so as to lift it into the dung-pots slung upon the horses' backs, for packing out the manure to the distant parts of the farm? Even driving the horses after they are loaded, is by no means an employment proper for such girls, being altogether incompatible with the household and more domestic duties they ought early to be made acquainted with.*

What is more, 'the girls, too frequently, from an early dislike to their avocations, and in which they well know they are not hereafter to be continued, cannot well be supposed to have much emulation or desire to excel in them; hence premature connexions are formed, and which by marriage terminates their servitude,

RIGHT Transplanting Brussels sprouts near Pershore in Worcestershire, 1956

out at work

but without their having acquired in it those domestic qualifications upon which the comforts of a peasant family so essentially depend'.

By the early years of the twentieth century the sight of women field-hands was increasingly rare, except in times of war when landgirls took on the work of men serving in the forces. In Northumberland you would still see women bent over their hoes in the turnip fields and here they were known as a bondagers. In the old days labourers who had the benefit of tied farm cottages were bound to bring an assistant with them into the fields, and this would usually be a woman, traditionally dressed in kerchief and big straw hat; there would be gangs of women at work in the mud.

The towns sent casual job-seekers out into the countryside at certain seasons. In particular there was the great annual exodus of hop-pickers, with whole families from the cities coming out to the hop-growing areas for what was a combination of fresh-air holiday and the chance to earn some money. These crowds of women and children came by rail on 'Hop-picker Specials' and camped in fields and barns at the farms. The work was hard (they were paid by the bushel, monitored by a tally man with his wooden tablets) but good-natured, and many hop-pickers look back wistfully to happy times in the field, despite the very basic amenities of their living-quarters. Pulbrook waxed quite lyrical in 1922: 'When dusk has fallen and the evening mists begin to rise the twinkling fires breaking out in lines and groups turn a Kentish valley or a Hampshire hill-side into fairyland; the smoke billows upwards, and the children pass to and fro in the flicker like elves in a garden lit by glow-worms.' Glow-worms? Now there's a sight that has become rare in the countryside.

Harvesting flax

POOR RELIEF

Life could be very hard for working women. Hannah Cato, of Kirtlington, was still working as an agricultural labourer at the age of seventy-two when she applied for outdoor poor relief. Unfortunately, her family was of bad repute: various members of it appeared regularly before the magistrates for poaching. Hannah was earning four shillings a week in 1871 but had broken her arm in an accident and could therefore no longer work in the fields and had become destitute. Relief was refused, as it had been many times before, and she was given an order for the workhouse, which, as many times before, she would not accept. No wonder her family continued to poach to keep body and soul together.

out at work

MUCH LESS HAPPY were the gangs of casual workers, again many of them women, who came to dig potatoes and harvest other vegetables in the huge market gardens that were so often found on the outskirts of the cities. They worked in the cold and the wet for very low wages and often at the mercy of unscrupulous gang masters; their countless untold stories would make miserable reading. This system continued well into the twentieth century.

Where women gained full equality was in marrying the farmer. Farming was necessarily a partnership – in the good and the bad of it – and the woman's role was just as important as the man's. Quite apart from the shared physical work, she was frequently entrusted with the finances, chasing creditors, paying bills, paying wages and so on. Quite a few women were farmers in their own right as well, even several centuries ago. Today family farms remain one of the few industries in which husband and wife work in partnership, and most of the women have such shrewd business sense that they could succeed in running any other business they choose. Equality for women came to the farm a long, long time ago.

IN SERVICE

Field-work was not the only work, of course. Many village girls went into service as soon as they left school, perhaps to work in the big house, or for the local parson or doctor. Here they would be fed in return for their work. One such woman, aged seventy-six and suffering from rheumatism when she related her story, had gone into service at the age of twelve in the 1820s:

> *It was a carpenter's family, and there was eleven children. Yes, that was my first place, for a year. I didn't get no wages, only my food, one frock and one bonnet, and a shillin' to take home. Then I was hired for a year to go to a farm where the master was a widower, and after that at another farm where there was two ladies. They was the particularest ladies I ever knowed. It'd do any girl good to go and live with such as they. There was the oak stairs – it was always a clean pail of water to every two steps; and I'd as much pride in it as they had. My wages never got as fur as four pound. Best place I ever lived in was at Mr Woods's at Hambledon. Quietest and best master I ever lived with. There was the red-brick kitchen-floor. I used to flow he down with a green broom; best of brooms for bricks; makes the floors red. You makes 'em of the green broom as grows on the common. After I left, there was always a bit of green holly at Christmas, and any win'fall apples he always give me. Ah! he was a good master. He minded me when I was married, and time and again he sent me a bit of beef – till he died – and then my beef died. He was the best man. One day after I left him I was at his place, and he had a cold leg of mutton, and what does he do but take a knife and cut'n in two and give me one piece. And one time when bread was so dear he says, 'Here's a shillin' to get a loaf' – Ah! we soon cut he up.*

OPPOSITE
Plum-picking in Kent

out at work

Cleaning the silver

HOUSEHOLD SERVICE IS WHERE women would have satisfied Fraser's polemic about learning good domestic skills in order to keep their own households once married. Richard Jefferies told of the editor of a local paper who was in the act of going to press when there was a timid knock on his door. A poor cottage girl, who had walked six or seven miles from her hamlet, had come to ask about the address of a lady who had advertised three weeks ago for a servant; it had taken the girl that long to make the momentous decision to apply for the post, no doubt long since filled.

During the two world wars many women left their villages to join the armed services or for all sorts of work in factories as well as on farms where they replaced the absent men. Their lives and attitudes changed forever. Society itself changed dramatically and the scope for domestic work altered completely. Live-in servants virtually disappeared; instead ladies of the manor hired a 'daily' or learnt how to clean and cook for themselves, and they hired nannies and au pairs to look after the children. Those who had been their servants learned different skills, such as office and shop work, or became self-employed in the domestic work they knew. There are many of the older generation who can still remember going into service straight from school, but most of them are in their eighties and nineties now.

HIRING FAIRS

The old hiring fairs, well described by Thomas Hardy, were the usual market place for country women looking for work. The 'mop' fairs were named for the way in which applicants sported some symbol of their trade; for housemaids this might be a mop in their hand, or a spotless white apron. They would parade in their best clothes, like show cattle in the ring, trying to keep an eye on their battered baggage and hoping desperately that somebody would hire them (albeit at a yearly wage that was hardly worth earning), then trailing off to another fair if no one did. Hiring fairs no longer served their dubious purpose by the First World War, though there were still a few here and there even in the early 1920s.

CLOTHES

Clothes in the country were more for practical wear than for fashion and glamour (even today, except for town dwellers not yet fully adapted to country life) and in the nineteenth century you could still work out whereabouts in the country you were by the type of clothes people wore.

In the north, rather than the south, women tended to wear a shawl and kerchief; in the south-west they sported pinafores. Market women always wore white aprons; older women continued to wear their frilled caps inside their bonnets in the early decades of the twentieth century and sunbonnets for working in the hayfield. In the eighteenth century, working women would wear a shift, an ankle-length petticoat, a waist apron and leather stays. The shift peeked out beneath an overgown whose low neck was demurely filled with a big kerchief of cotton or wool, according to the season. In 1797, Lord Egremont was informed that to clothe a woman in Suffolk would cost about thirteen shillings for a red gown and two coats.

By the 1820s many working women were wearing out-of-fashion clothes handed down by mistresses to their servants and then sold on, but country women still wore their shift, petticoat, leather stays and kerchief until the mid nineteenth century. Others wore cotton print gowns and used the offcuts for making patchwork quilts. Gertrude Jekyll remembered that in her youngest days the typical outfit was a print gown and apron, with either a cotton print sunbonnet (usually in pale lilac) with a deep curtain, or a plain straw bonnet with a ribbon under the chin, and kerchief shawl over the shoulders. Women wore mob caps, indoors and out; outside the cap would be covered with a straw hat, and by the 1850s both cap and straw hat were discarded in favour of a stiff, ruched and frilled sunbonnet that covered the neck and shoulders as well as the head. There would be a flat black felt cap over the top on market days or a black satin bonnet for church.

Typical nineteenth-century bonnets, worn here after their time, in the coastal village of Staithes

Indoors, working women continued to cover their hair until the twentieth century, but it was not until about the Second World War that women took to wearing head scarves. In Wales some of the fishwomen continued to wear those tall steeple hats that had been seen in other parts of Britain in the seventeenth century. The women of Llangwm, for example, wore them as they walked to Tenby to sell oysters and prawns. Working skirts were shorter than fashionable ones, showing at least the ankles, and some women would tuck their skirts up to knee level to make working in them easier. Skirts were frequently bunched up out of the way; women cocklers generally pulled up their underskirts between their legs with a string, almost forming culottes. And women always had aprons, indoors and out, often wearing two at once and generally without a bib. In the twentieth century those aprons were replaced by flowered cotton overalls or pinafores.

In the 1890s some of the older women farmworkers took to wearing trousers, and during the First World War trousers became common, as they and dungarees were among landgirls in the Second World War. By 1900 most of the old country sunbonnets had been cast off in favour of hats to keep of the sun and the weather.

Feet would be shod in boots or stout shoes. Women also wore pattens (clogs with a wooden sole, leather toe piece, leather bands tied over the instep and an oval iron hoop fixed underneath on two short legs) to keep their feet out of the mud before rubber galoshes became useful in the 1920s.

IN THE COMMUNITY

SERVICE HAS COME TO MEAN SOMETHING RATHER DIFFERENT. IT IS MORE A MATTER OF SERVICE TO THE COMMUNITY AT LARGE THAN TO AN INDIVIDUAL OR A FAMILY AND THE SCOPE FOR COMMUNITY SERVICE IN RURAL AREAS IS HUGE.

'... if you want to change the world but cannot, join your parish council and change what you can in the village.'

COUNTLESS WOMEN TAKE up the challenge as volunteers, be it serving 'meals on wheels', helping with a local driving pool to get villagers to their doctor's surgery or into town to collect their pensions, creating and running a wide variety of village activities ranging from lunch clubs for the elderly to playgroups for the children, helping out at the nurse's baby clinic, or generally making sure that, as far as possible, villages do not suffer from lacking amenities that town dwellers take for granted.

It is probably that very lack that gives a village its community spirit – villagers cannot rely on 'them' to provide the services and therefore get on and provide what is needed themselves, without charging for their time and skills. And it is usually the women who do so. In the early 1960s, Miss Farbridge of Dalston, Cumberland, for example, started and ran a small orchestra for the youth of the village. The children were so eager that they would spend hours of their spare time practising, and no doubt their talents would have gone unfostered without Miss Farbridge's encouragement. In the late 1990s, Mary Turton of Milland, Sussex, conceived and produced an annual pantomime, all its actors, sound operators, lighting experts and others being the young of the village. One highly gratifying result was that children who had seemed to be shy and awkward found self-confidence and talents they never knew they had, and another was the sparking of enthusiasm among adults as well for taking part in drama, dancing, singing and music.

Delivering the milk in the snow at Hastingleigh, Kent, in the exceptionally hard winter of 1946

Many women serve at the grass roots of government by becoming members of their parish councils, finding that they can have quite a strong and active influence on very local matters that affect people directly and personally. As someone once said, if you want to change the world but cannot, join your parish council and change what you can in the village. The legislation allowed women to serve on parish councils right from the start, when the councils were created in 1894 – long before women were admitted to other levels of government.

WOMEN'S INSTITUTUES

In 1915 the English followed the Canadian example when Mrs Aldred Watt founded their first Women's Institute. The timing was apposite: with Britain in the throes of the First World War there was a need to boost home food production and there was also a big emotional gap in the lives of the many women whose husbands, sons and brothers were fighting in the trenches. By 1951 there were more than 7,000 WI branches in England and Wales, with a total membership of about 400,000; by the golden jubilee in 1965 there were 9,000 branches, all under the protective umbrella of their National Federation (inaptly based in London). Today, there are about 9,200 institutes in England and Wales: Scotland has its own Scottish Rural WIs.

The aim of the institutes, which saw themselves as 'brightening the lives' of women in the villages, was 'to give countrywomen opportunities to improve conditions in their own homes and villages, and to increase their enjoyment of life'. The monthly meetings were (and are)

in the community

6

Fierce concentration in the cake-decorating class

divided into three parts: transaction of WI business, a talk or demonstration on a subject of general or local interest, and social activities after a cup of tea. Many institutes also organised drama or choral societies, art and handicraft classes or courses of lectures in subjects such as cookery and home-making. Others became interested in further education; for example, in one village the mostly middle-aged wives of agricultural labourers chose medieval history as the subject they wanted to study. The village WI might walk the local footpaths, welcome foreign students studying community development, run a WI group in the local mental hospital or prison, sell members' produce in a weekly market in the nearest town – once a group of women got together, the scope was endless.

The essence of the WI was that it was for women in rural areas and that it embraced all levels of village society as equals, be they the rector's wife or the roadsweeper's. These groups often became, as well, guardians of local history, listening to each other's memories and sometimes taking care to record them on paper, or even on tape, for future generations. Several WIs recorded on film, moving or static, and in paintings and needlework, creating visual records as well as verbal ones that local historians find invaluable. In these 'terribly British' groupings you would find examples of every clichéed character, which was part of the fun. There was always a woman with a loud voice and domineering manner ruffling everybody's feathers, but there were enough of you to put her in her

WITCHES

In the 1870s, the villagers of Souldern (near Banbury) convinced themselves that seventeen-year-old Mary Ellen Rouse, a poor uneducated girl of delicate health and 'perverted' mind, was bewitched. In another Oxfordshire village Ann Tustin, the wife of a pauper, died in 1875 and was widely believed to be a witch; mind you, she was a bad-tempered and eccentric woman so it was not difficult to pin such a label on her. It was said that she had bewitched her own daughter, who died within the year, despite taking every precaution to keep witches out of her home by sticking pins in sheep livers and putting crossed knives across any small crack through which a witch might try to enter.

Ann Tustin died of natural causes (whatever the villagers thought) but less fortunate was another witch, Ann Tennant of Long Compton, the sharp-tongued wife of a shoemaker. At the age of seventy-nine she was murdered by a near neighbour, farm labourer James Hayward, who was convinced that he was haunted by witches. Mrs Tennant was always blamed by the locals for every animal that unexpectedly died, or crop that failed, or child that sickened. People would say, 'Hey! old Mother Tennant's at the bottom o' this 'n. 'Tis that evil eye o' hern for sure.' At least by her time witches were no longer put on trial and hanged, burnt at the stake or drowned; the authorities dismissed the whole idea of witchcraft, even if the locals continued to believe in it because, after all, they had to blame something.

IN THE COMMUNITY

place. There was always the rather fey, arty woman seeking to enlighten the masses.

Let us take one that shall remain anonymous, one of the earliest of the WIs, founded in 1919 by the always splendidly hatted lady of the manor. It began with 49 members; by the following year there were 104. Meetings were held alternately at opposite ends of the long, large but sparsely populated parish, which meant everybody had to walk a considerable distance at least every other month 'and many a time rather stout and breathless members ... have had to be helped up the hill with the pressure of an encouraging hand in the small of their backs', wrote the institute's historian. But in those early days there were no local buses and most of the women were used to walking seven miles to town and back. This very democratic early WI decided that members should take it in turn, in alphabetical order, to take the chair at monthly meetings. (Their founder was married to a Liberal MP.) 'This prevented any feeling that some members were more important (or more pushing) than others. It was also a valuable training. In those days before the wireless, people in the country had little idea how to present their views or preside at meetings, however valuable their wisdom and common sense might be.'

Women's Legion parade

They decided to have informal weekly meetings as well, where women could have classes in glove-making, basketry, singing and other interests or could simply chat over their sewing or play cards before joining in communal dancing and singing. In the days when there were no buses, no cinema, no wireless or television, they welcomed this regular opportunity to make their own entertainment, and a local farmer remarked that there had been more friendship in the parish as a result. They would put on plays and children's parties, celebrate May Day with processions and competitions and folksinging on the green and much more. But they did have their disagreements. On one occasion a member who had been asked to second the vote of thanks to the retiring committee 'seized the opportunity instead to unburden herself of all her grievances during the past year and tell us exactly what she thought of all our failings!'

COURTSHIP AND MARRIAGE

In most villages, and in some even now, most people were related to each other, however distantly. The choice of marriage partners was not very wide but there were rules. For example, 'trade' was a superior stratum in village society, and it did not do for trade to marry beneath them – it brought disgrace on the whole extended family.

Newly-weds setting off from Micheldever, Hampshire, in a horse-drawn brougham in 1935

'It was hard to escape all those knowing eyes, and all those eyes did know you.'

Adultery was frowned upon if you were caught. When George Coggins, a baker, committed adultery in the 1870s with a willing woman in a railway carriage while the train was stationary, the guard caught them at it and the word quickly spread in the village. The remedy was traditional: the villagers gathered plenty of old iron and tin utensils and loudly played 'rough music' outside the culprits' homes for three consecutive evenings. Then they made effigies of the couple and carried them round their respective villages on poles before setting the dummies on fire, to a great deal of noise from rattling their utensils and shouting. It might have taught the adulterers a shaming lesson, but it shamed the innocent Mrs Coggins as well. Rough music would also have been the village's response to wife-beating; it would be preceded by a warning in the form of a trail of chaff being left during the night from the roadway up to the culprit's door, meaning that it was known that 'thrashing' was going on in there.

Courtship was generally the talk of the village; it was hard to escape all those knowing eyes, and all those eyes did know you. Dances were the highlight of a young person's week – the village hop, or preferably a dance in another village or in town, where you had a chance to meet someone you hadn't known all your life. Incidentally, the government's own statistical review for 1939 showed that, nationwide, one bride in every six was pregnant on her wedding day and that nearly 30 per cent of all firstborn children were conceived out of wedlock.

Weddings were generally simple affairs in the country until the end of the nineteenth century, when Jekyll remarked with horror on seeing a 'lamentable' photograph of a labourer's wedding in which the bride had a veil and

courtship

'Sex education was non-existent – people simply did not talk about such matters.'

orange blossoms, a shower bouquet, and pages!' She saw this as undignified burlesque. 'Such wedding parties do not walk to church; the bride's party, at least, hires the closed village fly, which for the occasion is called "the brougham". A wise old woman remarked, "When I was married we walked to church; and then walked home, and I cooked two chops. And then we changed our clothes and went to our work!" '

Sex education was non-existent – people simply did not talk about such matters. Women born about the time of the First World War might be quite shocked by their first period, having no idea what it was all about, and if their mothers did think to explain sex to them they didn't believe a word of it. Yet if you fell pregnant before marriage the penalties were severe: most girls would be sent in disgrace to a boarding establishment for the duration, and after the birth would have the baby removed from them whether or not they wished to keep it. Nobody ever counselled or consoled them; they had done a dirty thing and their feelings were irrelevant. Nobody explained what they would go through during the birth, though many country girls had seen it in the cowshed and lambing pens or had seen their own mothers giving birth at home.

Babies were born at home; childbirth was not seen as an illness (though it often turned into one) and was such a regular event that it became an annual habit. Friends and families would help and fathers were often on standby to summon the village nurse or midwife – they would probably set off on bikes at the first signs of labour, as of course there was no telephone to ring for help, and it was a matter of 'hunt the nurse' until they found her. Women paid pence a week to belong to their local nursing association, giving them the right to call out the district nurse when needed, and this was the situation until the National Health Service was created after the Second World War.

A Romany woman proudly displays her newborn baby, delivered in her beautifully kept caravan

BIRTH CONTROL

Birth control was non-existent, and the very idea of it would have shocked most country women in times when many children died young and you needed plenty of them to replenish the family stock and help to bring in the wages. Families remained large – some more so than others: Sarah Powell of Bucknell, Oxfordshire, for example, produced 5 children in 11 months and her total tally was 23 (including six pairs of twins and one lot of triplets). By the time she was 51, only 7 of her children were alive and her husband Samuel was 'ruptured & quite unable to work'. In the 1870s a 'most masculine kind of woman' who was an excellent ploughwoman fell pregnant while acting as under carter, the head carter having been 'rather too familiar with her'. The moral of the tale was not concerned with her pregnancy, but that there was 'either a deficiency of labourers or a superabundance of work, or both, to render it necessary for women to undertake men's work'.

SPORTS

In Chobham, Surrey, they started a ladies' cricket team after the First World War. They played in long white dresses, which made bowling interesting. Each woman paid an annual subscription of half a crown, and once a year they played against the men, with tea provided by the ladies. A more typical team game for women was stoolball, said to have evolved from milkmaids using a leg from their three-legged milking stools, or simply their hand, as a bat and the stool itself as something for the bowler to aim at. The game has a long history in rural areas and is still played seriously today, especially in Sussex. In the 1960s, one Sussex villager remarked that her team was a mixture of all ages, ranging from young girls to those who had been playing for years, and that 'married women enjoy the evening matches, a change from the house ...'.

In 1860 (note the date), The Field published an impassioned and feisty letter from 'A Riflewoman' on the subject of outdoor recreation for the 'fair sex':

> Gentlemen are gallant, but why should that prevent a woman's being able to load and fire a gun or a rifle, and to shoot either at game or at an enemy? I see no occasion for a woman's leaving England to fight, but why should she not be found doing her best in the defence of her country? Why should she be excluded from using her rifle behind a hedge? And where will she ever appear to greater advantage than by her husband's side in an action loading his rifle, or firing her own? I do not see why a woman is not to fish, or, in fact, to join in any healthy, useful out-of-door amusement, as long as she fulfils all her home duties. I only hope that, should an occasion ever present itself of defending England, I (with many others) may be found 'the right woman in the right place'.

She was responding to correspondence about whether or not it was ladylike to participate in certain outdoor pursuits other than 'a gentle walk out on a clear road for two or three miles, and home again' or 'a ride round the neighbourhood, by the roads, for an hour or two, and back again', or even a chance to fish 'after the hook is baited for us, placed where a fish is likely to be caught, but we are neither to see the bait we know to be there, nor the fish killed we know was intended to die and for which we have been angling'.

Well, things have changed a lot since then, and not just in sport. In all aspects, country women are now in charge of their own lives. They look outwards as much as inwards; they have been open to many influences over the last century or so; but they still form the bedrock of village life and, despite the commuters and the power-dressing and power-games of city women, those in the villages (whether of country or urban origins, whether married or single, whether young or old or middle-aged) understand the realities of life, know how important they are to their local community, know that their contribution is valued and relish the challenge of keeping the whole thing together.

6 Country Children

country children

SWIMMING IN SECRET PONDS, paddling in streams, tickling minnows and sticklebacks, gathering frogspawn and blackberries, hiding to watch the foxes at dusk, collecting birds' eggs, harvesting blackberries and whortleberries, hazel nuts and acorns, meeting the gang at the signpost, having adventures, playing games in the woods, following the cows, catching pincher-bob beetles ... 'You had to make your own fun in all sorts of various ways and we really enjoyed ourselves. We had nothing else but what we did ourselves and I think it was a good thing,' said Frank Burningham, old enough to remember quite a lot about the First World War when he was a boy. Nearly all his memories were of being out-of-doors – watching the 'thrashing' machine, tagging along with the village band as it marched down the village street on the evening of Armistice Sunday carrying acetylene lanterns for the bandsmen so that they could read their music, carol-singing with the band ('I remember we played one foggy night in front of a hay stack thinking we'd been playing in front of a house!'), joining the Cubs, going to the seaside in an open solid-tyred coach wrapped in coats in the middle of summer – so many golden memories of childhood in the country.

country children

20TH-CENTURY MEMORIES

ELSIE COUSINS RECALLED HER CHILDHOOD IN THE EARLY 1930S: 'I WENT TO SCHOOL AND I USED TO HAVE TO DO AS I WAS TOLD. I NEVER USED TO ANSWER ANYONE BACK – MY MUM ALWAYS USED TO HAVE A STICK FROM THE HEDGE AND HIT OUR FINGERS IF WE BEHAVED BADLY AT THE TABLE. BUT THERE YOU ARE, IT DONE US NO HARM, NONE AT ALL.'

'...a typical boy of three or four years old, dressed by his mother in the morning but then turned out of doors to take care of himself.'

OTHER WOMEN REMEMBER playing chase in the village streets, going on summer church outings (and coming home with oranges and apples), picking primroses, walking to town until you got a bike at eleven if you were very lucky, collecting Grandad's jug of ale from the back door of the pub or collecting milk in a jug from the farm ('You'd go home with steaming hot milk all frothy on the top, you'd stand it to set and cream it off'), buying as much milk as you wanted for tuppence on Saturdays and making a rice pudding 'big enough to feed your family, because money had run out on Saturday and you didn't have anything until you had your roast on Sunday', buying delicious little penny buns at the baker's, dad taking you piggy-back through the floods wearing his wellingtons (wellingtons were new then), going to the village flower show and seeing all the cattle there.

Percy Heath, whose father was a shepherd, roamed the countryside with his brothers when they were young and knew every tree, every hedge, every damp patch in the fields, every ditch, every pond, every cow, every pig, every path, every birds' nest, every fox den and rabbit hole. He remembers his very deaf old granny: 'Used to have to talk to her through a rolled-up newspaper tied with bits of string – you had to get it up to her ear. She used to sit us up on the old copper edge (with the lid on) and get hold of your hair to wash it, and scrub your face hard.' He also remembers the pranks he and his brothers would get up to, and playing football among the cowpats in the meadow. Dad had Dexter cows and an old mule when Percy was little; the boys would gather big bundles of bracken as bedding for them, and would drive the small two-wheeled mule cart to collect firewood and sheep.

memories

LITTLE ONES

Harking back to the building of the railway network, an old man said that the area was 'chock full o' navvies, very near every 'ouse 'ad lodgers ... and there was more babbies in the place then than there ever 'ad been afore, or ever 'ave been since, an' I could name a few wot come in the Pig's 'Ead of a night now who 'ouldn't be 'ere at all if it 'adn't been fer the railroad.'

Richard Jefferies, in the 1870s, described the labourer's child. He had noted that the style of walk of the Wiltshire labourer was caused by 'following the plough in early childhood, when the weak limbs find it a hard labour to pull the heavy nailed boots from the thick clay soil. Ever afterwards he walks as if it were an exertion to lift his legs.' He talked about a typical boy of three or four years old, dressed by his mother in the morning but then turned out of doors to take care of himself. Wearing his father's greasy old hat (well over his ears and down almost to his shoulders), a jacket that used to be white, a belt, and a pair of boots like his father's in miniature with iron at the heel and toe, his legs bare and sturdy, he would toddle off to the nearby farmyard to watch the big horses being harnessed, hiding behind a tree or rick so that he was not spotted by the carter. Then he would watch the steam engine, or the shovelling of grain in the great barn. Or he might pretend to be a ploughman, dragging a small log by means of a piece of string.

Soon his morning-scrubbed skin was boyishly grimy. In due course he might go home for a slice of bread and dripping; his little sister would be trying to look after the crawling baby.

Jefferies marvelled how 'those prosperous parents who dwell in highly-rented suburban villas, and send out their children for a walk with a couple of nurses and a "bow-wow" to run beside the perambulator' would be eaten up with anxiety should their little darlings have ventured where the little labourer's son played – under the hoofs of cart-horses in the field, or floating twigs in the stream to pretend they were boats, or mingling with the cows and the bull in the meadow, the big sows with their young, the carts rumbling to and fro, the steam engines ploughing the furrows: the little boy, all by himself determinedly out in all weathers, the freezing wind whipping tears from his eyes and reddening his skin, the rain plummeting on him as he splashes happily in the puddles, the sun blazing down on him in the fields.

Yet he not only survived; he seemed to thrive and be happy out there, happier than the sister already burdened with household work. The little girl, like him, would be locked out of the cottage during the day but she also had to be in charge of her younger siblings as they played outside. In summer her life was pleasant enough, sitting by the brook with the toddlers around her, picking flowers to make dandelion chains, plaits of rushes and cowslip balls. She might take the children down to the hayfield. Later in the year she would take them to forage for blackberries and other wild fruit. All the while she would be alert for suitable pieces of fallen wood to drag home for the fire – even in London children in the nineteenth century were constantly scavenging for burnable bits for the home fires.

Catching toads

'... the rain plummeting on him as he splashes happily in the puddles, the sun blazing down on him in the fields.'

CLOTHES

IN COUNTLESS OLD PICTURES IT CAN BE HARD TO TELL WHICH OF SMALL CHILDREN ARE BOYS AND WHICH ARE GIRLS. IN THEIR YOUNGER YEARS, THEIR CLOTHES WERE OFTEN INTERCHANGEABLE; OR, MORE PRECISELY, SMALL BOYS WORE THEIR SISTERS' CAST-OFFS. TO ADD TO THE CONFUSION, GIRLS UP TO ABOUT EIGHT YEARS OLD USUALLY HAD THEIR HAIR CUT SHORT LIKE THE BOYS AND WORE SIMILAR ROUND BLACK FELT HATS.

'Small boys wore short trousers until a certain age – usually about thirteen – when they graduated to long ones.'

MOST SMALL GIRLS in the late nineteenth century wore frocks that were short-sleeved, whatever the weather, made of cotton in summer and 'stuff' (coarse woollen cloth) in winter. Helen Allingham's paintings show the typical cotton print frocks with long pinafore and plain sunbonnet worn earlier in that century. Those pinafores could be quite a problem if you were in a hurry to get to school: they had countless fiddly buttons down the back. Buttons also featured on boots for both girls and boys – horrible things to deal with when your fingers were cold and wet.

At one time country boys often wore 'gabardines', which were short round-frocks (like smocks), over corduroy suits. Gertrude Jekyll was amused when an aged and long-retired schoolmistress, pondering her pupils, said, 'Let me see, which boy was it that used always to speak of his gabardine – was it Jushingto Earl? No, it was Berechiah Gosling.' Many a child had an extraordinary Christian name in the nineteenth century, and even in the twentieth; typically the parents would open the Bible almost at random and pick a name from it, and in the late Victorian period they might also choose fancy names from cheap novels.

In the twentieth century, there was the ritual of the trousers. Small boys wore short trousers until a certain age – usually about thirteen – when they graduated to long ones. They considered themselves to be tough in their shorts; long trousers before your time were wimpish. Open to the elements, knees were constantly cold, grazed, grass-stained and muddy, but these were badges of pride. The shorts were baggy and generally just down to knee-level; often over-large hand-me-downs, they would be held up by braces or string, or by those elasticated striped belts with an S-shaped metal 'snake' clasp that had so many other uses as well. In many a household a boy would have only one pair of shorts, but that didn't restrict him from forgetting, in the rough and tumble of daily life, to keep them clean and not to rip them when he climbed trees and scrambled through hedges.

HEALTH

IT IS HEART-RENDING TO VISIT OLD GRAVEYARDS, OR GO THROUGH THE PARISH REGISTERS, AND DISCOVER JUST HOW MANY CHILDREN DIED VERY YOUNG. SOMETIMES YOU WILL FIND A SUCCESSION OF CHILDREN IN THE SAME FAMILY GRAVE, THEIR NAMES GRADUALLY ADDED TO THE HEADSTONE AND THEIR DEATHS RANGING FROM A FEW DAYS TO THREE OR FOUR YEARS OLD.

IN THE CHURCH REGISTER of one very small rural parish it was recorded in the year 1836 that the Heath family lost three children on 10 January (aged seven, four and nearly three); within the next two months five more toddlers and babies in the parish were dead. In the same parish half a century later a smallpox epidemic buried five people in quick succession, their ages ranging from eleven to seventy-one.

Scarlet fever was one of the killers. In the 1870s, George Dew reported: 'Scarlatina and Febricula [little or small fever] very bad at Islip. In several houses three & four children are ill with it, but no case has yet been fatal. It is said thirty children have it.' Two or three years later Dew reported the deaths of several children from scarlet fever, ranging in age from two to four years old.

Smallpox was another highly contagious killer, described by Dew as a 'fearful disease'; he spent much effort in trying to persuade families to vaccinate their children against it (one of his many local jobs was to keep a register of vaccinations) and was empowered to take out summonses against parents who failed to do so. A journeyman painter by the name of Prosser was sent to Oxford Gaol for seven days for not having his child vaccinated; in the meantime the Anti-Compulsory Vaccination League paid his fine. The league was formed in 1866 when it realised that the arm-to-arm method of vaccination in use at the time presented a high risk of cross-infection, and many parents believed that healthy babies could become fatally infected through the vaccination process. There was much heated correspondence in journals such as the *Field* about the dangers and advantages of vaccination.

'There was much heated correspondence in journals such as The Field about the dangers and advantages of vaccination.'

Dew was quite shocked when William Abel Ryder, a grocer, was sent to prison for seven days just like Prosser. Ryder had been before the magistrates several times for the same reason and had always put foward a very sound case

Mobile diptheria vaccination unit for children, 1944

health

'Whole families were dying of typhoid in the 1870s.'

against allowing what he saw as an 'experiment' on his child's body. He subsequently became a Guardian under the Poor Laws but continued to be 'an energetic Anti-Vaccinator'. In 1898, after years of controversy, a new act was at last passed that admitted that the medical profession may have been wrong; it replaced the old humanised lymph arm-to-arm method with glycerinated calf lymph instead, and also allowed parents to apply to local magistrates for exemption on the grounds of principle.

The third major killer was typhoid fever, usually due to appalling sanitation and contaminated drinking-water. Whole families were dying of typhoid in the 1870s.

Florence Brooks remembers catching 'a fever' at the age of three or four and going to hospital, where her parents were only allowed to look at her through the window. Elsie Mumford remembers the terrible 'flu epidemic just after the First World War, when many villagers died; the church bell would be tolled once for the death of a man, twice for a woman and three times (or the small bell) for a child. Another woman remembered catching scarlet fever in 1901 and being bundled into the enclosed black horse-drawn 'fever cart' to be isolated at the fever hospital, from which the incarcerated children could only wave at their families on the other side of the road. All her clothes at home were burnt and the incarceration lasted for six weeks, which seemed a lifetime to a small child. Sometimes the isolation was reversed: another woman remembers her mother being taken to the tuberculosis hospital, and they were physically separated for months at an age when the child really did need her mother.

Fred Beard (born about 1877) remembered how you had to get a note from the doctor if you could not go to school. But that sick note cost a shilling – a day's wages for a woman stone-picking in the fields at a time when the family income for a week was less than a pound.

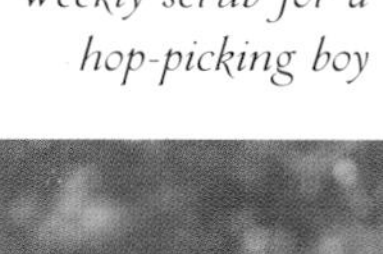

Weekly scrub for a hop-picking boy

SCHOOL

AS SOON AS THE CHILDREN WERE CAPABLE OF WALKING THE DISTANCE, THEY WOULD BE OFF TO SCHOOL IN THE VILLAGE, USUALLY IN GROUPS COMING TOGETHER FROM VARIOUS COTTAGES ALONG THE WAY AND PLAYING AS THEY WENT.

'I BE'ANT NO SCHOLARD,' the old folks would say, meaning that they could neither read nor write. William Cobbett, thundering from his soap box on the subject of cottage economy in the 1820s, said that the very act of growing your own food and raising your own livestock was 'the best possible foundation of *education* of the children of the labourer' and that it would 'teach them a great number of useful things, add greatly to their value when they go forth from their father's home, make them start in life with all possible advantages, and give them the best chance of leading happy lives. And, is it not much more rational for parents to be employed in teaching their children how to cultivate a garden, to feed and rear animals, to make bread, beer, bacon, butter, and cheese, and to be able to do these things for themselves, or for others, than to leave them to prowl about the lanes and commons or to mope at the heels of some crafty, sleek-headed pretended saint, who while he extracts the last penny from their pockets, bids them be contented with their misery, and promises them, in exchange for their pence, everlasting glory in the world to come?'

Cobbett, ever practical, did not have much time for those who preached that all labours and exertions in this world were in vain. Indeed, by diligence, industry, care, skill and excellence, a parent could rise from his present station, and his children would rise further, so that 'by and by, the descendants of the present labourer become gentlemen'. The duty of parents was to give their children book-learning, but not until they had first 'taken care to make them capable of earning their living by bodily labour. When that object has once been secured, the other may, if the ability remain, be attended to. But, I am wholly against children wasting their time in the idleness of what is called *education*; and particularly in schools over which the parents have no control, and where nothing is taught

Musical chairs at Wavendon Church Sunday School (near Milton Keynes) with the parson playing the fiddle

but the rudiments of servility, pauperism and slavery. ... Education means breeding up, bringing up, or rearing up; and nothing more. This includes every thing with regard to the mind as well as the body of the child; but, of late years, it has been so used as to have no sense applied to it but that of book-learning, with which, nine times out of ten, it has nothing at all to do.' He was disgusted that the aim of education seemed to be to give children enough book-learning for them to live upon the labour of others instead of their own. Polemic or what?

Cobbett apart, book-learning is what schools taught. Most country parents in the nineteenth century agreed with Cobbett and felt that their children would learn much more of value by working in the fields or at the family's cottage industry, contributing to their income, than sitting at a school desk learning by rote. The farmers agreed too: children should be available on demand to help with the harvest and haymaking, sheep-shearing and poultry-plucking, not glued to their books in a dusty school room, growing pale out of the sun.

'Education means breeding up, bringing up, or rearing up; and nothing more ...'

school

Class at a village school in the 1930s

'...and oh, what dire penalties there were if you arrived with dirty shoes or boots, despite the fact that you had been walking miles along the muddy lanes and fields to get to school.'

IN EARLY VICTORIAN TIMES, school was voluntary and for most village children that meant no school. Villages were free to choose whether or not they would have a school, and if so what sort of a school and how it should be run. It was not until 1876 that attendance at what were still voluntary schools became compulsory, and it was not until 1891 that free education (no more paying your school pence – a penny or tuppence a week to attend and twice that if you failed to turn up) became available to all, up to the age of fourteen.

In Scotland, which has often been ahead of England and Wales in education, the Reverend John Steward reported on the parishes of Blair-Atholl and Strowan in 1845 in his contribution to the *Statistical Account of Scotland* that described every parish: 'The Gaelic is the language of the country. There are few, however, under thirty years of age who cannot read, write and speak the English language. The manners of the people, as well as their dress, resemble those of their low-country neighbours, and no power can resist the assimilation of their language. ... Schools are more numerous, newspapers are abundant, and general knowledge is more widely diffused.'

Finally, the 1902 Education Act put the seal on it, with the State taking control of local education so

LOCAL DIALECTS

By 1890, schools were already frowning on the use of local dialects, and there were the beginnings of the loss of the rich vocabulary of old. Since 1870, children had been reprimanded for slipping into dialect at school and in Wiltshire they were told to 'ta'ak oop and vurget their mother tongue' – except that the teacher would have pronounced this instruction in clipped tones. Who was to say what the 'right' language was? Many dialect words had been used for centuries before 'proper' words came into being – words like 'chimbley' instead of 'chimney', 'turmut' rather than 'turnip', and so many more. How are you supposed to know a person's roots (no pun intended) if they all speak 'correct' English? A huge number of children's words for this and that started to be lost from the playground – phrases like 'I ballows that', 'Barley me that', 'Pike I'; words like coggy, shigs, laggy, croggies, screase, scribs, mardy and spahs. Why drum them out? Why couldn't they all be bilingual? The language became greatly impoverished when there were no longer a thousand different ways to call someone a fool. Keep correct English for the written page; but don't lose the spoken dialect. Of course, even Victorian strictness couldn't keep language wholly in its place; children, and adults, continued to create new words and always will do.

school

that everybody had to conform. No longer could children take the day off because the travelling circus was coming through the village or there was a local farm sale to be enjoyed; no longer was the farming calendar the dominant one. Timetables and term times applied to town and country alike, and children could not be released from their desks to help in the fields. In theory, the employment of children in agriculture had been regulated since the 1870s anyway, but in practice it was a different matter in the villages and even the village worthies often felt that children benefited from starting work very young, as young as seven, much more so than going to school.

But to school you had to go, sitting on hard planks with nothing to lean back against, scraping a pencil across a slate or scratching away with an inky nib, dashing across the yard to stinking earth closets when nature called, shivering with cold in the class room unless you were next to the stove, which steamed, being draped with everybody's wet clothes – and oh, what dire penalties there were if you arrived with dirty shoes or boots, despite the fact that you had been walking miles along the muddy lanes and fields to get to school.

Lessons were basically the three Rs and the parson's scripture class; later you might learn a little history and geography, needlework and basic science; in the villages you would probably learn something more relevant to your life as well – nature, weather, agriculture, practical gardening and poultry-keeping. In the early twentieth century practical lessons included handicrafts, cooking, laundry, butter-making and woodwork, but the range was hardly adequate to meet Cobbett's ideals.

Harry Rapley started going to school in 1905 and right from his first day he walked two miles there and two miles back again. Doreen Styles remembers that the playground was separated: the boys didn't play with the girls and there was a wooden fence between them. Rosa Ratcliff, born in 1909, remembers walking to school along a main road that was so quiet they ran along the middle of it. They would usually stop along the way to play with the goats that were kept on the common. There was a coke stove that they called the 'donkey' to warm them up in winter and there were coal fires in each class room. At dinner time they would unpack their sandwiches (most of the children had walked quite a long way to school) and watch the big mill wheel turning, the water rushing down the slip; farmers would bring their corn to be ground. Her village was a farming one and most of the lads went on the farms as soon as they left school, or took up gardening. In the holidays the children would cycle to the common and play hide and seek among the trees.

Herbert Bannister shared a school allotment with an older boy The school would always break up at midday on Fair Day for the summer

'Lessons were basically the three Rs and the parson's scripture class ...'

SCHOOL PUNISHMENT

School punishments were usually beating, detention, black marks or standing in the corner. Many a village school's old punishment books record the stroke of the cane, generally on the hands, for what today might seem petty misdemeanours – careless work, dirty hands, 'idleness during singing', 'running out of lines', being cheeky, not paying attention, dawdling into school after the bell had rung and so on. Before the First World War, one poor young lad simply could not read out the word 'signed' properly; he always pronounced it 'sig-ned', which was perfectly logical. Eventually his teacher's patience snapped and the boy was 'caned on the bum'. His mother was furious and marched round to the school to tell the teacher exactly what she thought of the punishment, loudly and threatening violence. In the 1870s the master of a village school in Oxfordshire was summoned before the magistrates and charged with excessively beating a small girl but the case was dismissed as she had evidence of only one stripe of the cane across the shoulders 'although she swore she had four'.

BELOW Hamming it up at Chilton Foliat in Wiltshire. School punishments were not really so extreme!

school

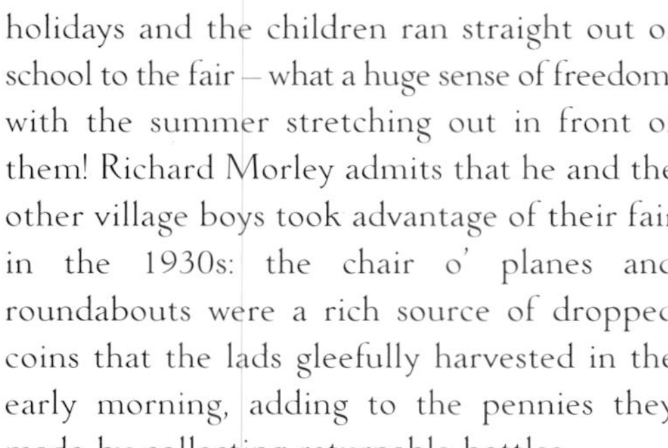

'The schoolroom had two rows of desks, then a screen to separate them from another class ...'

holidays and the children ran straight out of school to the fair – what a huge sense of freedom, with the summer stretching out in front of them! Richard Morley admits that he and the other village boys took advantage of their fair in the 1930s: the chair o' planes and roundabouts were a rich source of dropped coins that the lads gleefully harvested in the early morning, adding to the pennies they made by collecting returnable bottles.

The school in the small Wiltshire village of Biddestone was built soon after 1844, the year in which a piece of land was conveyed as the site of a school and schoolhouse. The exact date of building is unknown, but it was clearly well established by the time of the first Log Books in 1873. Six years later there were more than sixty pupils, and at some stages in its history the numbers rose into the low hundreds. However, if there were more than 108 pupils the children had to take turns to attend, as there simply wasn't room for all of them. In 1884 several children were 'obliged to go to Hartham on Thursdays for soup' (there was no explanation in the Log Book as to why this was so, but perhaps a charity was involved). In that year, the timetable for one term was:

Lessons in the fresh air

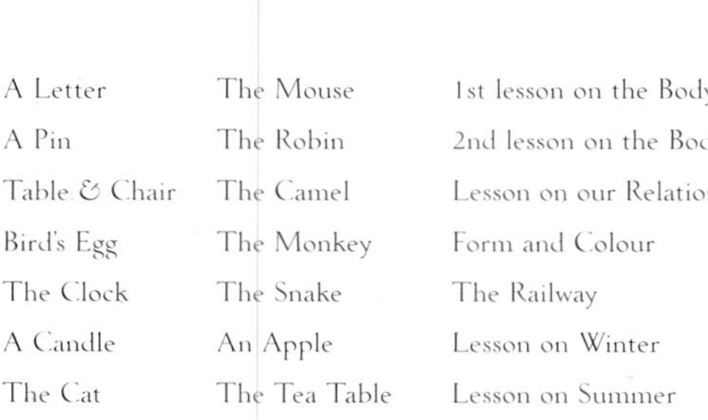

A Letter	The Mouse	1st lesson on the Body
A Pin	The Robin	2nd lesson on the Body
Table & Chair	The Camel	Lesson on our Relations
Bird's Egg	The Monkey	Form and Colour
The Clock	The Snake	The Railway
A Candle	An Apple	Lesson on Winter
The Cat	The Tea Table	Lesson on Summer

Alan Hayes attended Biddestone school in the very early years of the twentieth century, when the schoolroom had two rows of desks, then a screen to separate them from another class with its own two rows of desks, and so on. This was typical of village schools, many of which were simply one large room in which children of all ages were taught, the older ones often taking their turn in teaching the younger.

Village schools have suffered over the years, with instructions from on high altering the curriculum, dictating how the school should be run and the lessons taught, and closing down schools because numbers have dropped too low. The loss of a village school can tear the heart out of the place; no wonder people have fought so hard to keep their schools. At times teachers have come close to despair. In the 1960s a primary school at North Kelsey in Lincolnshire expressed its frustrations: the eleven-plus was about to be abolished, comprehensive education was coming to nearby Caistor and schools were likely to be reorganised into age groups that would probably sound the death knell for many village schools. Primary schools were being asked to incorporate many new subjects and teaching techniques (there were mutterings about the Initial Teaching Alphabet and 'new' maths) but if they did so something else would have to go. The parents and the rest of the community, as they always do for village schools, were still busily raising money and supplying voluntary labour for the extras, particularly swimming pools, but there were limits. Catchment areas were growing and there were justified fears that there would soon be no difference between rural schools and urban schools.

Flora Thompson, born in 1876 and writing her *Country Calendar* in the 1920s when living in Liphook, Hampshire, came up with the notion of appointing the school children of parishes to be local historians. 'What a multitude of little regarded facts, likely to be intensely interesting to future generations, those small, sharp eyes would note.' They would mark the passing of local landmarks – trees, tumbledown cottages and stories connected with them; they would report on village events and national celebrations; they would tell of weather, of wildlife, of work in the fields, of the planting of new woodland and the making of ponds; they would mention famous people who had passed through, or of their own villagers who had become famous elsewhere. She ended her fantasy as follows: 'It would make interesting reading for the people of the year 2,000, this "New Domesday Book; or Every Parish its Own History".'

FUN & GAMES

In 1908 Baden-Powell published the first edition of Scouting for Boys. Scouting was born in the days of Empire (as the handbook of the period strongly reflects) and Baden-Powell wished to foster an interest in 'Nature Study and Woodcraft'. 'We want to make the boy feel that he is a young backwoodsman and not an imitation soldier – still less a nonentity who does not count,' said 'Bee-Pea' in 1918.

Hand-turned rural merry-go round

He had already created a junior branch of the movement – the Wolf Cubs (ages 8 to 12), about which he said: 'The prevalence of Juvenile Crime among boys between the ages of ten and twelve shows that propensities are then already forming, and points to the need of shaping their characters at an earlier age than that of Scouts' (who were aged 11 to 18). He then instituted the Senior Scouts for the over-18s 'in sympathy with the changing psychology of the adolescent' and to retain the older boy 'under the good influences of the movement at the critical time of his life just when boyhood's pastimes cease to appeal and manhood's temptations are upon him'. He pointed out that scouting could be carried out in the towns just as well as in the country, and for many town boys scouting was their introduction to the countryside. The girls were not forgotten: the Girl Guide movement was only a little younger than the Scouting movement.

The range of self-made entertainments for country children seemed endless, as did their imaginations. There was an unbroken tradition of games, for a start, many of them with their own seasons for no apparent reason: skipping games, hopscotch, clapping games, ball-catching games, tag in all its complex variations, hide-and-seek, blind man's buff, grandmother's footsteps, leapfrog, trip-cat, king of the castle, sticky knife, baste the bear, war games, singing or nonsense rhyming games, cobble boobies, hatty, mud-flicking – there were so many simple ways of making use of the playground. In the

'The range of self-made entertainments for country children seemed endless, as did their imaginations.'

fun & games

Lake District in the 1880s they were playing chivy, with 'dens' at opposite corners of the village crossroads; or cosolary, with someone standing in the middle of the square trying to catch people as they sprinted past; or 'ickly ackly aiko', which involved hurling a ball over a cowshed between teams; or the elaborate rituals of minny cuddy, which seemed to involve boys clambering up on top of each other in pyramids and chanting their gang chants. Knucklebones and spillikins, marbles and conkers, tiddlywinks and spinning tops, hoops for bowling and horseshoes for tossing, mock hockey played with hedgerow sticks and walking-sticks, football and cricket if you could find a patch of green to play on, and scrapping, of course – every evening, the village would be loud with the high-pitched sound of children playing.

Then there were the sports days, at bank holidays or on other special occasions. School was school, but its rigours were occasionally broken with high days and holidays – teas at the manor house with Punch and Judy shows and races (you could win a penny for coming in third), May Day parades, jubilee and coronation celebrations. These were always occasions for stuffing yourself with food but they were primarily for joining in various activities. There might be 'catch the train' races, in which there were piles of clothes and you had to run and put on first your socks, then run and put on your pants, then on to the next heap to find your shirt and put it on, finishing up with your shoes and racing for the finishing line to be not just first but also the best dressed. There was 'tilt the bucket', in which someone sat in a barrow with a long pole with a bucket full of water on the end of it, and they had to get the bucket through a hole without spilling the water. There were wheelbarrow races, egg-and-spoon races, sack races (so easy to cheat if you knew how) and three-legged races (so easy to fall over if you didn't know how).

Cubs and scouts beat the drum …

And all that freedom to roam the countryside too – it was quite impossible for any country child to be bored. Today, when they have mountain bikes, skateboards, trips to swimming pools and skating rinks, and endless access to television and computer games, the kids complain of boredom and hang around the village hall looking for trouble. Strange, that.

John Moore, writing evocatively about his childhood in the late nineteenth century in a village he chose to mask with the name of Brensham, described how the only commodities of interest to him and his friends in the village shop were huge tiger-striped bull's-eyes which could be used as marbles, and thick square-sectioned elastic for their catapults. For the latter, they first had to persuade the shopkeeper that they would only be shooting at empty tin-cans and bottles; she would always lecture them on shooting at living things. 'If you hit a poor little fluffy bird with a stone you might hurt it *very badly*,' she would say, while the boys tried to look solemn and at the

A COUNTRY PRANK

There was all this and playing pranks – simple things like tying a pin to one end of a reel of black cotton and a heavy button a little further along, then secretly sticking the pin into a cottage window frame, reeling out the cotton while retreating across the field, and manipulating the button so that it kept going 'tink, tink, tink' against the window pane, irritating the occupants considerably.

fun & games

same time fingered the notches on the catapults in their pockets. Her strong black 'cattie-lackey' was just the job for what they really had in mind. Then off they would scatter, out of the village and up the hill past the last cottage, inhabited by 'Goaty Pegleg', who had a wooden leg and a long beard and kept a long-bearded billy goat in his garden. The old man always seemed to be leaning on the gate at the end of the lane and usually was in good enough humour to open it for the boys so that they could explore the wilderness of rough furze-bush fields leading to the old limestone quarries and their magic jungle of scrub woodland. Here they would hunt with butterfly nets, catapults and rabbit-snares, though the creatures they caught were usually imaginary ones. They saw merlins and goldcrests that were real; they saw grass-snakes, slow-worms, lizards and adders (even a blue-bellied one); they saw the fallow deer that belonged to the 'Mad Lord' – and once they saw 'the Mad Lord himself, only he looked neither mad nor a lord. He was disappointingly dressed in an old jacket and breeches which would have been moderately becoming upon a scarecrow' and he was tittuping along on a decrepitly ancient and skinny grey mare. The boys opened the gate into the larch plantation for him and he searched his pocket for pennies but found none, giving them instead a slow, gentle smile. They raised their caps, as they thought was fitting, and to their surprise he swept off his own battered hat in return.

All of that was the nineteenth century; the richness of local characters seems to have vanished since, along with the richness of the wildlife and the emptiness of the roads. Looking back to childhood in the 1950s, Valerie Grove claimed to be one of the 'last generation to experience what the young of today have never known: empty roads without yellow lines'. She and her contemporaries went on to recall farthings and three penny bits, stay-at-home mothers, free school milk, beetle drives and spelling bees, Sunday drives for pleasure, having just one pair of lace-up leather shoes and one pair of Clark's sandals (your foot was measured in that spooky X-ray machine) and black wellies, gob-stoppers, cold rooms, bucket-and-spade seaside holidays in your own country, freedom to roam without molestation, skipping games in the middle of car-free roads, the invention of fish fingers, rationed sweets (children stampeded to their local sweet shop when rationing was finally ended in February 1953), wind-up gramophones, snogging in the back row of the cinema, getting tiny samples of pink lipstick through the post from Yardley's – the experiences of country children were rapidly becoming identical to those in towns, and they shared their crazes.

COUNTRY COURTESY

John Moore highlighted another courtesy that has long since disappeared. Along a lane in the village were lots of very small cottages which belonged to the Colonel, who owned a farm at the top of the lane. Whenever the Colonel passed by sedately on his motor bike, all the little girls from the cottages would curtsy to him, bobbing as they clutched their print frocks at the hem. The Colonel's blue eyes would twinkle and he would wave back, somewhat endangering his own stability on his chugging machine. Young Moore was just as respectful, he would tug hard at the peak of his school cap as the Colonel went by.

WORK

UNDER THE OLD POOR LAWS, SMALL CHILDREN FROM THE WORKHOUSE WERE APPRENTICED TO FARMERS. IF THEY WERE LUCKY, THEY WERE WELL LOOKED AFTER AND RECEIVED A GOOD TRAINING IN AGRICULTURE. OTHERWISE THEY WERE NO MORE THAN SLAVE LABOUR. IN THE EIGHTEENTH AND EARLY NINETEENTH CENTURIES CHILDREN AS YOUNG AS SIX WORKED ON THE FARMS.

'Many children resented school as much as their parents and employers did, and welcomed their "duty" to escape from it to help with haymaking ...'

WILLIAM COBBETT, born in 1762, remembered being employed 'from an early age' as a bird-scarer. Soon he was weeding wheat and leading a horse to harrow the barley. Next he graded up to hoeing peas and finally attained the 'honour' of joining the harvest reapers, driving the horse team and guiding the plough. His father would boast that William's eldest brother at the age of fifteen 'did as much work as any three men in the parish'.

Although in some villages and in individual families the children might run riot, in many villages there seemed to be a general essence of home discipline that inculcated the work ethic. A farm labourer's young lads would have a good wash before the family meal and then stand in an obedient row until grace had been said, not sitting at the table until they were bid. In the nineteenth century they might have eaten off wooden trenchers if the family could not afford crockery, and the 'pudden' would be boiled in a cloth, not a basin – it would be a wholesome mixture of meat and vegetables wrapped in suet crust and each child would be given a helping of pastry, vegetables and gravy; the meat was kept for the next day.

Many children resented school as much as their parents and employers did, and welcomed their 'duty' to escape from it to help with haymaking and harvest, when all the village turned out to work hard but also have fun in each other's company. There was a buzz, a great sense of the importance of getting in the crop, the culmination of the growing year. In Wiltshire some of the boys had the thrill of the annual all-day cattle drive, a twenty-mile round trip through the villages to the market at Chippenham and back again, with all the excitement of rounding up animals along the way.

The labourer's children described by Richard Jefferies in the 1870s had their future mapped out for them almost from birth. On leaving school the boy would find immediate farmwork on the same farm as his father, or one close by, and his wage by then would actually make a difference to the family's income. Times were good for agriculture (for a while) and farm labourers could find work and good wages easily. The young began to travel in search of both, not just from village to village as of old but further afield, even to other countries. All over Britain they would turn their hand to other labouring jobs – find a spell of well-paid navvying on the railways, perhaps – and were not particularly interested in settling down with a wife and family yet awhile.

When they did so, it might well be with a girl from a different parish, even a different county, not known in their own village. The

HOUSEHOLD CHORES

Not all the work was done for employers. There were many jobs that children had to do at home – chopping firewood, digging potatoes, fetching in the coal, carrying water from the well, cleaning the rust from cutlery, looking after the babies and toddlers while mum worked elsewhere, pegging out the goats, milking the house cow, feeding the pig, scavenging for kindling and more, and possibly being boxed round the ears if you did your chores sloppily.

work

old ways of marrying within a small circle of families you had known all your life were vanishing quite fast, and the old allegiance to your own village was weakening.

The girls at that stage went less and less into the fields, though they might help their parents at harvest (payment was by the acre, and extra hands speeded up the rate of production). Girls were generally destined for domestic service, and most of them by this period wanted to find jobs in the town, not in the farmhouse and particularly not in the dairy. Farmers' wives complained that they could only get young girls, mere children, whose mothers wanted them to have early experience of a servant's work; the farmer's wife would teach them the basics but of course they would leave as soon as she had done so, and she would begin all over again with another youngster, or perhaps a slow-witted girl who could find no other work, or a girl who also had to look after an invalid at home or her own illegitimate child.

Aiming for the towns, country girls of the 1870s had begun to dress 'as flashily as servants in cities, and stand upon their dignity'. Jefferies was quietly amused, and also thought that one effect was to reduce the rate of illegitimate births: the girls had more self-respect than of old and were perhaps wiser in the ways of the world. They began to marry out; the men they met when in service in the town were earning far better wages than the farm labourers at home and were more 'refined', whether working as footmen grooms, artisans or general workmen.

When the girls first went into service, their cottage background was an obstacle that their employer had to overcome: they needed plenty of training if they had not already been through the hands of the farmer's wife. Mind you, should a girl choose to return to cottage life after marriage, she found her work a lot harder than it had been in service, because it was endless. Even Jefferies recognised that the lot of the agricultural labourer's wife was harder than that of her husband and that a woman's work was never finished. 'When the man reaches home he does not care, or will not turn his hand to anything, except, perhaps, to fetch a pail of water, and he is not well pleased if asked to do that.'

ABOVE LEFT
Domestic service often started at an early age

ABOVE RIGHT
Puddling clay (and note his belt)

LEFT
Coming home with the team

ONE OF THE MEN

C.H. Middleton was one of the many boys who still managed to duck out of school for a week in the 1830s to be in the fields at four in the morning to help with haymaking. He loved to think of himself as a man then, dressing in heavy hobnail boots (thoroughly practical in hayfields full of thistles!), donning a felt hat with a cord round it, and carrying his straw-and-canvas beaver bag or dinner basket full of man-sized hunks of bread, cheese and fat bacon to be cut up with a heavy pocket knife, just like the real men did. 'During that time too, although it often came more natural to run than to walk, I would adopt a steady and dignified gait with my toes turned out, and feel myself a man among men.'

work

By the 1920s schoolboys were no longer automatically taking part in harvest and haymaking, though they were more than happy to earn pocket money after school within the restrictions of the new laws about child work. They could deliver milk and groceries, for example. Children no longer went gleaning with their mothers, but they could still join their fathers under a hedge for tea at haymaking or help him on his allotment.

Chopping mangolds

MOVING ON

The problem of the young leaving the villages is far from being a new one. During the early years of the industrial revolution they left in their droves, seeking better opportunities in manufacturing than they could find in farming. The problem has persisted for generations. In the 1930s, F.G. Thomas said it was important to discover what it was that attracted the young to the towns. 'Any youth will gladly accept an opportunity of escape. In this he is supported by practically the whole village of younger people, the "mobile generation".' It began in the village school, with every head seeing the winning of scholarships as being the crowning achievement, putting a child on the first rung of the educational ladder to 'secondary school and the "black-coated" professions'. The brighter the rural child, the more likely it was that they would be pressed to aim for training colleges and university, preferably to become teachers themselves and preferably teachers in a major urban area. That was where the bright lights went and were.

'The brighter the rural child, the more likely it was that they would be pressed to aim for training colleges and university.'

In the village schools only one or two would ever win a scholarship. The best of the rest might aspire to become office clerks or garage mechanics; the others would be encouraged to take a job working on the land. Everything was designed to encourage children to believe that towns were vastly superior to the country, and most teachers and parsons had urban backgrounds or tendencies anyway. Surely in town, where there were pavements and street lighting, indoor toilets and bathrooms, cinemas and shops, there must be far greater opportunities for making a good living than in the materially poorer countryside, even if in the country you might pay very little rent for your cottage and be able to offset costs by growing or catching your own food. Above all, there was a certain snobbery: townsfolk were deemed to be more sophisticated and worldly than clod-hopping farm boys! It was hardly surprising that the young villagers of the 1930s were on the move, by bike, by motor bike, by whatever means they could find. They would travel some miles to get to monthly meetings of the Young Farmers' Clubs, especially those of neighbouring villages, where they could meet *new* people of their own age.

Teenagers have always said that there is 'nothing to do' in the country, and for many that may be so. In a 1998 Rural Development Commission report on young people in rural areas it was found that lack of transport caused enormous problems, especially as so few villages had their own social and sporting amenities or opportunities for further education, training and employment. Many of the young in rural areas expressed feelings of insecurity, isolation and loneliness as well as boredom and in an increasing number of villages there was fear, too: the vices of the

work

towns were making unwelcome inroads – drinking, drugs, vandalism and more, generally feeding on boredom and a degree of alienation, especially where incomers to the village seem automatically to be suspicious of the young and quick to complain about them.

Living in a small community means that everybody has their eye on you, benignly or with hostility. It also means that your pool of friends is limited and quite intense, unless you have independent transport to widen it. (In the RDC report, it was noticeable that teenagers seemed to expect motorised transport. Getting on your bike, which was the great escape vehicle for their grandparents and great grandparents, was not considered as an option.) Within a small circle of friends, a falling-out with one person can lead to ostracism by the rest of the group, and that is when the loneliness of village life can really set in; that, and the age-old system of gangs, except that in past times the gangs would have only inter-village rivalry. Then, they were proud of their own village; now they might lose their identity with it and even turn against it.

Vandalism is certainly increasing, and some villages are taking very constructive steps to tackle it. For example, at Upper Beeding in Sussex they dealt with playground vandalism with a multi-pronged approach. First they found other things for the kids to do, as they believed that vandalism was bred by boredom. The parish council established and paid for evening classes and extra-mural lessons for primary school children in interesting activities such as gymnastics, playing the accordion, swimming, cross-country running and chess. Then they decided to involve children directly in parish affairs, getting them to open a new bypass, a new school extension and a new adventure playground.

Finally they told the children that the playground was not just for their amusement; it belonged to them and they must be its guardians, with responsibility for ensuring that their own children in due course would still have its benefits. And it worked. Other parishes make sure that the young are consulted on parish matters – and that their views are not just heard but also acted upon. Thus the young feel that they matter in their own village, and are more likely to take care of it.

Time and time again, in villages all over the country, teenagers are saying that there is nowhere for them to go in their own villages. All too often the youth club is beneath them and its age range too wide; there are no informal meeting places for them simply to be rather than do, or to do what they like when they like; and they move away to experience life in the towns and cities. They cannot find anywhere to live independently in their home villages or nearby – rents and property prices are way beyond their means. But very often the young who do escape come back again later to raise their own children in a rural environment, so that the whole cycle starts again.

Potato picking – back-breaking work even for youngsters

Young Farmers' Club supper at Trewithian, Cornwall

7
Country Animals

DO COUNTRY CHILDREN still poddle about in puddles to see what they can find? Do they still collect frogspawn from the ponds? Probably, but far less so than of old, partly because there are fewer children living in the countryside and also because there are fewer ponds and hence fewer frogs to spawn in them. Farm ponds are drained and ploughed in; village ponds become dumping places for anonymous rubbish or so full of bread-fed ducks and dumped pet terrapins that tadpoles are wiped out; ancient ponds once in the middle of nowhere vanish under new housing estates. Many other aspects of habitat erosion add to the decline as well, including mass squashings on the roads that frogs and toads continue to cross on their way to their traditional breeding ponds, innocently unafraid of the vehicles that are the new predators. Do children still tickle minnows and catch sticklebacks? Maybe, but the streams are more likely to have been polluted and the life throttled out of them by over-enrichment with run-offs of agricultural fertilisers and escaped silage effluent, or by industrial mishaps that leak chemicals into the waterways, or by road-salt or a build-up from household detergents; not to mention insidious contamination by hormones and drug residues (particularly antibiotics) as a result of the convenience of domestic plumbing. We are all guilty.

WILDLIFE

The population sizes and species richness of birds in the countryside fluctuate but the trend seems to be downwards. This is likely to be due largely to changes in agricultural practice, especially the relatively recent habit of planting winter rather than spring grain crops, so that the stubble is ploughed and re-seeded almost as soon as the harvest has been taken rather than being left for the birds over the winter.

'... many more farmers are sacrificing part of what are already minimal profits in order to protect wildlife and the landscape itself.'

RIGHT
Swallows and their young

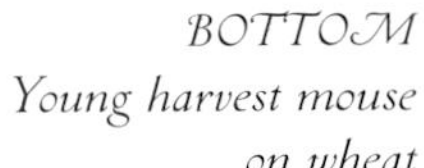

BOTTOM
Young harvest mouse on wheat

In tandem with the hugely increased efficiency of harvesting, which leaves very little to be gleaned anyway, winter pickings are poor indeed for the many seed-eating bird species that were once so common. Add to that the widespread use of pesticides that kill or poison the insects on which so many birds rely, and herbicides that wipe out the field-margin weeds where those insects once sheltered and fed, it is little wonder that many arable and even pasture fields are now silent.

The modern practice of making silage rather than hay adds to the problem, as silage is cut much earlier in the year and a silage field may be harvested twice or even three times or more in quite quick succession, making the field a restless and dangerous place for the leverets and fawns that seek to lie low in the grass and an impossible habitat for wildflowers and native grass species, which have no chance to set seed and reproduce themselves. Thoughtless hedge-cutting is another factor, whether by its timing that robs birds and small rodents of hedgerow fruits in the early winter or by its over-tidiness that deprives them of shelter, or for too long the practice of grubbing out hedgerows altogether to make fields big enough for increasingly huge machinery. The blame cannot be laid on the farmers: they increase their efficiency at the request of the rest of us who demand more food at lower prices. Again, we are all guilty.

There are roundabouts to set against these destructive swings. Above all, many more farmers are sacrificing part of what are already minimal profits in order to protect wildlife and the landscape itself. After all, they live there themselves and the majority have always cared for their surroundings – much more so than they are given credit for. (It would be fair to make comparisons with other businesses. How many manufacturers and service providers, whether mammoth corporations or small businesses, are prepared to put environment

wildlife

above profits? Think of the look of the buildings, the use of finite resources, the contribution to pollution by exhaust fumes and so much more. Farmers have the disadvantage that their factory floor and their work are out in the open for all to see.)

As for the rest of us, more and more people are putting out food for birds in their own gardens, whether they live in town or country, and thus many gardens are becoming refuges for the birds – provided they don't fall prey to the curse of all wildlife: the domestic cat. More and more people are creating ponds in their gardens, too, but many of those ponds are harsh towards the wild amphibians and pond invertebrates that would seek to use them, and many of those gardens are just too tidy to give food and shelter to wildlife. Even country gardeners are changing old habits and cleaning up every corner of their gardens, and even country gardeners are following the trend for carpeting large areas of their soil with patios, paving, decking and other hard surfaces that are barriers between blackbirds and their worms and gradually prevent the land itself from breathing.

Keeping up with the urban Joneses also removes habitats for small wild mammals such as hedgehogs and mice, and again road traffic takes a heavy toll on the former while domestic cats have a field day with the latter. Moles that have the temerity to heave up their soil heaps in the midst of too-trim lawns (lawn-mowing – what a waste of good grazing!) are ruthlessly exterminated; harmless grass-snakes are perceived to be venomous and promptly hit on the head; affable and intriguing animals such as bats 'terrify' people and are forced out of the roofspaces that have been their homes for generations; house martins and swallows are 'dirty' (how dare they leave droppings on the family car?) and their nest-making on the artificial cliffs of house walls is deliberately prevented; starlings and sparrows can find no access to the sealed eaves for nest-building and roosting.

Water voles (beloved 'Ratty' in Wind in the Willows) *are fast disappearing from country riverbanks*

RIGHT TO ROAM

Humans no longer tolerate the idea of sharing their homes or their land with other creatures, as quite recently they did; yet they insist that all other species allow humans to go where they will. Right to roam? Ask the doe trying to find a safe place to leave her fawn; ask the wild ducks nesting by the once-peaceful stream; ask the woodland badgers whose ancient setts are no longer secret and secluded; ask the moorland birds brooding their young amid the trampled heather. Ask any wild creature that seeks somewhere safe and private in which to live its life.

Rural hedgehog numbers are declining from a combination of road accidents and loss of habitat

wildlife

PESTS

RIGHT
Many cottagers kept caged wild birds, usually songbirds but often larger birds, such as jays, that were good mimics

Country people, living cheek by jowl with wildlife, have always sought to keep 'pest' species under a degree of control, but they are the first to be horrified at the thought of a countryside with no moving creatures in it other than humans and their chosen domestic animals. It will be a silent, empty, lifeless place. Countless older folk remark on how, when they were children, there were so many more birds, so many more butterflies, so many more of everything in the countryside. Where *have* all the flowers gone?

Jenny wren

Well, at least today's country dwellers do not still send gangs of boys out for the sport of wrenning, or set horsehair nooses to catch the bullfinches that peck at their orchard buds, or trap songbirds with birdlime and nets to make sparrow and blackbird pie. The eating of songbirds was often of necessity in poorer cottages; it was nothing like the continental sport of shooting anything that flies although in 1854 a correspondent wrote in *The Field* as follows:

> *I shot at a small bird with an air-gun last year out of a particular window. The bird was sitting on an iron fence; the bullet struck the hurdle and glanced back, and hit the window-sill close to myself and a friend who was sitting by me. We immediately put down the air-gun and resumed our bottle of port; a much more safe and agreeable pastime than playing with bullets.*

'So many species are on the wane, or have already vanished locally. It seems that even the grasshoppers and crickets are quieter and fewer now.'

Country families would catch live birds and put them in cages by the door for the sake of their sweet singing; this was quite common among cottagers, who also kept captive corvids for their mimicry, much as people keep parrots today.

Pigeon pie was another favourite. In 1854 somebody shot a wood-pigeon and examined its crop, which contained 937 grains of wheat and 94 tares. Farmers had good reason to control wood-pigeons, and still do. Some tried to keep pigeons away from pea crops by firing hard peas at them 'to make them smart', or by hanging up 'in effigy one or two of their own species' to warn them off. The expert who recommended this also said that larks should be shot 'by a good marksman' whenever they were seen in late-sown wheat fields; sparrows were 'the most injurious vermin of the feathered race, the most voracious and prolific' and should be netted in winter and their eggs and young destroyed in the breeding season, 'to effect which, some parishes or villages give a bounty of so much per dozen upon their eggs, and a higher bounty upon their heads'. This was in about 1800; there was still a bounty on sparrows during the First World War in some counties.

FOXES & BADGERS

Foxes are something else and attitudes towards them in the country are conflicting. On the one hand, they are hunted on horseback and are also accused by farmers and poultry keepers of all manner of devious deeds. Foxes

RIGHT
The Countess of Wessex with her tame badger at Lydstep House

tend to take whatever comes easiest in the way of food, and their tastes are catholic. Even those who suffer from their predations will sometimes admit to admiring this elusive and clever opportunist. The rest of us love to hear those strange night-calls and to see a russety fox slinking softly through the meadows, though in fact foxes are now more likely to be spotted in towns than in the country.

There are also different attitudes to badgers, especially among dairy farmers who have been told that there is a link between badgers and the tuberculosis that they so dread finding in their cows. Unlike foxes, badgers are rarely accused by country people of pilfering, though these very strong animals can barge in wherever they please and have been seen stealing eggs, sweetcorn and other delicacies. They also dig up your garden looking for leatherjackets, leaving the grass looking like a First World War battlefield.

SQUIRRELS

Squirrels, too, arouse mixed emotions. Foresters detest them for the damage they do; people who feed garden birds also sometimes detest them for stealing the bird food, but cannot help admiring them for the skill with which they do so. Red squirrels have lived in Britain for several thousand years, though they became extinct in Ireland for four centuries until reintroduced in the early nineteenth and their numbers dropped dramatically in Wales and Scotland in the fifteenth and sixteenth centuries, largely due to deforestation; in fact they were all but extinct in Scotland by the eighteenth century. They dwindled in England for similar reasons but to a lesser extent, and were quick to take advantage of the craze for planting lots of quick-growing conifers from the early nineteenth century. In 1889, the New Forest commissioners shot more than 2,000 red squirrels as pests, and by the 1930s the Highland Squirrel Club boasted that it had destroyed 82,000 red squirrels in thirty years.

So many species are on the wane, or have already vanished locally. It seems that even the grasshoppers and crickets are quieter and fewer now. And at night the sky in many parts of the country is never dark enough to appreciate the gentle glimmer of glow-worms or the spark of fireflies; never dark enough to see the Milky Way in its full glory. When will those towns and cities and motorways turn off their wretched lights? How can today's children ever come as close to nature as their grandparents were? How can they recapture the magic of it all?

BELOW
Red squirrels have been ousted by the alien grey in many parts of Britain

GREY SQUIRRELS

There was worse to come for the native red squirrel. In 1876 someone released two American grey squirrels in a park in Cheshire and over the next fifty years lots of other people followed suit, including, as ever, the owners of Woburn Park (the source of many introductions of species that subsequently escaped and spread in the wild). A combination of competition from these new, bigger American squirrels and overcrowding and disease among the existing reds, topped by much timber felling during the two world wars and some harsh winters, resulted in a drastic reduction in the number of red squirrels, which pulled back to take refuge in Ireland, Wales, Scotland and a few isolated areas in England. Those born in the 1940s and 1950s remember red squirrels in southern England, but there are none now except in the Isle of Wight.

GAME

In many country areas, the birds that have been really on the increase are gamebirds, especially pheasants. They are reared locally in their thousands, from eggs or chicks to young birds ready to fly. And then they are shot. Until well into the eighteenth century, the British only shot birds for the pot and on the ground; their weapons and their skills were not good enough to shoot birds on the wing.

'Poaching now is purely for profit, not for the pot of a family whose stomachs are knotted with hunger.'

GAMEBIRDS

In 1887 tests showed that partridge flew at 32mph and pheasants at 38mph. A year earlier, a covey of partridges had kept pace for 400 yards with an express train travelling at 45mph. In the 1940s, by perhaps more accurate methods, it was estimated that partridge flew at 39–45mph, pheasants at 40–51mph (in short bursts), geese at 42–55mph and wigeon at 50–55mph. So 'shooting flying' was quite a challenge but they learnt and their weapons improved; and then shooting became more of a sport than a pot-filler.

In the 1850s it was said in *The Field* that grouse, to the eye of an experienced sportsman, formed the chief features of a moorland landscape. 'Little does he care for beautiful prospects, rugged hills, or the wild scenery about him. The background of his picture is filled up by a covey of birds; whilst a couple of dogs, with himself and gun, may very conveniently form the foreground.' On 30 August 1888, Lord Walsingham took four Purdey 12-bore breech-loaders with him on to Blubberhouse Moor in the West Riding of Yorkshire. It was 5.12 in the morning when he fired his first shot and killed his first grouse. By the time he came home at 7.30 that evening he had fired 1,550 cartridges and had bagged 1,070 grouse.

In 1900 Lord Walsingham announced that the great bustard, long extinct in Britain, had been reintroduced from the Continent. In a letter to the *Norfolk Chronicle* announcing this fact, Walsingham said: 'It is hoped that the residents in Norfolk and Suffolk will agree to respect the birds.' What he meant was: he hoped that no Tom, Dick or Harry with a cheap gun and probably no gun licence

ABOVE
Retrieving the bird. Lord Normanton and his head keeper with a well-trained Labrador

A RUFFLED SPARROWHAWK

In 1916, in Kent, a bomb had been released from a trench mortar. A sparrowhawk spotted it, wheeled round and made a bee-line for its fleeing prey, attacking it from above and below. Within four seconds of the bomb's release and at an altitude of about 400 yards the missile exploded. The bird, trailing it close behind, escaped with no more than a temporary crumpling, from which it quickly recovered and beat hastily for the safety of nearby woodland to restore its dignity and reflect on the nature of human weaponry.

game

would go and shoot the birds in order to sell them for a few shillings to the nearest 'bird-stuffer'. Poachers beware! Gamebirds belong to the shoot! Not long after, the first of the new bustards was indeed shot.

In the harsh winter of 1708/9, somebody in the Sussex parish of Trotton shot a duck with a silver collar around its neck on which was engraved the arms of the King of Denmark. They ate the duck, and the Rector kept the collar; nobody told the Danes. In the years between 1786 and 1800, wildfowl shooters increased their chances by using seven-barrelled flintlock guns, mostly made by Henry Nock.

In 1848 there was the rare sight of a large sea eagle cruising the skies for several weeks in the Milland valley and roosting in some pollard oaks. Unfortunately the splendid bird grabbed a goose from a nearby farmyard one day and a council of war was declared; an alliance was formed between the farmer, the gamekeeper and the rat-catcher and 'the eagle was denounced'. They set up a trap, baited with a rat. End of eagle. In the nineteenth century in particular, the reaction to an interesting bird always seemed to be to kill it.

Country people are ambivalent about gamebirds. In days gone by, game of all kinds was a source of considerable friction; it 'belonged' to the privileged few, and was denied to the hungry many. George Dew, in the 1870s, wrote angrily: 'The Aristocracy hold game almost as tightly as gold, & every infringement of the game laws is proceeded against with the utmost vigour. The recent Act of Parliament passed for making the carrier of a gun take a yearly licence at a cost of 10/- is nothing but another cord thrown over the poor man to prevent his using a gun for poaching.' As a man whose many roles included that of a Poor Law relieving officer and an inspector of nuisances for the district sanitary authority, he knew more than most about the miseries of the rural poor.

Locals, being more often migrants from the towns than lifelong country dwellers, tend to tolerate rather than enjoy game shooting. Long gone are the days of touching your hat to the local squire and feeling that he had every right to do whatever he wished. Many do still become involved with the shoot, acting as beaters now and then as a good excuse to be out and about in the woods and fields in convivial company. But local people might question the scale of pheasant shooting.

Poacher on the prowl

A SPOT OF POACHING

The modern poacher is a very different story. Poaching now is purely for profit, not for the pot of a family whose stomachs are knotted with hunger. It is big-business poaching, carried out with an appalling ruthlessness. Sometimes you can walk the woods and come across evidence of poaching, often with crossbows (as they are silent) and dogs: you might find a terrified deer lying paralysed by a wound in the spine, quite unable to move, left behind by inept poachers, or you might simply find its guts left behind after disembowelment. Pheasants and other game are taken in large numbers, not just one or two here and there. Gamekeepers are often threatened with violence by what are usually city gangs pillaging in the countryside. There is absolutely nothing romantic about the modern poacher, any more than there is about the badger baiters.

game

WHERE THERE IS NOTHING more than a rough shoot, in which the birds are genuinely wild, albeit fed to some extent, it seems more sporting, more fair to the birds, which are often wily in the extreme. With reared pheasants, on the other hand, the birds have been coddled since birth and are sometimes shot at an age when they are barely able to fly properly and certainly have not yet learnt any of the skills that keep wild birds alive. Then there is the bother (or attraction) of having dozens of semi-tame pheasants invading local gardens, and the noisy intrusion of the shoot day itself, with beaters calling and bashing their sticks against trees and shrubbery, then the volleys of gunfire. Also, many of today's guns are not well versed in the ways of the shoot or of the countryside in general; they are more accustomed to being behind a desk but come out on corporate shoot days. Worst of all is the occasional day let to overseas guns who have little appreciation of the rules of sport in Britain and happily blast away at anything that moves, just as they would at home, including those small songbirds.

'Hares are increasingly rare now, even in places where they were common within living memory ...'

RABBITS & HARES

Birds, reared or not, are not the only game. Rabbits and hares are part of the picture, too. Hares are increasingly rare now, even in places where they were common within living memory, and all the marvellous old superstitions about hares are dying out as well.

Rabbits are not native to Britain and were originally introduced as a source of food; they were kept carefully controlled in warrens and culled when needed. But Britain suited them admirably and they soon ran wild. The profession of warrener persisted into living memory and rabbit meat was a valuable source of lean and wholesome protein.

At the end of the eighteenth century Richard Piers of Blankney, Lincolnshire, held a warren under Charles Chaplin Esquire (verily) and said that on a thousand acres, stocked at two hundred couple per acre, it was 'fair' to kill four thousand rabbits a year; they were sold at £13 per hundred in 1796. In winter the rabbits would be fed with ash boughs, gorse, oat straw, sainfoin and clover hay. The warren was very carefully managed, fenced to keep the rabbits in and with properly made sod banks capped with furze faggots, and could be highly profitable. But these were not just any old rabbits: they were a mixture of the hardy common grey and the more valuable 'silver skin' or 'silver sprig', which seemed to vary in colour from white to black according to the time of year at which they were bred. Skins were valuable: the rabbits would be netted and trapped for killing; then the skins would be carefully cleaned ('a useful woman will do it') and dried over charcoal. For a while silver skins in the choicest colours for the fashion of the time could fetch up to sixteen pence a skin; the problem was to keep up with the vagaries of fashion. Carcasses were much less valuable, mainly because a lot of Lincolnshire farmers were climbing on to the rabbit bandwagon and

Using a ferret to bolt rabbits into the purse-net

game

flooding the market, and also because nearly all the rabbits were killed in the six weeks before Christmas as that was when the skins were in prime condition. Still, Piers used the interesting term of land 'planted with rabbits': they were a crop, not a pest, except when they escaped to maraud a neighbour's crops. A good warrener of the period could earn as much as £35 a year plus a cow, a house and fuel, and on top of that overtime for killing over a sixteen-week period at eighteen shillings a week and other bonuses, bringing in an extra £18 a year.

In Sussex, at the same period, rabbits were described as 'the nuisance of a county; they flourish in proportion to the size of the wastes'. But considerable quantities were sold to London markets from the Horsham and Ashdown forests.

Rabbits are prolific breeders and survivors. In 1788, for example, there were apparently only five rabbits in Australia's Port Jackson; within a century they had overrun the whole continent and between 1914 and 1924 Australia exported 157 million rabbits, quite apart from the number that were eaten or destroyed at home. Those exports finally killed off the British warreners in the 1940s, even in barren sandy places such as Breckland in Suffolk where in the old days warrening had been the chief industry and poachers were hanged. Oddly enough, in the early 1950s the local Elveden estate workers were still lopping branches from the trees and carrying them to starving rabbits in hard winters, while at the same time the estate's owner Lord Iveagh was spending large sums to keep the very same rabbits off his farmland. Yes, they were a pest on the farm, but extermination disturbs the balance of nature and, anyway, rabbit meat had proved its worth during the war. It might be needed again.

By the 1950s, rabbits had become a plague in Britain as well, demolishing acre upon acre of crops, snatching grass intended for livestock and vandalising tree plantations. Some people were quite happy to see them almost wiped out by the gruesome plague of myxamatosis in the 1950s. It was a very ugly sight: rabbits with unseeing bulging or closed encrusted eyes would hop miserably about the fields, or sit there hunched and stark-furred, wholly oblivious to danger and taking a long time to die. The disease persists in pockets and in cycles but the population, despite being reduced by more than 90 per cent, did recover and in many places the fields are once again heaving with rabbits. Country gardeners learn to net their vegetable patches and flower beds.

Rabbit auction at Braintree, Essex, in 1951

DEER

Deer are also game and the ancient laws that protected them so that kings could hunt them were particularly harsh. Today most deer are regarded as wild, belonging to nobody if they are not emparked, and in some parts treated almost as vermin. Roe deer populations grew rapidly in the twentieth century and although many liked to see a few deer about, others resented their destruction of saplings and of garden plants and so every now and then local landowners would get together and organise a cull, or hire a stalker to keep numbers to acceptable levels. New deer species have begun to spread – in particular, sika deer, introduced originally from Japan and able to interbreed with red deer (to the detriment of the native species); and the odd little muntjac, introduced initially into Woburn deer park from south-east Asia at the beginning of the twentieth century and expanding since the 1950s in the wild.

BACKYARD ANIMALS

COUNTRY PEOPLE WERE PRACTICAL BY NATURE, AND IN GENERAL THEY KEPT ANIMALS BECAUSE THEY WERE USEFUL. MOST OF THOSE WHO LIVED IN THE COUNTRY WOULD HAVE ENOUGH SPACE OUT BACK TO KEEP LIVESTOCK ON A SMALL SCALE, THOUGH THEY COULD HARDLY CALL THEMSELVES SMALLHOLDERS AS THE 'SPACE' WAS PROBABLY JUST A PATCH OF GARDEN. BUT YOU COULD STILL BE REASONABLY SELF-SUFFICIENT EVEN WITH ONLY A PATCH.

'Almost any cottager would have a pig or two at the end of the garden, pig meat being a staple part of the diet.'

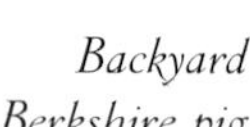

Backyard Berkshire pig

WRITING IN THE LATE 1930S, Frederick Smith said that the tragedy of the smallholder was that his more prosperous neighbours would watch his ventures into livestock with interest, watch him work all hours for a pretty modest standard of living, and then as soon as his ideas began to look profitable the neighbours would step in and start making profits themselves on a grand scale. This did indeed happen particularly with pigs and poultry, ideal smallholder stock but taken over by big business so successfully that there was no profit left in them for the smallholder.

Whatever the ingenious smallholder tried with success, someone else would grab the glory.

Quite apart from the value to the family larder, William Cobbett had a deeper and more interesting concern. He felt that a labourer's child who had been brought up to take care of cottage livestock would make a far better stockman on the farm, especially if given responsibility for the care of small animals in his own childhood. It was important for children to be brought up to value useful things, especially living things. In childhood would be instilled 'the early habit of fondness for animals and of setting a value on them'. Cobbett understood the importance of a child seeing that his parents took great care of their animals and treated them with great kindness; he also stressed the importance of now and then letting the child have 'a little thing to call his own', thus instilling a love and understanding of animals that would last a lifetime. A person who is actually interested in animals will care for them better and, in commercial terms, get better returns from them.

THE COTTAGE PIG

The idea of pannage is part of our history but it does still exist here and there. Pannage is the right to put your pigs into woodland to forage for acorns and beechmast, and the system persisted in the New Forest. It was recognised that acorns in excess could poison the Forest ponies and thus pannage for pigs was positively encouraged, in the interests of both species. The only problem today is the usual one of traffic. If there were no vehicles in the New Forest, pigs could be as happy as pigs in clover and swineherds would have a job for life.

Almost any cottager would have a pig or two at the end of the garden, pig meat being a staple part of the diet. The pig was kept in a pen and fed largely on household scraps, perhaps supplemented with meal bought from the mill or the village shop. Ideally the pig was grazed on the verges and then run on the commons and in the woods to forage and fatten, because that was food for free and, said Cobbett, 'if he be yoked , the occupiers of the neighbourhood must be churlish and brutish indeed, if they give the owner any annoyance'. In our own times, it is highly likely that the occupiers of the neighbourhood would indeed

COTTAGE ECONOMY

In his classic tract, Cottage Economy, published in 1823, William Cobbett exhorted his cottagers to brew their own beer, bake their own bread, make their own rushlights, plait straw for hats and bonnets, grow and mill their own mustard, make their own yeast cakes from hops, salt their own mutton and beef, grow their own fruit and vegetables and above all keep their own cows, pigs, bees, ewes, goats, poultry and rabbits. Goodness knows how they had time to bring in a wage as well.

LEFT
Feeding the pigs at Ipsden, Oxfordshire

give you annoyance if you let your pigs roam free. In some parts of the country there is a growing problem with feral wild boar, or more often crossbred pigs with some wild boar in them, which have escaped from wild boar farms and are now thoroughly enjoying their freedom.

Wild boar are the ancestors of domesticated pigs and are hardy, hairy and usually very lean beasts. The species was hunted to extinction as a native wild animal in Britain but has been reintroduced in recent years as livestock for its low-cholesterol meat. Until later in the twentieth century, British domesticated pigs were prized for the amount of fat they could produce. It was fat that provided energy, after all, and some pigs would be so fat that they could hardly stand. 'Lean bacon,' said Cobbett, 'is the most wasteful thing that any family can use. In short, it is uneatable, except by drunkards, who want something to stimulate their sickly appetite.' The cottager's pig was a hardy beast and would usually be something spotty, though not classy enough to take the name of a breed.

KILLING THE PIG

The pig was generally killed in the winter, before Christmas if the weather was coldish. 'To kill a hog nicely,' said Cobbett, 'is so much of a profession, that it is better to pay a shilling for having it done, than to stab and hack and tear the carcass about.' Most people did call in the pig-killer to do the dirty deed, but they often did their own scalding or scorching (to remove the coarse hair), butchering, salting and smoking. As well as all the generous produce from the carcass, you had lots of manure for your garden.

Flora Thompson graphically described the day the pig was killed by the travelling pork-butcher or pig-sticker, who happened to be a thatcher by day and so always had to kill after dark, by the light of lanterns and the burning straw of the bristle-singeing. The killing was a 'noisy, bloody business' and the job was often bungled. If you want the details, read the first chapter of Lark Rise (written in the late 1930s) and blench.

backyard animals

'A cow was even more generous than a pig: she gave you milk, cream, butter and cheese and, with careful management, a calf every year as well.'

Roadside goat at Coxwold, Yorkshire

THE COTTAGE COW

Fewer cottagers had cows, as they needed more space, though Cobbett claimed you could keep a cow if you had forty rods (quarter of an acre) of ground in which to grow cabbages and other fodder, and somewhere to build a small cowshed. Those who had access to the verges and commons had more scope for keeping a cow or two. A cow was even more generous than a pig: she gave you milk, cream, butter and cheese and, with careful management, a calf every year as well. A cow could also be trained as a draught animal to plough a field or pull a cart and still give you all of this. Calves could be reared for meat, so the benefits of cows were numerous – and all that dung as well.

Again, the breed was not a matter of much consequence to the cottager or smallholder; you went for what you could afford or what took your eye, and probably something small as it took up less space, ate less and was less likely to turn your grazing into a quagmire.

COTTAGE GOATS

Cobbett was very surprised that agricultural labourers hardly ever kept goats. They were tough enough to take care of themselves and were easy to feed (Cobbett claimed they would eat anything and would even 'make a hearty meal on *paper*, brown or white, printed on or not printed on, and give milk all the while'); they produced milk almost through-

backyard animals

out the year and kids besides, for many years; they did not ramble from home and stood no nonsense from dogs: they could be 'clogged, or stumped out' on the common or kept in a shed or let loose to browse where they wished (coming in regularly of their own accord in the evenings, or when called). Cobbett clearly adored goats and claimed that their only fault was their habit of debarking any young tree within reach.

In many European countries, goats are the poor man's cow, but for some reason they never did fill that role in Britain. They are not the sort of animal that is recorded in agricultural returns and so it is hard to know how many there were in the country at different periods, but it was never as many as their virtues warranted. There would usually be a few goats around any village, but only a few, and the situation remains similar today, though here and there people are farming goats commercially. In the 1980s there was a sudden fashion for keeping Angora goats, whose long, wavy coats are combed for their very fine fibre and who anyway look so pretty that they are often kept purely to decorate the garden.

Cottagers occasionally kept a ewe or two for milk, but the practice was not widespread. In medieval times almost all of England's milch animals had been sheep, not cows.

HUTCH RABBITS

Rabbits were instant meat in your backyard. They were easy to keep in hutches and prodigious producers of young, though Cobbett advised that a doe should not be allowed to have more than seven litters a year and that only six in each litter should be kept on the doe. Well, that makes more than forty rabbits a year! Their food was for free, easily culled from the wild or grown in the veg patch, and they were, said Cobbett, 'extremely pretty, nimble in their movements, engaging in their attitudes, and always completely under immediate control' – the ideal pet for small boys.

Rabbits were kept by many households for meat during the world wars. They could be fed on household scraps (bread and cake, scraps of meat and fish skin, potatoes, fruit peeling, tea leaves and the like) mixed with bran, with fresh weeds and grass cuttings. Some people literally cultivated dandelions for their rabbits, though in the country this was hardly necessary and you could grow kale, roots and clover to tickle their palates. Returns on rabbit pelts were still a useful source of income for smallholders in the 1930s and 1940s and there was also the production of silky Angora rabbit fur as a small business.

But children become attached to the softness of rabbits and now they are far more likely to be kept as pets.

'Rabbits were kept by many households for meat during the world wars.'

Taking the goats for a laneside browse

backyard animals

POULTRY

Backyard poultry included chickens, geese, ducks and turkeys. For most cottagers it was hens – for eggs and for the table. Anybody could keep a few hens, and they are what you usually see in Victorian paintings of cottages, scratching about in the lane or the farmyard, though they often made for bad relationships between neighbours when they started scratching about in other people's gardens instead.

'Geese needed access to grazing on the commons and verges, given which they could provide you with a hundred eggs a year and live to a great age.'

Cobbett found that chickens were prone to far too many ailments and said that fowls could seldom be kept conveniently about a cottage unless 'the wife' was at home most of the time. Bearing in mind that the birds are domesticated Indian jungle fowl, perhaps it is surprising that they do so well in the British climate.

Cottagers and farmers continue to keep chickens. During the two world wars they were particularly valuable, of course. Beverly Nichols, in a book published in 1933 describing his own attempt at cottage life in Huntingdonshire in the late 1920s, was typical: 'The obvious animals to get seemed to be hens.' So he asked the gardener to get him a few – two, he felt, would be adequate, if they were fairly large. 'Will you be wanting a rooster too?' asked the gardener. 'Of course,' replied Nichols impatiently, 'otherwise we shan't have any eggs.' The gardener realised that Nichols knew nothing about hens and carefully explained the facts of life. Although thrilled at the first egg he found, the novelty of his hens wore off after three weeks and he sold them at a charity fete. He then kept bees, and became enchanted by the poetry in them.

Feeding free-range farmyard poultry at Lambourne, Berkshire

Geese needed access to grazing on the commons and verges, given which they could provide you with a hundred eggs a year and live to a great age. To fatten them for the table you needed to provide corn, and Cobbett reacted in horror to the French method of fattening geese by 'nailing them down by their webs'. (He had plenty to say about French cruelty to geese and turkeys.) In some parts of the country, cottagers specialised in the production of geese and ducks for the markets, or for selling to farmers for fattening on stubble for the table.

Ducks also produced plenty of eggs, though you had to take care as to where they had been laid or you'd end up with food poisoning. They fattened well for the table on grass, greenstuffs and grain; apparently the Americans of Long Island fattened their ducks on a crab known as the horse-foot fish, and the meat gave away their diet in its smell and taste. In the garden and allotment, ducks did a marvellous job as slug-clearing machines as well as providing manure. Along with hens, ducks often feature in country cottage and farmyard paintings.

Turkeys, said Cobbett, 'are *flying* things', which might surprise some turkey farmers today – the ability has long since been bred out of them. Turkeys were native to America (how they came to be called turkeys is a long story), where they were often shot as game-birds in the wild, usually when they were peacefully roosting in tall trees. The biggest problem for the smallholder was the British climate: turkeys did not like the cold and young ones especially did not like wet weather and heavy dew. Turkeys also like 'room to prowl about', though if you raised the young under a broody hen she would teach them that rambling was not the thing to

backyard animals

LEFT
Taking a gander at the latest fashion …

do. Nurture would beat nature. Turkeys were reared purely for meat, not for eggs, and were therefore less useful to the cottager than other poultry.

In the late eighteenth century a few 'curious persons' kept guinea fowl. Like other poultry, however, they tended to be for family use, or as 'perquisites or pin money to the female part of the family'. This rather condescending description does highlight the point that many a farmer's wife kept poultry for a little income of her own.

PIGEONS

Wild wood-pigeons were shot as vermin and also for the pot, but for centuries pigeons had been 'farmed'. These were not wood-pigeons but were domesticated from a different species, the rock pigeon, and had come into Britain from France by the thirteenth century. At that stage only manor houses and monasteries were allowed to keep pigeons and they built substantial dovecotes in which the birds were able to nest and rear their young until the owner of the dovecote decided the young squabs were ready for the table. Then it was simply a matter of climbing the ladder, reaching into a nesting box and taking your choice. Queen Elizabeth I found a much more aggressive reason for keeping pigeons: their droppings were an important ingredient in gunpowder, as well as being useful manure.

Some of the manorial pigeon lofts were magnificent buildings in themselves, often built in stone. Farmhouses were more likely to have a simple wooden dovecote hanging on the wall, though some went to the trouble of making walls from clay mixed with straw, four feet thick or more, and cutting pigeon-holes into the walls while the mixture was still wet, then painting the whole thing white.

Cobbett urged cottagers to keep a few pigeons about the place, though in those early years of the nineteenth century there were probably more pigeon-keepers among town than country labourers. All the cottager needed to do was to put up a shelf for them in the cow shed or a board under the cottage eaves, shut them in for two or three days until

Free-range turkeys

backyard animals

'Many a cottager kept a few hives in the garden, usually in skeps made of rye straw as being warmer than boards.'

they knew this was home, and then enjoy them as 'very pretty creatures; very interesting in their manners; they are an object to delight *children* and to give them the *early habit* of fondness for animals and of *setting a value* on them'.

One problem with pigeons was that they tended to raid neighbouring crops. Charles Vancouver, in the very early years of the nineteenth century, took the trouble to calculate the damage. He had been told that there were about 20,000 dove-houses in England and Wales, averaging about a hundred pairs of 'old pigeons'. He estimated that during their predations these 'voracious and insatiate vermin' devoured more than 157 million pints of somebody else's corn annually, worth about 15 million pounds, in addition to the damage they did at seed time and the 'corn trod under and also beaten out by their wings' before harvest. He asked that this figure be set against the birds' value as a 'luxury for the table, their dung for the use of dyers, or the purposes of manure'.

Racing pigeons and carrier pigeons developed in due course from these domesticated meat birds, as did all the fancy pigeons that many people still keep as a hobby and the white doves that decorate country roof-tops, and also the 'wild' pigeons that haunt city parks and railway stations. Incidentally, did you know that the Romans and ancient Egyptians used pigeons for sending messages on the wing?

COTTAGE BEES

Many a cottager kept a few hives in the garden, usually in skeps made of rye straw as being warmer than boards. Straw was also cheap and therefore it was easily replaced every few months in the interests of hygiene. Apart from the hive, the cost of keeping bees was virtually nothing, either in expense or in time and energy. Honey was not just a useful sweetener in place of sugar; it could also be turned into mead. And apparently bee venom could relieve rheumatism. And little old ladies could set up a sideline in 'teas' – home-churned butter on home-made bread with honey from their own hives.

Towards the end of the eighteenth century, a lighthouse keeper at Dungeness made a small patch of garden despite being surrounded for miles around by gravel so deep that hardly anything would grow. He worked hard on his little garden and did manage to grow something, but more importantly he put up some bee hives and produced twelve pounds of honey of excellent quality in good years.

A postman taking due precautions: bees had swarmed into the pillarbox in the summer of 1937

PETS

SURROUNDED BY ABUNDANT WILDLIFE, EVEN IN THE NINETEENTH CENTURY, COUNTRY PEOPLE TENDED TO MAKE PETS OF WILD CREATURES. FAVOURITES INCLUDED SLOW-WORMS, TOADS, TADPOLES, BEETLES, SONGBIRDS, MICE AND BABY ANYTHING-THAT-MOVED.

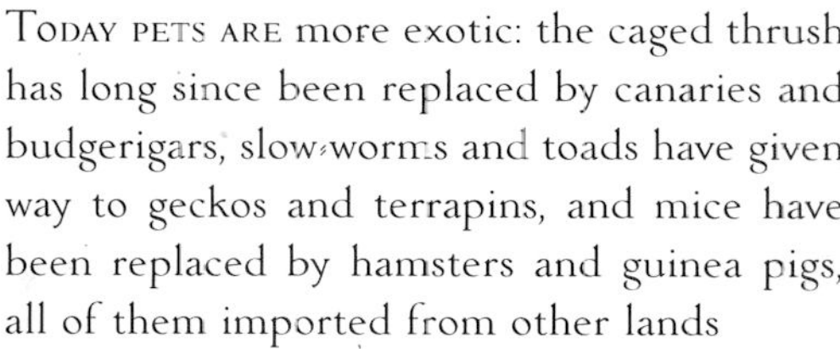

TODAY PETS ARE more exotic: the caged thrush has long since been replaced by canaries and budgerigars, slow-worms and toads have given way to geckos and terrapins, and mice have been replaced by hamsters and guinea pigs, all of them imported from other lands

A country favourite, at least of boys, was the ferret, which is basically a domesticated polecat. Ferrets have been known in Britain since at least Norman times, if not Roman, and were widely used in the medieval period for helping to catch rabbits for the pot. Ferrets in the pockets of boys and men would be frowned upon – not because of the distinctive odour of them but because their owners were more than likely to be poachers; ferrets work swiftly and quietly. Today quite a few men still keep ferrets for working the burrows, and, slightly to their disgust, there has been a growing trend towards the keeping of ferrets purely as pets. (In America, there are three million pet ferrets, kept in cosseted conditions that would shame an honest working animal.) Ferrets remain popular at country events where they 'race' through tunnels, actually taking their time to explore until they deign to come out the other end to claim their prize.

Cats were kept largely for their ability to keep down the rats and mice that plagued country homes and particularly the farms; but again, they became natural companions and are now valued more as pets, though in the country they are still expected to control the vermin. Dogs, too, were kept more for the work they performed in the country, especially with livestock or as gundogs, but now they are more often pets and companions.

LEFT
Old quarryman with a favourite terrier

BELOW
A ferreting partnership

DONKEYS & MULES

Donkeys (or asses) and mules were essential to the rural economy, and to that of the towns, for several centuries. They were ideal for itinerant hawkers, for all manner of farm work, for drawing carts and even carriages. Lady Massarreene, in the years just before the First World War, had a splendid team of white mules to draw her carriage about the narrow country lanes of Hampshire and Sussex (some claim that their ghosts still walk there), and she was by no means alone in her choice.

'All his farmwork was done by mules, and it was said that mules were capable of working "to the age of seventy, and upwards".'

In 1813 Pitt described how the late Samuel Skey, Esquire, of Spring Grove near Bewdley, Worcestershire, kept a good many mules, 'some of them a good size, to fifteen hands high or more, and some of nearly a milk white colour, the most beautiful of which were reserved for drawing his carriage, and for which a great price had been offered'. All his farmwork was done by mules, and it was said that mules were capable of working 'to the age of seventy, and upwards'.

Near Bromsgrove a Mr Carpenter used a 'strong gelding ass, with paniers' to carry turnips to his ewes in winter, and others copied his idea, creating cunning panniers with folding doors that could let out all the contents at once. They also used asses to pull light carriages on the roads, and even to haul canal boats, 'in which office their masters kindly assist, when the strength of the animal is insufficient'. Droves of thirty or more donkeys, each loaded with three bushel-bags of sand, would travel from the Wiltshire village of Cherhill in the late nineteenth century for journeys of fifty miles; one of the donkeys would be laden with pots, pans and blankets as the drovers slept rough along the way. The teams belonged to Old Aaron Angell and Levi Brittain, and when the two men died the donkeys were replaced with horses and, later, motor cars.

One-donkey power

In Devon mules and asses were in full-time employment carrying sand from the shores to other parts of the county. The poor, patient donkeys would be given loads that were no smaller than those on the accompanying big

donkeys & mules

mules and horses. They could be bought for about 25 shillings and seemed to live on thistles and whatever else they could glean from the verges, hedgerows and fields, but lived to a considerable age even on that regime. Mules, on the other hand, would cost about £15 to buy.

Mules are donkey/horse hybrids, bred by putting jack asses to mares; they cannot reproduce and so any mule breeder must always start again with a jack and a mare. Hinnies are the other way round: the sire is a horse and the dam a jenny. You can tell which species was the father by looking at the hybrid's head.

The New Forest became a centre for mule-breeding when the animals were much in demand in the United States – Southampton was a convenient port for shipment. During wars, mules became highly regarded by the Army and played a crucial role even in the Second World War, where they were notably used in Burma to carry weapons and other equipment over difficult terrain. After both world wars many a soldier remembered his experience of mules and recreated the partnership on the farm, using mules as agricultural animals. Now rather rare in Britain, there is a society for them and they remain interesting, useful and surprisingly amenable animals for those who understand them.

Donkeys were the cottager's friend as well as that of the itinerant, but were all too often abused with overwork and neglect. In some centuries they had unexpected periods of being in demand when wars requisitioned horses from farmers and they turned to the reliable old donkey instead. They probably reached their peak in Britain during the nineteenth century, both on farms and country lanes and as town pack animals. They were ridden by miners, they pulled lawn-mowers, they worked treadmills, they drew rubbish carts, they delivered the milk – and in London there was a substantial number of milch jennies who were taken to the houses of rather wealthy Londoners and milked in the street for the sustenance of their children. Famously in London donkeys were adopted by the Pearly Kings and Queens, who retain a strong affection for them to this day; they became costermongers' beasts of burden and cart pullers, and would take the family for outings on Bank Holidays. There was a thriving donkey trade at the cattle market in Islington, where donkeys had their own shows; they even took part in the International Horse Show and the Royal Show In Ireland they seemed to be everywhere, laden with goods on their backs or pulling carts. In England they found a new role on the beaches, giving rides, and they still do so now, though much less than fifty years ago.

The donkey's dramatic decline was really brought about by motorised vehicles; in the 1920s there were said to be only a hundred donkeys in the country (patently untrue, as there were more than that on a handful of beaches). For some forty years the donkey world went rather quiet, until in the 1950s donkeys suddenly became in demand as pets. They are rarely worked in Britain today, except by enthusiasts; they more often find themselves keeping lone horses and ponies company. Abuse through ignorance of their real needs persisted and countless numbers of donkeys ended up with rescue centres every year. For an animal that is so patient, loyal and uncomplaining, that is not a good state of affairs, but it is improving and the future for donkeys looks brighter. Maybe there will be new work for donkeys one day.

Mules were popular farm animals between the wars

HORSES

THERE HAS BEEN A MAJOR REVOLUTION IN THE STATUS OF THE COUNTRY HORSE. INSTEAD OF BEING MAINLY AN ENGINE OF WORK, ON THE ROADS AND IN THE FIELDS, IT HAS BECOME A PLAYTHING. IT IS SURPRISING HOW FEW OF THOSE WHO WORKED ON THE LAND ACTUALLY EVER RODE A HORSE.

'Ponies have always been useful animals for hill, fell and moorland farmers, but, like the horse, today they tend to be playthings.'

RIDING WAS A PASTIME for the middle and upper classes, unless you count plodding along on a donkey with your feet almost trailing on the ground, or straddling a plough-horse bareback as you both returned home tired at the end of the day. Gertrude Jekyll, writing in the 1920s, remarked on how seldom 'except in the wilder south-west' did she see a ridden horse.

An 1862 book about horses by 'Stonehenge' (editor of *The Field* magazine) detailed the breeds and types of horse of the period. Being a hunting man, he gave due prominence to Thoroughbreds, hunters and steeplechasers, but there was also a section on a wide assortment of 'half-breds, cobs and ponies' that included hacks and a range of carriage horses – the cars of their day. Many of these were town horses, or belonged to the professional classes or those who owned big country estates and could afford to employ others to care for the animals and drive them. The stables on those estates have long since been converted into desirable residences.

HORSIFICATION

Hunters and hacks continued in the countryside and there are numerous hunters today, though hunting has been a diminishing sport (too much barbed-wire now, for one thing). Many people now ride simply for pleasure, ambling the bridleways and lanes, or reviving the pleasures of carriage driving along the greenways.

The growth in horse numbers in some parts of the country has been phenomenal. With every sector of the livestock industry seemingly in trouble, barns become livery stables and indoor schools run by farmers encouraged to diversify; or the yonder grazing meadows of dairy and beef herds are coveted by people who buy up a few acres of green moat around

horses

their homes and put horses on the grass. Sadly, some of them have no idea that pasture needs to be managed, and the result can be rampant ragwort, thistles and docks or land virtually bare of all growth. They then pay a fortune for hay made by others from better managed land, which has the benefit of providing local employment. At least there is, potentially, plenty of good manure around for the roses, though passers-by are less likely now to scrape it, still steaming, off the roads – it is too soon flattened by passing cars.

Ready to win the racquet-and-ball race at the 1936 Aldenham House Club gymkhana

PONY GAMES

The increase in ponies is another phenomenon. Ponies have always been useful animals for hill, fell and moorland farmers, but, like the horse, today they tend to be playthings. Fifty or sixty years ago they were already popular with children, especially middle-class ones.

In the country, gymkhanas began to be held in villages, initially for cavalry soldiers, and many a village photo album has pictures of men in uniform at the local gymkhana, with not a mounted child in sight. Gradually, with the formation of the Pony Club in 1929, children on ponies took an interest in gymkhanas and this increased in the late 1950s when the first national Pony Club Mounted Games Championship was held.

Perhaps that was really the death knell for the old type of children's gymkhana, in which we all rode for fun, in the mad dashes of bending races, potato races, sack races, apple-bobbing and chase-me-charlies of the post-war years, when a cheap and cheerful rosette was just the icing on the cake and belonged to the pony, not its rider. The concept of championships introduced rules and cups and a much more serious competitive edge, to the extent that gymkhana organisers began to find themselves besieged by parents (usually mothers) complaining if their child failed to win. Winning seemed to be more important than taking part.

THE GYMKHANAS

In the 1860s, British soldiers serving in Asia allayed their boredom by adapting local mounted games, including polo. On non-polo days they had 'jollies' that they called gymkhanas (an Anglo-Indian word meaning 'a field day on horseback'), in which they rode camels, mules, donkeys and bicycles as well as horses, often with various wheeled devices behind them. The soldiers brought their horses and games back home with them, and polo and gymkhanas became fashionable regimental entertainments in the late nineteenth century. But that was mainly for Londoners.

horses

'Riding manners are improving as more riders realise that they, too, are part of the countryside but do not own it.'

VILLAGE GYMKHANAS COULD no longer cope with the stress and the one-upmanship of it all. Livery became expensive and the child who, with a pony or Welsh cob kept in a field shelter, happily rode bareback in the paddock and hacked to the gymkhana felt out of place among the expensive, elegantly groomed ponies (transported by boxes drawn by Range Rovers) and immaculate outfits of their pot-hunting rivals. Too many regulations were introduced and so gymkhanas were no longer a bit of light-hearted entertainment among friends. The laughter and innocence began to leave the games, and so did the villagers.

Pony express at Tregaron, South Wales. In 1935 the Natystalwen Horse Post took ten hours to deliver post to ten addresses in the Cambrian Mountains

RIDING MANNERS

Sometimes there is local resentment against the 'horsy set', who might be seen, often unfairly, as wealthier than most. Polo ponies exercise along the lanes in nervy strings, sometimes arrogant in their use of the road. A few hunts have forgotten that there are no squires now and that the hunt is a guest on the land, not a master. Simply by virtue of sitting higher than the average walker, some horse-riders seem to look down on the rest; others are thoughtless in their use of local tracks, churning them with hooves so that the humble walker can only stagger along them with difficulty. In the past riders have been disdainful of passing drivers, even those who, country bred, carefully slow down or wait patiently on the verge until the horses have passed. Riding manners are improving as more riders realise that they, too, are part of the countryside but do not own it. They also need allies on the bridleways, many of which are threatened by outsiders with four-wheel-drive vehicles and trail bikes that cause far more damage to the greenways than hooves ever did.

WORKING HORSES AND OXEN

The age of the working horse was surprisingly brief. The traditional working animal on British farms was the ox – a castrated bullock.

Sussex was one of the last bastions of working oxen. The deep-red, massive Sussex breed was ideal for the job and at least one pair of them was still being worked in the 1990s. Arthur Beckett, writing in 1909, described a ploughing match in which a team of six black bullocks yoked to a plough of the old type caught his eye on the South Downs. It was a fine sight but sadly he knew of only three teams of oxen even in Sussex by then: one at Chyngton near Seaford, one at Southover near Lewes and a team of 'dun-nut' coloured plough oxen on the Possingworth estate at Waldron. His description of the dignified black ploughing-match beasts with long, branching horns, marching up and down the furrows at a leisurely, steady pace harnessed with heavy wooden yokes and guided by a boy directing them with the slightest touch of a long pole, is superb. They were competing directly with equally splendid teams of horses that were 'sleek, fat and of great strength', their coats gleaming, manes and tails plaited with bright ribbons, polished brasses reflecting the November sunlight and their gait proud. As you read his story, you can almost smell the freshly turned soil and the sweat of the ploughmen as they followed their animals.

The Reverend Arthur Young, in his Sussex

horses

report more than a hundred years earlier, clearly thought oxen were there to stay and he went into pages of detail about their training, their uses, their yokes and collars, their shoeing and their 'distempers'. The number of oxen used in husbandry in the county was considerable. The famous breeder John Ellman (born in 1753) of Glynde deemed that for 200 acres of arable land you needed twelve oxen and nine horses, constantly working, but it varied according to the type of land that was being worked. The publisher Baxter, of Lewes, who knew Ellman well, simply said that the ox was 'an animal of great utility for various purposes of draught'. On the heavy tenacious Sussex clays, oxen were found 'equal to the best Suffolk horses for all sorts of work', be it in the fields or on the roads. To plough such land sometimes needed as many as twelve oxen, double yoked. The good Reverend Young, a Suffolk man as it happens, was so impressed by Sussex oxen that he considered horses to be irrelevant. After all, you could eat oxen once their work was done; whereas horseflesh, said Young, was only for dogs.

In Worcestershire the local oxen were Herefordshires, with their trademark white faces, red coats and Sussex-style horns; many writers lumped together the Hereford, Sussex and Devon cattle as the Middle-horned breed. Many farmers used working horses instead but the local breeds were in need of improvement. On farms, horses tended to be multi-purpose; for example, a hackney might be ridden but also used for draught work. At Lea Castle the splendid Mr Knight, when volunteer cavalry horses were needed, raised a troop locally and principally at his own expense, selling off his own heavy cart horses and buying cavalry horses instead, of the 'Yorkshire' breed Ten of his own servants and dependents were pressed into this private cavalry, ready to be called up for military services, and their mounts in the meantime did all his farmwork as well as occasionally being ridden or drawing his carriage.

PLAYING POLO

Polo, a game being played in Asia at least 2,500 years ago, grew in popularity in Victorian England, initially through the enthusiasm of nineteenth century British tea planters and those army officers coming home. It was first played in England by officers of the Royal Horse Guards at Hounslow Heath in 1869, and by the outbreak of the First World War there were sixty polo clubs in England. With its 'colonial' background, it was inevitably a game for the rich. Polo grounds and polo stables spread gently outwards from London to select parts of the country and tended to be owned by the very wealthy, who today often visit their stables by helicopter and play very little part in the local life of the countryside.

Teams of draught oxen were once a familiar sight in the fields and lanes

horses

A well-matched team drilling peas

'Young said that the "finest and best horses in the kingdom, chiefly of what are called the blood kind" were bred on the Wolds…'

IN THOSE EARLY YEARS of the nineteenth century, draught horses were essential on the roads, drawing stage wagons and taking heavy loads to the big trading centres on the one hand, and on the other dragging farmers' heavy loads over the terrible minor roads. The total number of horses in Worcestershire was estimated to be about 16,000 working on farms, 4,000 youngsters, and a further 4,000 'kept by gentlemen for pleasure, use, or amusement' or employed on rivers, canals and so on.

In North Devon the cattle, like those of much of southern England, were blood-red and stocky, ideal as draught oxen. It was claimed that the Devon breed was the best in the country for its 'docility, activity, and hardihood' as a working animal. But not just anybody could work a Devon ox. The local ploughboys had 'a peculiar mode of cheering them on, with a song he continually chaunts in low notes, suddenly broken, and rising a whole octave. The ceasing of the song is said to occasion the stopping of the team.' On flinty soils the oxen were properly shod: the smith would shackle the animal and throw it down on its side and accomplish the shoeing within the hour. The shoes lasted several months, as long as there was not much road work, and the price of shoeing was up to twenty pence per animal.

Arthur Young, in his Lincolnshire report published in 1813, said that once oxen would have been seen 'all the way from Grantham to Lincoln, now scarcely any; a pair of mares, and one man, will do as much work as four oxen, and two men'. He did find plenty of working oxen elsewhere, though; indeed most of the farmers on the Wolds had some, mainly used for carting, harrowing and ploughing. Mr Smith of South Elkington, and his neighbours, used oxen

horses

for 'leading manure, and corn, and hay ... and thinks that he can keep two oxen for the expense of one horse; but that the horse will not draw so much as the two oxen'. But he did find them too slow for ploughing. Mr Graburn of Barton had 'shod his oxen with horse-shoes reversed in putting on, that is, the heels of the shoes before; and they walked on stones perfectly well; but left off the practice, because the shoes came off, like common ones'.

The men of Lincolnshire bred very good horses for the saddle and for coaches, which they often sold at the great Yorkshire horse fair at Howden. Young said that the 'finest and best horses in the kingdom, chiefly of what are called the blood kind' were bred on the Wolds – even better than the famous hunting horses of Yorkshire or Durham. Every farmer in Holland Fen kept mares for breeding, and typically a good four-year-old cart-horse would sell for £30 at the famous Horncastle fair.

Overall, then, it seems that oxen were quite rapidly giving way to horses on the farms and the local roads as the eighteenth century rolled into the nineteenth. By the end of the nineteenth, there were about 2.6 million horses (out of the British total of 3.3 million) working in either agriculture or trade. In the late 1870s the breeders of those working horses were busily creating breed societies to promote their animals – the Clydesdale, the Suffolk and the Shire. In the First World War years Percherons from France also firmly established themselves with a British society of their own.

But after that war there was an agricultural depression and to cap it the combustion engine was in direct competition with horse power. On the roads it was motorised lorries; on the farms it was tractors. In 1920 the government census revealed that there were about 1.4 million draught horses in Britain, half of which were working in agriculture. After the Second World War the victory of engine over horse was virtually complete and the role of the heavy horse was pushed firmly to the sidelines. By the 1980s the total number of all types of horse in Britain was probably somewhere between half and one million (nobody really knows); of these, at a guess, perhaps 3,000 were heavy working horses. In the early 1980s the Shires began to fight back and, inch by inch, have been finding new niches for the working horses that served the country so well for more than a century and a half.

'Cart horse', incidentally, is not a good name for these big animals. Carts have only two wheels. The big draught horses were perfectly capable of pulling hefty great wagons with at least four wheels.

Horses were essential for pulling out forestry timber (commonly known as 'snigging') and are still used in places that machines cannot reach

'Oxen were quite rapidly giving way to horses on farms ... as the eighteenth century rolled into the nineteenth.'

LEFT
A wagonload of hops from Farnham, Surrey, once a famous hop-growing region

FARM LIVESTOCK

IN TERMS OF LIVESTOCK, THE FACE OF BRITAIN HAS CHANGED HUGELY DURING THE PAST THREE CENTURIES OR SO. BEFORE THE EIGHTEENTH CENTURY, FARM ANIMALS WERE FARM ANIMALS, AND THE BREEDING AND MANAGEMENT OF THEM WAS SOMETHING OF A HIT-AND-MISS AFFAIR. IT WAS A MATTER OF 'FOUR STIFF STANDERS, FOUR DILLY-DANDERS, TWO LOOKERS, TWO CROOKERS, AND A WIG-WAG'.

'In the eighteenth century Robert Bakewell developed a breed known as the Longhorn, and this magnificent creature quickly became dominant in many parts of the country.'

MOST OF THE ANIMALS would be killed off in late autumn and the meat salted down; there simply wasn't enough fodder to feed them through the winter. Then in the eighteenth century along came the 'improvers' – remarkable individuals who revolutionised British agriculture, including its livestock. Indeed Britain was way ahead of the rest of the world in the latter by the end of that century.

In the twentieth century, for the first time in Britain's history, the great majority of people have no knowledge or understanding of livestock. Those who have moved out of their towns and into 'the country' take offence at the everydayness of the animals – the dawn crowing of a healthy cockerel glad to be alive, the bawling of a bulling cow looking for a mate, the raucous squealing of pigs at feeding time, the braying of a donkey, all sounds that assault the tender ears of those reared on loud music and the roar of traffic. Then there are the country smells of sweet silage and of slurry spread on the fields to manure them and of acrid chicken litter. The incomers complain about the noise and the smell; they complain at a flock of sheep being driven along the lane and hindering their progress; they complain about dairy cows leaving pats in 'their' lanes; they complain that there are animals in the countryside at all.

CATTLE

In the eighteenth century Robert Bakewell developed a breed known as the Longhorn, and this magnificent creature quickly became dominant in many parts of the country. Before then, breeds were not really breeds, though local types often developed and became favoured in their regions. But Bakewell realised that the masses who were streaming into the towns with the industrial revolution would need feeding and he set about producing the beef, along with the tallow to make millions of candles.

The Longhorn's reign was not a long one and it was soon replaced by the Shorthorn, which became even more ubiquitous. The cattle fields of Britain began to take on

Feeding the cattle in winter

farm livestock

something of a uniformity, instead of the total ragbag of assorted colours, shapes and sizes of cattle theretofore. And that set a pattern. The reign of the Shorthorn was much longer and far more influential – it spread all over the world in huge numbers. But during the twentieth century it gave way to another, the Friesian, so that instead of being full of roan cattle the fields were full of black-and-white ones. Everywhere. Absolutely everywhere. With a few pockets of more interesting ones here and there, or regionally. Beef cattle of old were in suckler herds; the calves stayed with their mothers until they were weaned. During the twentieth century new systems became firmly established; calves from dairy cows were whipped away from their mothers at four days old and reared artificially, fed milk from buckets or bottles, though in hill country you would still see mothers and calves together as nature intended.

Dairy cows are still panting to catch up with what happened to them during the twentieth century. In Thomas Hardy's day, Tess of the d'Urbervilles was a typical milkmaid handmilking a few cows an hour in small herds of perhaps twenty, even in the great dairying country of Wessex. But then came milking machines, and now dairy herds are usually a hundred, two hundred or more cows, milked almost without human intervention. Very strange.

In many rural areas the local cow scene had altered dramatically within living memory. Where once a rural parish might be home to a score of small family dairy herds, of several different breeds or of none – Ayrshires, Jerseys, Shorthorns and Friesians, with some suckler herds of Hereford, Angus, local Sussex or Devon and so on – now there will probably be no more than one, or perhaps two dairy herds, big herds, all black-and-white and not even the good old dual-purpose British Friesian any more but a composite of Friesian and Canadian Holstein. As for beef, many of those herds have disappeared into huge sheds for intensive rearing, or have simply disappeared altogether. Cattle rearing became big business; there was no room for small family herds any more.

Farrowing: a farmyard sow and litter

Then in the 1980s and 1990s came that terrible disease, BSE (bovine spongiform encephalopathy) and the world went mad. British cattle, whether for beef or for milk, having been the best in the world for so long, were suddenly spurned and countless cattle farmers had the rug pulled out from under them, through no fault of their own, and went to the wall. Prime cattle were slaughtered in horrendous numbers. It has been devastating in the countryside and has brought British agriculture to the point of despair.

PIGS

Pigs used to be just pigs, any colour, any shape, any size, whatever you fancied or whatever you could get. Regional types developed, and there seemed to be a general trend for white pigs in the north, coloured spotted and splodged pigs in the Midlands and black pigs in the south (a very broad generalisation). Pigs belonged to cottagers or were in small groups on farms.

'Pigs belonged to cottagers or were in small groups on farms.'

Then pigs went commercial in a big way after the Second World War, partly because pig farmers (like poultry farmers) did not receive government subsidies and had to do something to save their industry. So they began to specialise; and in the 1950s and 1960s some gigantic pig-breeding companies developed,

farm livestock

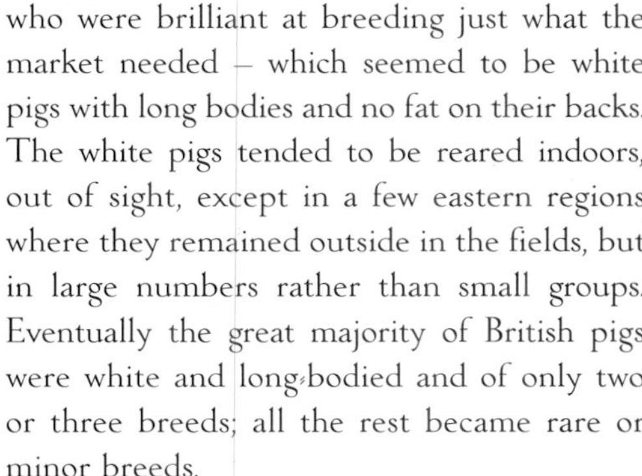

who were brilliant at breeding just what the market needed – which seemed to be white pigs with long bodies and no fat on their backs. The white pigs tended to be reared indoors, out of sight, except in a few eastern regions where they remained outside in the fields, but in large numbers rather than small groups. Eventually the great majority of British pigs were white and long-bodied and of only two or three breeds; all the rest became rare or minor breeds.

Some are now fighting back, and a bit of colour is returning to the pig scene. But, as in every other livestock sector, as the twentieth century turned to the twenty-first, pig prices crashed and for many it was no longer worth trying to continue in pig farming.

RIGHT
Sheep-washing from a coracle in the Afon Teifi at Cenarth

SHEEP

Sheep were once the source of many fortunes, in the long-ago days when they were farmed for their fleeces or for their milk. It all changed, and instead they were farmed for meat – initially good old-fashioned mutton but then lamb, lamb and more lamb. The sheep industry is now carefully stratified: you have hill ewes in the uplands where not much else can be done with the land; you draught older ewes down the hill a bit to cross them with meatier rams for meatier lambs; and you take some of those lambs down to the lowlands to fatten or to be crossed with what are rather alarmingly known as terminal sires – nice stocky breeds like the Southdown and the Hampshire, for example, to make even meatier lambs. The wool now is almost irrelevant, though sheep are still shorn. The inventor of the Woolsack would be appalled.

But at least there is still plenty of variety among sheep breeds, and strong regional identification with them. The big problem now is that people are putting large flocks of sheep on land wholly unsuitable for the poor animals – wet lowland fields that were once the kingdom of cattle but that now rot the feet of sheep and attract flystrike and the subsequent maggots that can eat a sheep alive. And here again the market for British lamb has crashed to the point where in the late 1990s hundreds of farmers were forced to kill their lambs and bury them, or dump them on the RSCPA and rescue centres, as it was costing them more to feed their animals than they could ever recoup by selling them. What a crazy world.

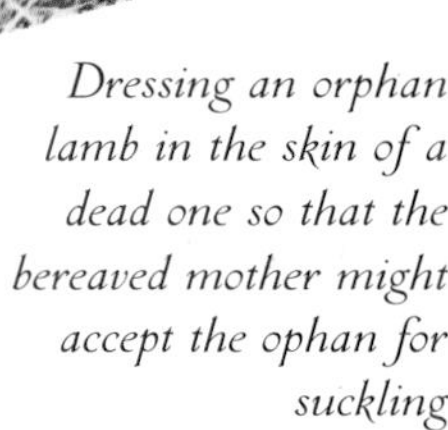

Dressing an orphan lamb in the skin of a dead one so that the bereaved mother might accept the ophan for suckling

Young Hampshire Down rams destined for Brazil

FISH

Quite apart from the sea-fishing industry which has always been crucial to the local economy in coastal areas, freshwater fish have also had a role to play. Every monastery had its stewponds for rearing fish for the table and it is sometimes forgotten what a considerable influence the monastic orders had on the landscape, with their large-scale general farming and highly efficient creation and management of pond systems for fish. In Lincolnshire in the 1780s and 1790s, Sir Joseph Banks would hold an annual fishing party on the river Witham. The parties (and they were hospitable occasions) lasted for four days and invitations were eagerly sought. The total party catch in 1793 weighed 2,644lb. The previous year the catch had included a salmon weighing 10lb and in Sir Joseph's kitchen was a picture of a pike weighing 31lb at thirteen years old.

Under observation, the travelling fishmonger fillets a fish

In the same period, freshwater fish were quite important in the Weald of Sussex, where there were innumerable ponds, many originating when that part of the country was a veritable industrial complex of iron-making, and others which were mill ponds. Unfortunately for the locals, a Mr Fenn in London had managed to become the sole monopoliser of all fish sold in Sussex. The fish were mainly carp but tench, perch, pike and eels were also 'farmed'. Because of Fenn's monopoly, just about all the fish ended up in London, where prices were high, and if you did not live on the coast you could rarely afford to eat fish, even though they were abundant in local ponds, unless you poached them.

Fenn's trick had been over a long period to rent the waters, which were managed in a highly scientific and efficient manner for the period and produced some very big fish. Apparently there were carp weighing 25lb a brace in Mr Milward's marl-pit ponds 'with two inches of fat upon them, but then he feeds with pease'. In Burton Park Mr Biddulph had extensive ponds (the Mill pond and assorted stew ponds and trout ponds) yielding a great abundance of fish; for example, on drawing down the waters of the 50-acre Mill pond on 10 March 1789 they took out 2,846 fish, including 1,517 carp, selling almost all the carp to Mr Fenn along with all the tench and 400cwt of pike.

Eels were often resident in mill ponds; they were often bought 'by the stick', as they would be hung from a stick through the gills – an ignominious end for a creature with a life history that involves spawning somewhere near the Bahamas, drifting towards Europe as larvae for three years in the Gulf Stream, loitering in British estuaries if they are males or swimming upriver as females to live for a dozen years or so (if they are not trapped) in rivers and streams, sometimes actually making their way to isolated ponds over land on wet nights, before returning all the way back to the Sargasso Sea to spawn and probably die.

In modern times, freshwaters are widely let to those who fish for sport; many a farmer has benefited from letting the local angling club manage and stock ponds that no longer quench the thirst of livestock or act as reservoirs for fighting rick and house fires. There is also a growing interest in the conservation of ponds for wildlife or as landscape features, including old fishponds, duck ponds, village ponds, amphibian breeding ponds, marsh ponds on heathland, and farm ponds that would otherwise be drained, filled in and ploughed up. Water is life, after all.

8

Country Work

country work

THE NATURE OF WORK in rural areas, or rather, the nature of the work of those who live in rural areas, changed dramatically in the twentieth century. Whereas in the Victorian village the great majority would have been working on the land and most of the rest in crafts and trades more or less directly connected with it, today the proportion of rural dwellers whose work has any connection with the land has shrunk to a small minority in all but the more remote parts of the country. Sad to say, the urban spirit often prevails even in the countryside because most people are divorced from the reality of land work.

Paul Jennings, writing in the early 1960s, reported that in 1851 there had been 1,778,000 farm workers in the country; in 1901 there were 1,399,000; in 1961 there were only 220,000 and the National Economic Development Plan of 1965 anticipated that the level would, and should, reduce even further: 'By continuing to improve its productivity, agriculture would continue to release substantial manpower resources to other industries.' Well, that's one way of emptying the villages.

Jennings also made the point that farming fluctuates wildly in the public estimation of its importance to the nation. During wars, when these islands are so vulnerable to blockade, people suddenly realise that if they don't eat, they die, and they want to plough up everything in sight. In times of peace, they decide that manufacture or services are far more important than agriculture and the whole country should be one big factory instead of one big farm. Or perhaps it should be just one big city, an endless stretch of suburbs, in which people are so much easier to control than those determinedly independent rural pockets of individualism.

country work

ATTITUDES

PREVIOUS PAGE
Broadcasting artifcial fertiliser by hand at Terling, Essex

IN THE 1960S AGRICULTURE WAS POISED BETWEEN TWO WORLDS AND HESITATING ABOUT WHICH WAY TO GO. THE DECISION IN FAVOUR OF MECHANISATION HAD BEEN MADE BY THE TIME OF THE SECOND WORLD WAR BUT THE NEXT DECISION WAS A MATTER OF SCALE. THE AVERAGE FARM WAS STILL A FAMILY ONE AND THE CHOICE SEEMED TO BE TO BECOME LARGE AND SPECIALISED OR TO REVERT TO SMALLHOLDING.

Agricultural protest march in 1936, during the depths of yet another depression. The 'shocks' of corn on the hat are a nice touch

INCREASINGLY IT WOULD be the former. Farming was becoming big business, run by those who were trained at agricultural colleges rather than those whose knowledge of farming was imbibed with their mother's milk. By the 1990s the family farm was almost extinct in many parts of the country, except in those regions where there were no large profits to be made.

Here and there they tackled it in a different way. In the Devon parish of Loddiswell in 1958 the local farmers and those of adjoining parishes formed a co-operative as a non-profit-making company to reduce their costs and improve their marketing techniques. Within a few years the company was supplying 800 farmers throughout South Devon, turning over more than £600,000 a year. It handled feed, fertilisers, seed, sprays and any farm or domestic equipment the farmers and their families needed. It sent calves to farmers as far away as Lincolnshire and Kent and weaner pigs to the Midlands, obtaining much better prices than individual farmers might. Its buildings department employed twenty craftsmen and labourers. It was felt that tighter economic circumstances were changing farming into an industrial business rather than a way of life. 'The farm labourer of the past is almost redundant, and staff with specialist knowledge is becoming essential.' With the increasing mechanisation of agriculture, farmers had to know about engineering as well as about crops and animals.

There used to be an urban assumption that country workers were simple people doing simple work. But in agriculture you need – and always did need – a complex level of skills and above all ingenuity. Many of the skills were and are highly technical, and there is also a much greater need for self-reliance than in many more 'intellectual' jobs.

Numerous rural communities in recent years have undertaken village appraisals, looking at every aspect of village life and making a genuine effort to listen to those who live there. The more useful of these appraisals, aimed at understanding villagers' needs, ask about the nature of people's work, how far they travel to it and what new job opportunities they would

attitudes

LEFT
Hand-broadcasting from a sowing-basket, a skill that relied on careful calculation and a good sense of rhythm

BELOW
Loading a mechanical seed-drill with barley

like to see in the village. It is also interesting to take stock of the different kinds of work that people do, and you can almost guarantee that those who work on the land in some way are no longer in the majority. Whatever the type of employment, in many villages the distance to work has increased considerably in the last fifty years, with often a high proportion of people commuting by train, bus or car to jobs in towns and cities.

The effects of the swing of the workers' focus from their own parish to the town are far-reaching. Absent from the village for most of their waking hours, they cannot contribute fully to its economic and community life, however much they might wish to do so. They shop in town, as they happen to be there anyway, to the demise of the village shops and services; they take advantage of the town's recreational facilities and so the village ones wither; they add to lane traffic by their commuting and are very often in a hurry, late for work or for delivering the children to school, so they drive at speed; they are simply not around enough during the week to notice the small details of village life, the little local difficulties and joys; they are not there to keep company with the old or the lonely or their own young; they have too little time at precious weekends to be involved in village activities, preferring to spend it at home catching up with the family or the mowing or household tasks or private leisure pursuits. In too many places the villages are almost dead during weekdays and then feel invaded by virtual strangers at weekends – strangers who are often highly articulate and tend to take over 'management' of the village, bending its ways to suit their own and sometimes claiming, somewhat patronisingly, that it is 'for the good of the village'.

'...they are not there to keep company with the old or the lonely or their own young...'

AGRICULTURAL WORK

MELON GREEN LIVED ON A SMALLHOLDING NEAR LISS, HAMPSHIRE, BUT WOULD CAMP ON THE SOUTH DOWNS AT ROTTINGDEAN. HERE HE GOT TO KNOW A PLOUGHMAN WITH TWO HEAVY HORSES, A MAN WHO NEVER TOOK A HOLIDAY BECAUSE HE SO LOVED HIS ANIMALS. THEN, IN THE LATE 1930S, THE FARMER FOR WHOM THE PLOUGHMAN WORKED DIED.

'"Perhaps a few years hence we shall no longer see the jolly teams of horses starting out for the day's work ..."'

A YOUNGER MAN took over the farm but said that by the end of the summer he would have to use a tractor, not the horses. Well, you can't say 'Woah', 'Gee-whut-ah' or 'Mither-wee' to a tractor, can you? Melon Green met the distressed ploughman that summer on the Downs, looking as white as a sheet at the thought of losing his horses. A while later he saw a picture in the local papers of the same man ploughing on the Downs, with the story that a thunderbolt had come out of a clear blue sky and killed him and his two horses stone dead.

Gertrude Jekyll, writing in 1925, noted that 'mechanical traction' was taking the place of horse power: 'Perhaps a few years hence we shall no longer see the jolly teams of horses starting out for the day's work or see them at work in the field or carrying the loads of farm produce along the roads. Are we to expect the extinction of those splendid breeds of heavy horse? Is all this living strength and beauty to give way to dead contrivances of unsightly iron?' Well, yes it would.

How often do you see the ploughman as he 'homeward plods his weary way'? How often do you see whole families in the fields, helping with the hay or the harvest? How often do you see people working in teams on the land? Consider the changes between the nineteenth century and the twentieth, especially since the Second World War.

In the nineteenth century, arable land was worked by oxen and heavy horses, at a slow and steady pace. The ploughman, his hand guiding the plough and his eye maintaining a straight furrow, knew every inch of the fields that he walked. With his boots tramping the soil (he walked on average about sixteen miles a day), he was in touch with the land and part of it. He worked up a sweat under the sun, he felt the jaw-numbing icy wind in his face and

Plough team at work. As this is a two-furrow plough, it needs three horses

agricultural work

the rain on his back; he smelled the earth, saw the worms, felt the wingbeats of the seagulls that followed him, heard the sudden twittering of flocks of sparrows and finches as they rose ahead of him, stumbled on the stones, slithered in the damp patches, and all the while kept company with the animals that helped in his work, their rumps methodically swaying and dipping in front of him. His eyes were always looking ahead.

That might seem lonely, but at least he had the animals and he constantly talked to them, in the traditional language that guided them to press on or draw to a halt, turn a corner, edge right or left. He was in touch with living creatures and his rhythm was their rhythm, the hooves plodding carefully and regularly, harness jangling gently, the occasional swish of a tail. Even if his thoughts were elsewhere, his whole being was focused on where he was, in the field, in the furrow, behind the animals.

In contrast, today the trundling tractor driver rarely uses his legs. He is isolated in his safety cab, insulated from the weather and from the living world that surrounds him. So he plugs his ears and links with another world, the world of the radio, its music jarring against the background of birdsong and his tractor engine's rumble travelling widely across the fields.

Both men will be tired and grimy by the end of the day; both will have their resentments and their worries; both will feel underpaid and undervalued; but perhaps the old ploughman will have had a richer life than the tractor driver, and he will have been much surer of his place in the scheme of things.

Meal break at Froxfield, Hampshire, for the men and their teams

The ploughman's day was a long one: he would see to his horse's needs in the stable as well as in the field

agricultural work

Steam threshing. The man on the platform (protected by a canvas windbreak) is feeding sheaves to a threshing drum driven by the steam engine; others are clearing away chaff, pitching straw and loading threshed grain into sacks. A wheeled water tumbril stands by to 'refuel' the steam engine

RIGHT Using hand-flails to thresh corn needed good team work, with each man swinging in turn, to prevent the freely rotating wooden 'sweple' from hitting a neighbouring thresher on the head

THE GREATEST CONTRAST is at the culminations of the farming year. Victorian haymaking and harvest often involved most of the village – farm labourers, women and children, grandads and grannies, aunts and uncles, school teachers glad to escape the school room on a summer's day, a few others deserting their normal work in order to join in with the hard labour and the good company of these great village occasions. There was a strong sense of communal purpose, a strong understanding of the rhythm of nature's seasons, a sense of urgency to make the hay or to harvest the grain before the weather turned, a sense of celebration and security when the crop was finally in and winter could be faced in the knowledge that there was fodder for the animals and corn for the mill. And then, of course, there was the harvest-home supper, highlight of the year and the chance to stuff yourself silly.

Today haymaking and harvest are of concern only to the farmer and the farmworkers. The village might watch, and perhaps complain, while the crop travels along the lanes; the children might thrill to the majesty of the huge combine-harvester wheezing into life in the morning and then relentlessly moving up and down and around the field to fell the head-heavy stems and devour them, spitting out the straw. They might hear the chunter of the baling machine scooping up hay or straw, packing it tight and tying it with brightly coloured twine as if there were a hidden gang of gnomes working within its bowels. They

agricultural work

might watch the bales being loaded on to trailers and carted away; they might watch a succession of tractors individually shadowing the combine to catch cascades of grain in their trailers; they might watch trailers loaded with wilted silage haring along the lanes in busy convoys. But they would only watch; they would not take part. The men in their machines would be working more or less alone in the landscape. The community spirit is no longer at work in the fields; hence it is hardly surprising that much of the community is divorced from the farms and no longer understands or sometimes no longer sympathises with them.

Farmers now employ very few workers. A farm that might have had a team of a dozen men within living memory now has only one or two. In the parish of Bedingham in Sussex at the end of the eighteenth century, there were 25 households. One farm maintained 23 labourers from the parish (all but three of them married, with 41 children between them); another maintained two labourers, both married and with a total of eight children; at another it was 16 labourers supporting 38 children. The farmers themselves had in their own families 11, 5, 24 and 20 people. Three men, 4 women and 18 children were maintained by the poorhouse, which was a very small proportion of the total population of 252 people – everybody else was on the farms.

Gertrude Jekyll watched the changes in farming practice with interest 'Nearly the whole of the change from hand labour to machine work in agriculture has taken place within my recollection,' she wrote in 1904. She could remember when hay was mown with scythes and made with forks and wooden hayrakes – you only needed these three tools to make hay, and they would hang in the labourer's back-kitchen or outhouse. But for haymaking in late Victorian times they needed a number of horse implements: mowers, kickers and tedders to air the hay for drying, swathe-turners for turning it and finally horse-rakes. All of these mechanical tools needed plenty of maintenance, repairing and space for storage, on top of which you needed at least a pair of horses to work them. And all of this would be used for perhaps only three or four weeks in the year.

Jekyll also remembered using a reaping-hook, or rip-hook, to harvest corn. A healthy, strong child in the late 1840s and early 1850s, she had delighted in any bodily exercise and thoroughly enjoyed a day in the harvest field with her hook. 'Anyone who has never done a day's work in the harvest field would scarcely believe what dirty work it is. Honest sweat and dry dust combine into a mixture not unlike mud. Hay-making is drawing-room work in comparison.' A man could, by working very hard indeed, reap an acre in a day by hand.

THRESHING CORN

Jekyll remembered how corn used to be threshed by hand with leather-hinged wooden flails on the barn floor. It was work that could be done at any time from harvest to the following spring, giving occupation for many in the winter months. The hand-winnowed corn was stored in beautiful old granaries, usually built over a wagon shed and standing on staddle-stones so that vermin could not break in. Today all the tools that Jekyll used and remembered hang uselessly on pub walls, mere decoration.

agricultural work

ABOVE
Delicate weeding amid the crop, in strong contrast to modern crop spraying. The weeds were carefully put into the 'plough apron' worn by each worker around the waist

OPPOSITE
Three generations of hop-pickers

BELOW LEFT
Sorting and polishing apples
BELOW RIGHT
Spraying a commerical orchard

AFTER THE HARVEST came gleaning, with women and children picking up the often substantial quantities of grain left in the fields. The wives and children of farm servants were allowed to glean on the fields of the father's employer before the sheaves were lifted. If anybody else came along, they were roped off into an area where the sheaves had already been removed: there would be a horse at either end of the rope to move the line down the field as the sheaves were taken off. The gleaners popped their bounty into apron pockets and kerchiefs, threshed what they had gleaned and then took it down to the mill for grinding, free of charge. They could gather enough to keep them in bread through most of the winter.

Jekyll wondered if the days of cheerful gangs of haymakers and harvesters had gone forever – all those lovely memories of well-earned meals eaten sitting under the shady side of the hedge or a large oak. Mowers had regular breaks: they started work at daylight (the first man there got a pint of ale) then took breakfast at six, lunch at half-past nine, dinner at noon, afternoon lunch at four and supper at seven. The farmer usually gave each man a bottle of beer or cider, carried in wooden harvest bottles like miniature barrels, holding a gallon and slung from the shoulder by a leather strap, and the drinking became a ritual, with the farmer calling a halt at the appropriate times. Sometimes a thirsty man would stand with head thrown back, both arms raised, pouring the liquor straight from the bottle into his mouth by way of a projecting spout rather than pouring it into a communual horn mug. While the men's bottles were kept replenished with beer, the women were offered watered-down homemade wine.

Hop-picking in the traditional style of numerous families descending on the hop fields from the towns died out during the twentieth century. In the 1960s, in the Kentish village of Pembury, only one farm still used its oasts for their original purpose of drying hops, and only one family came down from London: the hops by then were picked by machine and the family joined about fourteen local women merely to do the final checking for quality and the absence of leaves. Local orchards of cherries and plums had mostly been grubbed out by 1960 and replanted with apples, mainly Coxes, which were sprayed thirteen or fourteen times in a growing season.

agricultural work

agricultural work

In the 1871 census return for Lower Heyford, 25-year-old farmer Henry Hone employed nine labourers, four boys and three women on his 281-acre farm, and two more as resident maids in the house. Today a similar farm will probably employ two men, and no maids. In 1870 a neighbouring farmer, W.P. King, had bought a new reaping machine for nearly £30. It was calculated to do the work of sixteen men with only one man and two horses. That was fine for Mr King, but it immediately lost work for the men and, as George Dew put it in his diary, 'it transfers labour from agricultural labourers to engineering mechanics. I believe the use of reaping & other farm machines does really make more work, but it is the transfer just mentioned & the concentration of trade in towns which may for a time be rather injurious.' How prescient he was! By 1877 all the hay in his area was cut by mowing machines, though they were said to 'bruise the grass rather than cut it in two, & hence the after crop is not near so good as when it is hand mown where the scythe must be sharp & make a clean cut'.

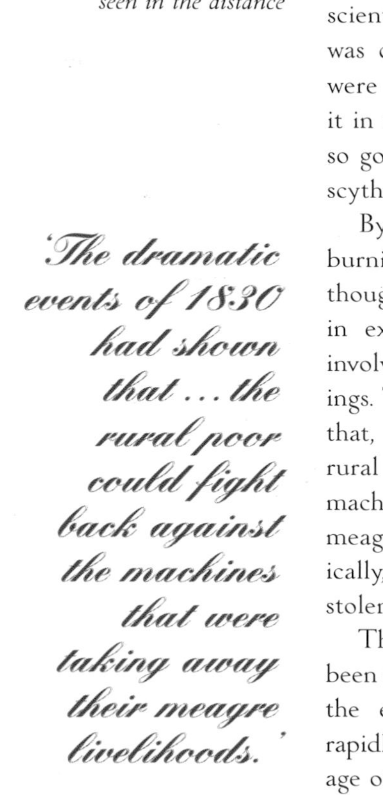

Stooks of parsnip seed drying at Cressing Temple, Essex. The wheat and barley barns can be seen in the distance

'The dramatic events of 1830 had shown that . . . the rural poor could fight back against the machines that were taking away their meagre livelihoods.'

By then the emotionally charged rick-burning riots of 1830 were a generation ago, though some agricultural labourers were still in exile in Australia as a result of their involvement in those 'Captain Swing' uprisings. The dramatic events of 1830 had shown that, compelled by appalling poverty, the rural poor could fight back against the machines that were taking away even their meagre livelihoods. What they attacked, physically, were threshing machines, which had stolen their winter employment.

Threshing machines, the first of which had been invented in Scotland in the second half of the eighteenth century, had spread south rapidly because of an increasingly acute shortage of labour during the Napoleonic wars. At first the machines had been static, driven by horses or water-power, but in due course they became more portable, worked by one or two horses, and might be owned by an itinerant contractor who would hire out the machine to farmers when needed, the farmers providing the horses and the labour. A rather surprising fact about the 1830 uprising was that the labourers who smashed the machines had the sympathy of many farmers, who had felt com-

agricultural work

pelled to use machines in order to get their corn to market as quickly as their neighbours, putting the whole farming community on a keeping-up-with-the-Joneses' treadmill of mechanisation from which it was difficult to escape. When the labourers trashed every machine in the area, everybody was back to equality.

In 1872 agricultural workers were again feeling their muscle and going on strike. They were joining labour unions, holding open-air meetings in the villages and getting the sack for it. Unions for agricultural workers were something new in 1872, when Joseph Arch, a hedgecutter from Warwickshire, was the leading figure in the first National Agricultural Labourers' Union.

BELOW
Threshing a corn stack on an Essex farm. A local lad is standing by with a stout stick, ready to dispatch any rats that scurry out

agricultural work

'If you look at old field names you will usually find a Furze Field next to a lime kiln...'

IN MAY THAT YEAR in the village of Upper Heyford, about 300 men, women and children gathered to hear about unions and 50 of them joined on the spot at a subscription of tuppence a week. The main aim of their union was to increase the standard wage to sixteen shillings a week. Two months later, in another village, all except two of the agricultural labourers joined the union after their meeting, and this began to happen increasingly over a widening area. Then the farmers began to create their own unions in self-defence at the growing power of their workers. Oh dear. In 1872 these farmers applied to the military authorities at Aldershot for soldiers to work in their harvest fields at Wootton, so determined were they not to employ union members.

A farm worker's caravan

In 1873 Shadrack Edmunds applied to the Board of Guardians for medical relief: he was ill, with a wife and four young children dependent on him. But he belonged to the NALU and received tenpence a day as sick pay, so the Board refused his request, saying that by belonging to a union he had forfeited his rights to relief and should go into the workhouse. It was not long before one or two union members took to burning ricks, or at least they were accused of doing so, though there was no sound evidence.

A new Agricultural Children Act that came into force in 1875 stated that no child under the age of eight could be employed in agriculture, except by its own parents, and that those between the ages of eight and twelve had to attend school for a certain number of days each year, though they could gain permanent exemption from attendance even below the age of twelve as long as they had reached the 'fourth standard' at school. The Elementary Education Act of the same year said that where 'out relief' was given to the parent of any child aged between five and thirteen years, it was only on condition that the child received elementary instruction in the three Rs. The legislation became more severe under the Education Act of 1876.

Well! Many a farmer had children as young as six working in the fields, and many (farmers, parents and all) deeply resented this new legislation and largely ignored it. Families continued to work together at peak seasons in the fields. In 1873 a woman named Savin, whose husband had deserted her, had a son of seven years old who went to work. When she applied for relief from Bicester's Board of Guardians, most of its members said it was good for children to begin work young and would do them more good than going to school. In 1874, farmer Charles Brown on the same Board said he could not bear the thought of poor children having to go to school! In 1878, farmer Thomas Tuffrey was prosecuted for illegal employment of his own ten-year-old son to help him with the ploughing; he was fined eight shillings.

LIME KILNS AND SMUGGLERS

Where soils were light and sandy, the practice was to spread lime in some form. Typically a farm would have its own circular open-topped kiln for burning lime and you sometimes find their remains, built into steep slopes near the road so that loads of chalk could be delivered to them. Large blocks of chalk were built up inside the kiln like an arch, with smaller pieces above – not unlike stacking a charcoal kiln. Furze faggots were crammed into the space under this chalk arch to burn the chalk into lime. If you look at old field names you will usually find a Furze Field next to the lime kiln, unless the kiln is by a common. Furze, or 'fuzz bushes', blanketed many an area and found many uses. They were also valued by several species of songbird that have now become rare.

Most lime kilns had fallen out of use by the middle of the nineteenth century and became things of mystery to country children: their low, rounded entrances hiding under a cover of bramble bushes looked as if

agricultural work

they must lead to secret tunnels. Of course there *were* secret tunnels as well, especially those used by smugglers, and some of these were quite extensive. There is one in Wiltshire which, if you ventured along it as a child, would scare the living daylights out of you halfway along: when you looked up to a glimmer of light, you saw a carved face staring down at you. Smuggling was at its height at the end of the eighteenth century and the beginning of the nineteenth. If you met a rider who looked particularly stout, he might well have had yards of smuggled silk wrapped around his body under his coat. Many are the local tales about lost kegs of brandy, or about horses disappearing from your field one night and being replaced by tired nags that had beaten up the secret tracks from the coast – there would usually be a small gift of spirits to thank you for 'lending' your fresh horse

People alive in the 1890s could still tell tales of smugglers they had known, or had themselves been. If you came across smuggled goods hidden in the countryside, the custom was that you marked a few of the articles with chalk: the smugglers would leave those items for you when they collected their booty, in thanks that you had not reported your find.

Harvesting oats in Herefordshire, on the slopes of the Black Mountains. This horse-drawn binder would later use tractor power instead

LIVESTOCK FARMING

One of the big revolutions in the countryside has been the change from mixed farming – family farms that grew a bit of this and a bit of that, generally in small fields, and had animals as well as crops, partly for sound husbandry reasons, partly in order to be self-sufficient and partly from a dislike of putting all your eggs in one basket.

'Those who tend livestock of any kind deserve considerable respect but rarely received it...'

STOCKMEN

The feeling, and experience, was that if cattle prices were disastrous, corn prices were likely to be good; if pigs crashed (as they often did and do) then sheep would see you through. Today, mixed farming is rare; most farms are either arable or livestock, and the latter specialise in either cattle or sheep, pigs or poultry, but not usually a combination of them.

With animals, you can form a relationship, whether of mutual respect or affection, dominance or distrust; it is a two-way affair. Because it is a living relationship, good stockmen cannot be clock-watchers: they are responsive to the needs of their charges as they arise. Animals need to be fed and watered every day of the year, including Sundays and Christmas Day – days when they invariably create a crisis by escaping from the field, falling ill or dropping dead.

All that is changing, of course. Mechanisation is distancing the stockman from the animals. It might be making the daily work easier, but it has also meant the loss of many jobs among those who used to look after the animals, so that in turn there are fewer agricultural families in the countryside. Their individual voices are becoming fainter and fainter, and they feel increasingly isolated in rural society.

Those who tend livestock of any kind deserve considerable respect but rarely received it. Many were deeply knowledgeable about their charges, even when their 'knowledge' was merely acceptance of what had gone before, however erroneous. There was often cruelty, but more through poverty, neglect, or ignorance of an animal's needs or of the more subtle ways of encouraging it to go where you wanted it to go, than through a desire to inflict deliberate physical or mental pain.

With two world wars, Britain looked to its livestock farmers to produce more and to produce it quickly. In fact this intensification began during the rush from country to town during the industrial revolution – hence the great interest in scientific breeding of livestock in the eighteenth and nineteenth centuries. Farming methods changed in order to produce large amounts of meat and milk to meet the demands of towns and cities that could no longer produce them for their own inhabitants, and the countryside became a factory for urban areas. It has remained so ever since, with subsequent governments encouraging more and more intensive production of cheaper and cheaper food, putting the pro-

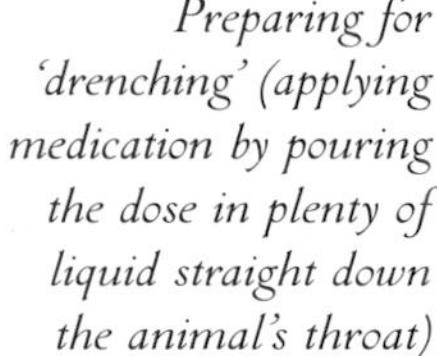
Preparing for 'drenching' (applying medication by pouring the dose in plenty of liquid straight down the animal's throat)

livestock farming

LEFT
Taking winter food to outlying cattle by sledge in the Dales

ducers on a treadmill that they cannot escape. This has had enormous ramifications in the countryside – for its landscape, for its social structure, and for its attitudes.

MILKERS

Ma Snooks, born in Dorset in the first decade of the twentieth century, was fond of harking back to her girlhood, when she milked cows by hand. She could manage seven cows an hour (if they behaved themselves) and she loved it, but to the end of her life she would drink only tinned evaporated milk; she was too well aware of what else had gone into her pail.

Those of us who have hand-milked house cows appreciate how hard on the hands it must have been to milk at Ma Snooks's rate, but there are far fewer of us now. Recently a cry went out in my own valley for a hand-milker or two to help on a smallholding, whose owner had been rushed to hospital leaving two Jersey cows and four goats with full udders. Eventually two of us were found, both rusty as it had been years since we had milked an animal. Fifty years ago there would have been countless villagers able to turn their hand with practised ease to milking.

Milkers' tales are many, usually involving recalcitrant cows that knock over brimming pails of hard-won milk just as the session finishes, or play up so much that milking is impossible. Cows are not machines and they are very responsive to individual humans; they will 'let down' their milk for some people (usually those they know well) and absolutely refuse to do so for others. The more a frustrated milker shouts and bangs about, the tighter a cow holds back the milk in her bag.

George, in his eighties, remembered the day when his dad Joe came home from the pub, not in the best of moods. Joe was a faster milker than Ma Snooks; he could get through eleven cows in an hour, and had taught George milking at an early age on their own three or four house cows. So on this day he took nine-year-old George out to milk the cows, one of which was a known kicker. The cow sensed Joe's mood but dad put George on the milking stool anyway. Sure enough, George had drawn half a pail of milk out of her when he felt the kick coming, but he did not act fast enough; her hoof sent the milk, the pail, the stool and George flying into the gutter. Livid, Joe threw a rope around the cow's horns and heaved upwards so that both her front legs were clean off the ground. 'Now you milk her, she's only got two legs to stand on!' he said, with never a thought as to whether the little lad had been hurt.

It was often said that women made better milkers (think of Tess of the d'Urbervilles – Thomas Hardy writes most evocatively about milking and cows) as they had more patience and a gentler touch. The same was said for the skill of calf-rearing: it takes a special sense of caring to persuade a calf, deprived of its mother as all dairy calves are at four days old, to suck up milk from a bucket. Bert, a strong, barrel-chested man in his seventies, is unusual among cowmen: he is a gentle genius with bewildered young calves and always immensely proud of that first moment when he can successfully withdraw his fingers from their sucking mouths so that they unwittingly find themselves lapping from the pail.

Swaledale farmer John Rew coming down Kisdon Hill to Muker, with a back-can of milk from his morning milking

livestock farming

THINGS HAVE CHANGED for the dairy farmer. In Ma Snooks's youth, the cow herds were still small enough for a family to manage – often no more than a dozen. Those of an older generation can certainly remember a time when every local farm and most smallholdings had a few milking cows, even after the last war. Today the cows are milked by machine in herds of at least a hundred, often twice as many, managed by one person. In the old days it would have taken one person about fifteen hours to milk a hundred cows, non-stop, or eight milkers to do what one machine can do in two hours. The milkers no longer have jobs; the cows no longer have names, but numbers; the cowman has a computer and the cows wear transponders around their necks so that their allotted rations are delivered automatically – in some parlours the cows are even milked by robots. Cowmen usually work alone, with their robots and machines, and you'll never see the likes of Hardy's singing groups of milkers again. It is a much lonelier job now.

SHEPHERDS

Among stockmen, shepherds have always been held in higher respect by their employers and regarded more romantically by dreamers. Shepherding has changed much less than dairying. There isn't the scope for mechanisation and the old dog-and-stick method often persists in the hills except that, now, the shepherd often rides a quad bike. He (or increasingly she) relies on well-trained dogs but he has a mobile phone to summon help in remote areas (if he is lucky enough for the mobile to get a signal there) and he probably practises preventive medicine on his sheep to a far greater degree than even thirty years ago.

Most of the old remedies have been cast aside or forgotten in favour of antibiotics and suchlike. Young shepherds would look at you blankly if you asked them about bleeding sheep when there had been a case of pooke, or dosing sheep with turpentine for fluke, salting their hay to prevent 'the rot', grinding up hellebore for scab, using a mixture of train oil and brimstone or of sulphur and lard for fly strike, or chalk in milk for scouring and, better, a glass of gin with ground pepper for colic. But shepherds remain better stockmen on the whole than cowmen, because they remain closer to their animals, with no mechanisation to distance them.

A major controversy in recent years has been the regulatory dipping of sheep in persistent insecticides, which many claim are highly damaging to the health of the sheep farmer, let alone the sheep. In dipping, the aim is to ensure that the animals are wholly submerged, albeit

livestock farming

LEFT
Sheep-washing in a stream

briefly, in the dip mixture. The dip is deep enough to force them to swim, in which they need to be encouraged to keep going as sheep hate water, hate getting wet – hardly surprising when you consider the weight of a wet fleece.

Sheep were being dipped even in the eighteenth century. John Ellman, born in 1753 and a famous breeder of Southdown sheep, described how to dip lambs to avoid problems with ticks. The mixture consisted of water (boiled in an iron kettle over a fire), soft soap and arsenic. Each lamb was seized by two men, one holding its forelegs and the other its hindlegs, who then immersed the lamb upside down ('taking care that its head is kept from going under the mixture') long enough for its wool to be thoroughly wetted with the cooled dip mixture. Then the lamb was lifted out and put, still on its back, on a cradle over a draining tub while excess dip was pressed from the wool (more to save on the dip than to dry off the lamb). Some flock masters insisted that the whole flock be dipped in this way, twice a year. Ellmann did point out that arsenic was poisonous and not to be ingested 'by any creature whose life we value'; he suggested that an infusion of tobacco would be equally effective, though more expensive.

Not to be confused with dipping was sheep-washing, usually in the local river or stream. This took place in June about a fortnight before shearing, when the 'yolk' or lanolin grease had risen in the fleece. Washing was a tiring, cold, wet job and required several helpers. For example, two men might be suspended in barrels anchored to posts in midstream in a tidal river, rising and falling with the surge of the tide. The sheep were driven into the water and urged by the rest of the team, with the help of poles, to swim between the two men, who would grab them and rub the fleeces with their hands, then dunk the animals under the water for a thorough cleansing. Many places had special sheep-washing pools, some of them complete with a huge stone plug so that the water could be drained away.

After washing came shearing, and here there has been mechanisation in recent years. The older shepherds used hand-shears to clip the fleece; modern shearers use high-speed machines instead. The older shepherds placed a high value on the fleece; today wool is usually a negligible proportion of the sheepfarmer's income.

Shearers now are as likely to be teams of migrant Australians and New Zealanders as local shepherds. The teams are also taking over other aspects of shepherding in some areas, hired for a month or two here and there, usually at lambing, and always on the move. They no longer live alone for several

Shearing by hand. The wattle hurdles in the background were ideal for setting up temporary lambing pens or sheep-handling areas

livestock farming

weeks in isolated wheeled huts at lambing time, or build temporary lambing pens by hand on the hills and downs with wattle hurdles and thatch. It is more likely that the lambing ewes will be brought indoors to a barn close to the farmhouse – much more convenient when things go wrong.

Flocks of sheep pouring along the lanes on their way to market or to fresh pastures are now a rare sight in Britain. They are more likely to be piled into double-decker livestock lorries, packed tight so that they do not topple over with every bend in the road, noses pressing between the slatted sides for fresh air and a few querulous bleats plaintive above the sound of the engine. Some farmers do still move their flocks along the lanes on foot now and then, to the outrage of motorists in a hurry; the flock might be preceded by children, checking that every garden gate along the way is closed to keep the sheep out of the flowerbeds.

Downland flock filling the lane. The bearded collie was traditionally a useful sheepdog

PIG AND POULTRY FARMERS

'Pigs used to rootle the fields but for the past thirty or forty years most of them have been confined indoors . . .'

Perhaps the saddest change in the countryside is the disappearance of the livestock that bring landscapes to life. The fields are emptier and dull. With intensification, many animals have moved indoors since the Second World War: beef cattle are finished in yards and barns, out of sight; pigs used to rootle the fields but for the past thirty or forty years most of them have been confined indoors, hidden from the general public to such an extent that people are surprised by just how big a real pig can be; chickens that used to scratch in farmyards are now, notoriously, reared intensively in cages or, at best, on deeplitter straw in barns. The public no longer connect the animals with their products.

Both pig and poultry farming have become major industries. In 1990, for example, some 80 per cent of all breeding sows in England were on only 2,500 units, with an average of nearly 250 sows per unit. Thirty years earlier the average pig herd size was 8 animals and there were 110,000 pig farms, run by families rather than companies.

Therefore, the pigman's job is very different now from that of the traditional swineherd caring for pigs on pannage, or even of the pigman of the immediate post-war years caring for outdoor saddlebacks. Today he is likely to work with a very large number of animals, probably all indoors and probably all white. In almost impossible circumstances, pigmen struggle to retain their husbandry skills – for husbandry requires a recognition of individual animals and their needs. With intensification come all the diseases of stress and of too many animals together in one place. Modern pigmen sometimes know more about regulations and drugs than about what makes a pig contented, and rarely have time to stand and stare, which is such a crucial part of animal husbandry.

The poultry industry has developed along similar lines and for similar reasons. After the Second World War, in contrast to sheep and cattle farmers, pig and poultry farmers were without subsidies and had to become supremely sufficient to survive. Scientific breeding was the secret of that survival, combined with scale, and during the 1960s in particular some very large pig and poultry companies began to develop, dominating the two industries. They did so by producing hybrids, bred for maximum production in intensive environments.

Hybrid hens were developed for battery units, in which all the birds' energy can be channelled into laying eggs; meat birds were developed for equally intensive broiler units. Poultry farmers no longer needed to shift homemade wooden arks around the field, scattering food on the grass and dust to supplement what the birds could find naturally. They no longer needed to collect eggs warm from the nest by hand, or search for them under the hedges. Everything was mechanised and, as with pigs, the nature of husbandry altered radically. Pigs and poultry, in a very few decades, have changed from being essential backyard animals for feeding the family to being factory animals produced to

livestock farming

LEFT
Orchard pigs

provide the supermarkets with cheap food.

In the past it wasn't all backyard farming, of course. In the 1870s the Oxfordshire villages of Fencott and Murcott were famous for duck-rearing. George Dew of Lower Heyford visited these hamlets and wrote: '... of all the miserable places I ever saw these two are certainly the most miserable. ... All the land lies so low that during winter it is partially inundated ... and when the water has subsided the fishy smelling miasma is to strangers almost unbearable. ... There is only one sight worth seeing in either Fencott or Murcott, and that is their ducks in the several muddy pools; hundreds of white Aylesbury ducks as white as snow and altogether beautiful creatures contrasting strangely with the surrounding objects.' These ducks were destined for Smithfield market, and the locals could earn good money from the duck trade. By 1914, some of the local rearers were making a net 11 to 15 shillings per pair, which was handsome money at the time.

As for geese, in Lincolnshire in the late eighteenth century they would be plucked five times a year. The feathers of a dead goose were 'worth 6d, three giving a pound' but 'plucking alive does not yield more than 3d a head per annum'. The thought of a goose being plucked while it is still alive is a truly alarming one. The boatman for Sir Joseph Banks on East Fen explained that he had a stock of eight score geese; in 1797, which was not a good year, he reared 500 (in a good year it would be 700, averaging eight in a brood), selling at 2s. He plucked four times a year at 4d a time 'because he thinks more hurts the old ones'. He plucked the young two or three times and would get ten quills from each goose. His net profit for the year would be about £40 but his interviewer thought he was exaggerating wildly.

'The thought of a goose being plucked alive is a truly alarming one.'

SMALLHOLDERS

A SMALLHOLDING CANNOT REALLY BE DEFINED. TO GOVERNMENTS, IT IS GENERALLY A FARM OF LESS THAN ABOUT 50 ACRES – OFTEN AS LITTLE AS JUST A COUPLE OF ACRES. IN 1801, AFTER THE ENCLOSURES OF THE EIGHTEENTH CENTURY HAD DEPRIVED MANY OF ACCESS TO GRAZING LAND, THE BOARD OF AGRICULTURE DECLARED THAT ALL WOULD BE WELL IN THE RURAL WORLD IF EVERY FAMILY HAD 'THREE ACRES AND A COW'.

Pigs exercising commoners' rights on the green at Guns Mills, near Flaxley, Gloucestershire

THAT PHRASE BECAME well used, and was adopted by Eli Hamshire, born in 1834 as the seventh son of an agricultural labourer at Ewhurst Green, near Cranleigh, Surrey. Eli was a great one for writing to politicians and the like and had grown up on his father's smallholding of three acres; at the age of only fourteen he rented a field for himself (a little less than three acres) at £4 per annum, though for the first year all he managed to grow on it was horse-mint and clover. Three years later he had become a chicken dealer as well.

Eli was a wily young man. For example, he also traded as a carrier and had a useful ruse for passing through toll-gates: he would unhitch his horse from the cart, take the horse through on its own (for free) and then pull the cart through himself for a charge of only a halfpenny, instead of the sixpence it would have cost for ,horse and cart to go through together. Then he would give what he had saved to the first poor fellow he met on the rest of his journey. And if he decided his load was not worth putting the horse between shafts for, he simply packed the goods into a wickerwork frame strapped on his own back and walked the nine or ten miles to Guildford, bringing back in the same manner whatever the local shopkeeper needed from town, which was often a hundredweight of sugar. This was a man destined to do well in life (despite always wearing a slate-coloured short smock) and by the time of his death in 1896 he was a man of property who owned four houses, including a five-bedroomed bungalow he had built for his wife when she became wheelchair-bound after giving birth to a fourteen-pound baby in 1881.

'... all would be well in the world if every family had "three acres and a cow".'

Above all Eli Hamshire became an author (and self-publisher), writing under the pseudonym 'A Carrier's Boy'. He was a man with strong political views that have variously been

smallholders

described as Liberal, Socialist and Communist. In numerous pamphlets and in his books *The Source of England's Greatness and the Source of England's Poverty* and *The Three Great Locusts*, he wrote about machinery, he wrote about vaccination, he wrote about the agricultural labourer and the oppressed in general, and threw in his views on nicotine, 'young women pinching their waists in', intermarriage, labourers' cottages, illegitimate children, homes for heroes, the game laws, pollution, the cost of fish, drinking, swearing, hunting, the workhouse, allotments, stepmothers ... This particular smallholder had a very active mind indeed.

In a survey of English life and leisure published in 1951 and based on 'case histories', Mr R. was described as a smallholder in his late fifties 'who has risen to his present position by virtue of the fact that as a farm labourer he married the daughter of a moderately well-to-do farmer'. But he was an industrious and kindly man of modest habits who probably deserved the share of his wife's inheritance that had enabled him to buy his smallholding. He was almost illiterate (his wife conducted all his correspondence for him), a very keen churchgoer and intensely superstitious – always looking for omens. He would not dream of starting any farming operation (such as harvesting) on a Friday, as that would bring bad luck. His vices were few; he did not smoke, though he liked a pint at the pub two or three times a week; he did not gamble, but he enjoyed playing dominoes or cards and cheated quite openly, as did most of his fellow players.

His way of life was in strong contrast to that of the pastoral (almost alpine) Scottish Highlanders described by Thomas Pennant in 1771:

> *Ride eastward over a hill into Glen Tilt, famous in olden times for producing the most hardy warriors; it is a narrow glen, several miles in length, bounded on each side by mountains of an amazing height. Ascend a steep hill and find ourselves on an Arrie, or tract of mountain which the families of one or two hamlets retire to with their flocks for pasture in summer. Here, we refreshed ourselves with some goats' whey, at a Sheelin or Bothay, a cottage made of turf, the dairy house, where the Highland shepherds, or graziers, live with their herds and flocks, and during the fine season make butter and cheese.*

In the New Forest, it is still possible for smallholders to thrive, as the Stride family continue to do. They have commoners' rights which not only keep the family tradition going but also help to maintain the Forest in its familiar form. There have been Strides exercising those rights for at least 650 years and its ways are in their blood. Outside the cottage they have a few pigs, cows and calves, and of course they all ride and help in the annual round-up or drift to check the state of the free-ranging ponies and mark them to show that the grazing fee has been paid. In the New Forest and on many commons of old, rights included grazing for specific numbers of specific animals (ponies, cattle, goats, geese and so on), pannage for swine, and the right to collect firewood or to up dig turves (turbary) for fuel.

Successful smallholder sisters Angela and Elizabeth Reece picking their own gooseberries near Newent, Gloucestershire

HOME INDUSTRIES

SMALLHOLDING IS A WAY OF LIFE AND A WAY OF ACQUIRING THE BASIC ESSENTIALS BY SWEAT RATHER THAN CASH, AND IT COULD BE SAID PROUDLY THAT SMALLHOLDERS WERE BRITAIN'S PEASANTS. AS WELL AS GROWING CROPS AND RAISING LIVESTOCK FOR THEIR OWN TABLES, SMALLHOLDERS GENERALLY NEEDED PAID WORK OR TURNED TO A RANGE OF COTTAGE INDUSTRIES.

THEY WERE INGENIOUS at converting cheap or free raw materials into something that could be sold. They were also typical of the many Victorians who had fingers in many pies – not for them a single job that was the same day in, day out, year in, year out. They believed firmly in diversification.

For example, there was besom-making – creating brooms from birch and heather on the commons where so often smallholders had grazing rights for their animals. The materials cost nothing, the brooms were quick to make and at the end of the nineteenth century they could be sold direct to the customer at three-and-sixpence a dozen for birch or half-a-crown a dozen for heather. In some parts besom-making became quite a well-organised trade, with loads being carted to the railway station for shipment to other parts of the country. Broom-squarers, or broom-squires, made for themselves the simple equipment they needed and usually worked under a heather-thatched shelter. The story goes that they often stuffed their money into the thatch for safe keeping and this could be the considerable sum of several hundred pounds.

Wood is a highly adaptable material and woodland crafts were numerous, all needing only simple home-made equipment along with cutting edges fashioned by the blacksmith or adapted from old tools. Some fashioned walking-sticks or shepherd's crooks; some created clappers for scaring off marauding birds; some made oaken pegs for pinning tiles to the roof; some made oak shakes, skilfully splitting the wood for use as tiles; some made thatching spars from supple lengths of hazel; some were good enough to split long hazel rods for making barrel hoops, or to split chestnut poles into fencing pales, or twist split hazel to weave wattle hurdles. Others made simple pole-lathes – springy poles with a string to turn a lathe for making wooden bowls and spoons.

Among the more organised woodland crafts on a larger scale were bodging (turning chair legs) and clog-making. Bodgers usually worked in pairs and on pole-lathes, setting up camp in the Chilterns beech woods to supply the big Windsor-chairmaking industry at High Wycombe. Clogging gangs were itinerant groups living in home-made shelters wherever they were working (generally in the northern counties and Wales); they made roughly shaped clog soles by the stack, usually of alder or sycamore, to sell to the village clog-makers, who would smooth the blocks into shape and attach leather uppers and sole irons. Charcoal burners also travelled in gangs, camping in the woods to mind their gently smoking kilns.

All around them, more serious timber felling was in progress. Trees have always been essential to house-building and ship-building, and for many centuries the crucial species was oak, found growing naturally in the ancient Wealden forests i1n particular. The act of felling large trees required considerable skill and also, for a long while, considerable strength and endurance as the work was entirely by hand, using axe and saw. The big two-man saws needed a good degree of team-work (and presented something of a challenge when you cycled to work with the saw along your crossbar). Next you had to get the timber out of the woods, and this is where oxen and horses came into their own, dragging felled tree-trunks between standing trees and then drawing massive wagon-loads of timber along the terrible roads.

In the twentieth century there were two major revolutions in the timber industry: the replacement of animal power by firstly steam

home industries

and finally the internal-combustion engine; and the invention of the chainsaw in the 1950s (though it was not in general use until the 1960s), which made the job a hundred times quicker and less tiring, but which also brought premature deafness to a whole generation of woodsmen before it was appreciated that ear-muffs should be worn. As for traction, the wheel is gently turning (so to speak): heavy horses are once again working in the woods to drag out timber from places that tractors and other machinery find impossible to reach.

Much of the timber would be taken to estate sawmills, and again the type of power used to drive the saws that turned tree trunks into planks evolved through animal and steam to petrol-driven and later electric engines.

In the villages you might find specialist workshops where craftsmen turned wood into rakes, or snaked scythe handles by steaming the wood until it was malleable enough to be curved gently into shape. The same system of steaming wood in hot sand was used to curve the backs of bentwood chairs and the rounded handles of walking-sticks.

Some of these woodland skills are still practised today, but the maker's income comes as much from demonstrating at country shows as in actually selling something that people want to use. At Milland Rural Fair, for example, the demonstrations of peg-making, pole-lathe turnery, besom-making, hurdle-making and every conceivable conversion of hazel and chestnut draw large admiring crowds – mainly to watch the quiet rhythm of traditional skills and only sometimes to buy. The travelling 'Yesterday's Farming' show put on by the South Somerset Agricultural Preservation Club demonstrates the use of old equipment and methods with eye-catching displays. There are beautifully maintained steam engines, Shire horses, vintage tractors, horse-drawn binders, old threshing machines and so on, but also bodgers making chair legs, blacksmiths forging iron, men thatching hay ricks and every kind of country craft you can imagine – and the crowds love it all. But how often do you still see a serious thatcher at work, making a new cottage roof? These highly skilled craftsmen are definitely a rare breed today, even in regions where thatch is the traditional hat for a house.

At a more basic level, the old skill of turning straw and hay into rope died out during the twentieth century, though there was a time when most farms had throw-crooks or rope-twisters in the barn. In some parts of the country rope-making was a more serious business and there were still some old rope-walks dotted about the villages in the 1920s. One of the last of the rope-makers died at the age of ninety in 1975; he used to spin his own hemp and then twist it into ropes on a system of T-shaped posts and geared wheels. But most of the cottage rope-makers had given up by the end of the nineteenth century, including those that lived and worked in the Castleton's Peak Cavern in Derbyshire. They had been a tourist attraction even in the seventeenth century, when travellers detoured to take a look at this cavern village, complete with livestock and haystacks.

Another home industry was working with rush, in areas where the raw material was plentiful. The work included making seats for chairs, weaving labourers' dinner-baskets, making mats and so on. During the First World War rush dinner-baskets were hard to find in Hampshire and the women of Micheldever decided to revive the craft of making them, turning it into a thriving little village business.

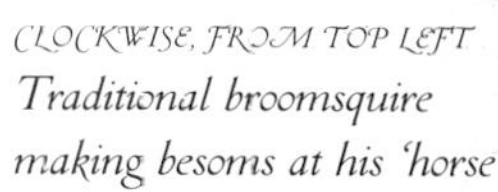

CLOCKWISE, FROM TOP LEFT

Traditional broomsquire making besoms at his 'horse'

Two-man cross-cut saw, in the days before chainsaws made wood-cutting so much easier and faster

Hurdle-maker and his workshop in the coppice. This is a light-weight gate hurdle, used for penning sheep

A Gloucestershire thatcher making his harvest knot to decorate the top of his rick

Making ropes for farmers

TRADES

THE SUSSEX PARISH OF GLYNDE, IN THE 1780S, HAD A POPULATION OF 212 LIVING IN 30 HOMES. ACCORDING TO JOHN ELLMAN, ALL OF ITS TRADESMEN AND ARTIFICERS WERE 'CONNECTED WITH AND DEPENDENT ON AGRICULTURE', SUCH AS CARPENTERS, WHEELWRIGHTS, BLACKSMITHS AND BRICKLAYERS. HE DID NOT SAY HOW MANY OF EACH, BUT THEY WERE ALL IN THE PLURAL.

RIGHT
Turner making bowls on a pole lathe near Wellington, Shropshire, in 1920

OPPOSITE
Cobbler mending boots in 1908 (top) and a saddler at Burford, Oxfordshire (below)

IN HIS 1791 statistical report on the Perthshire united parishes of Old Atholl (an area 18 miles wide and 30 miles long, including high mountains, glens, lochs, heath, peat-bog, pastureland and 'here and there a green spot, with huts upon them, to which the women, children and herds retire with the cattle for the summer season'), the Reverend James MacLagan numbered local 'mechanics' as: 6 smiths, 27 carpenters, 38 weavers, 32 tailors, 9 shoemakers, 16 flax dressers, 3 masons and 2 midwives. He noted that there was no physician, surgeon or attorney.

C.H. Middleton could remember his small boyhood village as it was a century later, when the horse still reigned along with the squire and there was a village harness-maker who took apprentices, a tailor, a shoesmith, carpenters working round the sawpit, and so much more. By the 1930s, he felt that the spirit of village life had departed – the saddler and tailor had gone, the golden harvest fields were down to grass along with the old village allotments, and the bus took people to buy bacon in town instead of having their own pig.

Farm workers making rope from straw in a barn at Lyth in the Lake District. The man in the foreground in using a throw-cock, or spindle, to twist the straw

Middleton described the good old countrymen that used to inhabit his village, 'ripe old gaffers, most of them with clean-shaven upper lips and a fringe of whiskers round the lower part of their faces; hale and hearty, bubbling over with wit and wisdom, and capable of emptying a quart pot without taking breath or flickering an eyelid'. But above all they were craftsmen, and they took a pride in their work and in each other's.

Ollie Baker, born before the First World War, was the son of a well-known harness-maker in the village of Northchapel, where Ollie, now retired as a market gardener, has lived all his life. His home overlooks the village green and he is saddened at the demise of cricket there. The village team was once highly esteemed – Noah Mann, the first 'swerve' bowler to play for England at Broadhalfpenny Down, Hambledon, was landlord of Northchapel's Half Moon inn during the eighteenth century. Ollie also regrets that, today, employment opportunities within the village are limited. In earlier centuries it had thriving glass and iron industries as well as agriculture, and in the nineteenth century a charcoal factory employed many local people.

In an intriguing study of countryside crafts

trades

published in 1958, W.M. Williams of Dartington Hall wrote about the organisation of rural industries in England. Since 1925 there had been official Rural Industries Organisers at large, and there was a Rural Industries Bureau, arising from the 1909 Development and Road Improvement Funds Act, all vaguely connected with the Rural Community Councils (first formed in 1921 at a time of rural crisis) and under the eye of the Development Commission. People really were trying to save rural industries. Incidentally, that 1909 Act listed, among the many types of rural industry it supported, the cultivation and preparation of tobacco.

Williams, in 1958, was still able to assume that most people had seen a rural craftsman at work, 'a farrier making a horse-shoe, a wheelwright building a wheel, or a weaver at his loom'. Yet in the 1940s Michael Tilley spoke in the past tense of the time when most villages had a farrier, an ironmonger, a saddler, a carpenter and a wheelwright, and the larger places might have a tannery, a brewery and a builder's yard. He reckoned that these village trades had been hit very hard since 1900 because of the changing structure of agriculture, as much as general economic trends. Cheaper mass-produced articles made in the towns were flooding their markets and squeezing out the craftsmen who had been the backbone of the village and who had made it self-sufficient. You could still quite easily find a farrier or black-smith and perhaps a thatcher in the 1940s, though it was more rare to find a wheelwright or a saddler, but nearly all of them were by then old men whose business would die with them, there being no apprentices or sons interested in continuing it. Farriers, wheel-wrights and saddlers had to adapt if they wished to service the tractors that were replacing horses. There might still be a demand for their services for repairs in the countryside, but not for making something new, and they were increasingly relying on the well-to-do and the connoisseur as their clients, rather than farmers and the village in general.

trades

RIGHT
Thatching in the 1930s

'To the young, farriery seemed to be a dead-end, dirty, smelly, sweaty and monotonous job...'

OPPOSITE LEFT
Capping a drystone wall in Derbyshire

The travelling farrier

WILLIAMS INTERVIEWED CRAFTSMEN in several parts of the country in his 1950s study and found many of them disheartened. Farriers in particular seemed to be ready to chuck their horse-shoes over the nearest hedge: it had become a low-prestige trade and many of them seemed to hate doing it anyway. 'You can keep it,' said one, who blamed farmers for no longer understanding their own horses. 'If I put the shoes on backwards most of the farmers round here wouldn't know the difference. You can't blame the horse. A live thing is a foot and I don't like it. Only on Monday one kicked my cap off. I'd be glad if I never did another horse.' To the young, farriery seemed to be a dead-end, dirty, smelly, sweaty and monotonous job and they didn't want to know. Blacksmiths fared better in terms of status, income and optimism, diversifying into making agricultural implements and repairing machinery, and often becoming full-blown agricultural engineers.

But iron, wood and leather were leaving the village workshops. What has happened to the village coopers, who used to make and mend all manner of essential everyday wooden containers – barrels and vats, tubs and bowls, casks and buckets, butter churns and barrel-shaped chairs? Once, casks were built to contain just about any commodity from butter, fruit and fish to beer, wine and gunpowder. Today, such coopers as remain are making decorative garden tubs and furniture and in most villages the art

has been lost of hollowing out the staves, banding them together with hoops, steaming them and trussing them into shape until they fit together so perfectly that they are leakproof with not a drop of glue or solder in sight.

Steam was also familiar to village wheelwrights, who usually set up shop not far from the blacksmith as their skills were complementary: red-hot iron bands would be fitted as wheel tyres and shrunk tight to the wood in a steaming hiss of water, and there were many other iron parts needed in making and fixing a wheel. Some of the wheelwrights were also wainwrights, making wagons and farm carts, and in due course turned their hand to making trailers and converting lorries and other vehicles for various rural uses in farming and the timber industry. Others developed a useful trade in making poultry-houses, bee-keeping equipment or ladders; many were general carpenters and often also coffin-makers and undertakers. There was something very personal about having a handmade coffin tailored just for you by the village coffin-maker who had known you for most of your life.

These were crafts and trades that directly served the needs of the agricultural village. Many other crafts are now only 'rural' because they happen to be carried out in a rural area. Whereas in days gone by these craftworkers might indeed have relied on their own area for raw materials and custom, today they might buy their materials from anywhere and their customers might be anywhere. They are often

trades

not indigenous villagers, related to other long-standing village families, but have chosen to move into the area. Typically these are 'artistic' crafts; for example, in many villages there are small potteries turning out mugs and jugs and plates and bowls, or basket-makers weaving things for the garden as well as things for the house, dreaming up new applications for old skills and methods.

There is quite a revival of interest, usually as a hobby, in spinning and weaving, which are skills that have been practised in Britain for several thousand years. In medieval times the

woollen industry was dominated by town guilds but during the sixteenth century it came out into rural areas on a big scale. Clothiers employed home-workers but the industrial revolution snatched back the looms from the cottagers and centralised the industry in places like the West Riding of Yorkshire during the eighteenth century, creating new towns such as Huddersfield out of what had been hamlets.

In 1849 Angus Reach visited the West Riding and went up to the moors to see the cottage weavers:

> *High up on the hillside above Delph I counted from one point of view a couple of dozen cottages, in each of which the loom was going, and around each of which the kine were grazing. It was a glorious sunny afternoon, and amid the fields and by the roadside, the weavers with their wives and children were many of them stretching out their warps upon a rude apparatus of sticks to dry in the genial air. The gay tinting of many of these outstretched meshes of thread, glancing along the green of hedges or the cold grey of stone walls, made quite a feature of the landscape.*

The weavers were unhappy; power looms threatened to take the work away from them. Yet they were a lot better off than their counterparts in the town factories, especially in the terrible shoddy mills where the workers permanently wore bandages over their faces to save themselves from breathing in lungfuls of omnipresent dust.

BELOW
The wheel-wright's yard near Luton at Breachwood Green, Hertfordshire. The blacksmith is helping to fix an iron rim to a wooden cart wheel

BOTTOM
Wheetwrights and blacksmiths were kept busy again when wartime petrol shortages encouraged a temporary reversion to horse-drawn vehicles

WORKING CLOTHES

Many trades wore distinctive clothes, such as the red caps of brewers' vanmen. Smiths were practical with their leather aprons. The traditional carpenter's outfit until about the 1860s was a short white jacket in thick baize or felt, an apron and a tidy paper cap (many other tradesmen wore paper caps). White was remarkably popular, considering the washing problems. Ploughmen and farm labourers at the beginning of the twentieth century still sometimes wore the white summer 'slop' jacket that drovers had worn a hundred years earlier, and white corduroy was a favourite. Corduroy and fustian (another cotton-based material) remained the everyday standbys for most working countrymen.

White smocks were usually kept for best wear; everyday versions of this practical linen garment were in greys and greens and browns, and they were worn by most agricultural workers until the 1860s or 1870s, and by some even into the twentieth century.

A typical outfit in the early nineteenth century for those who could afford it would be knee-breeches under a longish coat and waistcoat, or a full-length greatcoat in adverse weather. Leather spats might be worn over the shoes but leather gaiters seem to have been worn by only gamekeepers and slaughtermen. Low shoes, stockings and knee-breeches were commonly worn in the countryside until the 1820s or so; thereafter workers compromised on breeches (which had been thoroughly practical for working men) by tying their corduroy trouser legs below the knee with straps or string, variously known as lijahs (elijahs), yorks, whirlers and the like. The trousers generally had a front flap for convenience, fastened to the waist on either side, rather than flies. Waistcoats were usually worn and rarely removed, though they would be unbuttoned when working. Even in the hottest work men never took off their shirts. A neckerchief almost completed the picture but the missing item was what no working man was ever seen without: his hat.

You could always tell a man by his hat. In the eighteenth century, farmers and gardeners wore something like a top hat, but gardeners adopted bowlers during the nineteenth century and some head gardeners still wore them into the twentieth. Farm workers and others usually sported soft felt hats with low

TOP RIGHT Essex shepherd wearing a hard felt hat and a practical apron fashioned from an old sack; ABOVE LEFT The well-dressed shepherd; ABOVE RIGHT An Ayrshire forestry worker; RIGHT Leather gaiters worn over laced corduroy breeches; OPPOSITE Dairyman in a well-worn smock, photographed in 1928

crowns and a wide brim that could be bent in various directions to suit the owner; if you flung a wet felt hat of this type on to a peg as you came home, it would dry into interesting shapes and became a very personal item. The hard felt billycock hat (said to have been named after William Coke, nephew of the Earl of Leicester) had become standard wear by the mid nineteenth century. Cloth caps were not worn until the end of that century, but became universal in town and country by the 1930s and are still worn occasionally by elderly farm workers even now.

Once you had chosen your style of hat, you stuck to it. Middleton remembered a pair of old countrymen he knew well in the 1920s: one of them always wore a flat, clerical type of black felt hat with a small bone horse-shoe on one side of it; the other always wore an old high-crowned bowler, green with age and with what seemed to be a rat-chewed brim. The local schoolmaster always wore a ridiculous square-topped bowler; old Bob Hall always wore an ancient top hat minus the flat part at the top, so that his crown was exposed to the weather (when he lost the hat, he found another and carefully cut the top out). Nobody in the village would have recognised them in anything different.

Fishermen might wear woollen caps shaped like a night-cap. Rather than smocks, fishermen's waterproof canvas or oilskin over-shirts were known as slops; along the east coast they were usually blue, unless you happened to be a Yarmouth herring fisher, in which case your slop was brown, though oilskins were at first black.

'The old working mill would have been a scene of constant activity, with the noise of horses whinnying, wagons rumbling, men shouting ...'

MILLING

Mills always seem to appeal to the romantic in people, be they water mills or windmills. The father of the painter John Constable was a miller, and probably one of Constable's best-loved paintings is 'The Hay Wain', with its horse-drawn wagon fording the millstream by Flatford Mill. Constable painted it in 1821, at a time of agricultural depression (those times have been many in recent centuries) when the farmworkers of his native Suffolk were rioting and burning ricks and being confronted by troops – hardly the peaceful scene of the painting, but then Constable was probably recapturing the better times of his boyhood. The mill was built in 1733 and its working life ceased about 165 years later; today it belongs to the National Trust, who have preserved the building since 1943 and try to maintain the original view, more or less. The miller's house, built about 1600 and unoccupied for most of the twentieth century, was in Constable's time the home of one Willy Lott, a farmer who was born in the house and died in it, and apparently left it for only four days in his lifetime of eighty-eight years.

Millwright dressing a millstone

Watermills for grinding flour, once at work non-stop in every valley in the country where there was a decent stream, were already falling into disuse in the 1920s; though during the Second World War some old mills were brought back into use, and some were converted to generate their own electricity. The old working mill would have been a scene of constant activity, with the noise of horses whinnying, wagons rumbling, men shouting, hoists creaking, all against the background sounds of the wheel turning, the stones grinding and the busy working water splashing and rushing over its wheel.

Today the sounds are but memories, save for the chuckle of the millstream and the chattering of ducks on the millpond. Mills seem to be favourite targets for conversion into homes and that is their usual fate, but one old watermill has been rebuilt, stone by stone, at the Open Air Museum at Singleton in West Sussex, where you can watch the water driving the machinery and buy unadulterated wholemeal flour fresh from grinding. It is intriguing to see the cogged wheels turning and interacting, like the workings of some huge clock.

Windmills remain a feature in some exposed landscapes but not usually as working mills any more unless they too have been restored. Most were corn mills, like watermills, but the wind could also be harnessed to pump up water, typically in East Anglian fens.

Watermills could also pump water. The late Paul Adorian (a well-known name in Independent Television in the 1960s) bought an old mill in Sussex on the River Arun in the mid 1950s. It had ceased to grind corn at the turn of the century, though it had been at the peak of production in the middle of the nineteenth century, with the Wey and Arun canal only a few hundred yards away. Adorian used the millwheel to pump water from a well and from the river up to a domestic storage tank in the attic of the farmhouse 300 yards away and to water the garden. The mill also generated all the electricity for the mill house, farmhouse and three cottages, producing enough for lighting, water-heating and even running

trades

the radio and (fittingly) television set.

Adorian described his mill as probably the oldest hydro-electric station in the UK, in that it was first converted into a generator in about 1901, operating at 48 volts at that stage and controlled by a handsome switchboard with brass measuring instruments. In 1946 the dynamo was changed and the voltage increased to 110 volts. But never in his time there did Adorian meet the mill's resident ghost, a young girl dressed in black who was said to appear from time to time simply to help those who needed it.

Wind and water were not the only powers that drove wheels and pumps. On the Isle of Wight at Carisbrooke Castle there is a huge treadwheel in which a donkey would trudge to draw large pails of water from the castle's deep well; other devices were treadwheel cranes used to raise chains of buckets to lower the water level in mines, or to hoist building materials and dockyard loads. At Earlham Hall, Norwich, and in many other places a horse-powered wheel was used for pumping water. In some farms, horses or dogs worked devices that were very similar to the running machines you find in fitness gymnasiums, walking against a moving belt; dogs also ran on treadwheels to turn roasting spits in the farmhouse (there was even a 'breed' of dachshund-shaped dog known as the Turnspit), or to work the butter churn. Horses and donkeys might trudge in circles to crush cider apples or soften the pug for brick-making or work colliery winding engines or mint coins or saw wood or thresh corn or crush anything from ore and corn to gorse for fodder.

A wind-driven water pump at Chetney Marshes, Iwade, Kent, used for dyke irrigation and to water cattle in dry seasons

Running repairs to the water wheel at Twyford Mill, Bishop's Stortford, during the Second World War

BEER AND CIDER

Since the early 1990s there has been concern about the accelerating closure of rural pubs. By 1995 only one-third of England's 9,823 rural parishes still had their own pub. In 1999 it was estimated that village pubs were closing at the rate of 6 a week; 300 closed in that year alone.

Taking a refreshing draught of cider from a field firkin in the 1930s

Partly the demise of rural pubs has been due to the 'drink-drive' laws, partly because people are drinking less beer anyway, but also it is because of the trend towards 'themed' pubs and the modernisation of town pubs vying directly with country publicans, who are hard pressed to adapt their premises and provide the high-class food that so many pub-goers now expect. Countrywide more than 100,000 village pubs have already been converted into private homes.

So people put on their thinking caps as to how to save these important focal points in village life. For example, in Devon some pubs are also shops and post-offices and can offer rooms for use as doctors' surgeries and community centres. New ideas are to allow pubs to install computer terminals so that villagers can renew their road-fund licences or apply for driving licences and social-security benefits; or to allow the setting up of mobile banks at the pub. With the growing disappearance of proper village shops, these new uses for pub rooms should be welcomed.

That would have shocked the old boys like Henry, who bet some pompous strangers in his pub that he could drink a glass of beer without any of it passing down his throat. The bet was taken at half a crown. Henry stood the glass of beer on the floor, stuck a drinking straw in it, lay flat on his stomach on the table and leaned down over the side to drink through the straw. 'But that went down your throat,' said the stranger. 'Oh, no, it didn't, sir,' replied Henry, 'it went *up* my throat.' He won the bet.

Cider-making remained a rural industry on a very local basis (often farm-based) into the twentieth century. In that century's early years it was still being made in old wooden presses. All sorts of apples, many of them

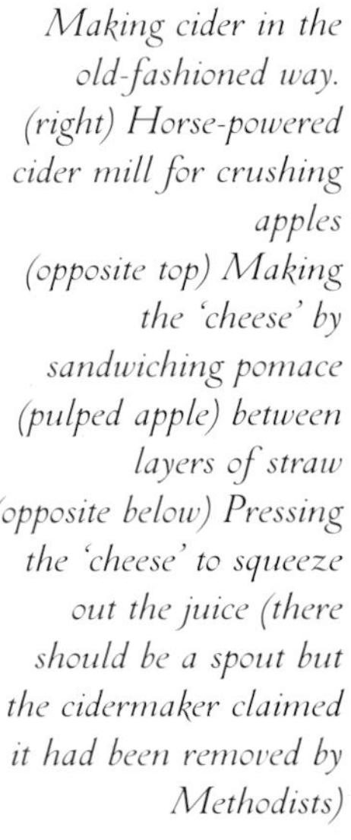

Making cider in the old-fashioned way. (right) Horse-powered cider mill for crushing apples (opposite top) Making the 'cheese' by sandwiching pomace (pulped apple) between layers of straw (opposite below) Pressing the 'cheese' to squeeze out the juice (there should be a spout but the cidermaker claimed it had been removed by Methodists)

beer and cider

muddy and bruised and certainly not washed, would be crushed by rollers in the cider mill, worked by two men turning the handle; on a larger scale the mill would be a massive stone turning in a solid stone cistern, powered by a horse plodding in a circle. The crushed apples were then put into coarse fibre bags, packed together in the press between boards and squeezed by screwing down the presser to extract the juice.

Farm cider was not made for sale but to whet the thirsts of farm labourers, especially as a reward during the peak activities of haymaking and harvest. Cider was one of the perks, and a daily ration of two or three litres would be transferred from the farm's barrels into wooden harvest bottles or firkins for the workforce. Often the men drank considerably more than that daily ration, sometimes three times as much, and it has been estimated that the farmers of Herefordshire alone were producing up to 13 million litres of cider a year during the 1870s.

The thoroughly pressed bagged pulp during cider-making is known as cheese, and indeed the pressing process is broadly similar to that used for making dairy cheese. Cheesemaking was becoming increasingly important as a rural industry in the late 1870s, when Richard Jefferies noted the 'enrolment of a cheese show on the list of annual exhibitions in London'. Throughout the West Country there were cheese shows and cheese fairs, very well attended by both buyers and sellers, and cheese-making on the farm was an increasingly popular diversification. Jefferies called it essentially a 'connubial occupation' – he doubted whether a widow or widower could ever make a good cheese, 'and as for an old maid, it is a maxim beyond dispute in the West Country that the milk would turn sour under her eye'! He thought that the duties involved in cheese-making were divided naturally between a man and a woman, the one to do the athletic 'hard' work, the other to do the 'light or head' work, and the teamwork was only successful in the couple that was 'united in the staid and homely bonds of conjugal felicity'. Well, now!

NEW RURAL INDUSTRIES

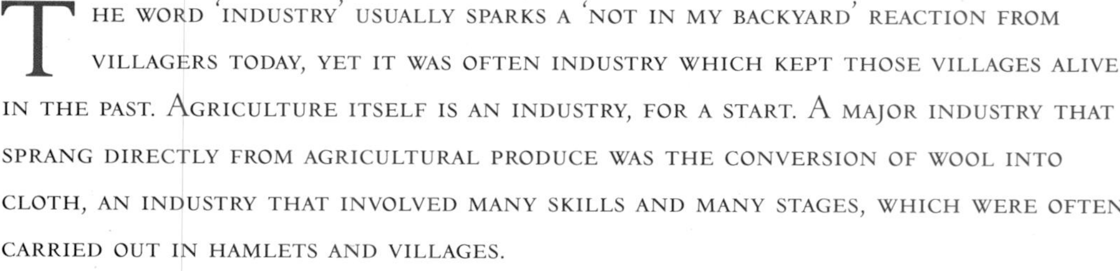

THE WORD 'INDUSTRY' USUALLY SPARKS A 'NOT IN MY BACKYARD' REACTION FROM VILLAGERS TODAY, YET IT WAS OFTEN INDUSTRY WHICH KEPT THOSE VILLAGES ALIVE IN THE PAST. AGRICULTURE ITSELF IS AN INDUSTRY, FOR A START. A MAJOR INDUSTRY THAT SPRANG DIRECTLY FROM AGRICULTURAL PRODUCE WAS THE CONVERSION OF WOOL INTO CLOTH, AN INDUSTRY THAT INVOLVED MANY SKILLS AND MANY STAGES, WHICH WERE OFTEN CARRIED OUT IN HAMLETS AND VILLAGES.

Weaving tartan on a hand-loom

'For much of the twentieth century, villages all over the country have been crying out that their economies are slowly dying...'

IN SEVERAL IMPORTANT wool regions this led to the setting up of rural fulling mills, especially in hilly districts where there was adequate water power to drive the big hammers for thickening and cleaning woven cloth (there was such a mill in Cumbria in 1135).

Then there were all the mining industries on which so many villages depended – coalmines in County Durham and South Wales, for example. Elsewhere there were brickworks that extracted local clay, glassworks and cementworks that depended on local minerals, or ironworks that depended on local iron-ore deposits and the power of the streams to drive the iron hammers. The Sussex Weald, now so rural, was the centre of charcoal-fuelled ironmaking in the sixteenth century and right up to the end of the eighteenth, when it ceded its position to the coal-rich Black Country. All of these industries were situated in 'the countryside', not the towns, and provided alternative employment for the villages. As Michael Tilley put it in the 1940s, 'Not every farm worker's son wants to work on the land or the railway, the only two alternatives open to him in many districts.'

The history of the small parish of Highley, in Shropshire, has been described in Gwyneth Nair's study of the development of its community from 1550 to 1880. Highley is situated in an area that provided coal, ironstone and building stone but is mainly agricultural. Farming was virtually the only occupation until the local mineral resources of Highley and neighbouring parishes began to be exploited in the 1780s, leading to a more than doubling of Highley's population by the early nineteenth century and considerable changes to the social and economic life of the village. New stone cottages were built for the influx of those who worked in the mines and quarries. The building of canals in the 1770s had increased the river traffic and new jobs were available to wharfmen and bargemen, along with the trades needed to sustain the boats. By 1811 more families were engaged in manufacture and trade than in agriculture, though there was a major hiccup in this trend when a local colliery closed and from the 1840s to the 1870s most men were once again working in agriculture and in services related to it such as milling and tree-felling. In the 1861 census there was a new category of worker: the railway navvy, with a large number of men helping to construct the Severn Valley Railway (opened in 1862). Twenty years later the majority were working in the mines and quarries again. The women, meanwhile, continued to go into service as domestic servants (the younger single women), and in the second half of the nineteenth century more and more women had jobs as nurses, housekeepers, charwomen, lacemakers and dressmakers (one of the latter was described quaintly as a 'mantua maker'), as well as teaching, shop-keeping and inn-keeping, quite apart from part-time and casual field work.

Throughout all these fluctuations in the main source of work, various trades could flourish: Highley had its own glazier, plumber, joiner and bricklayers in the village's building boom during the early years of the nineteenth century, and the increase in population at that time meant there were also shoemakers, blacksmiths, a tailor, a weaver and several seamstresses. After 1815 there was a butcher and a chandler; three pubs opened in the 1840s and a small grocer's. In the 1850s, in spite of mines and quarries, Highley could still be described as a pleasant rural village 'noted for its extensive orchards and the excellence of its cider'.

For much of the twentieth century, villages all over the country have been crying out that their economies are slowly dying and that they are increasingly peopled by those who work

new industries

elsewhere. In some villages the trend has been reversed deliberately. Between the two world wars, for example, new industries were set up in the countryside, such as sawmills, canning factories, agricultural engineers, joinery shops and milk-processing centres, usually in larger villages. They gave the villagers better wages and working conditions and brought new money into the village's existing trades.

Lapford is about ten miles north of Exeter. It was a farming village, with Crediton and Chulmleigh as its markets, and most of its young either went on the farms or left the village as there was no other choice of employment. Even when the railways and, later, buses made local travel possible, agricultural wages were inadequate for more than the very occasional journey. There was nothing in the village to attract tourists or anybody else. Then in 1927 the Ambrosia Milk Company established a milk processing factory at Lapford, in spite of many initial local objections as people anticipated some smoke-blackened factory in their midst, or that the new factory would lure all the men off the farms and all the girls too. When the company offered to supply the whole village with electricity it was refused ('Oil lamps are good enough for us!') and when they offered to buy milk from the farmers many of them refused too – 'I've never sold milk, and butter will always be made on this farm while I'm still here!'

But the factory was duly built, and it employed about ninety people, about half of whom were born within ten miles of Lapford. It set new standards in local employment: the working day was eight-and-a-half hours and there was a half-day holiday each week and a fortnight's paid holiday as well – unheard of in such a rural area. The men earned as much as £2 to £2 10s a week, the girls about £1 7s 6d, which meant that girls could often take home more money than their fathers who were working long hours on the farm. The 50 per cent of the employees who were not immediately local, the 'foreigners', came to live in the village as householders or lodgers, all of them spending some of their wages in the village and boosting its economy in general. New houses were built; farmers had a market for their milk right on their doorstep and farm rents rose. The company provided various welfare schemes for its employees, including a social hall which was made available to the rest of the village as well, sparking off several new activities and interests, especially for the young. The girls began to wear smart clothes instead of their habitually dull and dowdy ones; the boys owned bicycles, motor-bikes and occasionally an old car. Lapford had come alive, and would remain so as long as this single major local employer survived.

Then there was Dartington, also in Devon. In the 1920s Dartington Hall was derelict and roofless and its estate of some 2,000 acres was thoroughly run down, but Leonard and Dorothy Elmhirst had a dream and took it in hand and created something unique there. They wanted to develop all the resources of the estate (not just agricultural ones) and they wanted to discover if rural resources could yield a reasonable return on capital invested, given adequate capital and efficient organisation. To do this, they worked under normal industrial conditions, sold on the open market and struggled through ten years of disorganised international trade. They did not expect immediate returns: for example, they had 200 acres

Out-of-work Welsh miners planting potatoes on a farm

A builder's gang of stoneworkers

new industries

Looking after fir seedlings at Dartington nurseries

of woodland doing nothing in particular and had problems in finding adequate information about exploiting this asset without impoverishing it. The first ten years were exploratory in this respect and this was so of the many other small industries that they wished to locate on or near the estate – weaving, pottery, woodland crafts, poultry-breeding and so on.

Social values were as important as economic ones in their vision and they created an experimental co-educational boarding, day and nursery school and developed schools of art, drama, dance and music that extended their services to local villages, several of which developed outstanding drama and dance groups of their own. Then they thought about the many people working on the estate, initially as builders: should they be brought to live within the estate? Should trade unions be encouraged? Should wages be higher than elsewhere in the area? Should they organise 'welfare work' for the employees? They worked through the ideals and the problems and by the late 1930s Dartington Hall had reinvigorated a declining rural area and was influencing the cultural and economic life of local people in many different ways. Its story continues to this day.

'Farming remains a way of life for many in rural areas and they have been fighting to preserve it.'

DIVERSIFICATION

Despite the sharp decline in agricultural jobs, farming remains a way of life for many in rural areas and they have been fighting to preserve it.

In the 1980s the new buzz word was diversification and, to survive, farmers had to jump out of the age-old rut of corn-and-horn and try something new. They looked at what they already had – buildings, land, skills with livestock and plants, and so on – and then thought laterally. Some tried different livestock (everything from snails and trout to llamas and ostriches) or different crops (a sudden rash of pretty blue flax and a few stabs at hemp). Some created farm parks open to the general public, who came to look at rare breeds of farm livestock or to watch cows being milked and lambs being born. A few went further and became showmen, creating full-scale travelling sheep shows, perhaps with a collection of all the breeds, or becoming professional demonstrators of their sheepdogs' skills, or working up the theme of 'back to back' – from shearing a fleece to producing the finished garment, with all the necessary processes in between. Others simply let in the film crews to use the farm and farmhouse as a period set.

Many of the new enterprises were based on welcoming the public on to the farm, which for some was a radical change of attitude from keeping people off it by fair means or foul. Old farm buildings were converted into living accommodation that could be let out to holiday-makers and week-enders in ventures that demanded a much greater input of capital but were less onerous in terms of daily work and less intrusive in the farmhouse than the good old bed-and-breakfast business. Farm walks and trailer rides were devised; farmhouse lunches and teas were offered. Some opened farm shops, selling their own produce (fresh, or 'value-added' by processing on the farm) direct to their customers and usually selling produce from other farms and craftworkers as well. Some started mail-order businesses selling their own farm-processed ham, bacon and cheese or frozen meat. Many started pick-your-own centres, again bypassing the retailer and also avoiding the need to pay wages to picking gangs. Others invited groups against whom in the old days they would have almost taken up their shotguns: they offered facilities to cara-

new industries

van clubs, or for trail-bikers and four-wheel-drive vehicles to have a bit of fun; they set up clay-pigeon shoots, or allowed businessmen to play paint-ball games in the woods.

For those who continue to rely on livestock in particular, however, the future at the very beginning of the twenty-first century is looking very black indeed and many are close to despair. For much of the 1990s the levels of suicide among farmers remained alarmingly high and the feeling of alienation from an urbanised nation has become acute. The beef industry is almost as dead as meat on the slab; lambs and weaned pigs have been selling for far less than it cost to produce them; dairy cows have been slaughtered in huge numbers as a result of the BSE crisis, which has cost farmers (and to some extent tax payers) some £3 billion.

Rules and regulations emanating from Brussels and London are tying farmers in impossible knots and ruining what is left of their livelihoods; supermarkets absolutely control the prices they receive for their produce and lay down impossible production standards, and farmers no longer feel they have any control at all over their own industry. It is even worse for small producers, staggering under the onslaught of bureaucrats that seem determined to aggregate farming so that they do not have to bother with the irritations of smallness of scale. Everything must be big and centralised. Countless local abattoirs have been closed in favour of the very large ones that can afford to meet new standards; the result is that livestock, already under stress in any abattoir, certainly cannot be slaughtered in familiar surroundings and have to endure much longer journeys to the abattoir, with the added stress of being handled with the necessarily greater impersonality of a large concern.

Writing in *The Times* in the summer of 1999, Roger Scruton railed against what was happening in the countryside. The manufacture of fertilisers required far more energy than could be yielded by the crops on which they were used; even more energy was wasted by the centralisation of food distribution which demanded the transport of food on already overcrowded roads over great distances (the average distance travelled by a food item on a supermarket shelf was 3,000km). Local economies were dying from the emphasis on centralisation and scale. The very landscape was under threat because family farming was no longer practicable in so many places and the personal interest of those families in their surroundings was beleaguered from every side; and because the cry had gone up that huge numbers of new homes must be built in what was once the green and pleasant countryside.

And there was more. With suburbs, new towns and motorways spreading relentlessly across the land, more and more farms found themselves too accessible and suffered from vandalism and worse in the late 1990s. Poachers and livestock rustlers had become professionally ruthless armed gangs whom no farmer dared to confront; thieves swiped whole rows of newly planted trees and stretches of dry-stone wall (they took the latter from old churchyards, too); children would burn barns for fun; joyriders would dump scorched-out vehicles, and lorry-loads of rubbish would be fly-tipped in the fields; gangs would steal expensive farm plant and machinery to order, for selling overseas (the Home Office estimated that vehicles and plant worth £66.25 million were being stolen every year) and then return to steal the replacements.

In 1999 a BBC survey found that 55 per cent of farmers had been burgled, 45 per cent had suffered from vandalism, 33 per cent had been verbally abused and 10 per cent physically abused, and 20 per cent had suffered from arson. It is little wonder that, here and there, farmers have resorted to paying for security companies to patrol their land. And no one should be surprised if in the end the farmers give up altogether. Who, then, will care for the countryside?

Farmworkers can turn their hand to anything: concreting the top of a piggery's sludge tank

Splitting slate in Wales

9
Country Fun

EVEN FOR THE TOILERS of the field, it was not all work. Country people knew how to enjoy themselves; in particular they knew how to make their own entertainment. One of the biggest changes in country fun is that, then, they did it; now, they watch other people doing it. The other big change is that the town now considers the countryside to be its playground.

It was probably the First World War that finally broke the chain of tradition in rural areas. After those four grim years, most of the old feasts and celebrations lapsed, despite attempted artificial revivals by individuals with more of a sense of nostalgia than of real life. Some customs did persist, like always planting your potatoes on Good Friday in Devon, though that was the most unlucky day of the year to plant anything if you lived in the north. But Plough Monday lost its meaning quite quickly after the war, especially when tractors took over from horses – somehow driving a decorated tractor through the village wasn't quite the same as taking a handsomely beribboned Shire horse with you to collect money.

Haysel, which used to be connected with St Barnabas Day, lost its meaning when girls no longer came into the meadow with wooden rakes to make 'sweet hay' with their lovers. Rush-bearing at Ambleside, Shenington and Old Weston had no meaning when churches were no longer regularly strewn with rushes; dressing the well, another ceremony with church connections, persisted at only a few places, such as Tissington, with any real vigour.

CUSTOMS, TRADITIONS & FESTIVITIES

'Do young men still race up Dunkery Beacon at Easter for luck in love and work? And... do they know why?'

PREVIOUS PAGE *Spectator sport: watching cricket on the village green*

THE DOLING OUT OF FLOUR AND BREAD – THE TICHBORNE DOLE, THE BIDDENDEN CAKES, THE LENTEN DOLES OF BREAD AND HERRINGS AT DRONFIELD – SEEMED SPURIOUS AS POVERTY BECAME LESS ABJECT. THERE WAS A TIME WHEN A WILY TRAVELLER COULD FIND A FREE MEAL EVERY DAY OF THE YEAR IF HE WAS IN THE RIGHT PLACE AT THE RIGHT TIME. WHAT HAPPENED TO PAIGNTON'S AMAZING PUDDINGS (SEVEN YEARS TO MAKE, SEVEN TO BAKE AND SEVEN TO EAT) OR THE MAMMOTH DENBY DALE PIES, AND COLCHESTER'S OYSTER FEASTS AND THE GREAT BUCKINGHAMSHIRE CHERRY PIE FEASTS? WHO STILL GIVES THEIR LANDLORD A GOOSE AT MICHAELMAS?

WHAT HAPPENED TO THE candle auctions at Tatsworth, Chard and Upwey, or the drawing of balls at Yarnton? Do they still 'bump the mayor', or do they still bump new freeholders on the dunting stone on the Northumberland moors at Newbiggin? Do the boys of Helston still beat the bounds and place a clod of earth and a sprig of hawthorn on the boundary stones? Do they still ring the church bells of Kirton-in-Lindsey to guide people home from market? Do they still ring the pancake bell, and do Midland cottagers still throw the first pancake to their chickens to make sure of good luck and plenty of eggs?

The ancient festival of Hocktide, celebrated in the village of Hungerford, Wiltshire

What about Mothering Sunday: do they still eat frumenty and simnel cakes; do they still make special wafers in Chilbolton? On Palm Sunday do they still eat figs in Northamptonshire or eat fig cakes on Silbury Hill? Do young men still race up Dunkery Beacon at Easter for luck in love and work? Do they still go Peace Eggin at Easter in West Yorkshire, and do they still scramble for hare pies and penny loaves at Hallaton on Easter Monday before playing football with a small beer barrel?

Do the hobby-horses still prance at Padstow on May Day, and does the Minehead horse still have a long tail of knotted rope to chastise those who don't put coins in the collection box? Do they still understand the Horn Dance at Abbots Bromley, or the Furry Dance at Helston? Does Abbotsbury still take flowers out to sea on Garland Day as an offering to Neptune, and do they bury cakes and ale as luck for the fishermen? Do they roast lamb on the bed of a dammed stream at Kingsteignton on Whit Tuesday? Do children go souling in November in Shropshire? Do they still observe Salmon Sunday at Paythorne Bridge? And if they still do these things, do they know why?

Traditions may be broad, encompassing whole countries or at least whole regions, or very local indeed. The wider traditions included celebrating various royal occasions, such as jubilees and coronations, and this the villages did with great vigour (any excuse for a party). In the Sussex village of Cowfold, they set up a committee, of course, to organise celebrations for the coronation of Edward

customs

VII in 1902, and the parish records include a detailed list of subscribers to the celebration funds, along with a note of thanks for 'the willing manner in which many Gentlemen and Farmers gave assistance by lending useful materials for the day, giving Faggots for the Bonfire, Carting materials, &c., and the Cricket Committee for use of Field. The Ladies in particular deserve our best thanks for the excellent Cooking.' Personal contributions ranged from threepence from a widow to £10 from F.D. Godman Esquire, and one fat sheep from a farmer. Expenditure included the hire and erection of tents and tea urns, prizes for the children, 'Milk and Faggots for Tea', sports materials, fitting up coppers for tea, preparing the field for sports, fireworks and assorted food.

Food was important for such events; many a parish celebrated a coronation with a 'Tea' (children's tea, knife and fork tea, a 'good meat tea'), combined with sports and games and usually a bonfire with a few fireworks. Others were more practical; Victoria's jubilees prompted many of them to open a parish reading room, dedicate a stained-glass window in the church or plant a tree.

Participants in the Abbot's Bromley Horn Dance, Staffordshire, which celebrates the granting of the 'Charta de Foresta' by King Henry III. The charter returned some forest land to agriculture and lessened the penalties for contravening the rules of the 'chase'

LEFT
Triking off with the bread-and-cheese dole from the church at Biddenden, Kent

In 1999 many villages were encouraged (and succumbed) to celebrate 'the Millennium' and this they did in a wide variety of ways – planting boundary yew trees, writing books or making films about themselves, improving the village hall or the playground, restoring war memorials, taking parish photographs, producing village calendars (some quite saucy), and a host of other creative and lasting projects in addition to whole-village parties. The general effect was to prove that the community spirit is alive and thriving in the countryside, in spite of the cynics.

The new community spirit has not yet regressed to inter-village rivalry. In the nineteenth century, there was a traditional Whit-Monday fight between the 'Kaffirs' (originally Cavaliers) of Coneyhurst Hill, in the Surrey parish of Ewhurst, and the Diamond-topped Round-heads of Rudgwick, a Sussex village just over the border. It always took place on neutral ground, at the Donkey Inn at Cranleigh. Countless villages had regular rivalry with neighbouring ones, though usually on the more informal basis of a gang from one village taking it into their heads of an evening, probably after a drink or two, to go and sort out the other.

customs

'Neighbours were also important at burials ... they must make sure that the deceased left his home by the front door, feet first.'

IN CUMBERLAND, many old customs persisted into the mid twentieth century, though only just. For example, if a farmer was selling off his stock and implements, he provided a meal for everybody who attended the farm sale and he supplied stronger liquid refreshment for those who spent a good deal of money there or were his neighbours; each neighbour, by tradition, would buy something at the sale (often the piece of equipment they had most often borrowed) and would pay more than it was worth.

Neighbours were also important at burials, for it was they, never members of the family, who bore the coffin, and must make sure that the deceased left his home by the front door, feet first. At weddings, the bride and groom would find the church gate firmly tied when they came out of the church, or a flower-decked rope stretched across their way; the custom was for the groom to throw copper coins to the village young before they were allowed to pass.

FEASTS

Richard Jefferies was bemoaning the demise of village feasts even in the early 1870s:

> *Here and there the clergyman of the parish has succeeded in turning what was a rude saturnalia into a decorous 'fête', with tea in a tent. ... A village feast consists of two or three gipsies located on the greensward by the side of the road, and displaying ginger-beer, nuts, and toys for sale; an Aunt Sally; and, if the village is a large one, the day may be honoured by the presence of what is called a rifle-gallery; the 'feast' really and truly does not exist. Some two or three of the old-fashioned farmers have the traditional roast beef and plum-pudding on the day, and invite a few friends; but this custom is passing away. In what the agricultural labourer's feast nowadays consists no one can tell. It is an excuse for an extra quart or two of beer, that is all.*

Feasts and festivals used to punctuate the vil-

The annual silver-ball hurling game at St Ives, Cornwall. The ball is hurled to the crowd and then jostled, snatched and tossed from hand to hand

customs

lage calendar and had an important social role at both the community and the personal level that perhaps has not been widely acknowledged. They were a dramatic change from the daily routine that on the one hand confirmed community bonds, as they were essentially social occasions, and on the other gave individuals a moment to pause and lift their eyes from the everydayness of life, to reflect that there could be more to it and perhaps even to meditate on the meaning of it all.

CLUB DAYS

The biggest bash in the rural calendar had always been the harvest feast. It meant food and it meant drinking, both to extremes; it meant dancing to the pipe and fiddle, and it meant fully grown men bedecking their hats with flowers. A later innovation, in Victorian times, was the festivities held annually by local Benefit Clubs ('sickness societies' to which you subscribed your pence as a form of early health insurance), usually on the old village feast days. Jefferies described the annual village club dinners in Wiltshire at which farm labourers 'gormandized to repletion'. One man ate, in quick succession, a plate of roast beef, a plate of boiled beef, a plate of boiled mutton, a plate of roast mutton and a plate of ham and said he could not do much to the bread and cheese but devoured the pudding. Jefferies had heard of men who stuffed themselves silly and then retired from the table to take a mustard emetic so that they could come back for more gorging. As for beer, he had seen men lie on their backs and never take the wooden harvest bottle from their lips until they had drunk a full gallon.

The Benefit Club at Kirtlington held its annual gathering, with much feasting, drinking and general debauchery, and music from two bands for the procession, on the day of what had formerly been celebrated as Lamb Ale. At the Lamb Ale they would have had a Lord and a Lady (the community's most respectable inhabitants), with twelve attendants, processing with a lamb with a blue ribbon around its neck. This occasion of much merry-making had died out by the 1860s, but the Benefit Club annual days continued. The clubs soon added all sorts of stalls and amusements to their annual holiday, but the main activity seemed to be drinking and one Charles Hickman extended the idea of Lamb Ale by drinking himself to death on a non-stop week-long binge. On the day he died the local policeman said that he would have had difficulty in finding twelve sober jurymen in the whole of the village.

At nearby Chesterton they had an old feast known as the Chesterton Barrel on the same day as Kirtlington's Lamb Ale: they played all kinds of games with barrels of beer under a large tree along the old Roman road of Akeman Street. Everybody was given a day's holiday and would meet with friends and relatives from miles around, but in the 1860s the local parson decided the whole matter was a disgrace and he discontinued it. Parsons were always doing that. So much for tradition.

'Jefferies had heard of men who stuffed themselves silly and then retired from the table to take a mustard emetic...'

The two oldest members on the Fownhope Club Walk, Herefordshire, with their flower-topped staffs

customs

MORRIS DANCING

On his way through Kirtlington on Lamb Ale day in 1877, George Dew was quite surprised to come across 'a Morris dance' outside the pub. It was a tradition that had become almost extinct in those parts. A number of men were dancing to the tune of a whistle and a tambourine, but they had not bothered to dress up as of old in 'light or white trousers or rather breeches, spotlessly white shirts nicely made for the occasion, a tall box hat on, & jingling bells on the legs & wrists'. He remembered in his own boyhood during the 1850s watching Morris dancers accompanied by a Tom Fool, 'a fellow dressed in some outlandish, attractive manner to cause laughter', who 'acted as a general attendant to keep space for the dancers, his wand of authority being a largely expanded pig's bladder tied to a staff'. Did Dew know that Morris dancing is supposed to be pagan and Moorish in origin and was introduced into England from Spain by John o'Gaunt?

MAY DAY

May Day was celebrated throughout most of the nineteenth century with all the paraphernalia of maypole dancing by the children (and quite tricky it can be, too), crowning the May Queen, going a-maying to fetch hawthorn blossom (terribly unlucky if brought indoors), dancing and feasting. The 'tradition' was deliberately revived after the First World War, but by then it meant nothing. Gertrude Jekyll, who could remember the chimney sweeps' Jack-in-the-Green in the streets of London in the 1840s, when she watched an 8ft-tall tower of greenery dancing and revolving along the street, said of the twentieth-century May Day: 'The continuous chain of ancient tradition has been snapped and nothing can restore it.' That is why modern attempts to perpetuate Morris dancing and other 'traditions' always seem so uncomfortable, so unnatural. So many of these traditions were country ones, based on agricultural realities that people no longer experience or understand.

In the real old May Day celebrations, children would carry bunches of flowers on top of peeled willow sticks, chanting, 'The first of May is Garland Day, so please to remember the white wand; we don't come here but once a year, so please to remember the Garland.' Some would have a more elaborate arrangement of an intersecting double ring of hoops of flowers and foliage, carried on a horizontal stick by two children.

In the 1870s, George Dew described how on May Day the school children dressed in their best clothes 'in every gay colour possible ... with all the fine pieces of coloured ribbands for adornment they could obtain' and marched round the parish with their fresh flower garlands and flags to collect as much money as possible so that they could have a tea in the afternoon – cake, bread and butter, and tea. Then they played games outside and

TOP
Member of the Broadwood Morris dancers taking a break after climbing up to Leith Hill Tower, Surrey

ABOVE
Making paper garlands for Wadworth's maypole, a skill that is passed from generation to generation

in the barns and 'after having finished the cake & tea went home at a quarter past 8 o'clock at Evening' – so it was quite a day for them. And for their mothers: many a woman was up all night on May Eve washing and preparing the white frocks worn by most of the girls.

BONFIRE NIGHT

Bonfire Night was sometimes not quite the occasion it is now in many villages. At Lower Heyford in 1872 they had simply a peal of bells, not even a bonfire, though some individuals fired off several rounds of cartridges from their pocket revolvers in private remembrance of the Gunpowder Plot. In other villages they gave it the works, the village boys having been collecting money for the bonfire for some time before the day itself, and all around the countryside you could hear the explosion of fireworks and see the flare of the fires. In some places the blacksmith's anvil would be charged and fired. In general, though, the custom seemed to be slowly dying out – mainly because of the red tape that surrounded the sale and manufacture of fireworks and gunpowder.

Some villages had (and still have) a bonfire club, which did very little for the first nine months of the year but then would wake up and start its complicated preparations for the Fifth of November. There would be flaming torches to be prepared, hundreds of fireworks to be bought (and in the old days made, very dangerously), the display to be planned meticulously, and materials to be found for a carefully constructed bonfire, not to mention the guys to be burnt on it. Around the Sussex town of Lewes they took Guy Fawkes Night very seriously; and there are villages in other parts of the country that became quite famous for their November bonfires and fireworks.

Bonfire clubs often got involved in organising other village events as well – it is an indisputable fact of village life that once you become involved in one thing, you are automatically assumed to be willing and capable of organising everything else as well. This might be fairly simple carol-singing to raise money for a dinner for the old folks, or the much more complicated business of arranging a week of non-stop activities for all the village's children in the summer.

Pulling home a cartload of 'fuel' for the bonfire, in 1930

LEFT
May Day celebrations, c.1935

customs

'Isn't everyone's image of the traditional Christmas set in a village?'

IN THE SOMERSET village of Enmore they may or may not remember the will of my less-than-venerable ancestor, Jasper Porter of Bloxham. Jasper was smarting at being left out of his father's will in 1779 in favour of his sister. In his own will dated 1795 he instructed that the sum of £10 should be placed in the hands of the overseers in the parish of Enmore:

> *which they shall distribute equally amongst ten of the oldest men paupers of the said Parish, on condition that on the fifth day of November they make two effigies representing a man and a woman, which shall be fixed on two stakes, and a copy of my father's Will shall be fixed thereto with a label in large characters of these words: 'To expiate the crimes of fraud and perfidy and make some atonement to the treatment of the testator, we commit this effigy to the flames at the request and in commemoration of our benefactor.' The ten men shall assemble at the Castle Inn at Enmore and walk in slow procession to the beat of a drum through the village and carry the above-mentioned effigies and my father's Will affixed thereto, as far as the great elm on the crossings near the church, where a bonfire shall be provided for the purpose of burning the effigies. The eldest of the ten men, on arriving at the place, shall then commit the said effigies to the flames, and in a solemn and audible voice first repeat the words 'To expiate the crimes ...' etc. After performing the ceremony the men shall repair to the Castle Inn at dinner, and there receive the £10 divided amongst them.*

The curious might like to know that the bitter Jasper's brother, Thomas, who had also been left out of their father's will, was of a very different character. Always a generous and positive man, he took off for the West Indies in 1782, built a fine house called Enmore on his Porters estate in Barbados, married a general's daughter, then moved on to Demerara to found four substantial estates. At one time so great was his income from these West Indies estates that the tax inspector returned his papers to him, presuming that he had mistakenly entered his capital instead of his income. In 1795, out of one year's income, he bought for £57,000 the house and manor of Rockbeare, in Devon, with 900 acres. There the squire never had fewer than sixteen horses in the stable and drove the lanes in an open carriage drawn by four white horses, with two postillions in attendance.

BELOW LEFT
Acting out a Mummers play in Symondsbury, Dorset, in 1952

BELOW RIGHT
Boxing Day tradition in Haxey, Lincolnshire: two 'boggans' having a mock fight in the 1950s

customs

Whenever he visited the West Indies estates he charted a ship all to himself.

CHRISTMAS

Isn't everyone's image of the traditional Christmas set in a village? The village church, the carol singers, the handbell ringers whose brass tunes echo gently across the meadows, snowy landscapes with misty-breathed cattle and sunset-lit sheep, robins on the twig, skaters on the pond, frosted trees.

In the village, you knew all the carol-singing children and they took their rounds seriously, trained by the schoolmaster or the parson for weeks in advance but only giving the village the benefit of their carols on Christmas Eve, visiting every dwelling but especially the bigger houses where they would be given goodies to eat and home-made wine or ginger beer. Individual carols were often peculiar to a local area, unknown beyond it, but they've all been forgotten now.

Do any West Country farmers still wassail their apple trees? Does anybody remember the rhyming play of the Mummers and recognise the paper-clad St George, the Turkey land Knight, Father Christmas, the Doctor and the Old Woman, Betsy Bub? Read Arthur Gibbs if you want all the details about a Mummer's cure that involved eating a bucket of hot dry ashes, being groomed with a besom and drinking a yard and a half of pump water, recommended by the Doctor, who could 'cure the itchy pitch' and much else besides.

Ah, Christmas was Christmas then! Christmas in the village was a real excitement, followed by the Boxing Day meet of the hounds somewhere not too far away. Then at midnight on New Year's Eve the church bells rang out the old year and rang in the new; they had also pealed to mark the shortest day on 21 December, at 6 in the morning.

LEFT Christmas hand-bell ringers

Carol-singers in the 1920s

Wassailing at Carhampton, Somerset, in 1931

customs

The Silver Star Dance Band at Hartland, North Devon, in the late 1920s

DANCES

Oh, those village dances and hops! Can you imagine it when the lads who by day worked in the fields dressed themselves up in breeches and gaiters for the dance, but kept on their hobnailed boots? Can you imagine the noise of it all, the boots thumping on the floor and more often than not on other people's toes as well?

In Victorian villages you would often see a dancing booth set up in the square or on the green near the pub on one of the various feast days. It was popular with all age groups, married and single, male and female, sons and daughters and parents, of the labouring classes, all of whom had a merry old time. It was also another good excuse to get drunk.

Stealing a kiss at Yateley Fête in Hampshire

FETES AND FAIRS

The village fête – what visions that phrase conjures up! They don't do them like they used to, you know. There was a fête at Blenheim Park in the 1870s in aid of the Great Western Railway Widow & Orphan Fund, with excursion trains laid on from all parts of the country, and people came in their many thousands. Early shades of Woodstock, without the mud. It must have been rather more than the typical village smattering of stalls with bash the rat, home-made cakes and second-hand books. An August fête a few days later in Middleton Stoney Park was more typical: it rained.

Some villages had fiestas and carnivals, complete with people in fancy dress on floats mounted initially on horse-drawn wagons but later on tractor-drawn trailers (which also carried carol singers around the villages and farms). Other had elaborate pageants, perhaps telling the history of the village; these essentially outdoor plays involved as many of the village as possible, including the animals, and sometimes included a tableau. Some villages had their annual Revels, usually connected with May Day; others have invented new traditions such as rural fairs, raft races, duck races (with plastic ducks down the river), rare breed shows and revived goose fairs.

Local fairs were rapidly declining in Victorian times, though the bigger town ones and the county shows were still exciting and opened village eyes to the rest of the world and its goods and inventions. In the 1830s, for example, Deddington's Pudding Pie Fair had been celebrated for selling shoes, ready-made clothes, hats and horses; forty years later it had 'diminished to almost nothing'.

Today the big agricultural shows and county shows attract huge numbers from towns and cities as well as from the rural areas they originally served. That must surely indicate that the country exerts a strong pull on urban man even now, though they cannot really compete with the events that villagers would have attended in the twelfth century. Where Salisbury now stands, there used to be a large open space between the lofty palace of Clarendon, the fortress of Old Sarum and Wilton Abbey, and here they had a tournament ground. Villagers would set off from home a day or two before the great day dawned, to be there in time to see the host of armed men riding out from the castle in the early morning, banners fluttering and arms gleaming, while from the direction of the Abbey came the royal princesses (they were being schooled there) and the soldier-priests from the crusading knights of Jerusalem's establishment at St John's Priory at

customs

Ditchampton; and from Clarendon would come a horseback procession of gaily dressed courtiers. Villagers would be overawed by the richness of the clothes and the presence of queens, lords and ladies. The tournaments themselves would be full of excitement, colour and courage, with the knights and their horses gorgeously arrayed as they took part in these martial sports, and their retinue of pages and esquires and minstrels and heralds all dressed up to the nines as well.

There were tournaments here for four centuries, and four centuries after they finished the military theme took centre stage again in the form of searchlight tattoos in the grounds of Tidworth House from 1923. By 1938 the tattoos were attracting 150,000 people and excursion trains were coming from as far away as Wales, Cornwall and Wolverhampton. There were massed bands, pageants, physical-training exercises, sham tank fights and gunfire, circus episodes and a grand multicoloured torchlight procession. (Why 'tattoo'? Apparently it is from the Dutch 'taptoe', with 'tap' meaning alehouse and 'toe' meaning to close. When William of Orange reorganised the British Army in the late seventeenth century, the signal for troops to return to barracks was the sounding of 'Taptoe', at which the alehouses closed and the men had nothing better to do than come back for the nightly muster.)

TOP
New Forest pony sale, 1905, complete with fairground attractions

ABOVE
A Dorset farmer trimming up his entry for the local show

LEFT
The Grasmere and Lake District Athletic Festival in the summer of 1919

THE ARTS

RICHARD JEFFERIES ACCUSED THE ENGLISH NATIONAL CHARACTER OF BEING DULL, AND THAT THERE WAS 'NO COLOUR IN OUR MODE OF LIFE'. HE WAS EXCUSING AGRICULTURAL LABOURERS FOR THEIR LACK OF IMAGINATION IN THEIR SOCIAL ACTIVITIES; HOW COULD THEY HELP IT WHEN NATIONALLY THERE WERE 'NO PASSION PLAYS, NO PEASANT PLAYS, NO RUSTIC STAGE AND DRAMA, FEW SONGS, VERY LITTLE MUSIC'?

'Nobody bursts into song at the pub any more... or pulls out a fiddle or pipe and gives the locals a tune.'

HE CONTINUED: 'It is this lack of poetical feeling that makes the English peasantry so uninteresting a study. They have no appreciation of beauty. Many of them, it is true, grow quantities of flowers; but barely one in a thousand could arrange those flowers in a bouquet.' Harsh words indeed! But was he right? Was it an intrinsic flaw in the character of rural England, or simply a lack of opportunity?

MAKING MUSIC

Making music was very much a part of country life. People sang local folk songs and understood them; many an old boy had just the one song, which he could be 'reluctantly' persuaded to sing at the drop of a hat as his party piece, usually in exchange for a pint of ale. Children were always singing, especially girls in their games; women sang at their housework or in the field; everybody sang in church (with fewer people going to church these days, the joy of singing together is being lost); men whistled as they worked long before that became a catch phrase. Singing and playing music was an integral part of any march or procession. In Wales, if you were lucky, you might be wakened on New Year's Day by small children singing at your door – the old custom of *calenig*.

In recent years all that singing has disappeared, except in a more formal context such as the church choir or a local choral society or at school. Nobody bursts into song at the pub any more (unless they play rugger or support

Celebrating Founders' Day at Dartington Hall, Devon, in 1953

the arts

a town football team) or pulls out a fiddle or pipe and gives the locals a tune. They dont even tickle the ivories any more.

A man born in the Otmoor village of Beckley in 1888, who worked as a carrier and later as a woodman, met his wife at one of the village's fortnightly dances in the school, where they all danced the old dances – lancers, quadrilles and waltzes. The shoemaker and postmaster Amos Wing took over the piano-playing (once he had learnt how) from Obadiah Cripps; Mr Chaundy played the cello, Mr Haynes played the piano and all the young men wore white gloves and buttonholes.

There was a time, within living memory, when many villages had their own band – not just a couple of men with penny whistles and a shaky tambourine but the full works: brass instruments, big drums and all. Many a country church had a band of fiddlers and pipe-players in the days before they all had church organs. In 1878 Dew noted in his diary that a new organ had been installed in Lower Heyford church, replacing the old harmonium which had in turn replaced the 'fiddle, bass-viol, bassoon, clarionet, & such instruments' that had played in Rector Faithfull's time. When the harmonium first arrived, the Lower Heyford choir refused to sing, but then, that choir had always been a law unto themselves. Dew could remember their behaviour in the gallery during services '& all sorts of strange memoranda were written on the seats there; for instances such as when "Polly Hore", the landlady of the "Bell" Inn was last at church. But after the harmonium was placed in the gallery matters in this respect were much improved.'

Travelling bands visited Victorian villages too, including the old one-man band with cymbals on his knees, a drum at his back and a pipe to his lips. Another musical itinerant was the ballad seller, singing from the sheet-music that he offered for sale. There were also visits by itinerant acrobats (there is at least one hamlet where the crossroads is still known as Tumblers Corner for that reason), gypsies with dancing bears and organ-grinders with their monkeys.

RECORDED IMAGES

A favourite evening for Victorian villagers was the magic lantern show in the reading-room or village hall or a school room. From there it progressed to slide lectures and sometimes to moving pictures as well: in my own village there was a regular cinema in the village hall in the 1950s, showing films that you might have seen on the national circuit ('Riders of Death Valley' in several episodes, or 'The Way to the Stars' with Michael Redgrave and John Mills and even 'The Blue Lagoon' – a different film every Friday). The driving force behind this little cinema, in a village with a population of a few hundred, also set up a cine camera and made the village's own film of local events, scratchy copies of which can still be viewed; what is more he started a village newspaper, properly printed on broadsheet paper, at tuppence an issue, as 'the official organ of the Memorial Hall Committee'.

Life class in the farmyard

Today some villages are even more ambitious: most have their own newsletters (some of them produced very professionally); more and more have their own internet sites, despite having had their village names hijacked by entrepreneurs. Many villagers have appeared on local television, and whole villages have been the background for period films (Lacock and Castle Combe spring instantly to mind). Some villages even have their own radio stations. Whatever next?

the arts

'The activities that traditionally took place on the green have either died out altogether or moved elsewhere.'

VILLAGE GREENS AND RECREATION GROUNDS

There are two aspects to be considered in catering for a village's leisure needs: the physical and the cultural wellbeing of the villagers. The needs of the former can be met easily, as usually every villager is within a couple of minutes' walk of open countryside and can find their physical exercise and recreation there for free, be it walking, running, riding or cycling. Yet many villages were granted recreation grounds in the nineteenth century for the exercise and wellbeing of their inhabitants.

People also wanted facilities for more organised recreation, in the form of sport. Many villages already had village greens which were traditionally where village games were played and continued to be played, despite objections from newcomers who had bought homes overlooking the green and then got cross when cricket balls sailed through their windows. Well, what did they expect?

Village greens can be the source of considerable conflict, especially when ancient laws governing commons and such are suddenly flourished by lawyers in the faces of villages that have found better uses for their greens more in keeping with the times, for the good of the community in general, than leaving them empty. In most small villages there is so much 'open space' surrounding the built area that a patch of green in the middle of the village might seem superfluous. Also, the activities that traditionally took place on the green have either died out altogether or moved elsewhere. For example, the village green was above all the communal meeting place, but now people prefer to be indoors for their meetings and they go to the village hall, the church hall or the school. It comes as a surprise to many that there are rules deterring a village from building even a cricket pavilion on its village green, let alone a village hall, though the green would seem the obvious place for either.

Football pitches, cricket pitches and general playing fields were often established on the edge of the village, on a piece of manor-

READING ROOMS & PENNY READINGS

Many a landowner established a village reading room in Victorian times, to 'improve' the locals. These places were also built by parish institutes, providing a couple of warm and well-lit rooms in which anybody could read the newspapers or play bagatelle and other games. On the whole, they succeeded in attracting only some of the villagers – mainly tradesmen like the grocer, the shoe-maker, the tailor and the post-master, but rarely the broad base of agricultural labourers who might have benefited most.

The parish institutes would organise penny readings; they might pull together village plays or pageants; and they might encourage women to form sewing-bees for making things to sell in village bazaars. George Dew found penny readings 'seldom instructive, but almost always things of amusement'. In 1870 he had been to one at Middle Barton School room; it was 'an aristocratic show off – a display of themselves in their best humour & attire before the middle & lower classes, & yet strange to say pennies & threepences were paid to see them do this'. Almost all the readers and singers (it included a musical recital) had been aristocrats.

ial waste or the parish's old allotments or in a field released by a generous landowner to the community, and the same landowner often built a small sports' pavilion or club house of some kind. In other cases a squire or lord of the manor might have set up a village rifle range – this was particularly so during the Boer War, when it was discovered that England's agricultural labourers were not necessarily the best of shots, and needed some practice. Sometimes these ranges go right back to the times when soldiers used longbows rather than rifles: they were archery ranges. Whatever their history, they very often became the village playing fields.

A more recent introduction is village tennis courts, built with the help of grants or of donations or, more often, by the efforts of fund-raisers within the village. In my own village they set up a group aptly called MATCH (Make A Tennis Court Happen – we go in for acronyms here) which raised enough to build two hard courts at the heart of the village.

HALLS, CLUBS AND SOCIETIES

Every village needs a communal centre where the inhabitants can meet, informally or formally, and share activities and interests. Initially this was the village green (people were hardier then); next it was in the church vestry, which became the undercover equivalent of the village green. Finally it was village halls.

As the twentieth century rolled into the twenty-first, many villages marked the turn by building new village halls, or at least renovating what they already had. Over the years the hall has become increasingly important in village life, the centre for so many community events on whatever scale, but to be so, halls had to move with the times and meet new needs. They also needed to be in the heart of the village, where available building land tends to be rare.

Fund-raising is an important social feature of village life, for its own sake, and villagers are very good at it. Fund-raising pulls the village together in a common cause, almost regardless of that cause, and it usually generates plenty of new social activities which people enjoy so much that they hardly notice they are emptying their pockets at the same time. Looking back, fund-raising has always been a part of village life: countless traditional celebrations, such as May Day, Plough Monday and Bonfire Night, included people collecting money from as many households as possible

TOP
Making toffee apples

ABOVE
Children in a maze

TOP LEFT
Itinerant entertainers put on a show, with monkey and accordion, for the residents of Taplow, Bersкshire

the arts

'...good hunting grounds for marriage partners outside the village...the only regular dance nights for miles around.'

RAISING MONEY TO BUILD a village hall takes rather more. Many villages erected their first halls as memorial halls after the First World War but they were often no more than wooden or corrugated iron sheds, heated (if at all) by smoky stoves that cooked those close to them while the rest froze. These rough and ready buildings were greatly loved, and many a good dance and party would be held in them.

Between the wars the do-gooders were haunting the villages and there were many worthy people organising 'amusements' in the form of music, drama, folk-dancing (very false, that one), craftwork and all. The do-gooders meant well and tried to raise the standards to something approaching town levels. It was often a losing battle. For example, standards on village stages were usually so amateur that you could only put on a comedy: if you tried something dramatic or romantic, the audience would fall about laughing because they knew you far too well to believe the act. It could only be played 'for a laugh'.

Cubs playing a game of conkers, in 1919

OPPOSITE Auctioning produce at the Wavendon Flower Show held in the Parish Hall (top) and serious faces at a village social

There began to be a proliferation of clubs, societies and other groups in the village, all seeking to build up their memberships. There were so many of them that the village hall, should there be one, was solidly booked, hardly leaving room for more spontaneous entertainment such as village hops, socials and Christmas fairs. Quite apart from the Church and the chapel, there was the Women's Institute, the Men's Club, the Boys' Club, the Girls' Club, Boy Scouts and Girl Guides, Cubs and Brownies, the British Legion, Darby & Joan, the Horticultural Society, the Pathfinders, the Buffaloes (the what?), a variety of sports clubs (badminton in particular, which often dictated the size and shape of the hall), the youth club, dancing clubs (old time, ballroom, folk, tap and others) – oh yes, the do-gooders were determined that villagers should enjoy themselves, whether they liked it or not. Then there was the more practical side: baby clinics, weekly surgeries and the like. In due course there were monthly lunch clubs for the elderly as well as Christmas dinners for them; there were pop-ins and drop-ins, carpet-bowls clubs, band practice, drama clubs, choral societies – you would be amazed at the richness of village life once there was a hall in which it could be focused.

Halls could also be important centres for further education and for learning crafts and skills of all kinds. The Workers' Education Association (WEA) was financed by the Carnegie Trust to foster adult education, and though originally urban, it became active in many villages between the wars. Its efforts, combined with those of the local authority and of individuals within the village itself, meant that villagers could walk to lessons on subjects as varied as history and maths, metal work and soft furnishing, Scottish dancing and ballet, stick dressing and cake icing, cricket and car mechanics, French and flower arranging, hairdressing and basketry. They weren't usually seen as 'lessons' – more a friendly get-together in which you happened to do something very interesting and came away knowing a lot more than you did before.

But the village was increasingly looking outwards as well, especially its younger generation. With glee, they discovered Young Farmers Clubs (first created in 1928), meeting people in different villages with broadly similar interests, though today most Young Farmers have no direct link with agriculture at all. Then they discovered the Young Conservatives – groups which, whatever your politics might be, became good hunting grounds for marriage partners outside the village and which often offered the only regular dance nights for miles around. The time had come when simply dressing up in your Sunday best for the evening promenade through the village had lost its sparkle; when courting monitored by the whole village had lost its appeal; and when even lovers' lanes had lost their magic. The village was looking for something more.

Gradually people's standards within the village also became higher and they raised money to improve the hall they had or to start again with a more solid edifice in brick and stone, sometimes (though too rarely) designed in the vernacular style that fitted in with the villagescape. Sometimes there was unexpected opposition to the idea of any village hall being built in the first place; sometimes there was opposition to improvement, as if it were an insult to a much-loved old place that had seen better days. In recent years several villages have encountered quite bitter controversy when they have tried to extend the facilities of their halls. The opposition usually comes from people new to the village who think that a bigger hall means more noise, more cars, more teenagers hanging around, and 'Why can't they all go to the towns anyway?'.

It is natural that people's opinions on what a village hall is for should vary, but the essence of halls is that they are places where villagers can come together for any purpose they choose, even if it is nothing more than a cup of coffee. At Riding Mill, in Northumberland, they recognised this in the 1960s: 'Of all the activities at the Parish Hall none is more popular than the Saturday morning coffee, at which young and old gather to gossip,' they said, and the accompanying photographs showed more than sixty people enjoying themselves. That was more than 10 per cent of the village's entire population.

Halls are gradually expanding to become community centres. If they can work out what to do about their charitable status, some will include a small village shop to replace the one that has vanished, or an ever-open informal coffee room with comfortable chairs and home-baked cakes, or will offer community facilities such as photocopying, printing, computer lessons and access to the internet. The possibilities are endless, as long as the red tape doesn't strangle the initiatives at birth.

PUBLIC HOUSES

RURAL PUBS, IN CONTRAST TO MANY OF THOSE IN TOWNS, ARE IMPORTANT SOCIAL CENTRES FOR COMMUNAL LIFE. THEY GIVE VILLAGERS SOMEWHERE TO MEET INFORMALLY AND MIX FREELY WITH EACH OTHER, CATCH UP ON THE CHAT, EXCHANGE JOKES AND STORIES, SHRED A FEW LOCAL REPUTATIONS AND GENERALLY FEEL GOOD ABOUT LIFE, OR NOT.

'Gradually some of the ale-kitchens grew to accommodate more "friends"…'

THEY ARE NEARLY all called pubs now, but in days gone by there would have been ale-kitchens, ale-houses and inns. And there were a lot of them in the early Victorian period. Inns were places that offered food, lodging and stabling for a visitor's horses as well as drink; they tended to be sited on the road to somewhere, and often became the place where people did business, made deals, paid their debts to each other, found jobs and so on.

Ale-houses had been around forever, or at least since Anglo-Saxon times. They proliferated then, and in the tenth century a royal decree limited villages to only one ale-house each. They were really ale-kitchens, set up in private homes ranging from farmhouses to cottages where the wife sold her home brew to the locals and let them sit around and chat. They often paid for their drinks in kind rather than in cash and it was all very amicable for the most part – just friends dropping in.

Gradually some of the ale-kitchens grew to accommodate more 'friends', especially in homes that happened to be sited near places where villagers gathered anyway, such as the smithy or the village green. In Victorian times brewing had become an industry and the big brewers forced the homebrews off the market, either putting the kitchen brewers out of business altogether or taking over their premises. In 1850 (that date again) the term 'public house' was first used, confirming that the premises were often used as a general local meeting place, in the days before there were such things as village halls. By the 1870s most villages had at least two or three licensed pubs and soon they were welcoming the tourists that began to pour into the countryside by train, by bicycle, by motorbike and finally by car. By 1914 nearly all the pubs were tied to large breweries.

Lurgashall hoop-shaver William Pannell (left), aged 78, with smallholder George Humphreys, aged 81, at the Noah's Ark Inn

Mr Q. was about 75 in 1951. A bachelor living in a small country cottage, he was a retired labourer who devoted himself to his garden and lived in fear of the workhouse, knowing that when lonely old men were taken there they usually died within a fortnight. He was the last of his band of old cronies and his main recreation was to sit in the pub drinking a pint or two and smoking his clay pipe. White clay pipes, or parts of them – usually the delicate stems with a tiny airway through them – are often dug up in cottage gardens; they were first made in the sixteenth century (tobacco arrived in Britain in the late 1550s). In Victorian times they were mass produced and very cheap: you bought them by the gross, and pubs often gave them away for free.

Pubs provided other entertainments besides drinking, smoking, listening to old Joe on the fiddle and chatting. For many a country man, the ale-house was, as Jefferies put it

> *at once his stock exchange, his reading-room, his club, and his assembly rooms. It is here that his benefit society holds its annual dinner. The club meetings take place weekly or monthly in the great room upstairs. Here he learns the news of the day; the local papers are always to be found at the public-house, and if he cannot read himself he hears the news from those who can. In the winter he finds heat and light, too often lacking at home; at all times he finds amusement; and who can blame him for seiz-*

public houses

LEFT
Shove ha'penny at the Red Lion

ing what little pleasure lies in his way. As a rule the beerhouse is the only place of amusement to which he can resort: it is his theatre, his music-hall, picture-gallery, and Crystal Palace.

There was a wide range of traditional pub games, such as dominoes, draughts, cribbage, bagatelle, skittles and shove ha'penny, but pubs changed. Even in the 1870s new laws had practically forbidden pub-goers to play nine-pins and dominoes, in an attempt to stamp on gambling. The reign of 'skittle-sharpers' was more or less over. Yet skittles was usually played only for a quart of ale (to be drunk by the loser as well as the winner), which was hardly heavy betting.

Mr Leary was born in a little thatched Surrey cottage at Burrow Hill in 1923. He remembers the Four Horseshoes pub that he frequented after the war, an old-fashioned place then with no bar (the landlord brought out the drinks on a tray), the windows wouldn't shut, the chairs were rickety, the big round brass doorknob came off in your hand. It was a nice friendly pub, a family affair. Every Sunday lunchtime they would have a raffle there for the darts club. It was thruppence each and they would put the prizes out on the table: a packet of cigarettes, a box of chocolates, a bottle of beer (and you could get tuppence back on the empty bottle). One Sunday there was an enormous parcel on the table, done up with pretty paper and ribbons, and everybody thought they would like to win it so they bought extra tickets. The winner took ages to undo the parcel, miles and miles of paper and ribbon, and in the middle of it all was that brass doorknob. Oh dear. The next week all the darts club members were ready to protest that it had been one big fiddle, but they were each handed an envelope. Inside was all the proceeds from all the raffles in the darts club – four pounds and thruppence each, a man's weekly wage. It was surprising how many people wanted to join the darts club after that.

In more recent years some villagers have felt pushed out by the innovations – changes that seem to be designed to pull in outsiders rather than give the locals what they want. Outsiders bring their vehicles, and villagers start complaining about cars parking outside their homes. But the pubs are fighting to survive and will do what it takes. There just could come a time when the pub is no longer truly the 'local'.

'There was a wide range of traditional pub games, such as dominoes, draughts, cribbage, bagatelle, skittles and shove ha'penny…'

A pint for thirsty workers from Caroline Gibbs, a beer trader. Drinks had to be consumed outside as it was not a licensed house

SPORTS AND GAMES

CRICKET. THE VERY WORD SUGGESTS VILLAGE, AND THE GAME WAS BORN IN THE VILLAGE. EVERY VILLAGE HAD ITS CRICKET CLUB AND EVERY BOY IN THE VILLAGE ASPIRED TO SHARE IN ITS GLORY. MOST OF THE VILLAGE WOULD TURN UP TO WATCH THE SATURDAY INTER-VILLAGE MATCHES AND PASS JUDGEMENT ON THE PLAYERS AND OF COURSE ON THE UMPIRES. LITERATURE IS FULL OF WONDERFUL RURAL CRICKET MATCHES, DESCRIBED WITH PASSION AND WIT – THE PERVERSE PITCH, THE COWPATS, THE SUBTLE NEEDLING BETWEEN THE CLASSES, THE WAY IN WHICH THE CROWD COULD SO EASILY SWAY THE UMPIRE'S DECISION, THE WIFELY BICKERING OVER THE TEAS.

'The rest of the team included... "a somewhat fat and apoplectic butler"...'

THE YOUNG ARTHUR GIBBS, in his Cotswold village, thought that cricket was too energetic for hard-working farm labourers. But he remembered Peregrine, an 80-year-old yeoman farmer of the old type, who took cricket very seriously if his own sons were playing. He wouldn't speak to you for the rest of the day if you took one of them off the bowling. The rest of the team included a couple of farmers, the miller, two carpenter's sons, a footman, a 'somewhat fat and apoplectic butler' and the extremely tall village curate as captain. Another of Peregrine's sons, the local gamekeeper, was the umpire, always with a cigar clamped between his teeth.

Cricket had been much more fun in the earlier years of its four centuries (at least) of history, but then in Victorian times the killjoys came along, as in so many other old village games, and produced official rules. These tablets of stone were spread about the country by a rail-travelling MCC All-England XI. Maylebone? Isn't that somewhere near London? How dare they tell the villages how to play cricket (even if their club was established in 1787)! William Beldham of Hambledon would have turned in his grave, carefully minding his top hat or velvet cap as he did so. Incidentally, did you know that Julius Caesar played for England in 1861 against Australia?

In Nottinghamshire in the 1870s they claimed that the excellence of their village cricket was due to the local cottage industry of hand-frame knitting. It is difficult to see the connection, but it is a fact that the prevalence of this village industry in Nottinghamshire and Leicestershire could be judged by the endless long, low frame-shop windows that fronted row upon row of old cottages in the two counties.

Cricket clubs were often run by the parish institute, a committee of villagers of all classes and a wide range of occupations, from field labourers to schoolmasters, which evolved of its own accord in the days before lots of well-meaning sets of initials started coming into villages between the wars to improve rural lives.

Quite often a local lord would build a cricket pavilion for the village and then join in the match himself, as Lord Jersey liked to do in the 1870s – preferably with a band playing at the same time. Shortly after the First World War, cricket played in the grounds of the big house was quietly being eased out as squires turned their attention to golf or polo – hardly village games.

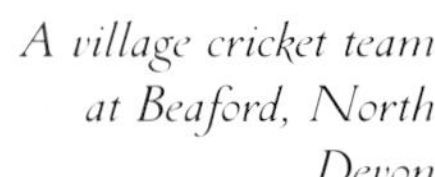

A village cricket team at Beaford, North Devon

FOOTBALL

It probably all began with an inflated pig's bladder being kicked about by the lads on the

sports and games

village green. Or did it? Several centuries ago, when Shrove Tuesday was the nation's favourite day for sports, a company of saddlers in Chester started presenting the drapers with a wooden ball decked with flowers, held on the point of a lance. In about 1540 the wooden ball was changed into a silver bell to be awarded to the man who could run 'the best and furthest on horseback' on Shrove Tuesday. Later, the shoe-makers of Chester started presenting the drapers with a leather ball, called a 'foote-ball', and naturally they started kicking it around. But the leather balls had a tendency to break windows and so the ball was changed for a silver trophy and was given for foot races instead of kick-abouts.

A more complicated version of football was played in the streets of the Derbyshire village of Ashbourne: they called it Uppards and Downards and it lasted for several hours. The Uppards team comprised native villagers born above the river; the Downards had been born down of the river. Others could join in as well but their goals wouldn't count.

SHROVE TUESDAY GAMES

Shrove Tuesday games also included tug-of-war and cock-throwing. The latter bestial sport involved tying live birds to a stake and throwing things at them until they were dead. In the Scilly Isles, having enjoyed a spot of cock-throwing, the local boys would then chuck stones at people's doors in the evening. In Dorset, on Shrove Tuesday, they went in for the similar pastime of 'Lent crocking'.

As for tug-of-war, that very villagy event is said to have sprung from an argument at Henry VI's siege of Ludlow. One group in the town supported the Duke of York, another group wanted to give in to the King, and this, it seems, led to an annual controversy which they would settle every Shrove Tuesday with a tug-of-war.

WRESTLING AND BOXING

Charles Vancouver, in his Devon survey published in 1808, said that the local 'young farmers and peasantry' were addicted to wrestling. Purses of up to ten guineas (a year's wages) would be put up by the promoters. A ring some fifteen to twenty yards across would be made in a field near a large village, marked out with stakes and a single rope, within which the winner had to throw down five of his adversaries before he could claim his purse. The rules seemed to be almost non-existent: it was a case of no holds barred or almost so: 'the collar, arm, or any part above the waistband, that most conveniently presents to the combatants during the contest.' The fun usually started at between two and three o'clock in the afternoon and often continued until midnight (by lamplight). Each bout lasted from ten to fifteen minutes, 'in which is displayed much activity, strength, and adroitness, whilst the shins of the party are often found streaming with blood from the sharp and violent blows they receive from each other, but which on no account are ever permitted to be given above the knee'. Well, that's a relief!

The first rule was to shake hands before and after the contest 'and it rarely happens that the play is followed with boxing, or that any grudge or ill-will is continued from the conquered to those that may have thrown them'. Then the rules get more complicated: 'In the outset of the play, every man who becomes a standard for the purse, must first throw two men on their back, belly, or side; eight of these standards must be made from the primary competitors for the single play; and when the standards are thus made, they each receive a crown. These eight playing, four of them must fall, the other four then engage, two of whom must fall; when the still standing two enter to decide the purse, and the second best man, or he who is last thrown, usually receives about one in five upon its amount.' There were three judges and no appeal against their decisions.

The men of the Devon moors were celebrated for their hardiness 'in bearing excessive kicking upon their shins'. It would have hurt – the Devon style allowed opponents to wear heavy shoes.

Contestants getting a good grip during the Heavyweight Sports at Windermere, Lake District

'... whilst the shins of the party are often found streaming with blood from the sharp and violent blows they receive from each other ...'

sports and games

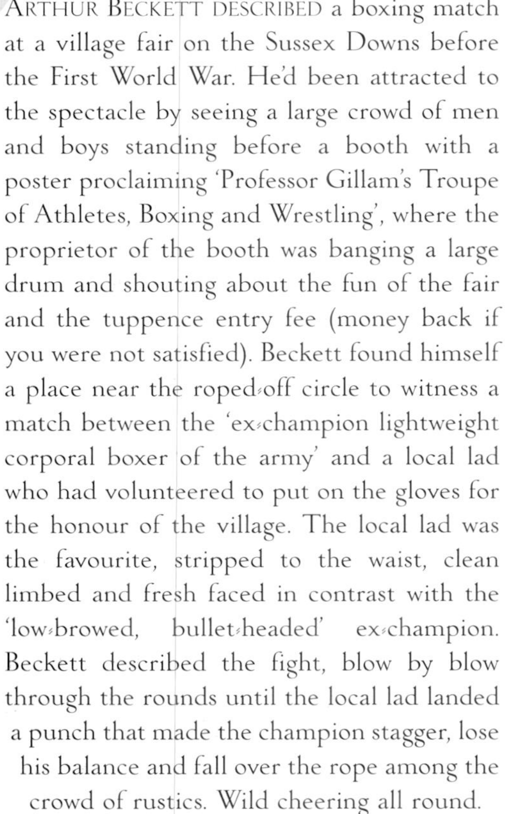

'...to land on the rough ice, falling over backwards and toppling the whole line, collapsing in a heap of sprawling laughter.'

ARTHUR BECKETT DESCRIBED a boxing match at a village fair on the Sussex Downs before the First World War. He'd been attracted to the spectacle by seeing a large crowd of men and boys standing before a booth with a poster proclaiming 'Professor Gillam's Troupe of Athletes, Boxing and Wrestling', where the proprietor of the booth was banging a large drum and shouting about the fun of the fair and the tuppence entry fee (money back if you were not satisfied). Beckett found himself a place near the roped-off circle to witness a match between the 'ex-champion lightweight corporal boxer of the army' and a local lad who had volunteered to put on the gloves for the honour of the village. The local lad was the favourite, stripped to the waist, clean limbed and fresh faced in contrast with the 'low-browed, bullet-headed' ex-champion. Beckett described the fight, blow by blow through the rounds until the local lad landed a punch that made the champion stagger, lose his balance and fall over the rope among the crowd of rustics. Wild cheering all round.

SKATING AND SLEDGING

As soon as the winter had set the ponds to ice, the whole village would take to sliding, with or without skates. In January 1879 the flooded valley at Somerton in Oxfordshire froze over and a large number of skaters arrived by rail to skate on it. Some brought small sleighs in which ladies sat while a couple of skating men propelled them over the ice. At Christmas the boys had been happily sliding about on the river Cherwell at Islip, and on Christmas Day the ice was 'as busy with sliders and skaters as a fair day'.

Mary Russell Mitford, writing in the 1820s, described a winter scene: the road was gay with 'carts and post-chaises, and girls in red cloaks, and, afar off, looking almost like a toy, the coach'. The walkers seemed much happier than the riders in the coach as they were all off to the glassy ponds for a bit of sliding and skating. The children on one pond had made 'two long, smooth, liny slides', skimming down the bumpy, snowy bank to land on the rough ice, falling over backwards and toppling the whole line, collapsing in a heap of sprawling laughter. At another pond it was all much more sedate: the lieutenant was skating elegantly with his little sons, on blades rather than boots.

MORE VILLAGE GAMES

In the early years of the twentieth century, some sports and pastimes could still be closely identified with particular regions. For example, hawking was popular on Salisbury Plain and its first day always coincided with the week in which the wild violets suddenly scented the Wiltshire valleys; the old hawking club's members always wore green velveteen coats. Wrestling was enjoyed in the dales of the north-west as well as in Devon and Cornwall, though to different rules; in Somerset they went eel-hunting with dogs; in Cumberland they had hound-trailing and fell-running; in Yorkshire it was arrow-throwing and billets; in Cornwall they hunted seals for sport. In Sussex they played, and still play, the old 'milkmaid' game of stoolball, which has affinities with softball, rounders and cricket, and may even be the forerunner of cricket, but is a much quicker game and much harder than it looks, as some men discover when they condescend to play.

There used to be a North of England quoits championship, in which teams of miners from Northumberland and Durham, shipbuilders from the Tees,Tyne and Wear and farm workers from the North Riding of Yorkshire all competed, but this had gone by the 1960s, though there were still the Dales League and the Hawsker & District. The game, also known as horse-shoes, involved iron quoits, made by the village blacksmith, and a 3in-high peg known as the hob, set in a square yard of moistened clay surrounded by a wooden platform. With a flick of the wrist, a player would send his quoit (which weighed more than 5lb) from the wooden platform to another hob 11 yards away; at the same time another player would probably be throwing

OPPOSITE Pitching to win at quoits, Goldsborough, North Yorkshire, in 1961. In the top picture a team member marks the aiming point for his colleague

sports and games

his quoit in the opposite direction. Two points for a quoit over the peg, and one if your best shot was nearer to the hob than your opponent's, though in fact the scoring was much more subtle than that.

Singlesticks was a rural game that harked back to the days of swordsmanship. You cut a slender stick of ash or hazel from the hedge, about 34in long and thicker at one end. The thick end was thrust through a basket-work hilt to protect the hand and, basically, you sparred with it. In the time of the first and second Georges, the stick was rather stouter and the 'game' was called cudgel-play.

Some villages have become famous for their particular games. At Tinsley Green they have been holding marbles championships for more than 300 years. At the model village of Ashton in Northamptonshire, built by de Rothschild in 1900, they have conkers championships. And can anyone remember the village that hosts the international tiddlywinks championships?

In the 1850s they were still having their 'pastime' in the Wiltshire village of Uffington, home of one of the famous white horses carved on the chalk hills. The main aim of the pastime was to scour the chalk horse so that his image remained clear and clean, but it was a great excuse for fun: they would have back-sword play (like singlesticks), they would climb a greasy pole to win a leg of mutton, they would race for a pig and a cheese, and old John Morse 'grinned agin another chap droo hoss collars, a fine bit of spwoart, to be sure, and the made the folks laaf'. Ah, the grand old sport of gurning! Those were the days when men in counties such as Somerset, Gloucester and Berkshire would bash each other's head with cudgels to win a gold-laced hat and a pair of buckskin breeches, or when donkeys raced for a flitch of bacon. In some villages they still have cheese-rolling.

Cottage-dwelling metal-workers and Black Country miners were passionate about pigeon-racing, and at one time also enjoyed the violent sports of cock-fighting and dog-fighting until their bosses dissuaded them and swung them around to playing in brass bands instead.

Much more to most people's taste was horse-racing. Thomas Garne, a Cotswold yeoman farmer born in 1784, was so incensed at the large crowds that marched across his corn-fields on their way to Bibury races that he sprinkled red sheep-raddle on the crop to deter at least the crinolined ladies. Bibury shopkeepers loved those races; they could let out their own bedrooms to racegoers for a princely sum, as well as selling their goods to this cheerful mob.

Garne's contemporary, Mary Russell Mitford, wrote that all people loved Ascot Races 'but our country lasses love them above all. It is their favourite wedding jaunt, for half our young couples are married in the race week, and one or two matches have seemed to me got up purposely for the occasion.'

During Royal Ascot Week, between the world wars, gypsies used to come from all over England to Chobham Common and camp there by the monument. They came in horse-drawn vehicles and would pick white heather on the common to sell at Ascot. The common was also a year-round home to tramps, and some can remember when the bodies of dead tramps from the common would be laid out at the Four Horseshoes.

'... can anyone remember the village that hosts the international tiddlywinks championships?'

FIELD SPORTS

HUNTING AND SHOOTING WERE FOR THE MOST PART THE SPORTS OF THE UPPER CLASSES. IN SOME REGIONS FARMERS AND TRADESMEN OFTEN RODE TO HOUNDS AS WELL, AND MOST OF THE REST OF THE VILLAGE FOLLOWED ON FOOT. MANY LOCALS FOUND EMPLOYMENT IN BOTH SPORTS – AS HUNTSMEN AND GAMEKEEPERS, AS KENNEL WORKERS AND STABLE WORKERS, AS BEATERS, AS LADS EARNING A FEW PENCE FOR HOLDING A HORSE OR FETCHING BUCKETS OF WATER, OR INDIRECTLY AS FARM LABOURERS HELPING TO MAINTAIN THE LANDSCAPE THAT SUITED THE SPORTS AND HAD OFTEN BEEN CREATED TO SOME EXTENT DIRECTLY FOR THEIR PURPOSES.

'...otters are now very gradually re-establishing in areas where they have not been seen for many years.'

TOP RIGHT *Hound-trailing at Wasdale in the Lake District: ready to start*

BELOW RIGHT *The fell hounds used in hound-trailing are of a rangy type*

THERE WOULD BE fewer spinneys, copses and hedgerows in the countryside if the hunt had not needed cover for foxes and the shoot had not needed cover for the birds; there would be much more barbed-wire in hunting country if it were better jumping material than hedges and gates.

HUNTING

The quarry hunted was not confined to foxes. There were and still are hunts that concentrate on deer, with staghounds. As well as foxhounds, there are beagles and harriers, bloodhounds and basset hounds; there are coursing hounds (lurchers and the like) pursuing hares (a species that has vanished from many of its old haunts), legally or otherwise. Deerhounds and wolfhounds used to be worked against larger prey; dachshunds used to be badger dogs.

There were working otter hounds until otters became virtually extinct, within living memory; otters are now very gradually re-establishing in areas where they have not been seen for many a year. At Rousham there is a marble tablet inscribed to the memory of a favourite otter hound. Otter hunters on the Cherwell wore a uniform of blue serge jackets and knicker-

The Vine Hunt meets at the Pineapple Inn, Brimpton, Berkshire

field sports

bockers with red stockings, caps and waistcoats; on the front of each cap was an otter's paw. Their followers would be on foot but were not adverse to hopping on a train to go home again at the end of the day; the hounds did the same.

Sir Archie James, a man who so loved hunting of all kinds, in England and in Africa and India, that he entitled his memoirs *Nimrod,* wrote a rousing piece in the late 1970s about how there would be no foxes in Britain without the hunts to preserve them, and how the very fact of hunting kept the species more healthy; then he spoiled it all by saying that meant nothing to him at all – he hunted purely because he enjoyed the sport, the thrill of the chase, the glory of the ride, and the good company of his friends.

Some thoroughly unpleasant 'sports' have been banned by law – horrors such as badger-baiting, dog-fighting and cock-fighting – but are still carried out, mainly by townsmen in search of an illegal and violent thrill.

field sports

SHOOTING

'Both shooting and hunting are seen as sports in which the countryman has a right to participate ...'

Shooting is now very big business indeed. John Moore, in his tales of the village of Brensham (a fictional place but based on real Midlands villages) in the 1930s, described the dreaded Syndicate that gradually took over much of the land for shooting. The Lord of the Manor was always close to bankruptcy and kept selling bits of land to the Syndicate to stave off his creditors, until finally he was isolated on his own island of the rabbity Park (home to gypsy caravans for years), the crumbling Manor with its ruined chapel and muddy moat, the Home Orchard and a handful of cottages and smallholdings. Even the lord's Folly fell to the Syndicate, who promptly evicted the harmless old hermit who lived there.

RIGHT Tom Wansborne, gamekeeper's assistant, with Charles Chandler, gamekeeper on the Eridge Estate, Kent, at the Crest and Gun pub in 1938

Then the Syndicate took over the river as well, sticking up 'Private Angling' notices where villagers had always been able to fish for roach and chub with home-made bamboo rods and bent pins. Those who ferreted for rabbits along the railway embankment, seeing it as their moral duty to keep down the plague-like numbers of the little beasts that were undermining the tracks, found themselves turned off so that keepers could snare and trap rabbits and sell them for ninepence a brace in Birmingham. Boys who had always collected rotting colic-inducing green windfall apples found themselves being prosecuted for theft; footpaths that the villagers had used for generations were suddenly closed. When the Stock Market plummeted in 1938, the Syndicate managed to grab the rest of the lord's land but allowed the lord to live in his own lodge along with the cowman's family. The trouble with syndicates was their shadowiness; they were not an identifiable individual you could punch on the nose.

Group of springer spaniels, a great team of gundogs

It is perhaps something of a left-over from the dominance of the squire that both shooting and hunting are seen as sports in which the 'countryman' has a right to participate, regardless of what others may think about it. The sports are divisive in that they tend to perpetuate the age-old anger of the peasant, feeling helpless against the power of the king and his 'barons' – it harks back to the days of

field sports

the royal forests when the abundant game was preserved as the sport of kings while the ever-hungry everyman was denied food for the pot and was punished with disproportionate severity when hunger led to poaching. The anger was refuelled by the equally harsh laws against trespass and against the traditional taking of game during the widespread enclosures by major landowners in the eighteenth century. More recently it has been fanned again by the sometimes arrogant behaviour of some shooting landowners whose sport impinges on the lives of those who happen to live locally. Thus the perception of this social divide lingers today, even though in many country areas people at all levels of society might be involved in the sports directly or interested in maintaining the traditions of them. There seems to be a gut reaction among those who live in urban areas against these major rural sports and it is unfortunate that such a strong urban/rural divide is seeking to dominate the debate about the countryside. There are far more important rural matters to be discussed.

Many modern gamekeepers know a great deal about the countryside in which they roam – they probably study wildlife more closely than most and many are excellent conservationists, but their job is to rear birds for the guns. The 'conservation' stance has been adopted in recent years by those who enjoy hunting and shooting but feel they must justify their sport. This has created a whole new area of antagonism, with the arguments being shouted loudly by both sides, in a strange mixture of emotion and 'science'. Looked at more dispassionately, both sports unsettle the balance of nature and that is always a dangerous game to play. Hunting is torn between destroying foxes, ostensibly on behalf of local farmers concerned for their young livestock and poultry, and protecting foxes so that the sport can continue. (A similar 'protection' argument applies to deer.) Foxes are natural predators; as such they will take whatever prey is easiest and requires the least energy to catch and kill. Very occasionally this could be lambs and piglets and quite often this could be poultry. Well, predators were around long before humans domesticated their animals and turned them into sitting targets. It is debatable whether war on a species is justified by the degree of the threat to livestock, and it could also be argued that the control of foxes has allowed rabbit populations to increase to 'pest' levels in many areas. Here again, the balance between predator and prey has been disturbed by human intervention

In the case of shooting, dispassionate conservationists and those who study nature point out the dangers of creating a monoculture in which one species – pheasants, for example – is reared in huge numbers in a limited area in which many other species are deliberately eliminated as vermin that threaten the monoculture species, thus creating a gross local imbalance with consequences that do not seem to have been studied seriously and without prejudice. And then those monoculture species are shot. It's a funny old world.

Mr and Mrs Hall-Watt at a pheasant shoot on their Yorkshire estate at Bishop Burton

'There seems to be a gut reaction among those who live in urban areas against these major rural sports . . .'

10

Country Estates

THE RURAL LANDSCAPE of Britain has been shaped by large-scale landowners who, until recent times, were individuals and hereditary families (including royal ones) rather than corporate bodies such as governments, local councils and limited companies.

In the 1790s, the population of the Scottish united parishes of Old Atholl was diminishing and quite a few farming tenants, in the face of rising rents, had become cottagers or moved into the towns to become general labourers; a few had emigrated to America. Most people were poor and even the larger farmers had little disposable income once they had paid their rents to the few landlords (the Duke of Atholl, at Blair Castle, owned at least half of the parish). Fifty years later the population was still decreasing; where on the higher ground there had been numerous tenants eking out a living at subsistence level, there were now sheep-walks and the families had moved to the large towns further south or, again, to America.

The people of Atholl were described as having a reasonable share of acuteness; they were 'disposed to be friendly to each other, hospitable to strangers, and charitable to the poor'. The country people were 'of middle stature, active and capable of enduring much fatigue', and they were now, it was claimed, more likely to convert their barley into money than to be involved in the once-widespread illicit distillation of whisky.

The 'gentlemen' were tall and handsome and 'fond of a military life'. Amongst the 'common people' there was still a 'deal of martial spirit remaining', and although they had learnt to despise a soldier's pay and to hate a life of servitude they still made 'very good soldiers ... being firm, hardy and brave, though not generally tall'. This description quite neatly encapsulates the old class differences, both in appearance and in outlook.

country estates

LANDSCAPES

PREVIOUS PAGE
Winter at Compton Chamberlayne, Wiltshire

In 1848 Robert Somers wrote in his *Letters from the Highlands*: 'So far as I can gather, the depopulation of Glen Tilt was effected between 1780 and 1790. This glen was occupied in the same way as other Highland valleys, each family possessing a piece of arable land, while the hill was held in common. The people enjoyed full liberty to fish in the Tilt, an excellent salmon river; and the pleasures and profits of the chase were nearly as free to them as to their chief.' But then the Duke of Atholl acquired a taste for deer.

THE HIGHLAND CLEARANCES

A large dyke was built at the head of the glen and those who used to take their cattle to a higher glen in summer were forbidden to do so. That outer region became the preserve of deer, which took to marauding the poor people's crops. The duke, pleased with his deer, extended their grazing grounds by a few thousand acres 'at the expense of the people, who now began to be peeled of their possessions like one of their elms of its leaves by an October storm'. In due course the last man left the glen, and the last cottage became 'a head of ruins'. The romantic Glen Tilt was deserted and its story was typical of countless other Highland populations in the period from the 1780s to the middle of the following century. Local people all over the region found themselves

Highland cattle in their natural environment

forced into an unwanted way of life as coastal crofters, or emigrated to find a better living overseas (often very successfully). The glens became empty of people, their places taken by not only the laird's deer but also his large flocks of sheep, and a noble Gaelic culture was virtually extinguished.

EAST ANGLIAN WASTES

In 1927 the 2nd Earl of Iveagh inherited the family's 23,000-acre Elveden estate in Suffolk.

Distinguished guests at Elveden, with King Edward VII at the centre of the group

Agriculture was in the depths of another continuing depression. A.G. Street, in *Farmer's Glory* published in 1931, wrote that the zest had gone out of farming. 'For any farmer to go round his fields to-day and view his crops brings him no pleasure. The larger and better the fields of wheat, the more useless the whole business appears.' Nobody seemed to want the food that British farmers were so efficiently producing.

Elveden's history was a colourful one. In 1863, for example, its occupant for the next twenty years or so would be His Highness the Maharajah Duleep Singh of Lahore, heir to the throne of Punjab, who had lived in England for most of his life and enjoyed playing the country squire. He was an excellent shot (on one drive, he killed 780 partridge with his own gun, using 1,000 cartridges) and was a good and generous landlord, held in high esteem locally in spite of converting the interior of Elveden Hall to resemble an Indian palace, its walls and ceilings covered with mirrors.

The 2nd Earl of Iveagh had inherited a very substantial fortune. He had no need to farm, at a time when farming did not pay and it was enough of a problem to maintain any large estate. Most major landowners of the period simply ran a home farm for milk and eggs and let the rest of the land to tenants, or appointed an agent to farm the land in order that the owner might have somewhere to shoot, as the 1st Earl had done. The 2nd Earl could perfectly well have continued to manage the estate for its amenities – it was one of the best shoots in England. The land was so poor that it made more sense to rear game on it than cattle or corn, and most people advised him to stick to pheasants, rabbits and trees. The Forestry Commission almost assumed that sandy land was theirs by right but Iveagh decided that food for the current generation and its children was more important than pit-props for a future one.

'...on one drive, he killed 780 partridges with his own gun, using 1,000 cartridges.'

landscapes

OPPOSITE
Clearing bracken for land reclamation. In many areas bracken was cut for use as livestock bedding

LORD IVEAGH FELT that the way of life of the great sporting estates would soon become an anachronism, and anyway he had a sense of vision. He actually believed in land. He did not agree with the view held by the majority for the previous fifty years that Britain should become 'the world's manufacturer', exchanging its goods for cheap foreign food. He felt that such a policy had been responsible for depopulation of the countryside and the ruin of British agriculture. He felt that, sooner or later, Britain would once again need to raise its own food, that there was great danger in staking the whole economy on being able to sell the products of urban British industry abroad in exchange for unlimited supplies of imported food. This, remember, was when the Second World War was not yet a black cloud on the horizon.

He decided to transform the sandy, windswept heathlands and vast rabbit warrens of Elveden into highly productive farmland. He sought advice from Sir John Russell about the use of organic waste, especially farmyard manure. He sought advice from John Hammond, Cambridge's top expert in animal breeding. He went to the National Institute for Research in Dairying to find out how to battle against mastitis in his cows and to learn that by growing lucerne on his light land many problems would be solved. Above all, in the foreword to a book about the Elveden enterprise written in 1951, he relied on 'my staff and all my workers ... No new experiment has ever daunted them ... Their loyalty has been never failing. If they sometimes shook their heads, I am told that their view was: "Well, he pays for it, so why shouldn't he have his fun."'

Within twenty years of inheriting Elveden he had succeeded in turning a desert into rich pasture and high-yielding arable land producing huge quantities of food – enough to feed several thousand people. By 1951 Elveden was the largest arable farm in England, with 8,000 acres under cultivation producing nearly 25,000 tons of grain and sugar beet; in addition there were 1,200

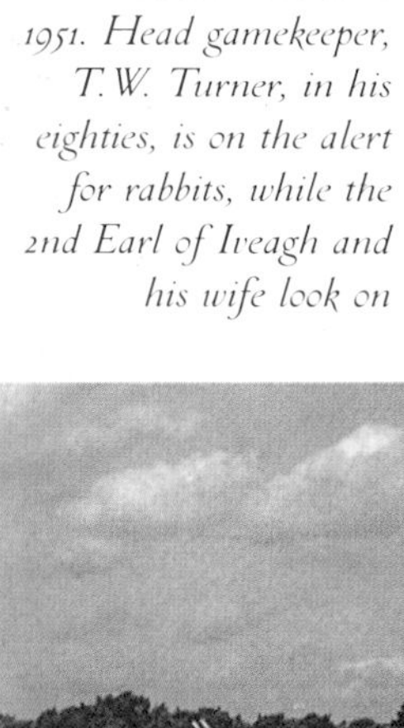

Combine harvester on the Elveden estate in 1951. Head gamekeeper, T.W. Turner, in his eighties, is on the alert for rabbits, while the 2nd Earl of Iveagh and his wife look on

landscapes

pedigree Guernsey and Shorthorn dairy cows, enabling the estate to sell more than 300,000 gallons of milk (Lord Iveagh was always at heart a dairy man), 500 beef cattle and enough sheep to produce a thousand store lambs. In spite of his little differences with the Forestry Commission, by 1951 his estate was growing more than 4,000 acres of trees and giving jobs to a large number of foresters, gamekeepers, engineers, sawmill workers, blacksmiths and other craftsmen as well as about 200 permanent farmworkers, many of whom had been working on the estate for fifty years or more.

LAND DRAINAGE AND TREE PLANTING

In the eighteenth and nineteenth centuries, many major landowners improved their land for agriculture, usually with noticeable effects on the landscape. For example, on the Hollycombe estate in Sussex much of the valley clay-land was wet enough to give rise to several local place-names ending in 'Marsh'. In contrast, other parts of the estate had always been described as 'wastes' – large tracts of sandy heathland growing nothing but heather, gorse, pine and scrub birch. The most challenging task was to drain the valley lands and this was done with the aid of clay land-drain pipes made at the village's own brickworks. Thereafter the valley became excellent pasture for cattle, supporting several dairy herds, and also grew good grain crops.

The owner of Hollycombe lifted his eyes beyond the valley and planted trees on the slopes of the small hills, clumping them artistically on one or two hilltops and clothing the steep hangers with useful sweet chestnut for coppicing. He planted oak woods and conifer plantations; he also planted specimen trees of the unusual species that were being introduced to Britain from America, China and elsewhere, and these have since grown to be some of the largest of their species in the country. Thus it was that the owner of the estate transformed the landscape, with great sympathy.

GOLF COURSES

In the latter half of the twentieth century, with many of the estate's lands long since sold off, new landowners had very different ideas. They built golf courses – precisely mown greens with little coloured flags punctuating broad swathes of fairway. Where once the commoners' animals had grazed and the reptiles had basked and the heathland birds had nested and sung, there are now tidy people walking methodically from one point to another, occasionally pausing to swing their club and thwack a small white ball that has done them no harm at all. There is something alien about a golf course in rural areas: it is too deliberate, too neat, too artificial, and above all it produces nothing in the way of crops or livestock. To a peasant's eye, that is a terrible waste of grass that should be grazed and soil that should be tilled for food production; to the commoners it is yet another erosion of their traditional rights to collect fuel and run their animals.

ESTATE VILLAGES AND FARMS

ESTATE OWNERS QUITE OFTEN BUILT COTTAGES, AND SOME OF THEM BUILT ENTIRE VILLAGES – MANY OF THEM VERY BEAUTIFUL BUT GIVING AWAY THEIR PLANNED ORIGINS IN THEIR UNIFORMITY OF MATERIALS, PERIOD AND OVERALL STYLE. THERE ARE FAMOUS EXAMPLES OF MODEL VILLAGES SUCH AS GREAT TEW IN OXFORDSHIRE, DESIGNED AS PART OF AN AGRICULTURAL IMPROVEMENT SCHEME IN 1808, AND THE DUKE OF DEVONSHIRE'S VILLAGE OF EDENSOR ON THE CHATSWORTH ESTATE IN DERBYSHIRE.

'They did not have an inborn sense of the rhythms of agriculture and village life but many of them had a vision ...'

MANY ESTATE VILLAGES were built or improved by new money rather than old. Especially in the nineteenth century, the old families of landed gentry with country pedigrees dating back many generations were being bought out by men who had made their money in commerce and industry and fancied the life of a country gentleman. They did not have an inborn sense of the rhythms of agriculture and village life but many of them had a vision and an urge to contribute to the rural environment in which they found themselves.

All over the country there are small villages that do not attract much attention but which the locals know owe their origins or their improvement to the local estate. Grittleton, in Wiltshire, is essentially a one-street village of attractive stone cottages snuggling under the skirts of a substantial manor house built in the mid nineteenth century, complete with elegant statuary in the house and scattered throughout the large gardens, a large underground ice-house, an extensive park, miles of stone

Beaulieu, Hampshire, in 1948. In this all-brick village the Montagu family's model Victorian cottages blend with older houses

estate villages

boundary walls, stables, home farms and woodland.

Evelyn Willis, now in a residential home for the elderly near Melksham, lived on the Grittleton estate when it belonged to Sir Audley Neeld (the Neeld family had built the big house in 1848). Between the wars, from the age of fourteen, she went into service at Foscote Farm for ten years, working for Judge Harding, whom she describes as 'one of those rich farmers': he rode around the farm on a horse and owned a prize herd of beautiful Shorthorn cows. The herd was the pride and joy of the staff as well as the judge:

> *They all had names, the Certificates won by them were pinned at the back of their stalls so that the cows could see them and be proud. The cows stayed in the sheds and yard during the winter. When springtime came, someone came to the door of the house and called, 'The cows are going out, come quickly!' We all ran to see them go out to the green fields. How they bellowed and galloped, seeing the green grass, the sunshine!*
>
> *The cows were brought in from the fields at milking time by Gillam, the head cowman. He used strong language but I understand that does not mean anything: the cowman is always fond and proud of his herd. There were five milkers, two carters, a man to wash the cloths and many churns. The milk was taken to Grittleton House in the morning, and cream, and on to Badminton Station by lorry, to go to Bristol and London. A busy time, it went twice a day, two milkings. There was a foreman; his son Willis groomed two horses and also washed and prepared the cars for use, driving them from the garage to the front gate when required by Judge Harding.*

Note that she is referring not to the lord of the manor but to a farmer, albeit a wealthy judge, who had all these employees and a fine large farmhouse (turreted and with a bell-tower) with flower gardens and lawns maintained by the gardener, a long driveway, a summer-house and a tennis court, and large cold-frames in which the daughter of the house grew violets to sell to shops in Bath. Another daughter, the same age as Eileen, was taught by a Scottish governess at home. Other members of the judge's family lived at Grittleton's home farm, where they kept a Friesian dairy herd.

Eileen remembers the long tree-lined drive from Foscote across the Park to the village; she remembers the post-office, the church, the village shop, the village school, the pub and the cottage wells and stone-walled gardens; she remembers the footmen and other staff at the big house too. Then there was the cricket team, a good one with (most important) a 'good tea-hut, run by Mrs Hopkins, whose sons and husband were in the team'. Next to the cricket ground there was a bowling green, where Sir Audley himself used to play and where in the late 1940s there would be bowling of a different kind at the village fête – bowling for live pigs and geese. After her marriage at the age of 24, Eileen was lucky enough to live in the more famously beautiful village of Castle Combe, a few miles away, with its often-photographed stream and bridges.

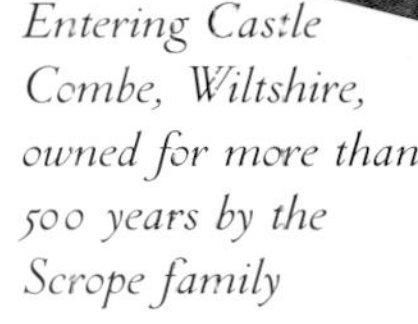

Entering Castle Combe, Wiltshire, owned for more than 500 years by the Scrope family

Today Grittleton House is a school (and has been for more than half a century); its spacious lawns have become playing fields and the stables have been converted into expensive homes. The Park is unspoilt and the estate village is superficially unchanged but there are smart cars parked in the street and clearly the present 'cottagers' are no longer farm labourers. The shop and village school have closed. Grittleton's way of life was radically changed when the M4 motorway was built almost within hearing, exposing this once-introverted village to a flood of commuters who were enchanted by its rural character but who by their very presence and way of life just might destroy what they came to enjoy.

'Then there was the cricket team, a good one with (most important) a good tea-hut ...'

ESTATE & VILLAGE

Because of the dominance by the estate or the 'big house', the relationship between estate and village has always been of immense importance to the village. It was usually the case that the livelihood of most villagers depended directly on employment on the estate, whether on the land or in the various village trades, or in service at the big house.

Lady Tavistock, who for the past decade has been adminstering the 13,000-acre Bedford estate that includes Woburn Abbey, said that living on the estate was like being inside a little country. There are about 400 cottages on the estate and some of their inhabitants are the third generation to have lived at Woburn. Like many estates, this one has diversified in order to survive: among other ventures there is a safari park and a stud farm.

In many cases, the nation's big landowners were philanthropical enough to benefit the villagers in a thousand ways in their everyday lives, by building a school or facilities such as reading-rooms and parish cottages, ensuring work was to be had in all seasons, playing lord and lady bountiful to the poor (and often the role was taken with great sincerity), finding doctors and nurses for the sick, building homes for agricultural workers and estate servants, and so on.

The major landowners often performed roles that today are played by the state. The village was a miniature kingdom and its welfare was in the combined hands of the landowner and the Church – powers that sometimes worked together but sometimes were in opposition to each other, harbouring petty jealousies that inevitably impinged on the lives of all in the parish. Some landowners were not benevolent, or, rather, took no notice of their 'subjects'. The problem is one that applies to everybody – the 'no man is an island' principle by which whatever a person does is likely to affect other people. It is a matter of scale: the more extensive your boundaries, the more neighbours you will have. A large estate thus has a lot more neighbours (and tenants and employees) than most of us; there are more people to be affected by the activities of the owner of that estate, which means that the responsibilities of that owner to the rest of the area are proportionately greater. Sometimes (and very often it was a case of new money not knowing its responsibilities, or of youth not accepting them), the obligations were forgotten and the squire lost his way, letting down the locals and blighting the whole neighbourhood.

THE SQUIRE

THE SQUIRE IS AN IMPORTANT FIGURE IN SOCIAL HISTORY AND THE INFLUENCE OF THE SQUIRE IN RURAL AREAS REMAINED STRONG UNTIL AT LEAST THE FIRST WORLD WAR IN MANY PARTS OF THE COUNTRY. 'SQUIRE' IS THE ABBREVIATED FORM OF 'ESQUIRE' AND WAS ORIGINALLY APPLIED TO LANDOWNERS WHO WERE OFTEN BUT NOT NECESSARILY LORDS OF THE MANOR, BUT IT CAN BE USED MORE GENERALLY TO INCLUDE THOSE IN RURAL AREAS WHOSE POWER OVER A NEIGHBOURHOOD WAS USUALLY BASED ON BEING A SUBSTANTIAL LANDOWNER.

Workers' outing in a charabanc for staff of Berkeley Castle, the Gloucestershire home of the Berkeleys since the twelfth century

THE ESSENCE OF the old-fashioned squire was that he was one of the gentry who came from an old and respected family and who preferred to live locally, involved with county society and village and farming matters, in contrast to the noble lords who preferred to live in the city and involve themselves in politics, court life, the arts and high society.

In 1850 squires were defined as 'lesser gentry' who owned between 1,000 and 3,000 acres of land and took an active interest in the farming of it. Their wealth was more in land than in other assets, and their land ownership gave them local power. There were about 2,000 squires in the country at the time and they were expected to have and maintain local roots. They were 'old money' – it was not until later in the Victorian period that 'new money' was accepted as being as valid as old.

A good squire, wielding that power justly and with a generosity of spirit, could command considerable loyalty and respect on his home territory, however much the urbane metropolitan aristocrats might sneer at his rusticity. Good squires were deeply concerned for the welfare of those who lived on the estate and in the village and they were supported in their role by their wives and families. The women would take a particular interest in the village's poor, sick, elderly and children and could bring genuine comfort to those in distress, though some unfortunately had a patronising air that could make your toes curl and some were downright arrogant or entirely cold in their manner. The family saw their concern for villagers as their duty, their responsibility, almost in payment for being better off than most and having what

The Duke of Westminster's gamekeepers at World's End, near Newbury

the squire

> *'The good squire would invite tenants, servants, employees and probably the rest of the village to celebrate joyful family occasions'*

some judged to be privileges even when they were in reality burdens. The good squire would invite tenants, servants, employees and probably the rest of the village to celebrate joyful family occasions; he would share the game-bag and ensure that every family had meat on the table at Christmas; he would put on 'teas' and fêtes on the lawns of the big house; and find countless other ways of mingling with the village while maintaining his family's own way of life and privacy.

Of course, the village tended to know everything that went on in the squire's family, as those in service at the house were often from the village and were not averse to gossiping. In his own household and on the estate the squire might have a bailiff for the home farm and a steward to look after the estate in general, who would discuss with the squire whether a certain copse should be cut that winter, whether the oak bark had been paid for at a proper price, how the Alderney cow was doing or the poultry at the home farm, whether the pigsty roof needed a few new tiles or a cart needed new wheels, whether a tenant should be allowed to put up another shed, and would then give him the local gossip to keep him in touch – farmer Smith's sheep seemed to be dying, old Mrs Brown had taken to drinking, and poor simple Sally had given birth to a bastard.

There would also be a gamekeeper, a head gardener, a coachman, a groom, a butler of course, footmen, a governess for the children, a cook, a housekeeper – most of these staff would have a team of lesser servants under their watchful eye and they would chat with the squire or his wife now and then about whatever it was they were responsible for. Then they probably grumbled behind his back. Each had their own little kingdom, jealously guarded, with many a petty rivalry between them and often a degree of ganging up against, say, the snooty governess: her past was mysterious and she certainly wasn't a local – probably from some distant metropolis like London or, worse, a foreigner from France.

An average squire might ride into market once a week, go regularly to church every

Outdoor staff of the 'big house' – gardeners, farm workers and maintenance men – with their tools

the squire

Sunday (always the best pew) and sit on the Petty Sessional bench weekly; he might ride to hounds in the hunting season, carry his gun about the estate to shoot rabbits at whim or pheasants on a shoot day, potter about looking at this and that, do his paperwork in the study or library, read the newspapers, talk to a tenant with a problem or complaint, pop up to London now and then, go to the seaside with his family, and perhaps even take a trip across the Channel once in a while.

The squire's role extended beyond the immediate village. For example, squires often sat as local magistrates in the towns, and when county councils were created in the 1880s many squires were elected as county councillors, which at the time seemed a natural progression.

Richard Jefferies described a young squire who was 'the magistrate most regular in his attendance at a certain country Petty Sessional Court'. The Petty Sessions were 'practically an informal weekly Parliament of local landowners'. The jurisdiction of this particular court covered an area that was 'somewhat populous' and included 'one or two turbulent places that furnish a steady supply of offenders'; the court therefore sat twice a week, on Saturdays and Tuesdays. In theory, the justices were each expected to attend twice a week; in practice, they often lived miles away and would only turn up on the Saturday. But the young squire always turned up, twice a week. He was from an old county family of good repute, though by no means rich; he was also known to have an excellent eye for good horses in the hunting field and to have done well at college. He proved to have a wonderful talent for business, which immediately put him high in the estimation of local farmers. He soon became widely known, as JPs also sat on numerous committees and were *ex officio* members of Boards of Guardians and similar bodies. He was hard-working and reliable; he had considerable natural charm and modesty; he had married a woman for her beauty and intelligence rather than her wealth and they both enjoyed London society but were equally happy in the country. They transformed their 'gaunt, commonplace country house' into something elegant and charming by exercising good taste rather than spending a lot of money on it. The squire improved his estate, looking after it personally (no go-between managers for him), studying its needs and strolling the fields, becoming a familiar sight to his farm labourers, whose cottages he repaired diligently but thriftly. Although much of this was in his own interest, the result was that the interests of his tenants and workers were also served. 'He beant such a bad sort of a veller, you; a' beant above speaking to we,' said the locals, approvingly.

The electioneering squire, canvassing at Alton, Hampshire

'He beant such a bad sort of veller, you: a'beant above speaking to we ...'

Thomas Barker was a Rutland squire, living at Lyndon Hall. In the 1730s, from the age of about eleven, he started to keep a weather diary and he maintained the habit for more than sixty years. It might seem a mundane thing to do, but today these diaries are helping scientists to refine their computer weather models in trying to predict the impact of global warming. Squire Barker's diaries preceded the official national weather records by more than a century.

It happens that Squire Barker's brother-in-law was Gilbert White of Selborne, one of the country's most meticulously observant and

the squire

esteemed naturalists. Barker was equally meticulous: he recorded temperatures and barometric pressures twice a day; he measured rainfall and wind speeds; and he noted cloud formation and the weather in general every day without fail for all those years, right through the little ice age of the late eighteenth century. Usually it was parsons who had the time for such occupations.

Barker's estate included the village of Lyndon and today the squire there still farms a thousand acres in Rutland, that defiantly smallest county which has just managed to snatch back its proper identity after nearly quarter of a century of ignominy as nothing more than a district of Leicestershire. Many of the old Rutland families can demonstrate the changes in rural society from their own histories. For example, their ancestors were moving money out of land and investing it in trade during the agricultural depression of the late nineteenth century that would last for half a century. Landowners in many parts of the country were in the happy situation of sitting on land full of minerals or on land wanted by companies building the Victorian railway network, and they could grow wealthier just by the accident of having land in the right place at the right time.

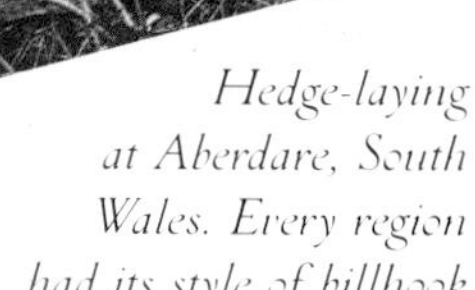

Hedge-laying at Aberdare, South Wales. Every region had its style of billhook

It went both ways: men who had made their fortunes in the railways, or in coal or in trade, decided they would like to become squires and lords of the manor. In a delightful study of Rutland written in the late 1980s, Nigel Duckers remarked: 'As Victorian capital became countrified, so the entrepreneurial spirit became gentrified; first generation wealth creation and industrial production became second generation consumption, and formerly productive capital languished in land. Britain was becoming less the "workshop of the world" and more the playground of the rich.' Oh yes.

In the 1950s and 1960s, Rutland was in trouble and its story was reflected in many other rural areas. With government encouragement and subsidies, landowners were grubbing out the hedgerows and putting more and more land down to intensively farmed corn; farms and their fields were becoming too large; workforces were being savagely reduced; villages were dying; the shops, pubs and schools were closing (more than 800 village schools were closed in the ten years after the Plowden report demanded that rural schools should be larger, fewer and 'better'); the young had moved out to find work elsewhere; the railway line felt Beeching's axe; the cottages were either falling derelict and being demolished, or being snapped up for almost nothing (£50 in some cases) by incomers who did them up or used them as weekend homes; and jarring modern housing estates were being dumped in old villages, their new occupants usually working in the towns rather than the villages or coming there merely to retire. Soon house prices were rocketing, way beyond reach of local young families; roads were made bigger and straighter for faster traffic that needed to commute or pass

through; and England's smallest county was rapidly becoming one big suburb. What was left they drowned under a reservoir.

Old Rutland still survives, though. During the First World War the Earl of Gainsborough's daughter Maureen was born; now Lady Maureen Fellowes, she grew up on his Exton Park estate in Rutland, an estate of some 6,000 acres. Exton Hall dominates its village and the Noel family that still live in it dominated the lives of those who lived there. Lady Maureen's father, the 4th Earl of Gainsborough, was the largest landowner in Rutland and her lifestyle reflected his status. She came out as a debutante in 1935 and for a while it was dances every night, her biggest problem being to choose which of a dozen handmade dresses to wear. The care of the dresses lay in the hands of her lady's maid, who travelled with her during the season. 'You were brought up to come out and go to the parties,' says Lady Maureen, and to find a good husband who met with parental approval and who would have a virgin bride. None of her fellow debutantes even considered working for a living in those pre-war days; it simply wasn't done.

That world was shattered by the Second World War, of course. Whereas she had been used to the presence of a dozen servants before the war, after it there was only one couple in the house and dailies who came in from the village and did the cleaning. 'So you had to be much more practical ... and not think that everything was going to be done for you. You had to hang up your own clothes.'

The warrener

Lady Maureen married at twenty-six and in due course hired a nanny to bring up her own children. She had moved to London, having very little interest in the country life of Rutland. In contrast, the 5th Earl, still Rutland's largest landowner, returned to Exton after the war: he had spent most of his childhood with his mother in her Park Lane flat and at boarding school in the south, and had then gone to America as a young man. In 1945 he was working on Spitfires in a Southampton factory when the government started to issue two gallons of petrol a week for 'pleasure motoring', and so he drove up to Rutland. It took him all day. He came of age in that year and the welcome he received from Exton was moving: people who had not seen him since he was seven years old came to welcome him home. He remembers that, apart from his own family, everybody in Exton village was working class except the vicar and the occasional colonel.

LEFT
Fox-shooting party, Sussex

Exton resisted the gentrification that came to most of Rutland in the 1960s, and it is still home to extended families that have a long history there. Like the Welsh, it was a case of having to give people nicknames to differentiate one branch of a family from another – Sweat Wallace, Bolsher Wallace, Boxer Wallace ('he was the roadman who you didn't dare speak to or he'd hit you over the head with his brush'), and a wonderful string of names like Scabby, Moocher, Porky, Eggy, Desher, Titner, Sidgey ...

THE BIG HOUSE

'It is a sad thing when the "big house" of the village is empty,' wrote Arthur Gibbs in 1898. 'The labourers who never see their squire begin to look upon him as a sort of ogre, who exists merely to screw rents out of the land they till. ... In some parts of England men who are not suffering from the depression – rich tenants of country houses and the like – are apt to take a somewhat limited view of their duty towards their poorer neighbours. To be sure, the good ladies at the "great houses" are invariably "ministering angels" to the poor in time of sickness, but even in these democratic days there is too great a gulf fixed between all classes.'

'A tea given two or three times a year ... does much to lighten the dullness of their existence.'

He went on to advise latter-day squires to remember that 'a kind word, a shake of the hand, the occasional distribution of game throughout the village, and a hundred other small kindnesses do more to win the heart of the labouring man than much talk at election times of Small Holdings, Parish Councils, or Free Education. A tea given two or three times a year by the squire to the whole village, when the grounds are thrown open to them, does much to lighten the dullness of their existence and to cheer the monotonous round of daily toil. It is often thoughtlessness rather than poverty that prevents those who live in the large house of the village from being really loved by those around them.'

Gibbs abhorred the fact that many large country houses were shut up for the greater part of the year, not even let to strangers to keep the place alive. 'Let these rich men who own larger houses and great estates live *in* those houses and *on* those estates.'

Repairs at Snowshill, a typical Cotswold manor house, famous for the Charles Wade collection and given to the National Trust in 1951. Workmen converting the stables to house the collection

There are countless histories of big estates and their big houses, some recorded in great detail that lets you imagine just what life was like for those who lived and worked in them. In recent years television has tried to convey that life as well, either in documentaries that look at how the estates work today, or in period dramas filmed on the estates. Some of them feature as the background to modern television dramas; for example, much of the 'rural soap' *Emmerdale Farm* is filmed on the Earl of Harewood's North Yorkshire estate near Leeds.

In need of income to maintain their ageing homes, many owners of the big houses now open them to the general public and so we all feel we know something about life in the big house. Wherever you live, there is bound to be such a house quite near you that is worth visiting to soak up its atmosphere and imagine how it used to be. Some of them deliberately

the big house

retain, for example, the old kitchen ranges and all the implements that would have been used there in times gone by, so that we can gasp in awe at the work of it all and the large number of staff needed to keep the whole place running smoothly behind the scenes without disturbing the tranquillity of the drawing-room – the classic vision of the swan on the lake, all serenity above but paddling like mad underneath.

A 'big house' of particular interest is Erdigg, now a National Trust property, near Wrexham in Clwyd. In the 1680s it was the property of Joshua Edisbury. From 1716 onwards it was in the continuous ownership of one family, the Yorkes, until they relinquished it to the Trust in 1973. That is a long record of ownership, and one of the advantages has been that they kept records and pictures of all the staff on the estate over the centuries. Today you can visit the estate and see evidence of this illustrated social history.

The big house at Erdigg is fairly typical in the scope of its various parts. There are the gracious living-quarters of the Yorke family, with dining room, drawing room, library, saloon, hall, a Chinese room, a Tapestry room and so on, and countless bedrooms, the nursery, a family museum, a Welsh Tribes room and a family chapel. The servant's quarters include the big servants' hall, the housekeeper's room, the butler's pantry, a huge kitchen, a stillroom, the agent's office and assorted storage areas. Out in the estate yards you will find almost a self-sufficient village of workshops, many of them in working order: a joiners' shop and store, the sawpit, a blacksmith's shop, a paint store, dovecote, dog yard, bakehouse, laundry yard (with its box mangle, drying racks, goffering irons and a wet-laundry area with a steam vent in the ceiling), the stable yard complete with carriages (and old bicycles) and a steam boiler and engine to power the sawmill and grind corn. There is an agricultural museum and a hay barn, wagon shed, lime yard and brick midden (dung-heap). In the grounds are orchards, beehives, a fishpond and a bowling-green, all adding to the feeling of the big house being a village in itself.

Furniture removal men at Highclere Castle, Hampshire, in 1946

The aspect of Erdigg that makes it stand out from most other estates is the collection of eighteenth-century pictures of the gamekeeper, the blacksmith, a woodsman, a housemaid, the gardener, the publican, a kitchen man, some carpenters and a negro coachboy. It is quite unusual to have this strong feeling that the 'servants' mattered to the family, that they were important enough to have their portraits painted and their names recorded for posterity, that they were, in effect, part of the family.

THE 'BIG HOUSE' TODAY

Many a 'big house' today has become too much for its owners to handle. Once-stately homes have been converted into schools, company headquarters, nursing homes, communes, flats and maisonettes, hotels, golf clubs, residential homes for the elderly, or country clubs. For example, in Ulgham, Northumberland, Longhirst Hall became an approved school, described in 1965 as being a 'practical and working partner in the village, and the benefit given to these boys by association with life in the village is most important'. A Georgian mansion next to the church in Goosnargh, Lancashire, became Bushell's Hospital 'for the benefit of Decayed Gentlefolks'.

In contrast, stylish young single professionals from London are increasingly taking refuge at mansions converted into country clubs, where, at a price, they can unwind and pretend that they, too, are country people.

11 Countryside at War

WAR PUNCTUATES LIFETIMES. People talk about 'before the war', 'after the war' and 'during the war', as signposts in their lives and in the history of their communities. Wars radically change people's lives, even those not directly involved in the fighting, even those who did not lose loved ones. Wars leave too many holes in the fabric of the community.

In the countryside, wars seemed to be part of a relentless pattern in which dramatically successful drives for agricultural improvements to feed the country at war were followed by disastrous agricultural slumps between wars that overturned the improvements so that farmers retreated into their shells and the whole village suffered.

Perhaps the countryside was changed more suddenly and more thoroughly than the urban areas by the two world wars of the twentieth century. It may not have suffered the terrible bombings that gutted cities and city lives, though it was by no means safe from the bombs, but the entire rural way of life was changed by those wars, probably more so than during any war since Harold fought at Hastings.

War altered the landscape in more subtle ways than the bombs. In the Napoleonic wars the Admiralty set up a system of telegraph stations on sight-line high points between London and Portsmouth and elsewhere – often the very same sites that had been used for signalling with beacons for centuries. The telegraph system was remarkably efficient, however Heath Robinson it might look. After the old 'shutter' method was changed to semaphore in 1816, the first station would display its message to the next, which would duplicate it to the next and so on down the line, by means of sail-like arms on a tall post, and a message could reach Portsmouth from London within fifteen minutes. At each station there would be living-quarters – just a wooden shack in the shutter days, but subsequently a proper though simple small building with basic conveniences, for the naval lieutenant who manned the station. With their hilltop positions, these later became quite desirable residences for private buyers prepared to modernise them. They are probably being eyed up by mobile-phone companies even now.

PREPARING FOR WAR

IN THE SECOND WORLD WAR, A HUGE DEFENCE TRENCH WAS DUG RIGHT ACROSS SOUTHERN ENGLAND BY THE PIONEER BATTALION, THE CANADIANS, ASSORTED CONSCIENTIOUS OBJECTORS AND ANY OTHER LABOUR THAT CAME TO HAND. ITS AIM WAS TO SLOW DOWN THE ANTICIPATED GERMAN TANK INVASION: THE TANKS WOULD TUMBLE INTO THE TRENCH AND WOULD BE BLASTED BY FIREPOWER FROM STRATEGICALLY PLACED PILLBOXES AS THEY STRUGGLED TO CLAMBER OUT AGAIN.

PREVIOUS PAGE Tommies dig for victory

'The labourer ... has fought the battles of England.'

PILLBOXES STILL LINGER: you come across them on the coast, of course, but there are also quite a few ruins sprinkled over the countryside, perhaps in a field beside a canal, where the cattle take shelter in them, or in most unexpected places beside narrow, unfrequented country lanes. There were lesser tank traps: here and there you can still find the concrete bollards that landowners were supposed to set across the lanes at the first hint of trouble.

'The labourer,' said Richard Jefferies, 'has fought the battles of England. He comes of a fighting stock. Fragments of the tongue of the hardy Saxons linger yet, and are used in his daily life. Against William the Conqueror how they whirled their heavy axes on the field of Hastings! These thanes and their men were farmers and labourers, nothing more. Under the Edwards and Henries they filled the ranks in the gallant if needless struggle with France. The Armada saw them once more ready for the field. Not a war but has called its thousands from the plough-share and the threshing-floor, from Hastings to Waterloo. Their blood has been freely shed the whole world over. To this hour the romance of war is believed in among the cottagers of the vale and the shepherds of the hill. The bugle sounds, the flag is unfurled, and the hearts of the young men are stirred.' Apparently all of this was because of a strong sense of adventure, which was exactly the excuse given by poachers.

Jefferies was trying to persuade his readers that there should be a return to the medieval system of constant practising at the butts: 'Could not the lads of the village be organized in some degree, as they were in the olden times, by these shootings at the butts and annual showings of weapons? ... The lads would be willing enough, and the young farmers also. Why should not a list be kept in every rural parish, revised once a year, of all males between certain ages, and not suffering from organic disease; and a rifle and accoutrements be provided ready for each of them? If butts were made for shooting and rifles found, the lads would subscribe for ammunition, and speedily become adepts at the targets; and glad indeed they would be of so congenial an amusement as shooting.'

And ready for the next revolution? Well, in some villages they did practise. On the Hollycombe estate in Sussex, for example, they set up a rifle range for just that purpose, at a time when it had been discovered that British riflemen in the Boer war were generally pretty poor shots. It was back to archery practice at the butts, but with firearms.

Land girls examining a tractor

THE NAPOLEONIC WARS

The battle of Waterloo in 1815 brought to an end fifteen years of war – a war which was won just as much in the fields of the countryside as on the playing fields of Eton. It was during those Napoleonic wars that British farmers had proved the country could produce all the food it needed, independent of imports from abroad, and this achievement was due to the great agricultural revolution inspired by men like Thomas Coke of Holkham, a good-looking, charming, well-educated and well-travelled man who inherited his country estate and substantial fortune when he was in his twenties. He took such an interest in farming (to the surprise of his friends and family) that he became the leading agriculturalist of his time, and his name became famous as far afield as Europe and America. With his wealth, his endless energy, his tenacity and his interest in experimentation on his own estate, he was able to put into practice many new theories to improve the land – reclaiming salt marshes, rotating crops, using new horse-driven implements, artificial manuring, breeding better livestock, sowing better grass mixtures, even growing wheat on the sands of Norfolk. One of the secrets of Coke's success was that he was rich enough to try out new ideas on his own estate first. If they worked, then he could set about overturning the prejudices of others, even those who said it was all very well for a rich man but ...

And there was a big but. During the Napoleonic wars prices for agricultural produce had been high and farmers were prepared to invest in the improvements that Coke and his ilk had shown them would succeed. Much new land was ploughed up and therefore much more grain was grown, to such an extent that they all got too good at it and supply began to overtake demand. In 1813, even before the war was over, an exceptional harvest slashed the price of wheat in half between January and November. When peace came, the country was faced with the typical aftermath of war: a labour market flooded with discharged soldiers, high taxation, unemployment and financial problems. A thumping great agricultural depression followed, with estates being sold off for half their value and thousands of farmers going bankrupt, abandoning all those new acres they had improved under the plough. The depression lasted for two decades, reducing farm labourers to paupery and putting into reverse all the advances that had been made in agriculture. But when it was over, and only the fittest had survived, with a new queen on the throne and the railways opening up new markets for farm produce all over the country, the innovations began again and there was a period of what came to be called 'high farming' that would last into the early 1860s.

Then it all fell apart again, this time triggered by a flood of cheap imported food, and another agricultural depression set in from 1874 which would last for most of the rest of the century. Frozen meat, butter, cheese and wool came pouring in from North America, Argentina and New Zealand; grain came tumbling in from all over the world and in 1907 only a quarter of the wheat consumed in Britain was home-grown. That was all very fine for British industry: cheap food meant low wages at home, and there was a rapidly growing market for their exports. It was fine for urban populations as well: the cost of living was low and there were plenty of jobs in manufacturing. Guess who suffered? Landowners, farmers, farm labourers and the village craftsmen and tradesmen who served the rural population. In the countryside, it meant poverty and despair. But the towns didn't care. Do they now? Again, many were ruined, and again, those who survived adapted by reducing production: the land in cultivation in England and Wales dropped by 20 per cent between 1878 and 1906, the wheat acreage dropped by half its area, and a quarter of a million farm labourers left the land. But it improved after 1906, to such an extent that farmworkers could earn a reasonable 14s 6d a week and the farmer's wife could even employ a couple of maids. It didn't last, of course. On a summer day in 1914 a bomb exploded somewhere in the Balkans and, quite unexpectedly, Britain was at war again.

THE FIRST WORLD WAR

THIS NEW WAR WAS VERY DIFFERENT TO ANY THAT HAD PRECEDED IT. THE CRIMEAN WAR, THE BOER WAR AND THE FIGHTING IN INDIA HAD BEEN DISTANT AFFAIRS CARRIED OUT BY PROFESSIONAL SOLDIERS AND NOT DIRECTLY IMPINGING ON LIFE AT HOME, EXCEPT FOR THE EXCITEMENT OF READING ABOUT THE BATTLES IN THE PAPERS AND OCCASIONALLY CELEBRATING A VICTORY. THE NEW WAR WAS FAR MORE SERIOUS.

'In the massive drive to feed the nation, everybody in the village from the squire to the poorest would be working out in the fields …'

OPPOSITE A 200-year-old windmill used as an ARP post

VERY SOON, there were recruitment drives in village halls and village schools all over the country. Many of those who joined up so eagerly would never come home from the trenches or, if they did, would be physically or mentally maimed. As the war took hold, farmworkers were not exempt from military service as they would be in the Second World War, and there was a constant flow of them out of the villages and across the Channel, younger men enlisting as soon as they were old enough to replace the huge numbers being killed. Every village family had at least one of its members or a close relation out there in the trenches or at sea, and many never came back.

It was not only farmworkers who headed for the trenches; many other estate workers and the servants in the big house went too, along with the sons of the gentry, and a whole way of life went with them. It would never again be the same in the countryside.

Apart from the soldiers and sailors (and a handful of airmen) and their families, the war was quite good for the countryside, especially when German submarines began to interrupt the imported food supplies on which the country had come to depend. Suddenly it was all systems go in the fields: grass was ploughed up, the downlands were ploughed up, committees were set up to tell people what to do, labour and machinery pools were created and, as the irresistible cherry on the cake, in 1917 farmers were guaranteed their grain prices for the next five years. Between 1916 and 1918 some two million acres of grassland were ploughed up (remember it was still horses), the production of wheat rocketed and, as they had in the Napoleonic wars, the British farmers beat the blockade.

The children did their bit as well, picking (at the government's behest) rosehips, crab apples and blackberries; they also gathered conkers for grinding into an alternative livestock feed so that there would be more grain for the people. Families knitted socks for sailors and collected eggs for soldiers; they raised money to buy tents for the troops and money to help wounded war horses in France. Everybody was much more involved in this war than in previous ones.

STRANGERS IN THE VILLAGE

In some parts of the country, enormous army camps were set up on commons and farmland and the nearby villages suddenly found large numbers of strangers in their midst. For some, this was exciting; for many, it was an invasion that disrupted their lives.

Then there were the women – the landgirl volunteers of the Women's Land Army that was formed in 1917 to put women in the fields to replace the men who had enlisted. They were joined on the land by urban women and public schoolboys taking working holidays on the farms. In the massive drive to feed the nation, everybody in the village from the squire to the poorest would be working out in the fields too.

The scale of 'invasion' of the countryside was as nothing compared with the Second World War, and in many villages there was little disruption to everyday life.

ON DUTY

Those who did not go abroad helped to defend the homeland. For example, those in the Cyclist Battalion of the Hampshire Regiment patrolled a wide area from Littlehampton to Selsey, the Isle of Wight and Bournemouth. Their aim was to prevent an enemy from landing unobserved

first world war

and unreported. The patrol was to watch for 'anything unusual particularly on the sea or in the sky'. The men must 'allow no one to approach without being certain of his identity' and must 'on no account enter into conversation with any person whatsoever' while on patrol. If they sighted an enemy, or anything unusual or suspicious, the men were to conceal themselves and observe. As soon as there was anything definite to report, one man would cycle as fast as possible to the nearest support or coastguard station, another should remain on the spot to obtain further information. They were told about key places to watch, such as where landing was most likely ('Landing is practicable in moderate weather from Littlehampton to Selsey except just SW of Bognor where the rocks are a source of danger,' said the battalion's printed list of duties – let's hope the enemy never came across this useful information), and the obstacles that might face the invader's inland advance. The patrols might usefully place themselves on good metalled roads, along the disused Arundel canal, or along Ryebank Rife in case of a winter landing between Littlehampton and Barn Rocks. They could always telephone Bognor Pier (on 77) or Pagham sub-postoffice (on Bognor 11) in times of need.

The Cyclist Battalion was fit enough to use two pedals. After the Second World War, and no doubt after the First, it was not uncommon to see men pedalling the lanes with one pedal immobilised. Only one leg did the work of propelling the bike; the other had been blown off in the war.

first world war

OPPOSITE Members of the Pig Club using a copper to boil up scraps for pigswill

LOCAL MATTERS

In some of the villages life seems to have jogged on through the war without changing that much. Take a look at the minutes of any local group. For example, those of the Ditchling Horticultural Society during the First World War imply that the 'Great War' was a mere sideshow that very occasionally caused minor irritations in village life – such as having to create new allotments to help with food production (in 1917 the government finally admitted that there was only six weeks' supply of food nationwide). After the war there would be other niggles: amid objections, the old cricket field was commandeered for the purpose of planting former army huts on it to relieve the post-war housing shortage; and the wartime allotments were bought privately for more building and the allotment holders were given a month to quit, far too early for them to harvest their carefully nurtured crops. But at least the ending of the war gave the society an excuse for celebration and they planned an especially good annual show.

'... in 1917 the government finally admitted that there was only six weeks' supply of food nationwide.'

If you read the minutes of parish councils (first formed in 1894) for the period 1914 to 1918 there is scarcely a mention of the war. The same people still served at this grass roots level of local government, carrying on the same mundane business of appointing overseers and questioning rates valuations and muttering about footpaths, blocked drains, the state of the roads and other crucial local matters. A parish clerk's claim for exemption from military service was unanimously supported by his parish council, who deemed him to be indispensible to the parish, though they did at one stage resolve that, should he be called up after all, his wife should take his place as clerk.

Occasionally there would be mention of the War Food Society (which one council promptly passed to the Flower Show committee) and at intervals the parishes would be chivvied by their county councils about food production: one parish council declined to be lectured about fruit preserving, owing to the smallness of the parish and the small quantity of fruit grown in it; another told the county that it just didn't have any surplus fruit and vegetables to sell, as had been suggested; a third, in some dudgeon reacting to a circular telling them how to farm, stated in the minutes: 'The farmers of the parish have done, are doing, and will continue to do their best to farm the land in the most suitable manner'; another, in response to a circular about rats (on whose tails there was a bounty) and sparrows, decided that 'considering the geographical configuration of the parish and the neighbouring parishes', the problem should be dealt with by the district council instead.

THE AFTERMATH

After the American Civil War, the phrase they used to express how life had changed was, 'Gone with the wind'. It was also an appropriate phrase for the British way of life that vanished with the First World War, and perhaps even more so with the Second.

In 1916 a concerned reader wrote to *The Field* for advice. The editor's response (the reader's question was not published) was:

> *Men are now acting as their own chauffeurs, who before the war thought they were too old to learn to drive a car. Others who had hardly handled a spade in their lives are now manfully digging over their kitchen gardens, and finding it not unexciting though laborious work. There is a piquancy about coming across stray potatoes in patches which purport to have been thoroughly explored long ago. When a man by force or circumstances becomes his own gardener, he realises a good many essential truths, one of which is that the proverbial slowness of the professional is due quite as much to the stubborn character of Mother Earth as to the restful proclivities of the sons of Adam. Orderly rows of vegetables represent a great deal of solid and patient labour, and some of us are learning this lesson for the first time now that we realise that*

first world war

the rows of vegetables are part of the country's economic strength.

Good gracious! Driving your own car and digging your own garden? Whatever next? No doubt the reader who had sought advice was hoping that, after the war was over, life would return to normal and he would have servants again to do these tedious things for him. Well, for a while, perhaps, if he was lucky, but not for long

MEMORIALS

With so many men having died during the Great War, many villages put up various kinds of memorials to their own dead. Some of these were war memorials of the kind you sometimes see on village greens – stone pillars and crosses, with the names carved into them, sometimes several members of the same family. Strangely, in many cases nobody now quite knows who it was that raised the money, found the materials, designed the memorial and took responsibility for its building; as a result nobody quite knows who is supposed to maintain it.

Other parishes preferred to put a stained-glass window or a tablet in the church, or to create a memorial recreation ground or build a memorial hall. In 1929 the parish council of Slaugham, in Sussex, received a letter signed by several ex-servicemen asking why the old German field gun that had stood outside the church since the end of the Great War had been removed. 'They honoured the gun ... Soon after its removal the Union Jack was flown, and while they honoured the flag they also honoured the Gun having fought in the war for both.' Apparently the Royal Sussex regiment had had a number of guns for disposal at the end of the war and the local rector had thought it would be nice to put one outside his church. Eleven years later he thought it was in too much of a state of disrepair and at one stage someone had tried to push the thing down the hill and into the pond, but the wheels fell off and it never got there. Eventually the rector simply removed a memorial he no longer valued.

THE PIG CLUB Not every response to the War Food Society's plea to increase food production was negative. One group of parishioners had expressed the desire to form pig clubs and the council wrote to the lady of the manor asking that her tenants should be provided with materials to make pig pens and that she might like to draw up some appropriate rules for a pig club. Some would contribute to the Prince of Wales's National Relief Fund from parish coffers but decline to set up a committee to deal with unemployment distress themselves.

first world war

ON THE FARMS

As ever, after all that effort to feed the country in times of war, in peace agriculture crashed. The government reneged on the five-year guarantee on corn prices and it would be a very long time, if ever, before farmers would trust politicians again. Among those who were hit hardest by the agricultural depression of the 1920s and 1930s were, sadly, the war heroes who had started a new life on the land with small farms and smallholdings. They often lost everything, and quite a few became tramps, trudging the lanes in ragged clothes and sleeping in farmers' barns.

'Three million acres went out of production in England and Wales between 1918 and 1932.'

Farmers in general abandoned intensive arable farming, dumped their implements and returned to pasture and animal husbandry, the old dog-and-stick way of farming, or set up their own milk rounds by pony-and-cart, or left the land for good. Three million acres went out of production in England and Wales between 1918 and 1932, half of it simply deteriorating to virtually derelict rough grazing land. Wages for farm labourers had been fixed during the war at quite a good rate, but after the war the farmers could not afford to pay them and simply shed their staff; one advantage of farming for meat and milk was that you could do much of it yourself, with the help of a cowman or two, instead of the dozen men who had helped with the crops. So it was back to unemployment in the countryside and, all around, hedges and stone walls and cottages became neglected and derelict. The countryside looked a mess.

'It was back to unemployment in the countryside and, all around, hedges and stone walls and cottages became neglected and derelict ...'

On top of the post-war agricultural depression came the devastating economic depression that hit Britain in 1931. There were 3 million unemployed and a coalition National Government was set up to sort out the mess.

The government's aims included rescuing agriculture from total collapse, by subsidising certain crops (and guaranteeing prices to a limited degree), controlling food imports under certain circumstances, subsidising the cost of land improvements and giving limited protection to pig farmers, market gardeners and hop-growers. The aim was to halt the decline in farming, just enough to keep it going, rather than boosting agriculture into a healthy condition. The First World War had taught a lesson: if it ever happened again, Britain needed to grow her own food and the land needed to be kept ticking over ready for that. The policy was to store up fertility in

peacetime so that it could be cashed in time of war.

By 1937 rural areas remained depressed, farming was regressing, land prices were rock bottom and workers were leaving the land for better prospects. But another war, always the saviour of agriculture, was looming and farming's twenty years of depression in the face of national indifference were nearly over. For a while. As George Martell explained in his story of the Elveden estate 'On 2nd September 1939 agriculture in Britain was still a relatively unimportant and depressed industry. By noon of the next day it had become a major element of national defence.'

Chaff-cutting with a steam traction engine near Tring, Hertfordshire, in 1928

THE SECOND WORLD WAR

It was said, during the First World War, that pheasants in southern England could hear the sound of the heavy artillery across the Channel: they reacted (as they do now whenever Concorde breaks the sound barrier with a gentle distant boom) by shouting their heads off in the middle of the night. And, yes, some people living near the coast could hear those terrible shellings too, though not the screams of the wounded. But the war did not come to Britain then.

'Every village experienced the influx of evacuees, mass troop movements, air-raid shelters …'

It did in the Second World War. The enemy crossed the Channel and invaded the air above Britain, so that very few areas escaped from the noise of the aircraft and the sound of bombs dropping on cities and docks. Every village experienced the influx of evacuees, mass troop movements, air-raid shelters in the garden, blackouts and of course rationing. This was a war that hit home, sometimes literally.

BY AIR, SEA AND LAND

Many people can remember watching the dogfights between aircraft in the skies over southern England. Many can remember the drone of German bombers heading for the cities and ports and airfields, the distant explosions and ack-ack responses, and the frightening sound of the bombers releasing their 'spare' ammunition at random in the countryside on the way home. Many have tales of planes crashing in the fields and woods, streaking like comets across the sky with their tails on fire before exploding as they hit the ground, and tales of parachutists tumbling among the mangolds. Many remember the terrible fear that, one day, their village would be bombed, and then how the thatch would burn! And sometimes it did.

In 1940 the village hall in Colgate was utterly destroyed by an unexpected and inexplicable Luftwaffe bombing raid that also damaged the church, the post-office and several homes and killed five people. Why, oh why? It was only a village.

At Smarden, in Kent, the WI diary recorded that every man, woman and child became fully involved 'as the Battle of Britain roared overhead, the skies streaked with white vapour-streamers from the planes'. Later in the war, and worst of all, were the incessant buzz-bombs, day and night: several houses were destroyed and ten villagers were killed, mostly women and children. The village was full of American airmen from various Thunderbolt aerodromes in the area and before D-Day many of them were encamped in the local woods. Soldiers were quartered in some of the bigger houses; refugees from the coast came to the relative safety of Smarden; a London girls' school was evacuated to the village. So, like many villages, Smarden was full of strangers, on top of the general strain of living in a country at war. They were 'crowded out, and almost too busy to be frightened'. The women continued their official WI work of jam-making and fruit-canning as part of the war effort: 'The first canning operation took place during the height of the Battle of Britain, in a farm outhouse, where the cans

Picking fruit for a local WI canning club in the Vale of Evesham

were boiled in a copper fed by billets of wood, while the planes roared and crackled over our heads.'

Those who could not join the forces served instead with the Local Defence Volunteers (later renamed as the Home Guard), prowling the countryside at night armed with shotguns and pikes and knives that they were expected to use against invading Germans, trigger-happy at the sound of a badger snuffling in the undergrowth, and training themselves to unaccustomed sweating activity by day after work.

Selsey was a Sussex seaside village where many evacuee children found refuge in the war. They could see the floating concrete mulberry harbours that accumulated along the coast there in the build-up to D-Day: the blocks were taken across the Channel and put together to form temporary harbours for support vessels after the Allies had gained a foothold on the Normandy beaches. Mock invasions for D-Day were practised on the coast at Climping, the Witterings and Bracklesham Bay, to the joy of the children who watched them; inland there were large numbers of troops in the woods, waiting to set off for France in landing craft that were being built at Itchenor's boatyards. Just along the coast the small village of Church Norton was next to an airfield, used heavily by fighter pilots before the invasion of France. Tangmere wasn't far away, and Thorney Island. For locals, the great excitement of the war was that Clark Gable had to land at Apuldram when his aircraft developed engine trouble. It was said that from the spire of Chichester's cathedral you could see nine airfields during the war.

Some villages, as in the First World War, resolutely pursued their everyday affairs. The minutes of the Ditchling Horticultural Society still largely ignored the whole thing; they continued with their annual show in defiance of the expected imminent invasion by the Germans (Ditchling being not far from the coast), though they wisely decided to hold it indoors in the village hall, just in case. However, it was not possible to process any financial matters for a while as the treasurer was inconveniently serving his country overseas for a few years.

Bombed out but business as usual at a Kentish forge in November, 1940

D-DAY DISASTER Brenda Lismer remembers how she nearly ruined D-Day: as a land girl at Lavant (a village between Midhurst and Chichester) she was taking a herd of cows in for milking but there was an endless stream of D-Day traffic, day and night, going right through the farm where she worked – lorries, jeeps, tanks rumbling along on their tracks, on and on and on, churning up the road and leaving it a yard deep in mud. She needed to get the cows across the lane but there was no gap in the traffic. Then an agitated cow panicked at this rude interruption to its placid daily routine and bolted, forcing a lorry to slam on its brakes – which no doubt meant that one lorry would be late in crossing the Channel that day.

second world war

IN THE MEANTIME, a Village Produce Association operated successfully in Ditchling during the war as a means of persuading people to grow their own food as part of the war effort. Its monthly lectures and films on practical matters such as pest control and the use of artificial fertilisers were immensely popular, and its popularity increased when the raffle prizes it offered included such treasures as live calves, cockerels, eggs, firewood, fertiliser, garden tools and bottles of gin and whisky. As there were many shortages at the end of the war, the VPA also thought about buying a canning machine for use by its members and had contingency plans for gleaning parties and harvest helpers even before the reality of the very harsh winter of 1946/7 hit the war-battered countryside.

'Why should a rat of an Austrian paper-hanger ... stop the continuity of an old English Flower Show.'

The secretary of the Ditchling society had been the man responsible for ensuring unbroken continuity through both world wars. When he finally retired from this post in 1946 he explained why he had persisted, saying that his incentives were both internal and external:

The internal part was from myself, as I did not want the continuity of the Show to stop after a lot over one century; the outside incentive was, and I got really cross over this, why should a rat of an Austrian paper-hanger, by name Hitler, stop the continuity of an old English Flower Show started years before he was born to be a curse on the world. I being Sussex bred and born and as pig-headed as real Sussex people are, was not going to allow a rat like that, at whatever cost or labour to myself, break the continuity of the oldest Show in England.

Bristol evacuees pulling turnips at Modbury, Devon

EVACUEES

In 1939, the government reckoned that more than 2 million children would die if they stayed at home in the cities. Thus Operation Pied Piper was born, at 7.30pm two days before war was declared. Parents took their children to the schools, carrying only a toothbrush and comb, hanky and spare clothes (nightwear, pants, socks and a mac), gas masks and enough food for the day. Over the first four days about 1.5 million evacuees were transported by rail up to a hundred miles from home, the government being certain that the enemy would begin bombing immediately. Many came back again by Christmas as the bombs hadn't materialised, but were re-evacuated when air raids began in May 1940. More than 3 million children were evacuated in the end, and some of them stayed away for 5 years, becoming strangers to their own families. It was not only children on their own; there were also mothers with their toddlers and babies, and the handicapped with their helpers.

June Arnold was impressed by the evacuees next door when she was a girl – they were so much wiser in the ways of the world. She would sneak next door to gamble at cards with them and was pretty shocked at the language they used. She shared her school with the evacuees: they would use it for half a day, and the church hall for the other half, turn and turn about. The local children couldn't help feeling sorry for their visitors, who had been separated from their families, taken away from their homes and had arrived on the railway station, clutching their gas masks and with their names and numbers marked on sacking satchels on their backs. A bus would bring them to the village hall, and there they were inspected like cattle, waiting for strangers to take them to a new home.

second world war

LEFT
Land girls after a hard day's work in the fields

The strangers had little option: billeting was compulsory, and this led to a fair amount of resentment. But at least you could choose which of the children you would take in, which sometimes meant that a child would be separated from its siblings. The government gave you 10s 6d for the first child, and 8s 6d for any others. The new country foster parents were often shocked at the state of the children; many came from the city slums and knew not even the basics of hygiene, and were crawling with lice.

The children were equally shocked by rural life. Some were terrified of livestock and even of rabbits – they had never seen such things. Many were frightened of going down to the privy in the middle of the night, and by the sounds of owls and foxes, and were scared of all that open space during the day. Some would never be happy, missing their families and friends and the urban environment that was home, and sometimes being with foster parents who were severely strict, or treated them as skivvies, or even beat and abused them. Others settled in remarkably well and fell in love with the countryside, making the most of the fresh air and the fresh food; they would return in adult life to live there.

LAND GIRLS

So many men (and women) were called up – the thatcher, the rat-catcher, the best bowler in the village cricket team, the squire's sons. The fields were emptying of men, as they had in the First World War, though for the Second agricultural workers were generally exempt – they were crucial to providing food at home. The absent men were replaced by teams of land girls – volunteers in the Women's Land Army, often straight out of school and straight out of the town. More than 10,000 women became land girls and sometimes they brought a breath of fresh air into the country, with their different ways, their different attitudes, their sense of fun in spite of the hard labour to which they were put, their new faces and new stories. In some places they were mocked for their inexperience and their horror at many of the discomforts of rural living; but generally the men who worked beside them came to admire their guts.

Land girls worked extremely hard: they drove tractors, loaded trailers, humped bags of potatoes, planted and weeded, pruned and harvested, milked cows, cleared out cowsheds and pigsties, caught rats and sometimes found themselves regarded as virtually slave labour by some farmers. After the war they were gradually demobbed over the next few years and the WLA was finally disbanded in 1951. Among many of the volunteers there was a sense of deep disappointment at the lack of official recognition for their contribution to the war effort.

BELOW
Land girls sinking a pint at the Black Horse, Teffont Magna, Wiltshire; and a land girl working a two-man cross-cut saw

second world war

LUMBER JILLS

Those who had joined the Women's Timber Corps felt even more unappreciated. Most people have heard of the land girls but very few realise that the 'lumber jills' worked just as hard in forestry during the war, in equally difficult conditions. Land girls were slow to volunteer for forestry work and in 1942 a separate Women's Timber Corps was set up. By the summer of the following year there were more than 3,000 lumber jills working in the woods and at sawmills all over the country. Like the land girls, many of the lumber jills were from the cities and towns, and from a wide range of social backgrounds. Some were straight out of school, others had been working in factories and offices. They were billeted with strangers in the middle of nowhere and found themselves clambering into an open lorry at seven on their first morning, wearing uncomfortably unfamiliar army boots, to be taken deep into the forest for training in how to swing an axe – which surprised those who thought all they would be doing was measuring trees and keeping records. Women chopping down trees? There was none of that in their nursery-rhyme visions of country girls milking cows and feeding hens.

'Whole plantations were felled over large areas, dramatically altering the landscape ...'

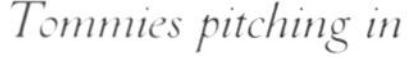

They also found themselves sawing (on their knees), debarking oak trees, loading telegraph poles and railway sleepers, driving haulage vehicles that pulled loads of timber on steep hillsides, steering motor boats that towed logs across remote Scottish lochs, and occasionally being caught out in the open by strafing fighter planes. Eileen Rawlinson was coppicing chestnut in Sussex in an area that was a local 'bomb alley' and the girls would watch as their own airmen, spotting V1 rockets on course for London, chased the missiles and tilted them with the wings of their plane so that the rocket simply dropped to the ground in open country. The pilots were usually quite unaware that there were a few agitated lumber jills out in that 'open country'.

The WTC's main task was to help to fell thousands of acres of standing timber to meet an insatiable demand for lumber, charcoal, pit props and poles. Whole plantations were felled over large areas, dramatically altering the landscape.

Tommies pitching in

PRISONERS OF WAR

Many of the land girls and lumber jills found themselves working alongside gypsies on piecework and also prisoners of war; very occasionally they had to fend off unwelcome advances from handsome Italians, but usually the men only flirted mildly. Many prisoners, though far from home and desperately missing their families, appreciated that it was better to be a PoW on the farms and in the woods than to be dead on the battlefield or lying seriously injured at a field station. Indeed, some of them were eating far more interesting and varied food than the land and woodland workers. Berta Gillatt remembered that the Italians had gammon, egg and chips for lunch every day, washed down with all-milk coffee drunk out of soup tins, while she and the other lumber jills had cheese sandwiches and cold tea.

In the late 1940s, on the whitewashed walls of the extensive cellars under Grittleton

second world war

LEFT Prisoners-of-war loading a hay wain

House in Wiltshire, you could still see pictures 'painted' with candle-smoke by the PoWs who had been billeted there. Others were housed in Nissen hut camps in various parts of the country. Locals did not necessarily have much contact with them, though they saw the work parties in the fields and woods or mending roads and bridges, but there was more of a sense of pity for the men than anger or hatred against an 'enemy'. Sometimes a parson or squire would extend hospitality to the prisoners in many small ways, to make them feel less homesick. In return, prisoners often made little gifts for village children – charming small baskets fashioned from bark and twigs, for example, filled with woodland violets and primroses. At Osmington in Dorset some German PoWs who were clearing mines made toys for every child in the village, and this much appreciated gesture has been commemorated in Osmington's very personal 'Parish Map', created under a scheme inspired by the environmental charity Common Ground in the 1980s.

After the war, a few of the prisoners made Britain their home; they had married local girls and set up as smallholders or builders or used other skills to make a living and a new life in the countryside.

THE FARMERS' WAR

When the nation heard Neville Chamberlain's declaration of war on Germany at 11.15 on the morning of Sunday 3 September 1939 (and almost everybody did hear it, on the wireless), more than 60 per cent of Britain's food was being imported. Self-sufficiency in food production at home became crucial to the outcome of the war and the farmers became heroes. Quite literally, within 24 hours of the declaration of war, the future of British agriculture was transformed because it had become an essential industry in everybody's mind, including the government's. The lessons of the First World War had been remembered and, once again, the ploughs came out but this time most of them were behind tractors rather than horses. In the first year of the war, in spite of a severe winter and a severe labour shortage with so many men joining the forces, 2 million acres were ploughed and cropped. By 1944 it was 6.5 million acres, reclaimed from pasture, derelict land and even from moorland, marshes and mountainsides that had never been cultivated before. The farmers did all that was required of them and more. By the end of the war, British farmers were the most highly mechanised in the world and were lapping up everything the agricultural scientists could tell them. The country's notoriously conservative farmers grabbed new ideas with both hands.

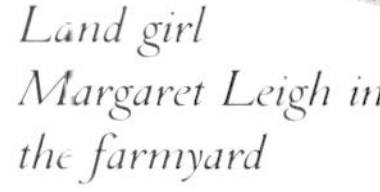

Land girl Margaret Leigh in the farmyard

Refreshments for English sailors helping with the haymaking

second world war

'Every parish in the country was given a quota of land to be ploughed and cropped ...'

WITHIN DAYS OF the declaration of war, local War Agricultural Executive Committees were inspecting farms. The committees, composed largely of leading farmers who had volunteered to help, had been delegated powers by the Minister of Agriculture to carry out the government's programme in the event of war. Every parish in the country was given a quota of land to be ploughed and cropped and the committees persuaded the farmers to comply; they also gave advice and assistance in procuring machinery where needed.

At Elveden, as elsewhere, they readily complied but were shocked when the War Office decided to take a large part of the estate as a tank training ground, churning up the land and the crops that were already growing there. Elveden Hall was partly requisitioned by the Army and then by the American Air Force, whose Lakenheath aerodrome was on the edge of the estate. Lord and Lady Iveagh had already removed themselves to a cottage on the estate when the Hall was used for evacuees. They never returned to the Hall even after the war, and a whole era of shooting parties, dances and lavish country weekends was gone forever.

The Women's Voluntary Service demonstrate emergency cooking with clay and stone ovens during the Second World War

By the end of the Second World War, the British thought highly of their farmers, who were of course delighted but wary, remembering what had happened after previous wars.

Everybody loves a farmer when they are hungry, but then what? For several years they continued to love the farmers, partly because there was a world shortage of food after the war. The government promulgated a new programme of agricultural expansion, with (again) guaranteed prices as long as farmers did what they were told. Confidence returned to the countryside, so much so that businessmen who had made money in industry were falling over themselves to invest in farms.

In 1941 Frederick Smith, advising those who wanted to live in the country, recognised as so many others did that the world he had known before September 1939 had gone for good. He had come to the conclusion that 'the land must play an increasingly important part in our lives. Many people who lived in towns prior to 1939 will find in the country the solution of at least some of their problems. ... We are many of us going back to the land. To my mind, country life today is an ideal life for better reasons than the worship of an antique but obsolescent rural England. ... I contend that the country life is a partial answer to reduced incomes as well as to war-weary minds.'

The optimism continued for quite some time, although there were no more wars during the twentieth century except for those fought in distant lands. Then towards the end of the century things started to go wrong again and the endless wheel of good times and bad turned sharply downwards. Again, only the best or the luckiest or the most determined will survive.

NEW WARS

After the Second World War those heroes and heroines in the services who could come home did, and the village welcomed them warmly but went on talking about crops and weather and rationing and horses and dogs and rabbits and cricket, as if the war had never been. But the lives of all of them had been changed, even those who had not seen active service. For a start, the women who stayed behind had discovered that they could cope on their own, they could handle the fieldwork, they could pay the bills, they could keep a trade going all on their own and still manage the household, and they could wear trousers, both literally and metaphorically.

The next war was the Cold War, with its unthinkable threat of the atomic or nuclear bomb. Despite the enormity of the mushroom cloud that we lived under for so many years, the villagers were ready for it. Parishes were encouraged to set up emergency planning committees, which they did with all the enthusiasm of boy scouts building campfires. If a threat is so huge and so unimaginably awful, you tame it by ignoring its scale and concentrating on the little things that you *can* control. Villagers found themselves learning about digging latrines, making field ovens, building nuclear shelters, setting up radio communications and using geiger counters to monitor local levels of radioactivity, just in case. They drew up plans to feed the village on stored provisions and to accommodate refugees from other areas in the village hall and the school and the pub. The pub even dug out the old air-raid warning siren, blew the dust off it and prepared to let the village know when a nuclear attack was imminent – though just what people could do about it in the allotted four-minute warning was difficult to say, except that the committee would have trained them to dive under the stairs and stay there, with a goat for fresh milk and a tin-opener and Calor gas stove and bottled water, and instructions not to eat the vegetables growing in their own gardens in case they were contaminated by fall-out.

Sometimes these emergency planning groups were unfairly mocked. In my own village our local war hero was featured in the national press (based in London, of course) when it heard of the plans he had drawn up to protect the village from any hordes that might pour along the London-to-Portsmouth highway intent on raiding the village's carefully hoarded rations. Pitchforks and yokels featured in the headlines among other unkind descriptions. Mock ye not, citizens of the Great Wen! The plan was in fact a sound one and highly detailed, relying on local knowledge of essentials such as water supplies, fuel supplies, which houses had cookers that did not rely on mains power, what useful equipment was held by farmers and householders such as generators, boats, thick ropes cutting equipment and horses, and all the other minutiae that would mean survival in the aftermath of disaster. When the nuclear threat was lifted, most villages retained their basic emergency plans in case of a different threat, and many have since put those plans into action – for example, after the major storm of 1987 that cut off countless villages from the rest of the world for a fortnight when trees blocked roads and brought down telephone and power lines, or when coastal villages became swamped by exceptionally high tides in stormy weather. Villagers always were self-sufficient, and sometimes they still can be even now.

'Villagers always were self-sufficient, and sometimes they still can be even now.'

Farm workers benefiting from a rural meat pie scheme in 1953

12

Country Villages

IN THE COUNTRYSIDE, every aspect of life is closely interwoven and it is difficult to divide a book such as this one into chapters, as so much overlaps. But all the strands come together in the fabric of the village itself.

The village is 'home' and remains the focus of rural life, even though quite a few people live beyond the village in farmhouses, woodland cottages and other scattered dwellings, and even though it has been said for generations that the village is not what it used to be. Villages are what people make them: villages are living, breathing entities that adapt to their inhabitants while at the same time subtly moulding those inhabitants to fit in with an evolving community that still has its roots in the past even if it believes otherwise.

For many centuries, the essence of the village was its self-sufficiency, a theme that has threaded its way throughout this book. For much of the twentieth century that self-sufficiency was eroded and eventually apparently lost. The urge for it still lurks beneath the surface and, when the need arises, the villagers rise to the challenge and once again stand on their own feet.

This I know, because the community spirit remains alive and kicking in villages today. It is different in detail from the old village's sense of kinship, in the days when most people were related to each other by blood or by marriage, and when perhaps many felt suffocated by the apron strings of the village as one big family. It is different in that agriculture is no longer the dominant employment that determined everything from the nature of the trades and crafts in the village to the calendar of social events. It is different in its social structure, which is far more multi-layered and mingled than the fairly rigid pyramid that existed right up to the two world wars, with the squire and parson at the top, then the professionals such as doctors and merchants and the yeoman farmers, then the village tradesmen and craftsmen, and finally a very broad base of agricultural labourers and what were termed 'servants', whether on the farms or in private houses.

BOREHAM
& CHELMSFORD

VILLAGE ACTION

OPPOSITE
Members of the Brimpton WI in Berkshire making jam for selling to local grocers during the Second World War

BELOW
Farmer's wife wearing her 'clout' bonnet

WITHIN THE LAST DECADES OF THE TWENTIETH CENTURY THOSE 'CLASS' BARRIERS ALL BUT DISAPPEARED. THERE IS STILL A DEGREE OF DIVISION BY WEALTH IN ITS EXTREMES BUT THERE IS A MUCH, MUCH BIGGER 'MIDDLE' CLASS, A GROUP OF PEOPLE WHO ARE NEITHER MAJOR LANDOWNERS NOR IN DIRE STRAITS. IN SOME PLACES THERE IS STILL A DEGREE OF DIVISION BETWEEN ORIGINAL VILLAGERS AND INCOMERS BUT THE LINES ARE BECOMING BLURRED, THOUGH PERHAPS THIS IS LARGELY BECAUSE THE INCOMERS GREATLY OUTNUMBER THE FAMILIES THAT HAVE LIVED IN THE VILLAGE FOR MORE THAN ONE GENERATION.

WITH THE BLURRING there is a loss of the great variety that once characterised the village. Too many people are similar now in their education, their general outlook on life, the type of work they do, the clothes they wear, the entertainments they enjoy and the aspirations they hold dear. The spread of easy communications in the nineteenth and early twentieth centuries injected a considerable dose of new life into villages that had been slowly dying, but ultimately good communications bred uniformity. And that might be a danger for the future.

It does seem that there are fewer and fewer 'characters' in the villages now, and far fewer of the eccentrics to whom 'conforming' was anathema. Without them life is duller. In their place, though, you will usually find that villages become motivated by a few individuals, whether old village or new, who dare to stand out a little from the flock; they are the people who are always proactive, always doing something for the village and always asking others to help. Perhaps in villages where people habitually say 'no', these motivators eventually give up and become hermits, or leave for fresh pastures, and so the dying village perpetuates its own decay by suppressing initiative; but far more often people say 'yes', and when they do a village can achieve whatever it wants.

The initiators are supported by a goodly proportion of those who are more than willing to serve their village by doing, but not by organising or taking responsibility. These are the ones who always say 'yes' when asked – and having once said yes, they will be asked time and time again. Without them, the initiators who do the asking would be useless. Many of those who say 'yes' are equally capable of quietly getting on with serving the village in countless small ways without anybody asking them in the first place.

It is hard to match the 'yes' people to the villagers of old: who would have fulfilled their role then? Ponder on it. But before doing so, take a look at the structure of the village as it was before the two world wars – the traditional village, as we now label it, though as villages are always changing it is hard to pin any such label on them. Then compare what it was with what it has become.

THE VILLAGE STREET

THE TRADITIONAL VILLAGE, THE POSTCARD VILLAGE, HAD A STREET WITH A MIXTURE OF SMALL SHOPS TO MEET BASIC NEEDS, INTERSPERSED WITH COTTAGES, AND HERE AND THERE A WORKSHOP – THE BLACKSMITH, THE WHEELWRIGHT, THE COBBLER AND SO ON. THERE WAS A VILLAGE GREEN, MAYBE WITH ITS STOCKS STILL IN PLACE AND A LARGE OLD TREE UNDER WHICH PEOPLE GATHERED. THERE WAS A CHURCH, OF COURSE, AND NEAR IT A LARGE PARSONAGE; DISTANT FROM THE CHURCH BOTH PHYSICALLY AND SOCIALLY THERE WAS A CHAPEL, OR TWO.

'There was a definition to the village, a sense that it had grown slowly out of the soil until it fitted snugly in its landscape ...'

SOMEWHERE THERE WOULD be the 'big house', either within the village, or set apart in its own parklands slashed by the long ribbon of its drive. There was at least one pub, a vaguely scruffy but friendly place that the regulars walked to, bringing their collies with them. There was a village school with just one large room, and a small playground outside. There was a handful of larger homes sprinkled here and there where you would expect to find a doctor, a retired army officer, maybe a banker and people of that ilk. The bigger cottages were home to tradesmen and craftsmen, and also their shop windows. The main village shop itself sold everything anyone could possibly need, but there would also be a butcher's shop and a baker. Somewhere there was a village pump, with a horse trough close by, and somewhere there was a place where people hung about and chatted – maybe an old market cross or a square.

The street had people in it, wandering, gossiping, going about their business. Occasionally a horse and cart plodded by, or a donkey carrying panniers, or perhaps a small group of cows or sheep on their way to somewhere, leaving tokens of dung in their wake. Maybe a farm worker pedalled slowly past on his old bike, tinkling his bell to a friend and wearing string around his ankles to stop his trouser-legs catching in the wheel. A couple of dogs lying in the middle of the street would lift their heads lazily to watch the world go by, having a thoughtful scratch now and then or dozing in the sun. Children played on the green and in the street, bowling hoops or skipping with ropes or playing games to traditional rhymes.

The Devon village of Sheepwash

There was definition to the village, a sense that it had grown slowly out of the soil until it fitted snugly in its landscape and then stopped, comfortable with its size and shape. Its buildings may have been of different ages but somehow they fitted together, they suited each other; there was an overall designer's touch that in reality was no more than local tradition developing the vernacular over a few centuries. They were made of local materials and you could imagine that, one day, when the village finally died, its materials would simply crumble into the landscape and become part of it again.

Well, forget all of that! The reality of many villages today is traffic, for a start – cars on the move with muttering engines, cars parked along every available inch of kerb, lorries shaking the old buildings and rattling the manhole covers and bridges as they rumble through and almost scrape against the walls. People hug

the village street

Snargate, Romney Marsh

the pavement and are in a hurry, looking faintly angry until they see a familiar face and pause to say hallo. If there is a village shop, it is self-service and sells mainly packaged goods, delivered to its back entrance by an enormous lorry. The smithy is now a garage, with cars choking its forecourt. The pub has been taken over by a brewery that likes background music, expensive food and no smoking. The cyclist wears lycra shorts, wrap-around sun goggles and a strange helmet. The dogs have more sense than to be anywhere near the street and the same goes for the cattle and sheep. There are signs everywhere – road signs, shop signs, advertisements, public notices, estate agents' signs. There are sodium streetlights and telephone wires, and white and yellow lines painted boldly on the road. Brash, brash, brash is today's village.

Some villages, that is. Some have managed to retain their charm, at least on the surface, and have only a few vehicles on their streets, but these are the ones that have probably lost their shops, their tradesmen and their crafts. They might, if they are very lucky, see a bus once a week, twice a week, or even once or twice a day, if only to ferry the children to a school a few miles away because the village school closed long ago. Most of the cottages have been 'gentrified', and very few of those who live in them were born in the village or work in the village. Television aerials or satellite dishes decorate the old rooftops; Helen Allingham would not have added them to her paintings, and the photographers would have airbrushed them from their pictures. Through the windows comes the faint bluish flicker of television sets and computer screens.

And the village has lost its proper shape. It stretches way beyond its natural boundaries, with newer and newer buildings straggling along the outgoing lanes – bungalows, little blocks of flats, council houses, modern estates in their own little worlds, all eagerly marching down the road to join up with the next village, and the next, to form one day a town of a sort to give people the urban security they have in theory tried to escape but in practice still seek. Oh, those streetlights! That tidiness! That Best Kept Village-itis!

'Some villages … have managed to retain their charm, at least on the surface …'

POPULATION CHANGES

'One Essex ploughman had been given a seven-year sentence for stealing a watch ...'

THE GREAT COUNTRYSIDE DRIFT TO THE TOWNS HAS ALREADY BEEN DESCRIBED, AND THE LATER DRIFT IN THE OTHER DIRECTION BY TOWN AND CITY DWELLERS TRAILING THEIR URBAN HABITS BEHIND THEM IN THEIR BAGGAGE LIKE SECURITY BLANKETS, AS IF THEY WERE SETTLERS HEADING FOR THE OUTBACK OR THE WILD WEST. HERE BE BEARS; HERE BE DRAGONS.

IN THE EIGHTEENTH and nineteenth centuries, many a rural family or disenchanted farmworker made the real journey into the unknown, emigrating to North America or to Australia and New Zealand in search of a better life and hastening the depopulation of the countryside. They continued to do so in the twentieth century but by then they were seeking employment and good weather rather than wanting to settle on a piece of virgin land and farm it.

In the 1830s much of that emigration was enforced. After the Captain Swing riots of 1830, nearly 500 men (and two women) were found guilty of crimes such as breaking a threshing machine or setting fire to a rick and were transported to Van Diemen's Land (Tasmania) and New South Wales, Australia. They were not criminals by nature and the Superintendent of Convicts at London Docks said that he 'never saw a finer set of men'. Of those sent to Tasmania, only one in three had ever been in prison, usually for things like trespass, poaching, fathering a bastard, petty larceny (one Essex ploughman had been given a seven-year sentence for stealing a watch), leaving their master's service or cutting a fence; of those who were sent to New South Wales only one in twelve had any sort of a record.

George Dew, whose work brought him in close contact with the poorest in the local villages, frequently mentioned emigration in his diaries in the 1870s. For a start, nearly all of his cousins living around Banbury had emigrated to America by 1871, and in that year he recorded in July alone that seven people from the small village of Lower Heyford had emigrated to Canada: 'Robert Cook, Junr., & wife & family left here by the mid-day train. He was a Farm Labourer & collected most of the money to pay their passages by subscription. I gave him 2/6. What farm labourer if he were wise would stay here & work for 10/- or 11/- per week when the New World is open to him? Emigration ought greatly to be promoted.' Three months later 20-year-old James Dunn left the same village and sailed for the United States. In the fol-

Hop-pickers packed and ready to return home after the season

population changes

lowing year Dew noted that there were more empty cottages in the village than ever before, all due to 'emigration to the north of England & America'. In 1874 he reported two ship loads of emigrants setting off for New Zealand in January, including two local families – a sawyer's and a farm labourer's. Within three months two more local families had left for New Zealand '& nearly all over the Bletchington District the Agricultural Labourers are on the move, emigrating to New Zealand or else migrating into the northern counties'. These emigrations had been arranged through the National Agricultural Labourers Union, whose local officials were recruited as agents by the New Zealand government.

A few years before the First World War, a special training farm was established at Woking Park in Surrey for those who wished to emigrate. At the time many people were emigrating to Canada with high hopes of wealth and adventure in the wide open spaces, but the 'farms' they leased there were often just a square mile of virgin prairie, perhaps with a basic log cabin if they were lucky (if not, you built your own immediately) and your nearest neighbour twenty miles away and the closest store a day's journey. Ah well, at least the Canadian government provided you with a telephone, even if it had not built a road yet.

Many of these hopeful emigrants to Canada knew very little about farming; many came from the towns and had done hardly any physical labour in their lives. The creation of the training farm at Woking Park was timely indeed and soon there was a similar scheme for the young women as well – most of them town-bred and middle-class, often used to having a servant at home in those days and certainly not ready to be a farmer's wife on the Canadian prairies. But the First World War brought an end to emigration and an end to the training farms.

NEW VILLAGE HOMES

The state of rural cottages was a matter of concern to many at regular intervals during the eighteenth and nineteenth centuries and for at least the first half of the twentieth. Some landlords couldn't care less but here and there the big landowners would take responsibilty for building new cottages for their workers, or tried to encourage people to help themselves. For example, Lord Rolle at the end of the eighteenth century was 'encouraging the peasantry to build and make small improvements' on the borders of commonland in the Woodbury region of Devon. The theory was that inducing the labourers to leave the village and settle beside the commons was 'by far the most likely means of promoting the comfort, and improving the morals of these people'. They were encouraged to enclose an acre of land about their new homes; if the improvements met with his lordship's approval, they were then allowed to enclose a further four or five acres of wasteland. Well, very nice, but the wasteland was aptly named and the poor labourer would have had quite a job to 'improve' it enough to make it in any way productive.

Other landowners were more generous and some really did seem to care. They built modern cottages – plain, perhaps, and maybe no more than one or two rooms on the ground floor and two above, but solid enough and new. Many an agricultural tome of the nineteenth century, in particular reproduced architectural diagrams of cottages for the workers built by the big country landowners, though not all were ideal. In *Youatt's Complete Grazier* in the 1890s there was a brand new single-story cottage built of corrugated iron, lined inside with wood. It was admitted that, after a severe frost, 'water from the melted ice beneath the roof is liable to find its way through the fissures in the matchboard of the ceiling'.

Immediately after the First World War, parish councils all over the country were expressing concern about the lack of good 'workmen's cottages' – affordable homes for the villagers. That concern persisted throughout the twentieth century and there were different ways of tackling the problem.

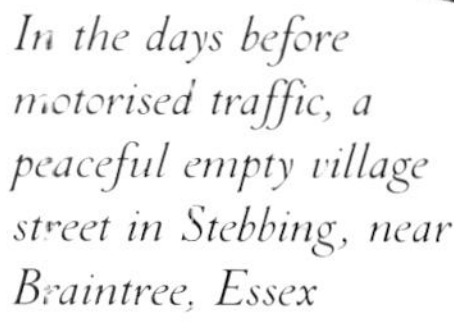

In the days before motorised traffic, a peaceful empty village street in Stebbing, near Braintree, Essex

'The state of rural cottages was a matter of concern to many …'

population changes

> *'By the 1930s many villages found that their boundaries had been stretched ...'*

HOMES FOR HEROES

After the First World War, every effort was made to welcome home the heroes who had been through so much. The government wanted to house them and find them smallholdings and jobs (subsidised with gratuities so that they could set up on their own), to give them a fresh start in civilian life and at the same time to help to revive rural areas. By the 1930s many villages found that their boundaries had been stretched: countless bungalows were built along the lanes leading out of the village, and at the same time old cottages were being knocked down and replaced by new houses.

In the 1930s, the pseudonymous Peter Simple wrote in the *Morning Post*:

> *I had an opportunity this week-end of examining some of the latest 'bungalosities' on the Sussex coast. Pink roofs and army huts, it appears, are now on the wane; and anyone who lives in a disused railway carriage is liable to be stigmatised as* demode. *The new fashion in domestic architecture is a mixture of Tudor and Rustic, with a dash of Hollywood added. Thatched roofs, latticed windows, and oak cocktail bars are now* de rigueur *all the way from Eastbourne to Selsey Bill; and the Best People are replacing their garden gates by rustic stiles.*

Some of those converted railway carriages were quite acceptable in the odd field here and there, and were an ingenious way of recycling whatever was available to make a home when homes were in short supply. The idea was romantic as well as practical, and the carriages seemed to fit better in the countryside than a modern caravan.

COUNCIL HOUSES

The first council houses were built in the 1890s, and thereafter in waves of enthusiasm,

Village pond on the Berkshire Downs

population changes

especially after each of the two world wars. The aim was to provide modern housing at affordable rents, and they were highly sought after by the many people in rural areas who lived in damp, cold cottages with no plumbing or any other conveniences.

There was a problem. Most of the council houses were built in styles that were often completely alien to the locality; what is more they were usually built en bloc, as estates, plonked on the edge of the village, rather than as individual houses scattered within the village envelope and thus integrated with everybody else. Then, although originally conceived as homes for the villagers, they were sometimes rented to people with no direct connection with the village. The combination of these factors often set the council house estate apart, storing up trouble in later years when villagers began to blame 'them from the estate' for petty crime and other problems.

HOUSING ESTATES

Planners and builders never learn, do they? In the last three or four decades of the twentieth century it happened all over again when developers were allowed to build new estates, this time of houses for private buyers. Again, the designs had no hint of the vernacular about them and could have been built anywhere in the country (and still not belong there), and the houses were crowded together in enclaves, cheek by jowl, sharing a private road. To the dismay of many villages, planning officers actually encouraged the high-density building that the developers preferred (for the latter, it made economical sense) but that created a feeling of overcrowding on the site and a vague sense of menace to an old village dominated by a solid block of newcomers. And newcomers they invariably were: villagers themselves could rarely afford the prices of these new homes. Older villagers began to say that they used to know everybody but now they had no idea who half the people in the village were.

And *still* the powers that be, based in towns and cities but dictating what happens in the villages, did not understand. First came the sale of the older council houses, which was good news for the tenants who could afford to buy them but which promptly lost the pool of affordable homes for rent in rural areas. So villages needed to find new ways of housing their young, who wanted homes of their own rather than continuing to live with their parents. With no new council housing being built to replace what had been sold, villagers eventually turned to housing associations for help. New affordable homes were built, but again the designs were alien to the village and again the homes were packed as tightly as possible and all together on a site. And so it goes on.

Fownhope Club Walk, Herefordshire

Some villages are trying to take matters into their own hands by somehow raising the funds to buy land that becomes available and then building homes that the *village* wants, in styles and at densities that the village can accept – provided the planning officers in the town will let them. Whose village is it, anyway?

It may well all be in vain. It is difficult enough for a village to fight against the demands of its own district council, which might be based more than twenty miles away in a large town or city and with members who are mainly urban in outlook, with very little understanding of rural life. It is that much more difficult when the demands come from a regional level of government, and almost impossible when they come from central governments who decree that, whether the rural areas like it or not, millions of new houses *shall* be built in the countryside, along with all the new roads, new shops, new industries for jobs and so on – the new infrastructure that so much new housing will need to support it. The people who will live in these new houses will come from the towns, not the villages. Those who live in the country are in such a minority that their views can simply be ignored, and certainly nobody thinks to ask the wildlife what it feels about these invasions into its shrinking habitat.

'Most of the council houses were built in styles that were often completely alien to the locality …'

VILLAGE CARE

PART OF THE SELF-SUFFICIENCY OF THE OLD VILLAGE WAS THAT IT LOOKED AFTER ITS OWN – INCLUDING THOSE WHO WERE IN TROUBLE. FOR SEVERAL CENTURIES, THE POOR WERE CARED FOR BY THE CHURCH AND THROUGH ACTS OF PRIVATE CHARITY, UNTIL THE ELIZABETHAN POOR LAWS EFFECTIVELY TRANSFERRED THE RESPONSIBILITIES TO THE VILLAGE ITSELF.

'In Victorian times, the sense of service to the village was strong …'

WEALTHY INDIVIDUALS CONTINUED to feel better about their wealth by giving money, food, clothing, homes, education and other services to the deserving in their parish, but the essence of the Poor Laws was that most of the village contributed as well. And being a village, everybody knew who was in trouble and what was being done about it.

In Victorian times, the sense of service to the village was strong among those at the pyramid's level of tradesmen, craftsmen, teachers and the like, many of whom played multiple 'official' roles in the village and its immediate neighbourhood. As well as paupers, their range of care embraced the sick, the elderly, the unemployed, orphans and bastards, widows, tramps and ne'er-do-wells.

Typical village get-together, celebrating in a local barn

VESTRY MEETINGS AND PARISH COUNCILS

An important part of village life was the vestry meeting, at which village worthies came together in the church's vestry (or more often adjourned to the nearest pub) to appoint each other to the various village care-taking posts that did not necessarily have anything to do with church matters. They appointed guardians and overseers of the poor, highway surveyors and waywardens, rates assessors and parish valuers, charity trustees, parish constables, parish doctors and medical officers, schoolmasters and others who were essential to the smooth running of the parish. They looked after almshouses, parish cottages and the parish workhouse; they distributed clothing, bread, flour, potatoes and other necessities to the parish's poor; they found things for paupers to do and dealt with vagrants; and they ensured that those who needed nursing were nursed (in some sets of vestry minutes there are references to the gloriously named London Truss Society for Relief of Ruptured Poor).

There was much more that the vestry meetings handled: they kept the parish roads in good condition, making sure that there were adequate materials, labour and draught animals to do so (some maintained parish cart-houses for this purpose); they maintained pounds where stray animals were held until their owners paid a fine for their release; they sold lane-dropped manure; they dealt with footpaths and ponds, flooding and drains. Many of them set up parish fire

village care

brigades (the engines, of course, had to be pushed or pulled by men or horses) and fire-fighting reservoirs; they maintained burial grounds and built schools; they kept an eye on the pubs and alehouses; they ensured that apprenticeships were available; they helped those who wanted to emigrate; they took adequate precautions to prevent the spread of smallpox or typhoid or plague in the village; they trod the bounds and cried the notices; they persuaded fathers to pay towards the wellbeing of their bastard offspring; they built reading-rooms and created recreation grounds; they paid the parish constable's bills, provided him with parish handcuffs and a parish lock-up and offered rewards on the heads of criminals. In fact there were very few aspects of village life in which the vestry did not become involved.

This system continued vigorously until the early beginnings of centralisation occurred in the late eighteenth century, when parishes were advised to combine with others in the interests of 'efficiency'; for example, by jointly buying or hiring a workhouse to cover a wider area than just one village. New maps were being drawn up by assorted authorities, carving the countryside into regions or 'unions' of parishes under Poor Law amendments, often in the face of overridden but vehement opposition from parishes that pointed out they had no natural affinity with some of those parishes and would rather be placed with others instead.

Gradually these more centralised groups began to take away the vestry's powers to look after its own, and the whole business became increasingly less personal. People in trouble were judged by people who no longer knew them and their histories.

By the time parish councils were created in 1894, the vestry system had long since withered to a shadow of its former self and the new councils could do very little for their own poor and other disadvantaged villagers. It was all in the hands of other bodies in the towns. During the early twentieth century, the villagers shrugged their shoulders and let 'them' get on with it.

DOING GOOD

Between the world wars a rash of initials came into the villages, full of worthy intent. The National Federation of Women's Institutes was formed in 1917, at first to organise women in the countryside to take a greater part in food production for the war effort.

In 1919 a National Council of Social Service was formed (it would later be called the National Council for Voluntary Organisations) to strengthen the 'rich and varied pattern of voluntary societies' by bringing them together under one umbrella, where they could work in partnership with the new statutory services that were being developed. Later in that year, the Council drew attention to the inactivity of parish councils (so soon? they had only been in existence for quarter of a century) and suggested setting up 'village social councils'.

In 1920 Sir Horace Plunkett appealed to the University of Oxford to take the lead in promoting a wider vision of 'better living as well as better farming and better business':

> *New ideas are stirring in the countryside. Men who have come back from service across the sea, women who have come back from work in munitions factories have learnt a new independence and a new vision ... The problem of making rural life as full of stimulus and as attractive as it ought to be can only be solved by educating village people themselves in the broad principles of co-operation in social and educational as well as in strictly agricultural matters.*

Well, that was a bit unfair! Villagers had lived in a society of mutual co-operation for centuries (though it had slipped a bit in recent years) – but he meant well. His appeal was heard by a Gloucestershire woman, Grace Hadow, vice-president of the NFWI, who in 1921 formed the first (Oxfordshire) 'rural community council', a group including leaders in adult education and spokespersons for various village clubs, to help the county's villages in social and educational work.

'New ideas are stirring in the countryside ... a new independence and a new vision ...'

village care

'The Welfare State finally relieved the villagers of responsibility for their own, indeed even responsibility for themselves ...'

The village bobby is now a rare sight. He used to know everybody; his presence deterred criminals and he could turn a young lad away from vandalism before it became a habit. There is now a move to revive the office of parish constable

In 1922 Professor W.G.S. Adams, a pioneer of the National Council, said:

> *The tendency has been on the one hand to give the village what was considered good for it and, on the other, to turn to someone else for help on all occasions. The essence of the country problem is to find means to enable country men and women to help themselves, and to bring together all classes in co-operation for the common good.*

It all rather smacks of condescension, doesn't it? But again, he meant well, and certainly the RCCs did pump new life into some of the villages. For example, there was immediate enthusiasm from voluntary groups of musicians and actors who went out to the villages to encourage an interest in the arts.

Then came the master stroke. The RCCs realised that the best way of bringing all a village's interests together was to build a village hall, or improve an existing one. With the help of the National Council, they managed to persuade the Treasury to provide interest-free loans to do so. In those days it was loans; in the 1930s there were grants (under the Physical Training and Recreation Act of 1937); today it is more likely to be grants from Lottery funds.

Eighty years from their inception there are RCCs in every county and they are an invaluable source of information and support for villages having problems with loss of services or in need of inspiration and cash. They have built up an enormous pool of expertise and knowledge; it is just a shame that they still base themselves in towns and that many of their staff are from urban, not rural, backgrounds who, albeit unwittingly, sometimes seem a little patronising towards their country cousins.

THE WELFARE STATE

A very big change after the Second World War was the creation of the Welfare State. Its effects have been largely beneficial but there are disadvantages as well. The Welfare State finally relieved the villagers of responsibility for their own, indeed even responsibility for themselves as individuals. Those in trouble are now taken in hand by people who have no connection with the village at all, and sometimes they feel like numbers, like ciphers, like part of a herd of cattle with no personal identity, just a case – a case to be dealt with until

village care

the file can be closed and forgotten. In the old village, even in the workhouse, that would not have happened.

The Welfare State also saw the final withdrawal of the squire from village life. Henceforth those in the big house and those with large land holdings became more self-centred and less willing to contribute to a village they perceived as being able to look after itself with the help of the state.

THE NEW VILLAGE

Yes, the village has changed, much of it for the better, some of it apparently for the worse until you remove those rose-tinted glasses when you look at the village of old, and some of it with genuine regret. The kinship has gone but so has the claustrophobic atmosphere it could create. The village bobby hardly exists, his place taken by the occasional passing patrol car whose occupants know none of the names or even faces of the villagers and certainly don't have the time or inclination to take a young lad to one side and point out the error of his ways before his petty mischief turns into something more serious. It is no longer possible to put a culprit in the stocks on the village green, to be ridiculed by those who have known him since he was born; instead he now goes to a town prison and disappears into a safe anonymity where nobody inside knows his mother.

The squire has gone, his place usurped by the state. The parson no longer dominates the village; again his role has been partly usurped by the state but partly lost through the reduction in his flock and the lessening of unquestioning respect from villagers who now are often as well educated as he is. But the village still cares for and respects its older folk, boasting with as much pride as they do themselves about their age, and listening to their memories. The village still cares for its children and raises money to ensure that they have a school and playing fields and playgrounds. The village still cares.

Parish councils are changing; they have been through too many years of nothingness and are now much more active, more alive to the needs of their constituents at all levels, more prepared to get up and do something about the problems that are thrown at them from elsewhere – that is, as long as they do not suffocate under the huge wadges of paper that arrive remorselessly with every post from the various higher levels of government, from district and county, from regional and central government, and increasingly from Europe. How can a bureaucrat in Brussels have any conception of what it is like to live in a village in England or to work on a Welsh hill farm or to chug out with the fishing fleet from a Scottish coastal village?

Stepping-stones at Chagford, Devon

There may seem to be more unhappiness, more abuse, more depression, more suicides in rural areas, especially at times of trouble for farmers, but in reality it is probably less than of old – it's just that the news of it is more widely broadcast. In the old village you might have known of such problems within the village (and possibly put it all down to a combination of witches and bad luck) but not elsewhere, so you would not have had the impression that the problems were on a large scale. Some say there is hidden rural poverty, but it is surely again a matter of scale: a nineteenth-century villager would not recognise it as poverty in comparison.

'People say that the spirit of village life is dying but in reality it is only changing.'

People say that the spirit of village life is dying but in reality it is only changing. There is still in many villages a strong desire to be involved for the general good of the community, albeit there are conflicts about what that 'general good' might be. The children in today's village will look back at their childhood in years to come and shake their heads, telling their grandchildren that life was wonderful in those days, those good old days, when there were still fields and woods and streams, before the village was engulfed by the tidy concrete suburbs of the town.

Oh yes, believe me.

BIBLIOGRAPHY

Adorian, Paul, *The Story of Gibbons Mill* (Paul Adorian,1970)

Allingham, Helen and Dick, Stewart, *The Cottage Homes of England* (Edward Arnold, 1909)

Baden-Powell, Sir Robert, *Scouting for Boys*, 9th edn (C. Arthur Pearson, 1918)

Baxter, J., *Library of Agricultural and Horticultural Knowledge*, 3rd edn (Baxter, 1834)

Beckett, Arthur, *The Spirit of the Downs*, 5th edn (Methuen & Co, 1930)

Birkett, Foster and Taylor, Tom, *Pictures of English Landscape* (George Routledge & Sons, 1862)

Bourne, George, *Change in the Village* (George Duckworth & Co, 1912)

Brill, Edith, *Cotswold Crafts* (Batsford, 1977)

Brown, Jonathan and Ward, Sadie, *The Village Shop* (Rural Development Commission/ Cameron & Hollis/David & Charles, 1990)

Chivers, Keith, ed., *History with a Future* (Shire Horse Society/RASE, 1988)

Clayton, Nick, *Early Bicycles* (Shire Publications, 1994)

Cobbett, William, *Cottage Economy* (1823; reprinted Landsman's Bookshop, 1974)

Cripps, Sir John, 'Christmas Coals to Community Care', 1984 Sir George Haynes Memorial Lecture (NCVO, 1985)

Duckers, Nigel and Davies, Huw, *A Place in the Country* (Michael Joseph, 1990)

Evelyn, David J., *Firegrates and Kitchen Ranges* (Shire Publications, 1983)

Fox, Ian, *Hampshire Privies* (Countryside Books, 1997)

Gibbs, J. Arthur, *A Cotswold Village* (Jonathan Cape, 1898)

Halford, David G., *Old Lawn Mowers* (Shire Publications, 1999)

Hammond, Martin, *Bricks and Brickmaking* (Shire Publications, 1981)

Harries, Mollie, *Cotswold Privies* (Chatto & Windus, 1984)

Hobsbawm, E.J. and Rude, George, *Captain Swing* (Lawrence & Wishart, 1969)

Horn, Pamela, *The Victorian Country Child* (Roundwood Press, 1974)

Horn, Pamela, ed., *Oxfordshire Village Life: the Diaries of George James Dew* (Beacon Publications, 1983)

Jackson, W.A., *The Victorian Chemist and Druggist* (Shire Publications, 1981)

Jefferies, Richard, *The Amateur Poacher* (Thomas Nelson & Sons, 1879)

—— *Hodge and His Masters* (Faber and Faber reprint, 1946)

—— *Landscape and Labour* (Moonraker Press reprint, 1979)

—— *The Life of the Fields* (1884; reprinted Oxford University Press, 1983)

—— *The Pageant of Summer* (Quartet reprint, 1979)

—— *The Toilers of the Field* (Longman, Green & Co, 1892)

Jekyll, Gertrude, *Old West Surrey* (Longman, Green & Co, 1904)

—— *Old English Household Life* (Longman, Green & Co, 1925)

Jennings, Paul, *The Living Village* (Hodder & Stoughton, 1968)

Jones, Sydney R., *English Village Homes* (Batsford, 1936)

Kerr Cameron, David, *The English Fair* (Sutton Publishing, 1998)

Kindred, David, ed., *In a Long Day: the Titshall Photographs of Farm and Village Life* (Old Pond Publishing, 1999)

Lansdell, Avril, *Occupational Costume* (Shire Publications, 1977)

Mann, John Edgar, *Hampshire Customs, Curiosities and Country Lore* (Ensign Publications, 1994)

Martelli, George, *The Elveden Enterprise* (Faber and Faber, 1952)

Maycock, S.A. and Hayhurst, John, *The Smallholder Encyclopaedia* (C. Arthur Pearson, 1950)

Meynell, Esther, *Sussex Cottage* (Chapman & Hall, 1936)

Middleton, C.H., *Village Memories* (Cassell & Co, 1941)

Mitford, Mary Russell, *Our Village* (Guild Publishing reprint, 1986)

Moore, John, *Brensham Village* (Collins, 1946)

Morley, Richard, *Red Roughs and Copper Kettles* (Ditchling Horticultural Society, Sussex, 1990)

Morris, Christopher, ed., *The Journeys of Celia Fiennes* (Macdonald & Co, 1982)

Mountford, Frances, *A Commoner's Cottage* (Alan Sutton, 1992)

Murray, Walter J.C., *Copsford* (George Allen & Unwin, 1948)

Nair, Gwyneth, *Highley: the Development of a Community, 1550–1880* (Basil Blackwell, 1988)

Nicholls, Beverley, *A Thatched Roof* (Jonathan Cape, 1933)

Olivier, Edith, *Wiltshire* (Robert Hale, 1951)

Pakington, Humphrey, *English Villages and Hamlets* (Batsford, 1934)

Pingriff, G.N., *Leicestershire* (Cambridge University Press, 1920)

Pitt, W., *General View of the Agriculture of the County of Worcester* (1813; reprinted David & Charles, 1969)

Porter, Valerie, *Field Book of Country Queries* (Pelham, 1987)

—— *Second Field Book of Country Queries* (Pelham, 1989)

—— *The Southdown Sheep* (Weald and Downland Open Air Museum, 1991)

—— *English Villagers: Life in the Countryside, 1850–1939* (George Philip, 1992)

—— *Life Behind the Cottage Door* (Whittet, 1992)

—— *Tales of the Old Woodlanders* (David & Charles, 1994)

—— *The Village Parliaments* (Phillimore, 1994)

Pulbrook, Ernest C., *English Country Life and Work* (Batsford, 1922)

Robertson, Una A., *The Illustrated History of the Housewife* (Sutton Publishing, 1997)

Seebohm Rowntree, B. and Lavers, G.R., *English Life and Leisure* (Longman, Green & Co, 1951)

Smith, Frederick D. and Wilcox, Barbara, *Living in the Country* (Adam and Charles Black, 1940)

Stempson, David, ed., *Three Acres and a Cow: the Life and Works of Eli Hamshire* (David Stempson, Cheam, 1995)

Svendsen, Elisabeth D., ed., *The Professional Handbook of the Donkey* (The Donkey Sanctuary, Sidmouth, 1986)

Thomas, F.G., *The Changing Village* (Thomas Nelson & Sons, 1939)

Thompson, Flora, *A Country Calendar* (Oxford University Press reprint, 1979)

Thompson, Paul, *The Voice of the Past* (Oxford University Press, 1978)

Tilley, M.F., *Housing the Country Worker* (Faber and Faber, 1947)

Toulson, Shirley, *The Drovers* (Shire Publications, 1980)

Vancouver, Charles, *General View of the Agriculture of the County of Devon* (1808; reprinted David & Charles, 1969)

Vidal, Mrs, *Rachel Charlcote: a Village Story* (Wells Gardner, Darton & Co, 1902)

Williams, W.M., *The Country Craftsman* (Routledge & Kegan Paul, 1958)

Willis, Gill, ed., *I Remember Chobham* (Willimms Publications, 1999)

Wilson, Geoffrey, *The Old Telegraphs* (Phillimore, 1976)

Wright, Geoffrey N., *Turnpike Roads* (Shire Publications, 1997)

Young, Arthur, *General View of the Agriculture of the County of Lincolnshire* (1813; reprinted David & Charles, 1970)

Young, Rev. Arthur, *General View of the Agriculture of the County of Sussex* (1813; reprinted David & Charles, 1970)

INDEX

index

ACKNOWLEDGEMENTS

The author would particularly like to thank the villages of Chobham, Lyndon, Grittleton and Milland for sharing their personal memories of the past.

The author and publishers would like to thank the following for supplying photographs:

THE COUNTRYMAN MAGAZINE: Jacket: front cover top rt (Kenneth Scowen); pp1 (Joseph McKenzie), 2 (John Tarlton), 3 (Eagle Photos), 4–5 (Russell Frith), 6 (John Gay), 7top (John T. Dray), 7btm (John Edenbrow), 8–9 (Gordon Watt), 10–11ctre (The Sutcliffe Gallery), 13top (John Edenbrow), 14, 15 (Leonard & Marjorie Gayton), 18, 19 (John Tarlton), 20, 24rt (Richard Gee), 25 (Mike Howarth), 31, 32 (Gordon Wood), 34 (John Tarlton), 40, 46–7 (Kenneth Scowen), 48–9 (J.P. Lyon), 50both (John L. Jones), 51top left (E.A. Janes), 51top & btm rt, 52, 53left (Guy B. Newham), 53rt (B.G. Furner), 54, 55, 56rt (Thomas Henshall), 57left (J.M. Boatfield), 57rt (Phyllis Kelway), 58–9, 60 (Thomas Henshall), 61top (Enid M. Pyrah), 61btm (Thomas Henshall), 63top, 63btm (John Tarlton), 64–5 (Bertram Unne), 66btm (Thomas McLeary), 69 (John Tarlton), 74 (Janet Bord), 74–5 (Thomas Henshall), 75 (H.C. Flashman), 77 (P.A. Macnab), 80top (J.G. Jenkins), 80btm, 81left (Kenneth Scowen), 81top rt (Eric L. King), 81btm rt (J. Hardman), 82btm (Bernard Wakeman), 82 (Clyde Higgs), 84top (David Hugill), 84btm (Valerie Bissland), 85 (J. Hardman), 89top (F. Thompson), 89btm (Douglas Murray), 90top left, 90btm left (Michael Walters), 92, 110left (Miss M. Wight), 110rt (Tony Boxall), 11top (Dr. Wyn Hughes, 111btm (Paul Popper), 114top left (Jim Bennett), 114top rt (Kennedy McCreadie), 119top rt, 120 (Bernard Wakeman), p121btm, 124 (D.A.E. Cross), 125left (Douglas Bramhill), 125rt (R.E. Balch), 127rt (E.S. Halliday), 132top 132btm (John Tarlton), 133top (Tom Parker), 133btm (Paul Popper), 134–5btm, 135 (David W. Jones) 137top, 137btm (Tom Parker), 138left (Miss B.L. Benson, 138rt (Claude Fisher), 139left (Miss M. Wight), 139rt (Carel Toms), 140left (M. Littledale/Poole Museum), 143 (Phyllis Walker), 146 (Peter Rosse), 145 (John Edenbrow), 150, 154 (Philip Acker), 155rt (Oxford & County Newspapers), 156 (Tom Parker), 157top rt (Eric D. Cheshire), 162 (John Saunders), 165 (Arthur Strong), 172top & ctre, 172btm (Phyllis Kelway), 173top (Ernst Bollinger), 173btm (Arthur Spragg), 174top left (G. Maclean), 174btm (Francis Pitt), 175top left (Llew T. Jones), 175rt (Scotsman Features Ltd), 177 (John Tarlton), 179btm (Paul Popper), 180, 181top rt (Clyde Higgs), 181btm rt (J. Goodchild), 182left (Alex Watkinson), 182rt (H. Wills), 183, 185top rt (John Gay), 187top left (Col. A. Greg), 187top rt (C. Horace Clarke), 187btm (Kenneth A. Coldman), 188btm (Francis Sandwith), 191btm (Ronald Lockley), 194top (John Tarlton), 195top (Rev. C.J. Parry-Evans), 197 (E.A. Janes), 198top rt (John L. Jones), 198btm (John Tarlton), 199 (Kenneth Scowen), 200–1 (John Tarlton), 203rt (Robert Miller), 206–7btm (John Tarlton), 207top (Robert Miller), 208top (W.J. Watkins), 209 (Jane Bown), 210–11both, 213 (John Tarlton), 214 (Robert Miller), 215top (Ron & Lucie Hinson), 219btm (H. Smith), 220 (Ray Cowmeadow), 221 (John L. Jones), 222 btm (John Tarlton), 223top (R. & J. Wakely), 226left (Clyde Higgs), 226rt (M.C.G. Hooton), 227left (H.Smith), 228top rt (John Tarlton), 228ctre left (E.O. Hoppé), 228ctre rt (William S. Paton), 229 (Edgar & Winifred Ward), 231btm (S.E. Mardon), 232top left (Miss M.Wight), 232btm, 233 both (John S. Beswick), 234 (The Scottish Tourist Board), 236 (Nicholas Horne), 237top (Robert Miller), 237btm (The New Studio, Milford Haven), 238–9 (G.G. Garland), 243 (Miss M.Wight), 244top left (Keith Harding), 247top left (John Tarlton), 249ctre rt (Archie Griffiths), 250 (Nicholas Horne), 256 (G.G. Garland), 257 (Miss Pennethorne), 260 (John Saunders), 261both (A. Richardson), 263top (Tom Parker), 263btm (David W. Jones), 266–7 (Kenneth Scowen), 268 Tom Weir, 274 (Christopher Dalton), 276 (G. Moore), 278left (George H.Hall), 278–9 (Messrs Parsons Ltd), 279top (John Edenbrow), 297ctre, 300–1 (John Tarlton), 302 (W.B. Redmayne), 304 (John Tarlton), 305 (Leonard & Marjorie Gayton), 307 (John Tarlton), 308, 309 (Miss M. Wight), 310, 311, 313 (John Tarlton).

BEAFORD ARCHIVE: pp 115top, 258

HULTON GETTY: Jacket: back flap (Maeers/Fox Photos), back cover: (Carl Sutton/Picture Post), front cover left (Val Doone), front cover btm rt (Charles Hewitt/Picture Post); pp 10left, 27, 28, 30, 35 (The Bettman Archive), 43, 68, 73, 79, 90rt, 91, 93, 100–1, 103, 104left, 104–5btm, 106 (Maeers/Fox Photos), 107, 118, 119btm, 149, 151, 155left (Topical Press Agency), 157btm, 158, 185top left (Maeers/Fox Photos), 186, 191, 192, 231top, 240, 241left (Topical Press Agency), 241top rt, 242, 244btm left, 244–5btm, 245top, 246both, 247top rt (Topical Press Agency), 249btm, 254, 259, 264top rt, 265, 273 (Charles Hewitt/Picture Post), 280, 281, 287, 292, 298, 303, 306 (Topical Press Agency)

RURAL HISTORY CENTRE, READING UNIVERSITY: pp 12, 13btm, 16–17 (G. Charles, Bangor), 21, 22–3, 24left, 26, 29, 33 (Dorothy Hartley Collection), 36, 37, 38, 39, 41, 42, 44, 45, 56left, 62, 67, 70, 71, 76, 78, 82top, 86, 87, 88, 96, 97, 102, 105 (John Topham), 108–9, 112both, 113both, 114btm, 114ctre, 115btm, 116–17 (Godalming Museum), 122, 123both, 126left, 126–7btm, 129 (Mary Evans), 130–1, 136, 140–1btm, 141rt, 142 (John Topham), 146, 147 (Royston Rowley), 152–3, 161, 163, 166, 167all, 168, 169both, 170–1, 174top rt (Hereford City Library), 178 (Fox Photos Ltd), 179top, 181top left, 184, 185btm, 188top, 189top, 190, 193 (Packer/Oxfordshire County Council), 194–5btm, 196, 198left, 202 (Sports&General), 203left, 204, 205top, 205btm, 206top, 208btm left (John Topham), 208btm rt, 212, 215btm rt, 216–17all, 218, 219top, 222top, 222ctre (John Topham), 223btm (Farnham Museum), 224left, 224rt (Wellington Journal & Shrewsbury News), 225both, 227top & btm rt (R. Whitmore Collection), 230, 235both, 247btm (Hulton Getty), 248btm, 249top (John Topham), 251, 252–3 (Taunt/Oxfordshire County Council), 253top & btm rt, 257 btm (William Boyer/The Science Museum), 262, 264btm left, 277, 282–3, 284, 285 (H.D. Keilor), 289, 290–1, 293, 294, 295all, 296, 297top left & btm rt, 299